Pompey the Great

Pompey the Great

The Roman Alexander

Lee Fratantuono

Pen & Sword
MILITARY

First published in Great Britain in 2024 by
Pen & Sword Military
An imprint of Pen & Sword Books Limited
Yorkshire – Philadelphia

Copyright © Lee Fratantuono 2024

ISBN 978 1 52679 570 0

The right of Lee Fratantuono to be identified as
Author of this Work has been asserted by him in accordance
with the Copyright, Designs and Patents Act 1988.

A CIP catalogue record for this book is
available from the British Library

All rights reserved. No part of this book may be reproduced or
transmitted in any form or by any means, electronic or mechanical
including photocopying, recording or by any information storage and
retrieval system, without permission from the Publisher in writing.

Typeset by Mac Style
Printed in the UK by CPI Group (UK) Ltd, Croydon, CR0 4YY.

Pen & Sword Books Limited incorporates the imprints of After
the Battle, Atlas, Archaeology, Aviation, Discovery, Family History,
Fiction, History, Maritime, Military, Military Classics, Politics,
Select, Transport, True Crime, Air World, Frontline Publishing, Leo
Cooper, Remember When, Seaforth Publishing, The Praetorian Press,
Wharncliffe Local History, Wharncliffe Transport, Wharncliffe True
Crime and White Owl.

For a complete list of Pen & Sword titles please contact

PEN & SWORD BOOKS LIMITED
47 Church Street, Barnsley, South Yorkshire, S70 2AS, England
E-mail: enquiries@pen-and-sword.co.uk
Website: www.pen-and-sword.co.uk
or
PEN AND SWORD BOOKS
1950 Lawrence Road, Havertown, PA 19083, USA
E-mail: uspen-and-sword@casematepublishers.com
Website: www.penandswordbooks.com

For Maren Jensen

Contents

Preface and Acknowledgments		ix
Chapter 1	On the Cusp of a Tumultuous Century	1
Chapter 2	Commencing a Career	17
Chapter 3	Sulla Ascendant	29
Chapter 4	Africa and Triumph	49
Chapter 5	From Consul to Rebel: Lepidus, 78–77 BC	63
Chapter 6	Pompey in Spain	71
Chapter 7	Spartacus and the Third Servile War	86
Chapter 8	First Consulship and Pirate War	93
Chapter 9	Pompey in Asia, Part I	104
Chapter 10	Pompey in Asia, Part II	124
Chapter 11	Toward the 'Triumvirate'	139
Chapter 12	The 'First Triumvirate' in Action, Part I	154
Chapter 13	'The First Triumvirate' in Action, Part II	164
Chapter 14	Consulship with Crassus	177
Chapter 15	54 BC	185
Chapter 16	The Three Become Two	195
Chapter 17	Consul a Third Time	208
Chapter 18	A Republic Rife with Tension	218
Chapter 19	Zero Hour	231

Chapter 20	How to Start a Civil War	238
Chapter 21	The Road to Dyrrhachium	251
Chapter 22	Dictatorship and Dyrrhachium	265
Chapter 23	Toward Pharsalus	287
Chapter 24	Endgame in Egypt	306
Chapter 25	*Magni Nominis Umbra*	325
Notes		329
Select Bibliography		353
Index		357

Preface and Acknowledgments

Pompey is an enigma. One of the first serious works of classical scholarship I read was Peter Greenhalgh's exemplary two-volume biography of the 'Roman Alexander' and the 'Republican Prince.' That happy experience as an undergraduate student of Roman republican history came after two very different encounters with the legend of Pompey, from avid film viewing and the rigours of Latin class. Pompey figures briefly in the 1961 epic *King of Kings*, where he appears in the prologue in the context of his conquest of Jerusalem; in the 1960 *Spartacus*, he is mentioned in passing alongside Lucullus as he arrives for the climactic battle between Crassus and the slave army. The 1963 *Cleopatra* commences with the aftermath of Pharsalus, and the arrival of Caesar in Alexandria, where he is presented with the grim trophy of the hero's head. Cicero's speech on Pompey's proposed *imperium* (the so-called *lex Manilia*) has long been a standard choice for the third-year Latin curriculum in American secondary schools. Between cinema and junior year Latin, one developed a sense of Pompey as a figure of considerable mystique, inevitably eclipsed (at least in the popular imagination) by Caesar, but of appreciable interest in his own right. He is a mystery well worth delving into for a better understanding of his age, among the less known (at least in the popular imagination) of the most consequential figures in Roman history.

Under the late Seth Benardete, I had the pleasure of reading closely one of the most extraordinary meditations on Pompey and Caesar ever composed, Lucan's epic poem *Pharsalia* or *Bellum Civile*. The Neronian Age poet Lucan offered a stunning appraisal of the civil war between the two great political and military rivals, a magnificent poem that reflects bitterly and brilliantly on Rome's seeming infatuation with internecine strife. Benardete was a splendid guide to both Lucan and Caesar's own commentaries on the civil war, and that spring, 1997 seminar at New York University offered a most welcome chance to spend a semester immersed in the problems posed by Pompey. Thanks to Benardete's exemplary mentorship and guidance, I was able to devote significant time to thinking about and writing on Lucan; readers of the present book may find my 2012 monograph *Madness Triumphant: A Reading of Lucan's Pharsalia* of interest for the literary afterlife of Pompey. In that book I offer a comprehensive quasi-commentary on the whole of Lucan's epic and his depiction of both Pompey and Caesar, considering Neronian Lucan as critic of the Augustan vision that seemed to offer a solution to the problems that exploded in the Roman civil wars.

Pompey the Great is a narrative history and biography, which attempts to provide a coherent introduction to its subject that is rooted in close consideration of the many surviving sources for the hero's life. It tries to be fair and impartial, both to the protagonist and the principal antagonist he faced. Pompey and Caesar were both extraordinarily talented military leaders, of brilliant ability and impressive record. Indeed, Roman foreign affairs (not to mention political life) would have profited from greater collaboration between the two, especially regarding Parthia. Both men were masters of intense planning, and both were capable of moments of true daring, even what the more conservative tactician would call daring. They had complementary skills (Caesar being more willing to take hazardous risks, Pompey sometimes too rooted in what he was certain was the theoretically better course), but militarily they were more alike than not, ultimately both pawns of fickle Fortune, testaments to how every battle is an excursion into the unknown, no matter the skill or the bravery of the commander. Pompey has been ranked by many military historians as second to Caesar, not so much because he lost at Pharsalus, but because for Caesar we have so much more information about many of his campaigns, thanks to the priceless (and problematic) testimony of his own commentaries on both the Gallic and the civil wars. Caesar was his own best promoter and propagandist; to read his *commentarii* side by side with Lucan's later epic on the same war is a richly rewarding exercise, as is examining Caesar alongside the later writers Plutarch, Appian, and Dio, not least as we try to glean some sense of how Gaius Asinius Pollio treated the civil wars, what the poet Horace called the '*motum ex Metello.*'

What follows in these pages is meant for a general reader more than for a specialist, though it is hoped that experts in the subject will find something of profit. It is planned to be the first of two volumes. The second, *The Sons of Pompey*, is intended to continue the story of the fortunes of his family and its place in Roman history from the death of Pompey the Great in the autumn of 48 BC to the death of Sextus Pompey in 35. The present volume thus offers no 'afterword,' nothing of the more or less customary summary of the 'ending' of the story; the eventful dozen or so years after Pompey's death in Egypt are reserved for that projected sequel. This book succeeds my 2017 Pen & Sword volume on Lucullus; it may be read in close conjunction with Gareth Sampson's work in the same Roman history series on the campaigns of Dyrrhachium and Pharsalus, as well as Philip Matyszak's study of the Alexandrian War. The bibliography on this period and its luminaries is immense; I have tried to recommend what I consider to be some of the best works for further research in a list appended to the volume. The notes attempt to give a guide to scholarly articles and books on specific problems as well as general topics. The topics addressed in this volume have occasioned a dizzying array of studies; Caesar alone seems to inspire a new biography or monograph on some aspect of his life every year. This is a testament to the enduring popularity of the subject matter; it is a burden sometimes pleasant, sometimes exasperating for the serious student. If an article or book is cited herein, I have found something of value in it, even if I disagree with the conclusions.

Again, Pompey was both loser and winner; for many more casual students of Roman history, he is remembered primarily for having been defeated in the civil war with Caesar, after having won so many memorable victories over Rome's enemies both at home and abroad (and, too, over Caesar). Our investigation seeks to explore how despite his sorry end with defeat in the Battle of Pharsalus and ignominious assassination the next month in Egypt, Pompey's principal legacy was to provide a blueprint for how to fix the recurring problems that had turned the first century BC into a seemingly interminable cycle of civil conflicts for Rome. Pompey emerges as nothing less than a proto-Augustus, a true *princeps* who provided the model for another *princeps*. A quarter of a century after his death, Pompey would enjoy nothing less than a vindication of his mode of management of the tensions and challenges of the republic. The murdered Caesar would enjoy deification, but the murdered Pompey would provide something of the blueprint for how to ensure that Romans would not experience another civil war. The Augustan settlement would be a success, and it would owe its justly celebrated achievements in no small part to the model that Pompey provided of how to reconcile competing ambitions in the unwieldy construct that was the republic.

Rendering gratitude to others is unfailingly pleasant. As ever, this book is the product of the considerable help and encouragement of colleagues and mentors. Phil Sidnell is among the most patient, kindhearted, and altogether understanding of editors. The late Gerard Lavery inspired not only my college reading of Greenhalgh's *Pompey*, but also my initial serious study of Roman history (especially of the first-century BC), and I am honoured to have followed in his steps in my time at Fordham. Among my teachers of Roman history and imperial literature, Robert Penella and Holly Haynes deserve special mention. Blaise Nagy, Thomas Martin, and John Hamilton remain cherished correspondents, models of the scholarly life, and friends. I have profited immensely in my academic life from my friendship and correspondence with Egil Kraggerud, Karl Galinsky, and Michael Putnam. Michael McOsker is a welcome scholarly accusing conscience. Above all, my academic work is made possible by my cherished affiliation with the Department of Ancient Classics at the National University of Ireland, Maynooth.

Pompey lived a cinematic life, one that more than merits serious treatment by the filmmakers' craft. He was an avid patron of the dramatic and other arts, alongside his many contributions to the betterment of countless locales and regions of the Roman world. Fittingly, this book is dedicated in honour of an exemplary actress, philanthropist, and entrepreneur. Maren Jensen has contributed to the betterment of health and wellness, to the world of the arts and music, and, not least, to the reception of the classics. Scholarly studies of the debt of film and television to ancient Greek and Roman mythology and history have highlighted the important place of the 1978–1979 *Battlestar Galactica* and its science fiction odyssey in the long history of the reception of Aeneas and Trojan War lore. Pompey the Great built his 'Minervium' or temple of Minerva Chalcidica as a dedication to Athena after his return home from his victories in the east. It is a privilege to offer this book on Pompey to 'Lieutenant Athena,' in appreciation for all she has done for culture, health, and wellness.

Lee Fratantuono
31 December 2023
Notte di San Silvestro

Chapter One

On the Cusp of a Tumultuous Century

The man we know best as 'Pompey the Great' was born in 106 BC, on 29 September. His celebrated contemporary Marcus Tullius Cicero was born the same year, on 3 January.[1] In his appraisal of Pompey as a skilled orator (indeed, one who would have been more distinguished in the art, had he not pursued military glory), Cicero notes how he was a contemporary of the storied general.[2] The Rome of 106 BC would be radically transformed by the events of the ensuing decades, such that by 6 BC one could assert with good reason that the Roman Republic had been irrevocably transformed into the Roman Empire. Pompey played no small role in the dramatic historical episodes of the first half of a century that merits such labels as tumultuous, chaotic, violent and unstable (at least with respect to its first two-thirds).[3] Pompey's career was of inestimable importance to the domestic and foreign history of the late Roman Republic. A man who knew the extremes of supreme power and abject loss, of glorious victory and humiliating defeat, his life would be inextricably intertwined with that of the celebrated Gaius Julius Caesar, his ultimate rival in the quest to ensure a more stable and secure destiny for Rome. Pompey died on 28 September 48 BC, on the eve of what would have been his fifty-eighth birthday. It would be for his sons (especially the younger one, Sextus) to preserve the legacy of their father. For more than a decade after Pompey's death, his family would continue to play a major role in the unfolding events that would only be resolved with the ultimate accession to unchallenged power of the man we know as Augustus.

Pompey's life is reasonably well documented, as are the lives of most of his leading contemporaries. That is not to say the evidence is always straightforward or bereft of contradiction, confusion, and lack of clarity. Students of ancient history quickly become familiar with the problems of source criticism, of how to weigh and evaluate the surviving literary and archaeological evidence so as to move closer to that seemingly always retreating goal of determining what exactly happened. For Pompey, we have one of many of the so-called Roman lives from the great collection of parallel biographies composed by Plutarch probably early in the second century AD.[4] Plutarch is an invaluable treasure trove of information; we have works of his on Marius, Sulla, Crassus, Caesar,

Brutus, Cicero, and Antony, to name only some of the most renowned figures in his library of lives. Alongside Plutarch, we may name from the start the vast extant writings of Cicero, in which Pompey is referenced often;[5] Caesar's pen produced priceless commentaries on his campaigns in Gaul, and on his civil war with Pompey, works that invite particularly attentive care in use as historical sources because of the prejudices of the author in describing events in which he participated.[6] What survives of Sallust's *Historiae* offers a rich and compelling supplement to the picture.[7] The reader interested in Pompey's life does not lack for material to study; the problem is one of interpretation and analysis.[8] Apart from ancient histories, speeches and letters, commentaries and works of military science, we also possess an extraordinary epic poem, Lucan's *Bellum Civile* or *Pharsalia*, which is devoted to exploring Pompey's war with Caesar in a meditation on the Roman penchant for self-destruction.[9]

Scholars have devoted considerable energy to trying to unravel the mysteries of Pompey's life. The bibliography on his domestic and foreign exploits is daunting. Not only have major works been devoted to Pompey alone, but his war with Caesar and, more generally, the events surrounding the decline and fall of the Roman Republic have been the subject of an enormous range of books and articles.[10]

What follows in these pages does not aspire to break new ground in the study of its hero. This book is designed for the general reader, a vaguely defined audience whose composition has changed with the fickle attentions of school curricula and endurance of classical education. On one level, this book aims to provide a readable and engaging account of an exciting life. On another, it seeks to illustrate how Pompey's ambitions and cause did not prove entirely unsuccessful, notwithstanding his defeat at the hands of Caesar and the circumstances of his sad end in Ptolemaic Alexandria. In short, it is a story with a not altogether unhappy ending, for all the reality of defeat and even desecration that its subject endured.

The title of this first chapter references the cusp of a tumultuous century. Not everyone, it could be argued, is born at precisely the moment to live through some of the most consequential events in history, not least as a major participant. Like Caesar, Cicero, and a handful of other key figures, Pompey had the fortune of being born at the right time to be active in momentous happenings.

Besides dealing with the perennial problem of source criticism, a biography of Pompey must carefully delineate its scope. A life of Pompey could easily become a life also of Caesar, of Sulla and Marius, or of Lucullus and Crassus. It is easy to become lost in the Sertorian War, or the Third Mithridatic. Pompey was so intimately involved in every aspect of Roman life in his age that his story is nothing less than a history of Rome at a pivotal point in what would prove to be the unfolding transformation of republic into empire. It is all too easy to become bogged down in the details of the civil and foreign conflicts of the age, and to lose sight of the particular role played by Pompey in the complicated events in which he was immersed both actively and passively.

We shall endeavour to remain closely focused on Pompey, with a caveat from the start: we do not know much about his life from his birth in the autumn of 106 to circa 87.[11] The first eighteen or so years of his life are largely obscure; while we know quite a lot about what was happening in the republic in that period (controversies notwithstanding), the upbringing and early years of Pompey himself are somewhat shrouded in mystery.[12] At best we can conjecture from what we know about the rearing and education of men of his age, social standing, and economic class.

Plutarch's life of Pompey opens with an interesting comparison.[13] The Greek biographer recalls the play *Prometheus Bound* attributed to Aeschylus, noting that the tormented hero of humanity lavished praise on Heracles (his saviour), even as he condemned Zeus (his oppressor). For Plutarch, the comments of Prometheus on Heracles the son and Zeus the father serve to describe the memory of Pompey and his father Strabo: Pompey was the object of widespread admiration and respect, while Strabo was loathed and detested.[14] One could argue that there is more afoot in this mythological comparison from the corpus of Greek tragedy than mere ornamental reminiscence and literary colour. Heracles was famous for his extensive travels, pacifying the Roman world by fighting against and conquering the foreign enemies of the Republic. In this, Pompey was not unlike Heracles from the annals of mythology, even as he was like Macedonian Alexander the Great in his eastern adventures and triumphs.

I hate the father, but I love the son: so speaks the Prometheus of the Greek play that goes under Aeschylus' name (its authorship has been the subject of scholarly debate).[15] In meditating on the life of Pompey, Plutarch opines that the Roman people must have felt the same way toward his subject as a beloved son of a problematic father.[16] We shall return to this prefatory, indeed programmatic statement of Plutarch, as we explore the question of the degree to which Pompey figures in what would prove to be the settlement of his tempestuous century, the coming to power and ultimately peaceful rule of Augustus Caesar.

Plutarch explains the principal reason why Pompey's father was hated: he was addicted to wealth, obsessed with the acquisition of treasure.[17] If we can believe the ancient biographer, the father of the future legendary commander met with a dramatic death: he is said to have been struck by lightning.[18] His corpse was abused and insulted; his funeral was bereft of honour, with his men finally able to indulge freely in the contempt and disdain they felt toward their despised commander.

Who was this Strabo, this avaricious military man and father of the subject of our story?[19] Gnaeus Pompeius Strabo was born sometime around 135 BC. The cognomen 'Strabo' means 'cross-eyed' or 'squinting'; Roman *cognomina* often recall some memorable, idiosyncratic trait of a family ancestor. In the case of Strabo, we may find an explanation for the ocular nickname in a passage of Pliny the Elder, where the polymath discusses striking instances of resemblance between individuals.[20] Strabo had a slave who resembled him; the cook in question had a squinting or cross-eyed look that his master imitated and, in time, acquired. The slave's name was Menogenes; Pompey's father was sometimes called by the same name on account of the physical resemblance, having earlier been accorded the name 'Strabo' because of the eye problem.

Pompey's family hailed from Picenum, a region of ancient Italy roughly corresponding in extent of land to present-day Marche and part of Abruzzo in the centre of the country, on the Adriatic coast. Roman *praenomina* were relatively few in number; Pompey and his father shared the named Gnaeus, which would also be that of Pompey's oldest son. The Pompeian *gens* was of respectable local nobility; the family was the dominant one in Picenum.

In Stanley Kubrick's 1960 film *Spartacus*, the fictional plebeian hero Gracchus tells the gladiatorial *lanista* Lentulus Batiatus that he is planning to go to Picenum in exile in the wake of the victory of Crassus after the suppression of the slave revolt.[21] Batiatus is incredulous, noting that Picenum is 'the dreariest town in Italy.' Crassus had informed Gracchus that a 'farmhouse' awaited his adversary as his abode in exile; in reality, Gracchus commits suicide after helping Batiatus and Spartacus' wife Varinia. The scene does not necessarily conjure a fair portrait of Picenum, but it emphasizes the provincial character of the place in contrast to Rome. Picenum was not exactly a hinterland at the time that Pompey was born, but it was by no means an obvious corridor of power.

The *gens Pompeia* was a plebeian family, not a patrician like the *gens Iulia* of Julius Caesar. Pompey the Great would be by far the most accomplished and celebrated of its members. We cannot be certain of the origins of the Pompeian clan, but we are able to trace the histories of several members of the various branches of the family in reasonable detail.

While the Pompeii were plebeians, one should not overinterpret or misinterpret this family detail when considering the eventual clash between Caesar and Pompey. If anything, of the two, Caesar would embrace what at least stereotypically might be called more popular causes, and Pompey more elite. This gross oversimplification does serve to remind us that both Pompey and Caesar were privileged in their origins; by the time both men were born, wealthy plebeians often had common cause with patricians, and in many regards the problems of the so-called Struggle of the Orders had been addressed if not resolved. Put another way, the political divisions and tensions of the Middle Republic had either given way to or been transformed into new crises, problems that would beset the careers and very lives of both men.

Plutarch's Strabo was a slave to his lust for money; Pompey, in contrast, is said to have been adorned with numerous virtues.[22] In the biographer's laudatory note about his subject, we may see a hint of what could be labelled the republican martyr image that has on occasion been applied to Pompey. Pompey is an easier hero to set up as an archetype of anti-imperial, traditional Roman republican virtue than Brutus, Cassius, or the other assassins of Caesar; perversely, in some regards one of the best things that would happen to Pompey in terms of his enduring reputation would be his assassination in Egypt. Unlike Caesar, Pompey fell victim to the court of a foreign potentate, not the daggers of his fellow Romans. Whatever we may come to think of Plutarch's positive endorsement of the virtuous character of Caesar's great rival, one thing is certain from the start: Pompey was born with certain material advantages, as the son of a successful, locally prominent man who would enjoy military and political career successes.

Pompey was destined to achieved considerable success and renown in both domestic and foreign affairs. In this he was by no means unique; the same could be said for both Caesar and the other man whose career would be closely intertwined with his own, Marcus Licinius Crassus.[23] All three men would die violently; all three would die in the order of age, with Caesar the last of the three to fall by the sword.

Plutarch makes an interesting remark about Pompey's appearance as part of his enumeration of his virtues and remarks about his popularity and success. He says that Pompey resembled Alexander the Great. But he qualifies this comparison of Pompey's looks to that of Alexander as depicted in portraits of the storied conqueror. He says that the resemblance was rooted more in the comments made by people, than in any actual physical similarity. We may recall here that the ancients could rely only on statues and paintings, and on comments in literary and historical works about appearance. Photography and the like did not exist to permit ready physical identification of even the most famous of men. Pompey would earn a reputation that he was a Roman Alexander, and at some point along the way, people began to say that the accomplished son of Picenum resembled Macedonian Alexander. Such comparisons are easier to make when the model of comparison is a portrait bust or mosaic image. Plutarch's comment is rooted in a familiar concern of historians, biographers, and philosophers: the relationship between truth and fiction, appearance and reality.

One thing leads to another: for Plutarch, it was an all too easy step for Pompey to start allowing people to call him 'Alexander.'[24] It was a nickname, and certainly a more majestic one than something like 'Strabo.' But it also came to be applied to Pompey as an insult, Plutarch notes. Here certainly there is a good example of the problem of how to maintain a lofty reputation. If you are supposed to be a Roman Alexander, you have little if any opportunity to rest on your laurels. Constant activity is demanded by the sheer magnitude of your aspiration. Although Plutarch does not say it, some of the people who started using 'Alexander' as an insult may have done so out of a memory of another Alexander, the son of the Trojan king Priam better known as Paris. He was a figure of handsome appearance, too, favoured by the gods and of fortunate circumstance. But he was also derided on account of his notorious affair with Helen of Sparta, and the dire consequences of his dalliance. And, at least to some extent, there are parallels to be made between Trojan Alexander and the would-be Alexander from the Italian Marches, and the name 'Alexander' remains a two-sided, problematic appellation. At the very least, the name could easily become a burden, for anyone who failed to continue to achieve success in the manner of the Macedonian king.

What parallels could be made between Priam's son and Strabo's? Here again we are treated by Plutarch to what amounts to a meditation on the nature of illusion and reality.[25] Pompey was said to have been passionately enamoured of a courtesan named Flora. One of Pompey's friends, Geminius, became fixated on her, to the annoyance of the woman. She rebuffed his advances repeatedly, noting that she would not submit to him on account of Pompey. Geminius went to Pompey and was forthright about his intentions. Pompey turned her over to Geminius, and never again had anything to do with her. Similarly, Plutarch notes that Pompey treated the wife of his freedman Demetrius with a rudeness and contempt that was quite unlike his normally affable, polite temperament, precisely because he did not want anyone to be able to say that he was smitten with her exceptional attractiveness. Two examples, then, are cited in support of the thesis that Pompey was capable of great restraint in the matter of seeming to be under the power of the seductions of physical attractiveness.

And yet, Plutarch proceeds to observe, Pompey nonetheless developed a reputation for being guilty of affairs with married women, to the point of neglecting his public duties for the sake of indulgence in his private, illicit pleasures. This is exactly the sort of charge and censure faced by Trojan Alexander in the matter of his behaviour with Menelaus' wife Helen. But Pompey is no mere libertine, no simple case of a man with a weakness for sexual indiscretions. He seems, instead, almost like some tragically flawed figure who always just misses the mark. Though possessed of a resolute spirit and determination not to succumb to the attractions of a beautiful woman, he was unable to escape the criticism of being inappropriate in his relationships with married women.[26]

At this juncture, Plutarch offers a related story about Pompey's attitude toward luxury.[27] He notes that once when he was sick, the doctor prescribed a meal of a thrush, which was unable to be found at the markets because the bird was out of season. Pompey's servants were only able to procure the menu item from the notoriously luxury-loving gourmand Lucullus. When he learned of this, Pompey made the witty remark that apparently he would have needed to die, were Lucullus not given over to such excessive, decadent tastes. Pompey decided to forego the thrush, and he ate simpler, plain food and recovered his health.

Plutarch tells this anecdote with the note that this episode was from a later time in his subject's life. It is likely that he presents it deliberately in conjunction with the matter of Pompey's reputation for indiscretions with women, as if to imply that the criticisms he faced were not entirely fair and justified. Plutarch offers us a chance to explore the inherent frustration of being someone who both aspires to lofty, exemplary virtue and achievements, and who succeeds impressively, only to be the subject of carping and a seeming lack of appreciation. At the same time, Pompey was admired more than he was condemned. He presents a maze of contradictions, an enigmatic life that defies simple and straightforward analysis.

We have noted that Pompey was destined to earn distinction in both domestic and foreign affairs. Indeed, his early life would be dominated by two exceedingly consequential conflicts: the so-called Social War in Italy, and the First Mithridatic War overseas. We may begin by examining the state of affairs in the Roman Republic when Pompey was born. 'Italy' did not exist in the strict sense as a political entity. Rome was but one of the city-states of the Italian peninsula. The Social War derives its name from the Latin word *socius*, meaning an ally; the brutal conflict that erupted in 91–90 BC would take its name from those allies of Rome who decided to cast the die in favour of armed engagement.[28] The inevitable question is why the allies were discomfited with Rome to the point of going to war. Historians debate the various theses that have been proposed to explain the dissatisfaction of the *socii*. Pompey's father Strabo would play an appreciable part in the war; Pompey's own first experience of conflict would come in the struggle that erupted when he was a teenager.

Some have seen in the Social War the seeds for the eventual decline and fall of the republic. The war would last until around 87 BC, even if most fighting was finished before then; Rome would be the victor, though some would argue that the victory came at a great cost, at least with respect to the health of the republic and the rise of what would be nothing less than a devastating series of civil wars that would convulse both Italy and the empire. Rome had been founded traditionally in 753 BC, and until 509 had been a monarchy. The republic was centuries old by the time Pompey was born, and in the Mediterranean world

Rome was on the ascendant. Carthage had been defeated in a series of three great conflicts, the so-called Punic Wars; Rome was far more than a small city-state on the Tiber, nestled with neighbours on the Italian peninsula. The Roman Republic already had what amounted to an overseas empire, even while Italy remained a patchwork of city-states connected to Rome by a complicated set of alliances, intermarriages, and extensive economic relations. It would be fair to say that Rome's overseas conquests were won in large part by the immense manpower contributed to her armies by her Italian allies.

Pompey's family occupied an interesting place in the interwoven circumstances of the age. The Pompeii were provincial in origin, to be sure. But they were Roman citizens, and when it came to conflict between Rome and her allies, there would be no question that the family's loyalties were with Rome. The family was wealthy, and economic strength guaranteed a certain prestige and power, provincial roots notwithstanding.

Strabo was destined to earn distinction in fighting for Rome against the allied confederation that rose up in arms. One of our main surviving sources for the Social War is the historian Appian, who flourished in the second century AD. From the start a key fact must not be overlooked: Appian (like Plutarch) is an appreciably late source. He wrote a Roman history in Greek, of which only some sections survive. From an original twenty-four books, we are fortunate to have Books 13–17, which focus on the Roman civil wars. Appian is valuable in that we are able to read a continuous narrative covering crucial decades in the history of Rome; our knowledge of the period would be considerably less if we did not possess his extant books. That said, like any ancient historian, Appian is not without his problems. In the case of the Social War, the pressing question for the reader of Appian is whether he is correct in his verdict that a major grievance of the Italian allies was exclusion from Roman citizenship. Certainly one of the most important consequences of the war was the fact that citizenship would, in fact, be extended to the allies: in this regard, the *socii* were victorious even in defeat. The war was unquestionably costly: the number of men killed on both sides was frightfully high, a harbinger for the slaughter that would recur in the ensuing bloody decades of Roman history.

Appian does not record any information about the activities of the young Pompey during the conflict. Pompey was only sixteen in the first year of the war. He was from a family that was deeply invested in the burgeoning economic enterprises of empire. The Pompeii had the undeniable advantage of being Roman citizens; wealthy investors and speculators from the Italian allies would covet such a passport, so to speak, to achieve even greater financial success in the heady times of imperial advances. It is not within the scope of the present study to explore in detail the many problems surrounding the *Bellum Sociale*;

the causes were no doubt many and varied, and economic considerations would have been prominent among them. For our purposes, it may prove more valuable to focus on the formative experience of Pompey in this maelstrom of what was in essence an Italian civil war. Here it will be necessary to trace the history of Strabo's involvement in the war in particular.

There were two main theatres of the Social War, dominated by the Marsi in the north of central Italy, and the Samnites in the south. The Italian allies were no mean assortment of foes; they fielded at least 100,000 men at the start of the conflict, and they were experts at dealing with mountainous, inhospitable terrain. One of the disadvantages of their situation was that they were divided geographically. There were benefits to the separation alongside the obvious problems: the war was close to Rome, and the distant allies allowed for threats to the republic to emerge with little if any advanced warning from multiple fronts simultaneously.

The first appearance of a Caesar in our story comes in 91, when one of the consuls was Sextus Julius Caesar; he was an uncle of the more famous Gaius Julius Caesar. He would play his own role in the Social War, eventually succumbing to illness while involved in the prosecution of the war in 89. His cousin Lucius Julius Caesar was one of the consuls in 90, in the first year of actual fighting; he was responsible for dealing with the southern front of the war. Lucius would survive the Social War, only to die in another civil conflict, in 87.

Lucius' consular colleague was Publius Rutilius Lupus. He was entrusted with operations against the Marsi in the north; Pompey's father played a supporting role on that front. Rutilius was fated not to survive the war; he was slain in battle in 90. Rutilius' most famous subordinate commander was not Strabo, but the celebrated Gaius Marius, the man renowned (or notorious) for serving seven consulships.[29] The day would soon come when Marius would be involved in his own civil war, with Lucius Cornelius Sulla; at the time our story begins, Sulla was serving under the consul Lucius on the southern front.[30] We can see the assembly of chess pieces already; the Social War was the laboratory in which so many celebrated men of Roman history first experienced that most dreadful form of conflict, a *de facto* civil war. Internecine strife was rooted in the lore of Roman history, from the time when Romulus slew his brother Remus. By the end of the century, Augustus would be calling for the celebration of a unified Roman Italy, one in which there was peace not only throughout the Italian peninsula that was the very heart of the empire, but throughout Rome's Mediterranean realms.

Rutilius' death on 11 June 90 BC marked a significant victory for the allies; Marius, however, was able to restore the situation so as to avoid full-scale defeat for Rome. The exact circumstances of the fateful battle are unknown; even the location is disputed in the surviving sources. The only reason we know the date of the engagement is because it coincided with a Roman holiday, and in his calendar poem Ovid alludes to the death of the consul.[31]

Marius' saving of the day after the death of Rutilius inaugurated an all too brief period in which Marius and Sulla were cooperatively engaged in the same military interests. The year 90 was not an embarrassing one for Marius in terms of his achievements and successes, especially given his advanced age. Especially if it is true that his health was beginning to fail, if there is one criticism that may be fairly levelled against him, it is that he did not know when to think about honourable retirement. Marius was not given a new command in 89; we are not entirely certain of why. One of the problems with civil wars is that they bring few undisputed, unsullied honours. The Social War was not exactly a civil engagement of the same sort as the ensuing conflicts that marked the fall of the republic, but it was still an all too uncomfortably Italian war, one fought in the homeland and heartland of the growing empire. Marius had earned fame fighting foreign tribes, and despite advancing age and the burdens of ill health, he was no doubt eager for another chance at overseas glory.

Plutarch, like Appian, records no experience of Pompey during the course of the dramatic events of 91–90 BC, as the Social War erupted and his father had his chance to earn distinction under fire. We know very little as to the particulars of Pompey's education, or of when exactly he commenced his military career.[32] Strabo was responsible for recruiting soldiers in Picenum to respond to the crisis; his success both in raising troops and in the military events of 90 secured his victory in achieving the consulship in 89, together with Lucius Porcius Cato. Like Strabo, Cato was not destined to live long; he was killed in his consular year, possibly by none other than the son of Marius, Gaius Marius Minor.[33] Allegedly Marius' loyal son was incensed at Cato's boasting that his achievements were comparable to the great Marius' epic victories over the Cimbri, and slew him at the Battle of Fucine Lake. Whether Cato died by the hand of one of his Italian opponents in the chaos of storming a Marsic camp, or by Marius the Younger on account of a perceived slight to his family honour, we cannot say with certainty. The historian and student of Saint Augustine, Paulus Orosius, claims that Marius was the killer in his great history *Adversus Paganos*, a key text for bridging the historiographic gap from late antiquity to the medieval period.[34] Orosius' detail is curious, and cannot be corroborated from Plutarch or Appian; some would argue that the silence of those sources on the matter is sufficient reason to suspect Orosius. On the other hand, given the connection of the Porcii Catones to prominent men like Sulla, there could be evidence here for why certain hatreds and vendettas would prove so intractable in the ensuing years. This much is clear: the consuls of 89 were ill-starred.

We may return to Cato's colleague Strabo. He was sole consul after the Battle of Fucine Lake, and, in fact, he would aspire to a second, immediate term as consul in 88.[35] His ambition matched his greed, at least in the appraisal of his rivals and adversaries. We have noted that covetousness was among the charges levelled against Strabo, and it is likely that the reputation was at least enhanced (if not acquired) as a result of his conduct during the war. In terms of the events of the Social War, Strabo is most famously associated with the siege of Asculum in November of 89.[36] Ancient Asculum is the modern Ascolo Piceno; it managed to hold out for some time against Roman forces, which in the history of siege warfare has often translated into significant bloodletting and looting when the city is finally taken. Strabo allowed his forces to run amok in destroying Asculum, and the commander profited greatly from the victory.[37]

The exact sequence of events that precipitated full-blown war cannot be determined from the extant evidence. Asculum was clearly a hotbed of allied activity as plans were made to foment war against the republic.

If we can believe the Tiberian era historian Velleius Paterculus, Asculum was the scene of an immense battle: he says that some 75,000 Romans engaged 60,000 Italians.[38] These numbers are likely inflated, but there is no compelling reason to doubt that Pompey's father won an extraordinary victory, if followed by a questionable outcome of the siege of the beleaguered town. The surviving historical record is both incomplete and contradictory as to the exact sequence of events, but the picture that emerges is reasonably clear: Strabo could boast of impressive successes, but he had a certain bloodthirsty and greedy disposition.

It is interesting that Strabo failed in his efforts to secure the consulship of 88, for all his achievements. The winners in that contest were Sulla and Quintus Pompeius Rufus. We cannot be sure of the full extent of the machinations and vicissitudes of politics and war that doomed the ambitions of Strabo. Sulla, to be sure, was a formidable rival for office, even if Pompey's father were not as unpopular as the surviving historical record would seem to indicate. Pompey was seventeen when Strabo met with political reversal; again, his formative years afforded him the opportunity to gain some knowledge of the inner workings of the Roman republican governmental apparatus, as well as of army life and the complicated relationships between urban Romans and provincials, citizens and allies.

The Social War pitted Rome against her allies. Before the crisis was resolved, another, foreign conflict posed its own threat to the stability of the republic: the first of what would be three wars between Rome and the wily eastern king, Mithridates of Pontus.[39] Here in the simplest analysis we find a classic case of the natural concomitant of expansion: you will one day brush up against a potentially deadly rival, a neighbour who shares your imperial dreams and is determined to be the dominant power in what he considers to be his sphere of influence. The First Mithridatic War would erupt in 89, a direct consequence of the growth of Roman power in western Asia. Again, it is not our subject to trace the origins of this foreign war in detail. Rome had been involved in Asia Minor for decades, and Mithridates was an exceptionally talented, ambitious potentate who had been eager to see the borders of his own kingdom of Pontus expand. Some might say that conflict was inevitable; indeed, the Mithridatic Wars would prove to be the first of a great series of struggles between the Rome of the west and the great powers arrayed in the vast territories to her east.

History might have been very different had Strabo and not Sulla been one of the consuls of 88. Sulla would be entrusted with command of Roman military forces in Asia in the wake of the disastrous opening salvos and episodes of the war with Mithridates.[40] It is all too easy to see the enormity of the crisis that enveloped the Roman Republic. There was a serious and costly conflict in the very heartland of Italy, and now a major war in the east, which threatened the vulnerable border provinces of the republic. The economic cost of prosecuting the war successfully would be astronomical, and manpower would pose a significant problem as Rome sought to muster sufficient forces to counter Mithridates.

The crisis of 89 affords a good opportunity to explore the problem of military and political rivalry. The threat from Mithridates was clear enough: he wanted to expand westward, and he was willing to slaughter Romans and Roman allies to secure his imperial ambitions. But for Rome, the problem was not only how to defeat a foreign foe. As would happen time and again in Roman history, the aggression of an overseas enemy did not necessarily unite Roman opinion in an entirely productive and healthy way. Rivalry was the word of the hour, as Romans jockeyed for such plum positions as the one entrusted to Sulla. To be commander of Roman forces in a theatre like Asia Minor was to aspire to amass both immense wealth and great prestige; certainly there were tremendous risks involved (as we shall see later in our story with Crassus and his own eastern ambitions), but the rewards were equal to if not superior to the hazards.

Sulla incurred significant jealousy among his rivals by virtue of his winning the Asian command. Marius, for one, was green with envy. While advanced in years relatively speaking, Marius was not the sort who enjoyed the prospect of a quiet retirement. Pompey was destined to have his own glorious career in the east; what his father was not destined to achieve, he would win with interest. The dangers posed by Mithridates were considerable, even if the war were confined to Asia. As it happened, jealousy and envy would prove to be all too capable conspirators: Rome would face civil war in direct consequence of the question of who exactly would be facing the King of Pontus and winning glory in far-flung lands. There was no time for ambitious men to rest or to reflect; the Roman Republic was in dire, potentially fatal crisis both internally and abroad.

The conflict between Marius and Sulla was in some ways a prelude to the eventual war between Caesar and Pompey. The Roman civil war that dominated the early careers of both men offered a bitterly learned series of lessons about the peculiar dangers of internal disorder. One could compose a parallel set of lives in the manner of Plutarch, pitting Pompey against Caesar, not least with respect to how the one would make a name for himself in eastern conquests, the other in the west with his expeditions in Gaul and even to the shores of Britain.

Despite the severity of the crisis in Asia, there was no way that Sulla could proceed immediately to handling overseas problems. At the very least, it would take time to prepare a proper force to face Mithridates, who had the advantage of position and initiative. Sulla was also not free simply to prepare for his war with Pontus. Marius very much wanted Sulla's command, and he was willing to be bold in seeking to take it.

There were still more problems. The Social War may have resulted in the extension of Roman citizenship to the Italian allies, but there were numerous questions as to how exactly the newly enfranchised Italians would be absorbed into the existing Roman political system. Disputes as to the actual details of the plan to expand the pool of citizens led to more violence and chaos. In another instance of where it might have seemed as if destiny were composing Pompey's life, Strabo was not fated to survive the turmoil of 87 BC.

But the loss of his father would be a mere footnote to the dramatic events that would engulf Roman political and military life.[41] Essentially, the problems that emerged constituted a fateful juxtaposition of two discrete issues, with ambitious would-be commanders and leaders igniting what amounted to a tinderbox. Domestically there was the question of how to incorporate new voting citizens into the existing political system. Overseas, there was the matter of who would win glory and secure significant wealth by taking the command against Mithridates. Sulla was poised to dominate in both arenas of activity, if only by virtue of his consular authority and strong senatorial support. But Marius, old age notwithstanding, was not ready to surrender his dreams of adding to his long list of achievements, and he, too, had significant backing from certain quarters.

One thing that Sulla's opponents in this period arguably failed to consider was that their adversary would be willing to push matters so far as to threaten civil war. Sulla would become notorious for daring to lead his soldiers even against the gates of Rome, one of the most unthinkable and sacrilegious of actions. Roman generals were not supposed to be marching into Rome at the head of armed legions; the whole concept of such a military action of occupation and showing of force was beyond the pale.

We may take a moment to consider what exactly the problem was with the newly enrolled Roman voters. Simply put, if you place numerous newly enfranchised Italians into limited voting tribes, you minimize the significance of their votes. If you distribute the new citizens more equally between existing voting tribes, you face a quite different election scenario. Sulla's political opponent Publius Sulpicius Rufus was tribune of the plebs, holding an office that was traditionally the classic bulwark in the republican political system against the authority of the senate and the magistrates.[42] Sulpicius saw a chance to checkmate Sulla by an alliance with Marius that would achieve mutually beneficial goals: Sulpicius wanted the new voters to be divided between the voting tribes equitably, and Marius wanted to take the field against Mithridates.[43] The backroom deal was an instance of classic Roman political negotiation: Sulpicius would secure the transfer of Sulla's command to Marius, and Marius would endorse Sulpicius' voting scheme.

Roman republican politics was a deadly serious game. Sulla would have none of Sulpicius' legal and political machinations. Sulpicius was no mere employer of political machinery; he had armed bodyguards, men he was willing to use as a sign of intimidation against the consuls. Sulla tried to fight political tactic with political tactic by proclaiming what the Romans called a *iustitium*, or a suppression of public affairs; Sulpicius and his mob responded by driving the consuls from the forum.

It was one of the lowest points in Sulla's career; there were stories that the consul had to flee for his life, forced to take refuge with Marius of all people. Marius attempted to play the role of negotiator, but for the moment, negotiation seemed to include merely guaranteeing Sulla's life. Officially, Sulla was still supposed to be commanding forces against Mithridates, and when he left Rome to proceed south to his armies, no doubt he felt that whatever domestic embarrassment he had suffered could be ameliorated by achieving impressive and lucrative victories in the east. It would have come as an enormous shock to learn that Sulpicius was interested in far more than Italian voting rights. The news that Marius was to take over the command against Mithridates was tantamount to an attempt to force Sulla into premature retirement, in favour of a man twenty years his senior.

Sulla was willing to bring troops into Rome to confront Sulpicius, and he crafted what amounted to an argument in defence of security and stability.[44] According to Sulla's propaganda, Sulpicius and Marius were dangerous rabble rousers; conversely, Sulpicius and Marius were free to condemn Sulla as a violent suppressor of liberties and democratic institutions. Again, probably neither Sulpicius nor Marius expected that Sulla would respond to clear provocations in such an unprecedented manner. Sulla surprised many by his willingness to march on Rome, and clearly it cost him support and stained his reputation.

Scholars debate the decision of Sulla to use force against his political opponents, just as the Romans of the hour argued for and against the daring patrician. There is no question that Sulla was the victim of chicanery and trickery. Most of the criticism he faced came in consequence of his shocking decision to march on Rome.[45] His supporters were not entirely wrong in arguing that he had little choice; his options were exceedingly limited. Sulla's forces were not entirely in agreement on the plan to threaten Rome in what amounted to a clear step toward a full scale civil war. One of the men who emerges at this juncture in support of Sulla is Lucius Licinius Lucullus, who was serving as one of his officers; he would remain loyal to his commander, notwithstanding the hazardous plan.[46] Sulla's argument was that he was not attacking Rome, not launching some ugly spectre of civil war.[47] Rather, he was freeing Rome from the tyrannical demagogues Sulpicius and Marius.

Sulpicius had nothing of the reputation of Marius, and was a far easier foe to eliminate. In the end, he would be betrayed by a slave and slain; his death in 88 BC took its place as one of the countless instances of civil violence in Rome in this chaotic period.[48] Marius and his son were able to escape Rome and to flee to Africa. Sulla had achieved a victory, after a fashion at least: so inculcated in the Roman psyche were certain traditional values and sanctions, that some would never accept his armed incursion into Rome, even if they were otherwise sympathetic with his points and programme.

The price that Sulla paid would come in the elections for the critical year 87 BC, the year in which the surviving historical record gives its first definitive glimpse of the young man Pompey had become. The elected consuls for 87 were Lucius Cornelius Cinna and Gnaeus Octavius, and Cinna for one made it crystal clear that he intended to call Sulla to account for his actions. The political situation with the consuls-designate of 87 offers a microcosm of the problems of the late Republic. Cinna was certainly a devotee of what could be called the popular, democratic cause.[49] He was in favour of distributing the newly enfranchised as widely as possible, to maximize the power of their votes. He wanted to see Sulla stripped of his eastern command. His colleague Octavius was by no means sympathetic to what Sulla had done in his Roman march. He disagreed with Sulla profoundly in terms of the means that the aggrieved would-be Mithridatic hero had employed to secure his goals. But Octavius was also suspicious of Cinna, distrustful of his popular politics. Cinna and Octavius were doomed not to cooperate in the governance of the troubled republic; matters would devolve to the point that one could argue that there was a civil war within a civil war. The so-called *Bellum Octavianum* would see the spectacle of consul against consul, and Pompey's father would play a significant role in the drama.

Suffice for our purposes to say, Cinna was more than willing to resort to mob violence to secure his political goals; there were riots in Rome. Octavius would seek to depose Cinna from his consular office, hoping to replace him with Lucius Cornelius Merula.[50] A student of this period could note that some of the same Roman officials who were horrified at the idea that Sulla would lead an army into Rome, were more than willing to tolerate civil unrest in the city and the use of what amounted to armed groups of thugs to achieve their goals. Octavius was no less culpable than Cinna in the matter of using deadly force; before long, Cinna had to flee Rome, and civil war was once again a Roman reality.[51]

We may heartily regret not knowing more about what Pompey Strabo was thinking, let alone doing, in this period. Cinna certainly had Marius as a strong ally; Octavius, one might say, was forced to take the Sullan side, even if he had serious reservations about some of Sulla's actions. The situation in Rome was not black and white, and Strabo may well have been hedging his bets, especially given that events were moving quickly, and as ever in ancient history, we do well to remember that news was not quite as instantaneous or nearly so as today. We do know that Strabo was one of the commanders who responded to Octavius' call for support in facing the threat posed by Cinna and Marius, who were in a position to try to besiege Rome. And we know that Strabo's son Pompey was serving under his father. Strabo would not survive the *Bellum Octavianum*, a somewhat obscure, relatively minor campaign in a series of wars both domestic and foreign. The Octavian War would be the first chance that we know of for Pompey to distinguish himself, not least as one of the young men who would espouse the cause of Sulla, certainly one of the most complex and ambivalent figures in a memorable century.

By his late teenage years, the world seemed eerily poised for Pompey to embark on his military and political life. On the domestic front, there was the Social War, and then the outbreak of what would be the devastating civil conflict between Sulla and Marius. Abroad, there was the war with Mithridates. 87 BC was a fateful year for both father and son; before Strabo's death under disputed circumstances, Pompey would have time to serve with his sire and to witness firsthand the hazards of civil war.

Chapter Two

Commencing a Career

We cannot trace with certainty the activities of Pompey in 89 and 88. By 87, he was undoubtedly serving in the Roman military, under his father's command. It is here that Plutarch records another exemplary anecdote about his subject, one whose lessons resonate through later episodes in Pompey's life.

The ill-fated consuls of 87 were Gnaeus Octavius and Lucius Cornelius Cinna. Neither man was destined to live long; Octavius would not survive his consular year, and Cinna would perish in 84. Pompey's father was also a casualty of 87, under circumstances that are somewhat mysterious. In a way, the uncertainty about how exactly Strabo died matches the charge that he was somewhat on the fence over supporting either Octavius or Cinna.

The story that Plutarch tells about Pompey is rich with commentary and reflection on his subject.[1] The context is the *Bellum Octavianum*, the scene the camp of Strabo in which his son was serving. Cinna is said to have bribed one Lucius Terentius to assassinate Pompey, while others were similarly suborned to kill Strabo. Somehow, Pompey learned of the plan to add both father and son to the ever increasing roster of men who fell victim to Roman civil strife. Pompey was made aware that he faced betrayal from one of his own tentmates in the camp, with Terentius planning to see to his death as part of a plot to help Cinna and Marius.

Despite the dangerous, shocking report, Pompey is said to have conducted himself as if nothing whatsoever were wrong. He dined as usual, and if anything were different, it was that he seemed especially relaxed. But late at night, armed as he was with the knowledge that there would be an attempt both on his father's life and his own, he secretly arose from his bed, prepared a guard around Strabo's headquarters, and waited for Terentius and the other conspirators to strike. Terentius did not fail in his plan to try to assassinate Pompey; he stabbed at the bed, not realizing that he had been fooled into thinking that his prey was under the covers. Soon enough there was chaos in the camp, and Plutarch is clear that part of the problem that Pompey faced was that there was widespread disdain, even hatred for his father in the camp. There were plenty of soldiers who were ready to support what Cinna had tried to set into motion; arguably many men would have happily killed their commander even without any bribes.

Pompey responded to the tumult by making an impassioned appeal, essentially offering himself as a casualty, even to the point of dramatically lying down and inviting those who would murder Strabo to do so by stepping over and on the body of the commander's son. If Plutarch's version of events is correct, we have an instance of excellent theatre; everything was calculated to inspire feelings of sympathy and shame in the presence of the loyal, devoted son who was exemplifying the cherished Roman virtue of *pietas*. This was like Aeneas, ready to carry his father Anchises to safety from the burning city of Troy, except the reverse. Pompey had no intention of fleeing the camp with his father on his shoulder; instead he rolled the dice, as it were, inviting these Roman soldiers to decide whether they were going to commit the shameful deed of killing a loyal son. Implicit in the rendition of the scene is the idea that Pompey was generally well-liked; for as much as the father was hated, the son was beloved. If anything it was like Virgil's Mezentius with Lausus.

Pompey's first stage role was a smashing success. The would-be assassins put down their arms, and most of the soldiers were reconciled to Strabo. It was a victory of diplomacy and oratory, of tears and a calculated play on the better sentiments of the Roman army. Strabo, however, was doomed to die soon enough anyway. Plutarch, as we have noted, would have his readers believe that a lightning bolt succeeded where Cinna's bribery had failed. It may be that Strabo died of illness, dysentery or the like on account of a poor hygienic state in his camp. Whatever the cause, Pompey's father died during the Octavian War, and it seems that very few missed him. We may never know the truth about Strabo's fate. Was his body desecrated, pulled from its funeral pyre and dragged about? Was Strabo actually murdered in the end anyway, notwithstanding his son's successful intervention on the night of the planned assassinations? What probably happened was that Strabo did indeed die of natural causes, and that he was not much lamented. The question for the student of Roman history, however, may be to consider not so much what did or did not take place, as the lessons that a biographer like Plutarch wanted to glean from the circumstances surrounding the death of the young Pompey's father. In short, Pompey is presented as a virtuous and loyal son, even of a disreputable father.

In a later period, Caesar's adopted heir Octavian would emphasize the concept of loyalty to one's father. The assassins of Caesar would be hunted down, because that was the obligation of an adopted son. It did not matter if the conspirators had done something that a reasonable, level-headed Roman might find understandable in terms of seeking to preserve what remained of the republic. A cynical critic might argue that the men who assassinated Caesar had helped to ensure the rise to power of Octavian, whatever their actual intentions. But in terms of the virtue of *pietas*, all of this was irrelevant. One owed a debt of loyalty and honour to one's father, and the record reflected such behaviour on the part of Pompey. *Pietas*, at any rate, is even more praiseworthy when one's father is not easy to love or to respect.

Pompey was not entirely free of his father's influence in the aftermath of his death. We are told that Pompey was charged in the courts in the wake of Strabo's death, accused essentially of having profited from illegal thefts and plunder from his father's activities during the Social War.[2] Pompey turned nineteen in 87, and he was already a veteran not only of the plots and perils of camp life during a period of near-constant civil strife, but he was also soon destined to gain experience in the Roman legal system, where he was compelled by his adversaries to defend himself in 86 against charges that probably reflected at least in part the lingering animus felt toward Strabo. Plutarch is clear: Pompey was a gifted speaker, able to defend himself with poise as well as recourse to the truth. Apparently Strabo's freedman Alexander had actually been guilty of wrongdoing, and Pompey was able to prove his innocence. When we hear that all the same, the young man was charged with having books and hunting nets in his possession that had been illegally acquired from the booty of Asculum, it is easy to think that there were those who were determined at all costs to cast aspersions on Pompey.

The manner in which Pompey finally acquitted himself in his legal troubles is a vintage example of Roman republican backroom dealing and secret negotiation.[3] The praetor in charge of managing the case, Publius Antistius, had a daughter. The magistrate so admired the competent and affable defendant, that he offered a deal behind closed doors: marriage to his daughter in exchange for acquittal. It was quintessentially Roman, in the sense that corruption could in certain circumstances be considered the right thing to do, a fair deal to end an ugly and ultimately tedious and pointless business. Plutarch offers a charming detail: when Pompey was acquitted, the people cried out *Talasio*, which was the traditional Roman hale and hearty greeting at a wedding ceremony.[4]

Plutarch explains the allusion for the sake of his readers. The cry *Talasio* dated back to the legendary abduction of the Sabine women in the time of Romulus. *Talasio* means 'For Talasius'; one of the abducted women was assigned to be the bride of Talasius, and the cry of the Romans on that ancient day was allegedly the origin for the use of the invocation at Roman nuptial ceremonies ever after.[5] Plutarch admits freely that the story about Talasius may be fictitious, but whatever the truth of the matter, Pompey married Antistia, the daughter of his judge. All the emphasis is again on how appealing a young man Pompey was; once again, he found success on account of the effect of his exemplary character on others.

But there were other pressing concerns beyond questions of possible embezzlement and nuptial resolution to legal jeopardy. Strabo had died as the commander of an army, one that was ostensibly supposed to be defending Octavius and Rome against Cinna's forces. Plutarch delicately proceeds from the anecdote about Pompey's marriage to Antistia to an all too rapid account of how Cinna met his end.[6] The swiftly dispensed with narrative belies the complicated chain of events that took place in the months and years after Strabo's death.

One of the sources of complication in this period is the propensity of so many for double dealing amid the chaos of civil war. The question of the exact circumstances of the death of Pompey's father is but one problem that a student of the period faces. We do not know what exactly Strabo was trying to do, or at least contemplating doing, with respect to the political situation in Rome. He had sided with Octavius against Cinna, but there is good reason to believe that he was not above negotiating privately with Cinna for his own benefit. We may recall that Strabo had been annoyed by his loss of a second consulship; it is more than likely that he was open to negotiating with Cinna for just such an office. Strabo's death put an end to any such machinations, and for the Roman senate as well as the military, there was certainly an openness to finding a mutually acceptable settlement to end the ugly scenario of consul fighting against consul.

Cinna was open to such discussions, but it seems that the real power behind his throne was the aged Marius. It was an era of pendulum swinging; one day the Marians might be in favour in a given place, the next day the Sullans. It is unlikely that Cinna was genuinely interested in any rapprochement with his enemies. Certainly there was talk to the effect that Cinna was willing to entertain not seeking the life of Octavius; this would have been the most basic sort of concession that he could have made. But in actuality, Cinna was almost certainly desirous of seeing Octavius dead as soon as possible, and there is no real surprise when we learn that Gaius Marcius Censorinus assaulted Octavius' paltry remaining forces and slew the onetime consul. The head of Octavius was presented in triumph to Cinna, such that it was literally a case of one consul's head being presented to his colleague in what was supposed to have been their shared consular year. It was an unforgettable moment of depravity in the catalogue of horrors that accompanies the long experience of Rome with civil wars.

Meanwhile, what happened to armies such as that of Pompey's father? It appears that in the wake of Strabo's death, his units simply came to terms with Cinna. This is not particularly surprising, given that Marius was engaged at the time in quite successful operations in support of Cinna, not least in terms of preparing for any need of a protracted siege of Rome. Octavius seems to have met his own death bravely; he had been warned by his friends not to trust Cinna or Marius, but he refused to leave Rome, arguing that he was consul and that the city was not for him to abandon. Nor was Octavius the only victim of the purge that followed on the apparent victory of Cinna and Marius. Merula himself was falsely accused, guilty it would seem of nothing other than having been named consul in place of Cinna. The fact that he abdicated his ill-starred appointment after the senate negotiated with Cinna was of no avail. He committed suicide, dead in the year 87 as yet another victim of his bloody age.[7]

'Purge' is a qualified term. In the end, Sulla would be the victor in the struggle, and the victors often enjoy the benefit of influencing history. Some ancient sources attest to nothing less than wholesale slaughter. There is reason to believe that the casualties may have been exaggerated, but there is no question that Cinna and Marius were willing and able to eliminate their political enemies. Sulla was now declared *hostis*: he was to be treated as a public enemy. Rome was by no means a remotely friendly place for those with loyalties to Sulla, even if there was no wholesale purge of his allies and those suspected of allegiance to him.

Cinna would enjoy one clear fruit of victory: Marius and he would be named consuls for 86 BC: for Cinna it was the second time in office, and for his older colleague an astonishing seventh term. Cinna owed much to Marius, and he would not need to worry about repaying the debts: Marius died less than two weeks after taking office, a victim of natural causes at the age of seventy or seventy-one, certainly a respectable longevity for his day and place. He was replaced by Lucius Valerius Flaccus, one of the most loyal of the Marians. Flaccus would enjoy his consular year in power, destined to be sent at its end to Greece, where the legal fiction of a leaderless army was the story of the hour. Sulla was a public enemy, and so his command of the forces against Mithridates was nonexistent to all but Sulla and his men. Flaccus' principal aide in his eastern assignment was Gaius Flavius Fimbria, who was perhaps the most savage and bloodthirsty of all the partisans of Marius and Cinna.

We have observed that Pompey was born at an auspicious time for an ambitious Roman. In the immediate circumstances, he benefited from being young enough to be able to escape much of the turmoil of the hour. We know little about Pompey's activities in 87 after his father's death, or in 86 apart from his legal troubles and his marriage to Antistia. It seems that Strabo's son returned to Picenum, ready to inherit the vast system of clients that his father had amassed as patron.[8] The Roman *patronus-cliens* system was one of the key mechanisms by which the business of the republic was conducted. The image of a wealthy Roman devoting time every morning to the *salutatio* or greetings of his clients with their various requests, duties, and tidbits of information offers a classic insight into the workings of daily life in Rome.

Pompey, in short, had much to do. If his father was less than beloved and he was in contrast widely respected and looked upon with favour, he was still quite young and relatively unproven. He had accomplished little by this point in his life, for all his exemplary virtues. In some regards survival was enough. We can be sure that Pompey was kept quite busy in this 'hidden' period of his life. There were business affairs to oversee, soldiers to recruit and oversee in training, and all the labour that had to be expended on the management of his extensive and lucrative properties.

We know nothing of Pompey's thoughts in this period as to the political situation in Rome. If he was already firmly convinced that Sulla was to be the saviour of the republic, this was not the moment to be vocal about his loyalties. When the time was right, the young Pompey would be ready to stand forth as one of the stalwarts of Sulla's regime. For now, Picenum demanded his attention, not Rome.

Some students of this period wonder why Cinna and his colleagues were not more forthright in dealing with Sulla. During the entirety of 86 BC, the Marians were more than occupied with managing affairs in Rome. There may have been an element of overconfidence: the Octavian War, for example, had been resolved relatively easily. The most ardent Sullans were either fleeing Italy to join their hero in Greece, or were keeping their partisan leanings more or less quiet. An outright expedition to go to war with Sulla would require time and planning, and that was supposed to be managed by Flaccus and Fimbria. If Cinna seems to have behaved either listlessly or without sufficient foresight in dealing with his ambitious target, we need not be surprised. Rome was still possessed of a visceral loathing for civil war. Cinna is certainly an enigma, but at least some of his actions can be attributed to the extremely long list of tasks and problems that confronted him and the usual problems of the time required for news to spread. Was he a mere puppet of Marius? Almost certainly not. Was he interested in maintaining an indefinite hold on supreme power? This question is more complicated. What is sometimes referred to as the *Cinnanum tempus* or *dominatio Cinnae* is one of the least well documented major political episodes in republican history.[9] We can blame the propaganda of Sulla for only some of our lack of understanding. It is possible that Cinna did not have a particularly innovative or detailed plan for what to do with the government of the republic. Certainly he hoped to maintain a steady tenure of consulships; he would continue in office in 85 and 84. As we shall soon explore, even Cinna's end is a mystery. Certainly he was murdered by his own, yet another victim of the bloodthirsty spectre of civil war. Revulsion in the face of civil war was a recurring theme in this period, as ever in such internecine episodes; in the case of Cinna, it would also be a significant factor in his downfall.

In the annals of Roman history, Sulla was among the most competent and successful, as well as the most notorious. While Cinna could not fairly be accused of dithering, there is no question that Sulla was more productive in these crucial years. He had a campaign to prepare against Mithridates, and he needed to be ready for the inevitable actions of his political foes in Italy. That second major problem would be especially urgent once Flaccus and Fimbria were on their way to Greece.

The story of Sulla's management of the First Mithridatic War (87–85 BC) is a book in itself. Mithridates was a formidable opponent, and Sulla was compelled to fight his forces in Greece; the siege of Athens and eventual fall of the city in 86 was one of the most challenging episodes of an arduous struggle. Cinna faced two problems in connection to the war: he wanted Sulla removed from command, but he also needed to deal with Pontus. Flaccus and his officer Fimbria were supposed to be the answer to both challenges. Arguably, Flaccus was a disastrous choice for so mammoth a task; his reputation for being quick to violence and eager for personal aggrandizement did not necessarily bode well for success in so perilous a set of circumstances. Then again, one of the perils of civil strife is that you are more or less obliged to reward those who have been devoted to your faction. Few men were as ardent in their devotion to the Marian cause as Flaccus.

Flaccus had a difficult task, and luck was not remotely on his side. For one thing, there was a financial and recruiting problem that hampered finding sufficient forces to confront Sulla, let alone Mithridates as well. Weather did not cooperate with the eastward voyage, and Flaccus' already smaller than advisable forces were divided. On arrival in Greece, some of Flaccus' men actually deserted to Sulla, an interesting comment on both the immediate situation and, perhaps, the pent-up feelings of those less than satisfied with Cinna's government.

Flaccus met his death in 85, a failure in his grand endeavours.[10] What happened is difficult to explicate with clarity. Certainly it was yet another instance of civil war within civil war: Flaccus and Fimbria had a serious falling out, with Fimbria attempting to seize power from his superior, even to the point eventually of hunting his former colleague down and having him decapitated. The reasons for this shocking turn of events are not entirely clear. Ambition was certainly a significant factor. The apparent failure of Flaccus to achieve appreciable success in his early exploits may be cited. There was probably also a serious concern about what might happen if Flaccus and Sulla resolved their differences. Again, there were many men in the Roman military who were not happy about fighting their fellow countrymen, especially when there was so great a threat from Mithridates, and so much wealth and glory to be won in eastern conquests.

If there were winners in the First Mithridatic War, they were Sulla and Mithridates. The King of Pontus would live to fight another day, and the resolution of the first war would be made on very reasonable terms for him. Sulla would enjoy the credit for resolving the major foreign policy crisis of the hour. Even if one were to make the reasonable point that it was clear that trouble would likely erupt again sooner rather than later, nobody could fault Sulla for realizing that the situation in Italy demanded swift attention. Only so much time could be spent away from Rome in a critical hour; this would be another of the recurring lessons to be mastered by would-be Roman potentates. Caesar and Pompey alike would face the challenge of knowing when their presence in the capital could no longer be delayed; both men would suffer the consequences of not being in the city when the hour demanded it.

The Treaty of Dardanos that ended the war with Mithridates in 85 BC was an impressive achievement for Sulla, though it was obvious to friend and foe alike that Sulla was eager to return to Rome.[11] Mithridates suffered the loss of the territory that he had seized, but he was able to survive as King of Pontus. Sulla would be given a significant amount of treasure, as well as a fleet of ships: the war would be profitable in terms of securing his position to face Cinna and his political enemies in Rome. As for Fimbria, his fate was no better than that Flaccus. Faced with the defection of his troops to Sulla, he was another of the dead of 85, a suicide at no more than thirty years of age.[12]

Cinna meanwhile remained consul, and for a colleague in 85 BC he had Gnaeus Papirius Carbo. Carbo was another loyal and trusted Marian, and in the immediate his principal task was to help Cinna prepare for the inevitable need to deal with Sulla.[13] The victor in the east had decided to commence his westward return to Italy in 84, after dealing with the necessary oversight of the new order of affairs in Roman Asia, and along the way making sure that Roman interests were secure in Greece. Toward the end of 85, Sulla made clear what he intended to do: he wrote to the senate, giving the traditional account of his military activities, and also making clear that he had been treated atrociously by Cinna and the Marian faction. He had lost friends to his enemies; his family had been compelled to flee Rome. He was honest that revenge was on his mind, and there has been no shortage of judges from antiquity to the present day who have argued that Sulla prioritized personal vengeance over finishing the war with Mithridates in a definitive fashion.

The senate was in no mood to see a civil war between the Marians and the Sullans. They were interested in compromise, concession, and conciliation. Cinna and Carbo had been planning for war; the senate urged them to halt such preparations. Sulla was to be sent legates who would try to negotiate some sort of settlement. In point of fact matters were probably too far gone, on both sides. Certainly Cinna and Carbo were not interested in seriously stopping their military preparations, whatever they told the senate. And it is likely that even the most mellifluous of ambassadors could not have persuaded Sulla to abandon his intention to exact revenge on his enemies.

The situation that unfolded with Cinna was not entirely unlike what Flaccus experienced. Like that ill-fated, would-be commander, Cinna faced significant difficulties in the crossing of the Adriatic that he attempted in 84 BC. Cinna would die in a mutiny early that year, under circumstances that remain shrouded in a fair degree of mystery. The twenty-one year old Pompey may have been a factor in the assassination of Cinna. According to Plutarch, a rumour began to spread that Cinna had murdered Pompey.[14] The news of the alleged killing so incensed men who were already less than delighted with the consul, that they decided to add Cinna to the growing list of the casualties of civil war. The story in Plutarch is of a piece with the general thrust of the biographer's introduction to Pompey that we have seen: the young man was so virtuous and so admired by his associates and among the soldiery, that there could be no question that they would be enraged at the idea that he had been slain.

It would be fair to say that Pompey had been spending the months since Strabo's death wisely and well, seeing to his family affairs in Picenum and making sure that he was in a good position to be of use to Sulla.[15] This second enterprise required a certain amount of faith in the man who would be a mentor to him. Sulla had performed impressively thus far, but he had formidable foes arrayed against him at every step of the conflict, and he had been the object of severe criticism even by those inclined to be supportive of his positions. Plutarch's judgment reflects this fact, when he notes that while there was widespread support for Sulla to return from the east and to set matters on a better, more secure and peaceful course in Italy, there was also a question simply of wishing to be slaves in a more attractive, tolerable state of servitude. Life in Rome had been so difficult in the wake of the Social War and the ongoing civil and overseas strife that it was not a question of aspiring to republican liberty, but rather to a more pleasant state of enslavement: better Sulla as master than Cinna and Carbo.

We can only reflect on the state of mind of Pompey in his early twenties. He had already seen and heard much in both political and military life, and he had lost his father relatively early. Perhaps he was jealous of those who had been able to go east with Sulla; the future Roman Alexander no doubt was prone to indulge in thoughts of eastern adventure and profitable conquest. The two choices that confronted an ambitious young man in the year 84 were Cinna/Carbo and Sulla, and Pompey would firmly ally himself with the victor over Mithridates. If we can believe Plutarch, he sought to be in a position to impress Sulla and to gain the attention of the *imperator*.[16] Hence he engaged in raising military recruits among his vast network of clients and connections in Picenum. Interestingly, Plutarch emphasizes that Pompey enjoyed being in the cities of his native land, where he was respected and was an object of favour and kindness. We begin to see the picture of a balanced man, one who would be willing and able to go to the far corners of Rome's far flung, growing empire, even as he also took real pleasure in remaining close to his provincial roots.

How accurate is Plutarch's appraisal of Pompey in these crucial days? While we may reasonably doubt the veracity of the story of the part played passively by Pompey in Cinna's death, we may be confident of the biographer's account of the young man's intentions in the period immediately before Sulla's momentous return to Italy.

At this juncture in our story we may make mention of another eminent Roman who would play a major role in Pompey's life: Marcus Licinius Crassus. Crassus was born in 115 and was thus appreciably older than Pompey, who like Caesar would become something of a goad to the ambitions of the man destined to be both fabulously wealthy and, like his two rivals, dead by violence. Crassus' family suffered greatly at the hands of the Marians; he would be one of Sulla's most devoted allies. Like Pompey, Crassus would spend the years of the *Dominatio Cinnae* busily raising soldiers for Sulla among the clients of his family; he was kept busy in Spain in this enterprise, ready to provide considerable aid to Sulla once the war with Mithridates was finished and the Sullan faction was ready to proceed to Italy. Crassus voyaged via Africa to Greece, ready to meet with Sulla and to become one of his key subordinates.

What of Caesar at this time? His background is of particular interest not least because his paternal aunt was the wife of Marius and the mother of Marius the Younger. We have observed that Caesar's family, unlike Pompey's and Crassus', was patrician and not plebeian. But there was by no means a straightforward dichotomy between patricians and plebeians when it came to political alliances, loyalties, and machinations. One could be a patrician with notably democratic tendencies, just as one could be a plebeian whose wealth and family accomplishments and prestige found it more natural and profitable to be inclined to stereotypically conservative, traditionalist Roman tendencies.

Caesar was probably born in 100 (some would argue for 102 or 101), certainly in the month that would one day bear his name (Quintilis would become July, just as Sextilis would be August). Like Pompey, he would lose his (homonymous) father at a young age: he was not yet sixteen. We do not know the exact cause of the death of Caesar's father (in 85 or 84); he was apparently putting on his shoes in the morning when he succumbed to what may have been a stroke or cardiac event. There are other mysteries in Caesar's early life. He may have been married originally to one Cossutia; scholars debate whether the union was merely engaged or finalized.[17] What is certain is that the union with Cossutia was exceedingly brief, and Caesar's first undisputed marriage was to Cinna's daughter Cornelia, who would be the mother of Julia, the only legitimate child Caesar would have.

From the start, we see an interesting array of rivals. Patrician Caesar had strong ties both to Marius and to Cinna from a young age, while Crassus and Pompey would be allied with Sulla. Caesar was no doubt fortunate in his relative youth; he could easily have been far more seriously involved in the deadly game of civil war between the Marians and the Sullans. As we shall soon see, Caesar was in fact in serious jeopardy as a result of his rather impeccable Marian credentials. Certainly the lives of all three future triumvirs were forged in the domestic disturbances and internecine turmoil in which Rome was embroiled.

In early 84 BC, the dead Cinna's consular colleague Carbo faced difficult choices in how to manage the inevitable clash with Sulla. The year would be a busy one, as the now sole consul made preparations for a military struggle. One of the time-honoured tactics of Sulla's opponents was to try to persuade the recently enfranchised Italian allies that a Sullan victory would spell the reversal of all that they had gained; the argument went that Sulla would seek to deprive them of their voting rights and to reduce them to exactly the state of second-class existence that had prompted the outbreak of the Social War. Manpower shortages would have been keenly felt given the slaughter of that conflict.

Carbo was consul in 85 and 84; for 83, the consuls would be Scipio Asiaticus and Gaius Norbanus. Carbo sought the proconsulship of Cisalpine Gaul, and he continued his strong efforts to induce the senate to condemn Sulla as an illegitimate enemy of the republic. Tensions must have been extraordinary on all sides; it was increasingly inevitable and apparent that it would be impossible to resolve the impasse without further bloodshed.[18]

There were veterans of the Social War on both sides of the simmering conflict, but Sulla had the advantage of battle-hardened veterans of the campaigns against Mithridates. The image of 'Sulla returning from the east' would be a terrifying one for years to come. Sulla had already made it abundantly clear that even such an unthinkable act as marching on Rome was not outside his repertoire, and after the years of the *Dominatio Cinnae*, he had an abundant list of grievances to seek to avenge. It became ever more certain that the spring of 83 BC would be the arrival time of Sulla in Italy, and the commencement of a new and more savage turn in the history of Roman civil wars. For one thing, the very presence of Sulla on Italian soil would be the impetus for many of his partisans to flock openly to his cause. There would be no need now for any pretence about where men stood. Those who were convinced that Sulla was the man to restore order to the chaotic republic would now throw off any mask of being open to negotiation or coming to some agreement with Cinna and his Marians.

The young Pompey had benefited from an extensive eyewitness education in the problems of Roman republican government. He had cast in his lot with Sulla, spending the time since the death of his father in solidifying his personal network of clients and friends, in particular so that he could contribute appreciably to the Sullan cause. For many in Pompey's position, the advent of Sulla was viewed in quasi-messianic terms. Sulla was to be the salvific figure, ready to restore the traditional greatness of Rome and to put an end to squabbling, dissension, and the perceived manipulation of the apparatus of elections and political offices to favour what was viewed by some as an increasingly radical democratic policy agenda. The calendar had worked in Pompey's favour. He turned twenty-two years of age in the autumn before Sulla's return, still quite youthful, but now able to contribute impressively to a cause he clearly believed in as the path forward for Rome. His older contemporary Crassus clearly shared his views on the matter of siding with Sulla. Caesar meanwhile was eighteen when Sulla landed in Italy, certainly old enough to play some role in the unfolding events, and in the present circumstances burdened with a quite close connection to the Marian cause.

Until the arrival of Sulla, prevarication was a possible strategy for the conflicted. Those of insufficient courage and mettle, or who were in awkward positions either on account of family ties, property holdings, and political office were more or less able to be forthright about their intentions and views. No doubt a good number of prominent Romans continued to hope to the end for a peaceful settlement. Civil war remained a ghastly prospect for a sizable percentage of the Roman ruling class, not to mention the soldiery. Not all military men were eager to wield swords against their fellow Romans. Looming over all was not only the still controversial question of the recently pacified Italian allies, but also the slave population of Italy and the empire, a brewing crisis in the making that would soon enough provide its own headlines.

Pompey would more than attract the notion of Sulla and his circle in the critical events of 83 BC. Plutarch notes that one critic of Pompey in Picenum noted that the young man had left his pedagogues to become a demagogue, eager to rally his ancestral homeland to the cause of Sulla.[19] The man paid for his verbal assault with his life, and not by Pompey's own hand. So persuasive was the oratory of the young man that the very crowd around him would repay hostile words with fatal blows. It was the hour for the son of Strabo to distinguish himself in a new crisis for the republic. It was an hour that would set the pattern for the breathtaking early years of Pompey's rise to ever more formidable power.

Chapter Three

Sulla Ascendant

Plutarch's tale of Pompey's encounter with a heckler is cast in the context of the efforts of the consul Carbo to rally support for his cause from the citizens of Picenum.[1] Pompey displayed unquestionable audacity and daring this period. The results are impressive: we are told that he managed to muster a total force of three legions, fully equipped.[2] For any who might have wondered what the son of Strabo had been doing with his time, the answer came as he simply assumed command of his homegrown force, an army that he was ready to use in service of bolstering Sulla's cause. The victor over Mithridates did not arrive in Italy devoid of forces by any means, but he would no doubt be delighted when he learned that the number of fighting men at his disposal rose appreciably thanks to the successful efforts of such as Pompey.

As so often in Roman republican history, we see here a clear instance of a would-be commander acting independently, with the law made legal, as it were, by force of arms. Pompey had no senatorial or other commission to raise three legions. He had no permit or mission sanctioned by any government authority or magistrate. He moved independently and decisively to raise men to defend his political interests, which in this case meant bolstering Sulla's army. By no means either the first or the last to employ such expedients to achieve a desired goal, Pompey was among the most efficient and competent in his enterprise.

Sulla landed his forces in that fateful spring of 83 BC in two units, one of which arrived at Brundisium, the other at Tarentum (the modern Brindisi and Taranto).[3] The goal of many in Pompey's position was to find their way to Sulla, either individually or, like the ambitious Pompey, with an army. The Adriatic Sea was a problematic eastern barrier for Italy. This was not an age where it was feasible to have such defence of the immense coastline that one could hope to prevent an enemy landing. It was often a case of one side crossing over ahead of the other. Landing in Italy gave Sulla an undeniable advantage, not least because it was far easier now for his partisans to declare for him openly and without much hesitation. Managing to make one's way to Sulla's camps might be difficult, but it was far more feasible than joining him somewhere in Greece.

Switching sides was by no means unheard of in this period. One notable figure, Publius Cornelius Cethegus, would survive to be able to tell of how he had been transformed from a committed partisan of Marius to one of Sulla. Such men always laboured more or less seriously under the charge that they had been fickle in their allegiances. Pompey had no such problem, at least not to any appreciable extent. Young and with relatively little experience, but already with a proven appetite for daring and decisive bravado, he was ready to be among the first in the ranks of Sulla's elite inner circle.

A sympathetic observer might have felt sorry for Gnaeus Papirius Carbo. The real power behind the consuls Scipio Asiaticus and Gaius Norbanus, he found himself in a situation that might well have looked bleak. All previous efforts to checkmate Sulla had failed, and now Italy faced upheaval reminiscent of the Social War, with the prospect of bloody, costly combat on Italian soil. The consuls were responsible for taking the field to deal with the man Carbo had denounced as an outlaw and enemy of the republic.

Pompey had the task of moving south from Picenum to intersect with Sulla. Plutarch emphasizes that Pompey made no effort to conceal his marches, and further, he made no real effort at speed: he was interested in dealing with any opponents who tried to hinder his advance, a tactic that would allow him both to destroy opposition forces and to give his men a taste of battle experience. In one sense, strategically what Pompey did was make it seem as if Sulla had landed in a third location; the forces that set out from Picenum constituted a potentially formidable new front in the civil war, and they offered a tempting target for the consular forces. Certainly Carbo did not want to see Pompey's three legions unite with Sulla's men in the south; arguably, Pompey also wanted them to attack him or hamper his progress. It would allow an opportunity for solo glory before any rendezvous with Sulla, and it would weaken Carbo's forces before they could be destroyed by Sulla's larger contingents.

There is some evidence that at least three discrete armies tried to converge against Pompey as he marched south; our knowledge of the youthful hero's actions is clouded by a certain tendency in the extant record to ascribe Sullan exploits to his protégé. Plutarch's account is characteristically dramatic.[4] One of the armies sought to engage Pompey, who gathered his forces together to prepare to make a stand of it. As for the tactics and progress of this first real taste of battle for Pompey, we are told that the commander took the lead with the cavalry, stationing them in front for a charge against the enemy. Celtic cavalry rode out to try to check his advance, but Pompey bravely clashed with the leading horseman of the foe, killing him in battle. The daring and reckless stunt worked; the cavalry turned and fled, which disrupted the infantry lines and allowed Pompey's forces to rout their adversaries.

The tale of virtual single combat in the midst of an equestrian engagement in what amounted to Pompey's debut performance in battle is Homeric in its colourful composition. According to Plutarch's narrative, the defeat of the first of the three consular armies caused such consternation that Pompey's adversaries withdrew to regroup and plan a next move, which led to more towns and locales coming over to Pompey's cause. In the biographer's estimation, the prevailing opinion was that the consuls were scared of Pompey, cowed by this successful young man who had performed brilliantly in his first clash. We are told that when the consul Scipio Asiaticus took the field against him, Pompey was hailed at once as commander by his would-be foes, who saluted him in a sign of defection to his banners. We are reminded again of how loathe many men were to engage in civil war, especially on what they perceived to be the losing side. To the degree that Pompey was supremely popular and widely admired, he had now displayed excellence on the field, and all in the service ultimately of the man who was increasingly viewed as the one to save Rome from the likes of Carbo.[5] Even if Sulla was viewed by some as at best a necessary evil, there is good reason to believe that the internal administration of the last years had engendered significant dissatisfaction with Cinna's regime and its aftermath. Roman public support could be all too transient and fickle, but for the moment at least, Sulla and Pompey were in the ascendant. What is clear is this: even if the extant record is no doubt exaggerated as to the accomplishments of Pompey, this was the hour in which the young man distinguished himself sufficiently so as to gain the attention of Sulla. It was the *kairos*, the critical juncture of his early career. He made the most of it.

The third army that Pompey is said to have engaged with was sent by Carbo himself; Plutarch offers minimal details as to the battle. This was actually the fifth force that had set out after Pompey: from the first three armies, one was routed and the other two withdrew, to be followed by the successive advances of the men under Scipio and then those commissioned by Carbo. Carbo's soldiers did not defect to Pompey; they acquitted themselves well in a strong attack, but Pompey's forces succeeded in routing them. Plutarch notes that the terrain was sufficiently treacherous so as to impede an easy flight; unable to escape on horseback, the men surrendered themselves, together with an impressive amount of horses and equipment. All things considered, it was an impressive series of accomplishments for Pompey in his first experiences as a battle commander.

We have no idea exactly what news arrived when at Sulla's headquarters, but he was clearly made aware that Pompey was on his way, and he appears to have been kept reasonably informed of the movements of the consular armies. Again, there was ample opportunity for anxiety: Sulla had no idea what to expect from this young man from Picenum, and the dispatches seemed to indicate that Pompey was facing significant opposition on his southward march. Plutarch relates that Sulla was worried about his young ally, and was on his way, planning to advance north to meet him along the way and to offer help. But the scene that emerges is more vintage Plutarch: Pompey succeeds in his mission, and when he learns that Sulla is approaching, he orders his men to focus on dramatic battle array and a splendid appearance, ready to impress Sulla on his arrival.[6] Here we see an attempt to portray Pompey as nothing less than a splendid manager of high theatre, with all the emphasis on spectacle and visual power. Pompey greeted Sulla with the title *Imperator*, as was his due. And Sulla returned the favour, hailing the young Pompey as *Imperator* in turn. The story may well be true; it is the stuff of instant legend, destined to be passed along and handed down as part of the mythic apparatus of the great commander. Plutarch draws attention to how Pompey was not yet even a senator; indeed, he held no official rank whatsoever. And yet from that day forward, Sulla is said to have treated Pompey with supreme deference, even to such significant Roman courtesies as uncovering his head and rising to greet him.[7]

Pompey had more than succeeded in his lofty goal of impressing Sulla. Sulla, for his part, had three more legions of veteran troops, personally loyal to Pompey and by extension to Pompey's hero. Plutarch notes that Sulla took note of the vigour and loyalty of the men serving under Pompey. Whatever reputation Strabo had, his son was widely admired and respected. These were men on whom Sulla could count for superlative service in the challenges ahead.

When Plutarch makes clear that none of Sulla's honours inspired any arrogance in Pompey, we see another hint of the adulatory tradition that surrounded a man who would end his life as something of a republican martyr. It is impossible to determine the truth of such appraisals of his character. Likely Pompey cultivated avidly such a reputation. In the immediate context, there was the question of his youth. Sulla had older allies, men who had more than earned their commands by years of dutiful service. Especially where Pompey outperformed them, there was ample room for jealousy and recrimination. No doubt Pompey was eager to avoid any such charge by being particularly zealous to appear humble.

For the moment, the first order of business was to determine what Pompey would do next, now directly under Sulla's control. The republic was a vast and somewhat unwieldy construct. Africa, Spain, Gaul, Greece and Asia, all loomed large in the political and military landscape, besides the heartland of Italy. Civil wars could be complicated by such vast geographical considerations; in another time and during another instance of Roman against Roman, Pompey would prove to be a master of manipulating the map to his advantage.

Pompey was apparently assigned two new challenges in quick sequence, both of them arduous. There is some indication that he was sent back to Picenum to raise even more troops. This was difficult both logistically and because it may well have seemed to be a somewhat dull (even if exceedingly important and necessary) assignment. No doubt the young *imperator* wanted to take the field again quickly. In conjunction with his meditation on Pompey's respect for his elders, Plutarch notes that he was unwilling to be sent to replace one of Sulla's senior loyalists and commanders, Quintus Caecilius Metellus.[8] Metellus was about twenty-two years Pompey's senior, and was to be responsible for the management of operations in Cisalpine Gaul. In the end, Pompey would be sent to manouevre with Metellus, ready to aid him as his cavalry commander.

Pompey would proceed north and muster more reinforcements in Picenum. Then he would join forces with Metellus, ready to display more of his exemplary work in horsemanship. Again we cannot be certain of every aspect of Sulla's thinking. Pompey certainly deserved a job, and Sulla's cause needed more men. Metellus was no Pompey in terms of brash bravery and reckless daring; by all accounts he was at least a relatively conservative commander. In other words, Sulla may have realized that Metellus and Pompey could help each other and learn well from serving as officers together.

Metellus was one of those Romans who acquired an honourific *agnomen*, a title that amounted to a fourth name. His father had been one of those banished in the days of Marius' ascendancy, and he was fortunate to have a son who never ceased labouring strenuously to have him recalled to Rome. His efforts were so herculean that he was called *Pius*, with reference to that quality of *pietas* that was so cherished by the Romans. It added to his mystique as a classic, conservative republican of the old school, one of those *optimates* fiercely opposed to the efforts of the *populares*.[9] Metellus in some regards had impeccable credentials for a partisan of Sulla, and whatever help he needed in successful prosecution of military campaigns, Pompey would prove to be a more than useful support and colleague. It is true that he was one of those prominent Romans who had waited to see if there might be some successful negotiation or settlement to avoid civil war, but this can be attributed to that loathing for civil war that was so palpable in Roman society. Even those willing to engage in acts of civil war were aware that they had to contend with managing armies that were sometimes hesitant to do battle with other Romans.

Metellus had cooperated with Crassus in the raising of troops for Sulla in Africa. There is some evidence that the two men were not entirely harmonious in their cooperation. Crassus, as we have seen, eventually travelled to Greece to join Sulla. Whatever difficulties were present, however, there is no question that the two men were devoted and committed to the success of Sulla's initiatives and programme. Metellus had his own series of adventures to be able to proceed from Africa to Cisalpine Gaul. Like Pompey, he was able eventually to manage to meet Sulla, offering troops and supplies for the cause.

Metellus was to be accompanied north by several prominent figures; besides Pompey, Marcus Lucullus, the younger brother of the more famous Lucius, would be present. Crassus had come from the east with Sulla, and whatever past differences he had with Metellus notwithstanding, he would go north as well. Sulla was also apparently occupied in sending notes far and wide in Italy, urging prominent men to support his cause and to contribute men and arms. There was a major engagement in November of 83, the Battle of Tifata or Casilinum, in south-central Italy. According to Appian, Sulla and Metellus confronted Norbanus and won an astonishing victory, losing seventy men and slaying 6,000.[10] The figures may well arouse suspicion as to accuracy (even with the detail that many of Sulla's men were seriously wounded); further, we are not certain of the exact chronology of events during the year of Sulla's arrival, not least in the prelude and aftermath of this major battle. We do not know, for example, exactly when Pompey was sent to raise more troops in Picenum. We do not have precise information as to the exact itineraries and calendars of the commanders in question, though the general course of events is reasonably clear. Certainly we lack details as to what exactly happened in this apparently costly battle. Tifata was fought in November, when Pompey was likely busy raising additional troops before joining Metellus and his entourage.

Norbanus was forced to withdraw after his devastating loss, but his consular colleague Scipio was nearby. Unfortunately for Scipio, his forces were apparently quite unmotivated to engage in civil war, and were eager for peace. Sulla learned of this and attempted to capitalize on his psychological advantage. Negotiations commenced; from Sulla's perspective, the intention was transparent: he hoped to win over more men and arms without fighting. One man who would play his own significant role in subsequent events was not open to trusting Sulla. Quintus Sertorius was a key member of Scipio's staff, and he was insistent that the consul should not put any faith in Sulla's intentions.[11] There is good reason to agree with the appraisal that Sertorius was one of the more competent and insightful members of the Marian faction; time and again his advice would be ignored, with perilous consequence. That said, Sertorius was also impulsive and reckless, ready to pounce on what he thought was the right opportunity at the right moment, whatever the risks.

While Scipio and Sulla were officially engaged in negotiations with the customary exchange of hostages, Sertorius (who was convinced that Scipio was not heeding his admonitions) decided to seize a nearby town.[12] This was exactly the sort of provocation that Sulla could take advantage of during difficult negotiations, especially if he was not sincerely acting in good faith. Sertorius' major problem at this juncture was that he was not in charge. Scipio's response to Sulla's objections about what Sertorius did was to return the hostages, which on the one hand was an honourable thing to do, while in another sense it was fatal to the already wavering faith of the consul's men. Scipio's men were ready to defect to Sulla, who was magnanimous in sending away the consul and his son, strictly enjoining them not to engage in further efforts against him, or to join Carbo's initiatives. Before long Sertorius would be sent by the Marians to manage their affairs in Spain, and when we return to his story, Spain will be the scene of his most lasting contributions to history.

The year 82 BC, like 83, was to be one in which Pompey was engaged in manouevres and battles as part of the ongoing campaigns of the civil war. The principal difference was that now he would be cooperating directly with colleagues, including his future fellow triumvir Crassus. The ill-fated consuls for the year were Carbo and Marius the Younger; both men would join the ranks of those who did not survive their year in office.

There is good reason to believe that one of the first of the major engagements of 82 was between the forces under Metellus and Pompey on one hand, and those of the Marian Gaius Carrinas on the other, in the so-called Battle of the River Asio.[13] The spring campaigning season barely commenced that March, after what seems to have been an especially harsh winter, as Appian reports.[14] Pompey had clearly spent the winter amassing more men and material, ready to commence the season for war with fresh forces. We actually know somewhat more about Asio than Tifata. The battle lasted from early morning until noon, some six hours of deadly fighting on a day in early spring. Carbo's subordinate Carrinas was routed after an exceptionally hard fought engagement, and the victory of Metellus and Pompey was sufficient to induce still more men to go over to Sulla's cause.

82 BC would be the key year for Sulla's ambitions. Plutarch reports that Pompey was invigourating for Metellus, encouraging him and inspiring him to renewed vigour. Frustratingly, Plutarch indicates that he is hesitant to delve into the details of these early endeavours of Pompey, since they were so eclipsed by his later, monumental achievements. This much is certain: while the task was difficult, the balance sheet at the start of 82 inclined heavily to Sulla's favour. The men serving under him were unquestionably more competent than Carbo and his commanders; Sullan propaganda aside, it is clear that officers like Pompey were a major key to Sulla's ultimate victory.

Sulla's opponents were deeply motivated by what they considered to be the inevitable reprisals against them if he should be victorious. If anything, Sulla was honest that vengeance would be the watchword of his coming to power. Appian notes that the actual war was not particularly long given its momentous nature.[15] For Appian, the principal explanation for this is that the adversaries were acting like personal enemies, determined to wipe out men they truly despised and hated. Sulla had been willing to engage in at least the pretence of negotiation with Scipio, and some have seen in this evidence that he was trying to improve his reputation, ever eager to see more men come to his banners without the need for doing battle. It was a delicate balance; one develops the impression that Sulla was willing to engage in profitable diplomatic discourse when it both benefited him, and when the men involved were not on his list of those destined to suffer his vengeance.

The spring of 82 was an auspicious one for Sulla, and the time for negotiation, at any rate, seemed long past. Metellus and Pompey disposed of Carrinas' force in their six-hour battle, and even the subsequent efforts of Carbo to come to rescue the situation would be doomed to swift failure. Sulla would be the victor in the Battle of Sacriportus, which took place in April.[16] His opponent was Marius the Younger, whose consulate was to be marred by so much failure. Once again we may be suspicious of any Sullan propaganda influence on the reports of the engagement. We need not believe that Marius lost 28,000 or so men, either killed, wounded, deserted, or defected. We need not think that Sulla's forces suffered barely two dozen casualties. Numbers are relatively easy to alter and to exaggerate, especially with the passage of time. But there can be no doubt that Sulla won another tremendous victory.

Appian records that Marius did not perform entirely badly and to his discredit, notwithstanding the final disaster.[17] He was said to have fought bravely and to have acquitted himself well in terms of courage and daring, but his left wing began to give away under enemy pressure, and when the battle seemed to be inclining toward Sulla, many of Marius' men defected. Marius was forced to flee to Praeneste, and barely escaped; Sulla pursued his routed army, and there was tremendous slaughter. Sulla had plenty of things to do, and to do quickly, throughout the peninsula; he ordered a siege of Praeneste and assigned forces to maintain the siege. Marius' son was to be forced to surrender by force of hunger and not arms.

Carbo had been on his way to try to confront Metellus and Pompey when he learned of the disaster that had befallen his consular colleague. This was a moment of crisis that would have taxed the resources and abilities of the most capable of commanders, and Carbo was destined for failure. Appian says that Metellus engaged Carbo's forces, winning another victory; once again we are told that a major factor in Sullan success was the number of defections.[18] Civil wars are difficult on many levels, and the Marians in particular were receiving a deadly firsthand education in its perils.

Gaius Marcius Censorinus is one of those many names in republican history that is known best because of his sorry end. Censorinus was a Marian commander assigned the difficult tasks both of confronting the forces of Metellus and

Pompey, and, later, of trying at least to bring supplies to the besieged consul at Praeneste. Censorinus clashed with Pompey in the Battle of Sena Gallica; he was defeated, and Pompey was able to plunder the town. The strategy in sacking the town was a harsh expedient: the idea was to convince other locales to open their gates freely to the Sullans, so as to avoid the same fate. Towns near Rome would learn this lesson, and when the time came for Sulla to draw near the capital, he would find a ready reception from civilians eager to be spared the ravaged of war. Meanwhile the ill-fated Censorinus attempted his relief of Marius the Younger, and he was swiftly ambushed by Pompey's cavalry.

Perhaps not surprisingly after two defeats, Censorinus' men began to blame him for the poor showing against Pompey. Once again the Marian cause suffered desertions; Censorinus was eventually compelled to retreat to Carbo, having lost most of his force to defections more than to battle. Our relatively scanty evidence of these military engagements does not permit us to render a definitive verdict on Pompey's merits as a commander. There is no question that he was a key figure in Sulla's successes in the field in 82. He was likely an exceptionally gifted cavalry commander in particular. This was one of the classic pursuits of a gentleman in arms; the famous fifth-century Athenian Xenophon authored handbooks on the maintenance of a cavalry force, as well as on horsemanship more generally. Young men in particular were encouraged to train in the effective use of the horse in both hunting and equestrian battles. The men who faced Pompey on the field were not renowned for their military acumen, and they suffered under the burden of engaging in a civil war. Under such circumstances, the winning side has a marked advantage in the game of bringing more men over to their cause without firing a shot. It is telling that Plutarch does not dwell on these early Pompeian battles; they were not the matter of a glorious record, not least because they were fought against his countrymen. All the same, Pompey was deservedly earning a reputation for competence, and for a great destiny.

After boxing in Marius the Younger in Praeneste, Sulla proceeded to advance on Rome. There were ugly scenes that would unfold, to the discredit of the Marians and as a reminder of the atrocities that can mar the actions of both sides in a war. When it became clear that Rome might easily fall to Sulla, there were assassinations and purges of those sympathetic to Sulla.

The situation had devolved to a point where Sulla by no means had won, but his victory must have seemed all but sealed. All military efforts to check his progress had been repelled. Metellus and Pompey had distinguished themselves in Etruria, even as Sulla had made his inexorable advance toward Rome. One consul was trapped under siege in Praeneste, while the other must have felt that he rarely could go far without feeling harassment from Pompey's formidable cavalry. Rome was indefensible, and the most that the Marians could do was to try to kill as many Sullan sympathizers as possible before they were forced to flee the city before Sulla's arrival.

Italy south of Rome was largely under Sulla's control by this point; Praeneste was holding out, but sieges are notoriously slow and tedious. Even after the fall of Rome (admittedly, without a fight), Carbo was still in a position to challenge the Sullans, and perhaps a masterful commander could have made a better show of it. Still, circumstances weighed heavily against him, and the situation was growing ever more dire. Carbo deserves credit and admiration for being willing to face Sulla; certainly he had decided that he was possessed of sufficient forces to try at last to defeat his perhaps overconfident foe. Further, this was clearly a life and death game, and Carbo was not ready to commit suicide.

June of 82 was the month of the Battle of Clusium, or more accurately the first such engagement.[19] One could plausibly argue that at least in some regards, Clusium was no means a disaster for Carbo. It was, one might think, a clash that might have inspired one to hope that all was not lost. On the other hand, Carbo had limited forces at his disposal. The engagement was fast-moving and complicated. The consular forces enjoyed a welcome reinforcement of skilled Celtiberian cavalry from Spain. It is conceivable that Pompey had developed a particular reputation for outstanding skill in equestrian manoeuvres, and that Carbo hoped to field the celebrated Spanish cavalry against his Sullan opponents. In any case, there seem to have been two stages to the combat. There was a cavalry battle in which Sulla performed well, and there were more defections: some of the new Spanish horsemen were ready to go over to the enemy. Appian reports that Carbo was reduced to slaying the remaining reinforcements, either because he was afraid that they, too, would be treacherous, or because he was simply so incensed at the initial betrayal.[20] Soon enough there would be a full-scale clash between Carbo and Sulla, a struggle that would last an entire day, only to end in what at best was a stalemate.

We say 'at best,' because Carbo needed a victory, not a draw. He did not have the luxury of losing significant forces in what at best was a delaying action. Carbo's mood understandably worsened as the series of defeats continued to mar the first half of his consular year, only to be crowned by heavy losses in an indecisive clash. There was no good news to report as the steady drumbeat of failures continued; indeed matters were about to turn even worse. Carbo decided to try to send some of his remaining forces to aid his commander Carrinas, but Sulla was able to ambush them en route, with a reported loss of 2,000. Carrinas was in dire straits because he was trying to evade Pompey, who had created an especially deadly force to face his enemy by joining up with Crassus.

Later history would take particular care in remembering what might otherwise have been yet another in a series of victories of the *optimates* over the *populares*.

It was the first time that the future colleagues in power collaborated in facing a common enemy. Carrinas was defeated in the Battle of Spoletium, with a loss, Appian notes, of 3,000 men.[21] Casualty figures aside, it was clearly another devastating loss, and another of the laurels for Pompey in this busy year of battle. Between the defeat and the subsequent ambush, it was increasingly clear that the Marian cause was doomed. Carrinas was able to escape his losses at Spoletium by virtue of taking cover in a severe rainstorm that made pursuit impractical.

Meanwhile, Marius could not survive indefinitely in the increasingly critical siege situation in Praeneste.[22] The fact that Carbo sought to send Censorinus to help him is understandable, but constitutes another instance of reaction rather than active strategizing. Now it was Pompey's turn to imitate his mentor Sulla and to set an ambush. Pompey defeated the relief force with additional great losses, and once again the vanquished Marians were inclined to blame their leader for the failure. There was a serious mutiny, and much of Censorinus' force dissolved. There are reports that Marius sought actively to try to break out of the Sullan siege, but those efforts came to naught.

Carbo cannot be faulted for a lack of boldness, even as one setback came swift on the heels of another. It must have seemed mad to some at least of his men when he announced his intention to launch an attack on Metellus at Faventia. Surely he was weary at this point of a reactive policy; once again he hoped to catch a Sullan force unawares. Joining with Norbanus, he planned a twilight surprise strike, anticipating that he could utilize his initiative to recoup some of his losses in a devastating attack. The story told by Appian records that the enemy Carbo faced on this occasion included vines: striking not long before dark, before long the Marians were contending as much with entanglement in the terrain as with the enemy.[23] We are told of 10,000 dead and another 6,000 desertions, figures that once again we may dispute. But propaganda did not conjure another defeat out of thin air: Carbo had lost in his bold gambit.

Cisalpine Gaul soon defected en masse to Sulla: the handwriting was on the wall. Marcus Lucullus won a victory over additional forces of Carbo at some point; Appian makes a brief mention of such a win near Placentia, with no details.[24] The sources that allude to Lucullus' activities in this war are difficult to reconcile; we do well to remember that the more famous Lucius Lucullus was managing Sullan affairs in the east in this period, with his brother maintaining the family's honour and distinction in Italy.

It is not entirely surprising that by September, Carbo was ready to withdraw from Italy in the hope of securing more forces and supplies abroad. Men like Censorinus and Carrinas had an unenviable task: they were in charge of maintaining the Marian forces in Italy. One can well imagine that Pompey spent much time reminding his men that they had defeated both commanders; there was no need to fear the clearly weakened enemy. It was frustrating that Carrinas had escaped, but however persistent the enemy was, the noose was tightening.

Carbo's decision to flee to Africa was an understandable one in context, and most men in his position would have done the same thing.[25] That said, it reinforced the notion that the Marian cause was doomed. It was also a harbinger of what would happen again and again in the history of the Roman civil wars. It was all too easy to depart for some other theatre of the empire, seeking support and time to restore one's fortunes. Pompey and his sons would have their own experience of just this sort of geographical gambit, one that at the very least caused immense frustration to one's foes.

In the course of 82 BC, domino after domino fell as Sulla's forces secured control of Italy.[26] If there was an overarching strategy, it was simply to confront the consular forces, either by provoking an engagement or by inviting attacks. Little by little, Carbo's available manpower was being whittled away, not least by wholesale defections to Sulla. Carbo still had appreciable forces, and the fierce and battle-hardened Samnites of south-central Italy favoured his cause. But defeat upon defeat weighed heavily on his morale, and for a consul to feel that he needed to depart Italy was a sure indicator of despair.

Carbo would never return alive to Italy. At the time he embarked on his journey, he probably had about 40,000 men still under arms, not counting his Samnite allies. Of the 40,000, some 30,000 were concentrated near Clusium. One battle there had already ended in disaster for the Marians, and there would be a second before the end of the fateful year. The Second Battle of Clusium is a mysterious one in terms of details of the engagement. The basic facts are clear: Pompey won another tremendous victory, in which Carbo's cause incurred further frightful losses. Appian claims that 20,000 were lost, as usual a number that should likely be taken *cum grano salis*.[27] If accurate, this would be the greatest single loss that the Marians suffered in the war. Whatever the death toll, it was another disaster that qualified as a nail in Carbo's coffin.

The Marians were in a desperate state, and there is no surprise in the extreme measures that they contemplated. Rome had been spared much of the ravages of war. There had been assassinations of Sullan supporters before the flight of the Marians, but the city had not suffered a siege or sack. Now the Marians and their Samnite allies conceived the notion that they could perhaps invade the city, taking it over in its state of light defence, able then to negotiate from a stronger position, and certainly able to bask in the glory of a much-needed victory, one that would be supremely symbolic as well as strategically valuable.

Was Sulla caught by surprise? Was the man who had shown no qualms about marching on Rome reduced to a state where he came close to suffering a significant blow just as he seemed to be on the verge of victory? Sulla was eminently pragmatic, and a masterful tactician. Certainly he may be criticized for not preparing for the possibility that Rome might be attacked, but from a military point of view, arguably there were far more pressing concerns elsewhere. All the same, in the high autumn of 82, Rome came dangerously close to being sacked for the first time since the Gallic invasion of 390. The remnants of the Marian forces, together with their Samnite, advanced on the city ready to pounce.

The first of November would be one of those days in history that matter. What became known as the Battle of the Colline Gate would enter the legends of Sullan propaganda, certainly. The man who had brought armed forces into the city in pursuit of his own cause would be able to boast that he had saved Rome from the Samnites, who were a more palatable enemy to highlight to those squeamish about Romans killing their fellow Romans. Regardless of whether or not Sulla had been caught by surprise, his response to the crisis was swift. Units of his forces were dispatched at once to Rome. The Samnites and other Italian allies who would be met in battle had a far better reputation as fighters than any of the Romans serving under the consul. Fierce warriors with the fresh memory and experience of the Social War in their favour, the Samnites could be expected to pose a serious threat to Sulla, notwithstanding the fact that he had quite qualified veterans of his own. One problem was exhaustion: Sulla's men had been busy in the period leading up to the battle, and they had had to make a rapid advance to intercept their enemies.

Appian records that 50,000 men would die in total on that November day.[28] Certainly it was one of the most ferocious and bloody engagements of the war, if not the costliest. The battle is said to have commenced in the afternoon; Sulla was eager to engage the enemy quickly, even at the cost of giving his fatigued men a chance to recover from their march and to prepare. The combat reportedly went on through the night. Sulla won, though apparently his left flank was repulsed by the enemy and fled to the city. We find here another of those instances where the defenders of the walls are frightened of the pursuit of the enemy as they chase down the men seeking to flee into the city; the crush of gates and efforts to keep the Marians and Samnites from entering Rome meant that there were heavy casualties on both sides on the very threshold of the city.

This was Sulla's dramatic day in combat; we hear tales of how he tried to restore his faltering left flank in person, drawing enemy fire because of his easily identifiable white horse, and nearly losing his life. Ancient battles were extraordinarily prone to confusion and the fog of war. On the left, Sulla did not save the day; the flank was defeated. The right was under the command of Crassus, and he was able to secure a victory. Sulla was not even aware of the success of Crassus for some time. Cynics might wonder if Sullan propaganda made the battle more than it was, exaggerating the difficulties to make it seem as if Sulla had faced an enormously challenging task with ultimate success. But the surviving records of the battle do not seem to reflect efforts to gloss over Sulla's failings, or to embellish his achievement. On the contrary, two major facts critical to Sulla dominate our knowledge of the fight. Sulla probably should have waited before commencing the battle. This point may be debated endlessly by armchair wargamers; one could, after all, argue that Sulla was right to take the initiative and strike hard and fast, tired men or not. Perhaps matters would have been no different had he waited; perhaps the Marians and the Samnites would have struck first had Sulla delayed. Second, Crassus is the one who succeeded in his sector; Sulla failed to win on the left. All told, we may be reasonably confident that the battle was exceptionally hard fought, with grave losses on both sides. Perhaps no one could have done better than Sulla.

Censorinus and Carrinas survived the battle, but not for long. Their escape did not get very far before they were captured. They were decapitated on Sulla's orders, their heads sent to Praeneste as a grim indicator of what had happened at the Colline Gate. It was a clear indicator in and of itself that Sulla was in no mood for concession or conciliation after the difficult battle: the Marians could expect to be given no quarter. Some 8,000 Samnite prisoners were also slain: again, Sulla was clearly in a mood for this war to be concluded with a definitive indicator of the price of attacking or threatening what he considered to be nothing less than the security of the republic. For Sulla and his supporters, the cause they were espousing was nothing less than the restoration of order. The Marians had proven themselves all too capable of acts of bloody reprisal; neither side could claim to be free of violent acts of vengeance.

Praeneste had no hope of holding out successfully. The victory of Sulla and Crassus at the Colline Gate sealed the fate of Marius the Younger; the long siege had no chance of finding some saviour. The surrender of Praeneste would come on the fourth of November. Marius had been born around 110; the ill-fated consul was about twenty-eight. He tried to take advantage of an underground tunnel, it seems, either to hide out or, more probably, to flee. In the end he committed suicide. Sulla's commander in charge of the siege, Quintus Lucretius Afella, would be able to present the head of the consul to his superior. This was Sulla's autumn; much of the work was now finished.

There is no question that many died in those early days of November, not only in combat, but in the reprisals and executions of prisoners. Some of this was no doubt a consequence of the difficulties faced at the Colline Gate, but Sulla had also been clear that he intended to seek revenge for what he perceived to be all the wrongs that he, his family, and his supporters had suffered at the hands of the Marians. Sulla had indeed returned from the east, and in the space of a year and a half he had successfully taken over Italy; by early November, 82 BC, the Sullans were in charge across the peninsula, and Marians left in Italy had every reason to fear that their names were marked down for elimination. Proscriptions were not exactly uncommon in the bloody history of the Roman civil wars and the decline and fall of the republic, but arguably no one would achieve quite the dubious, notorious reputation for savagery in utilizing the expedient as Sulla.

Late 82 BC was the advent of a time of what has usually been taken to be a period of severe reprisals against those who had taken up arms against Sulla, or who had in some way challenged him or supported those who did. One might well wonder how exactly Sulla and his followers argued for the legality of their actions. The answer was to be found in the title *Dictator*, one that certainly existed in the Roman system of traditional government, but which was exclusively to be used in times of great crisis and state emergency.[29] For all the problems and disasters that the republic had suffered, it had been well over a century since the office had been invoked. Critics of Sulla could argue that he was interested at this juncture solely in power. Certainly his supporters included both those who genuinely agreed that the republic needed a dictator, and those who simply chose what they saw to be the winning side: fear is a powerful motivator. References in the historical record to Sulla's capacity for mercy toward defeated enemies (both foreign and domestic) has often been taken to be little more than evidence of pro-Sullan propaganda.[30]

Sulla's dictatorship was absolute not least with respect to the calendar. There was no announced time limit to how long the crisis would take to be resolved. Especially since there had been precedent for a dictatorship, it was possible for Sulla to make the argument that republican institutions like the consulate would continue. Sulla was not *rex* or 'king'; whatever absolutism he exercised in his power, it was cloaked in the veneer of republican sentiments. The cynic might believe none of this, but that was irrelevant to the ultimate course of affairs. One of the examples that demonstrated the futility of objection was the man responsible for maintaining the siege of Praeneste, Lucretius Ofella.[31] He was incensed at what he correctly viewed as the sham state of elections in which the dictator actually dictated as to the candidates who would elected. Irritated that he was not a beneficiary of the fake process, he appealed to the people to rise up and support him in his objection. The pleading and indignant objection was all in vain; Sulla ordered a centurion to slay the objector on the spot. Appian says that Sulla told the people a chilling fable: a man was once irritated by fleas while ploughing, and every time he tried to shake them from his shirt, soon enough they returned.[32] At last he burned the shirt, so that he could continue his work without interruption. Be careful, Sulla warned the crowd, that your dictator not be reduced to needing to use fire to deal with you.

Sulla was well advanced in becoming one of the most complex personalities on the Roman republican stage. There were those who despised him as a king in everything but name, a tyrant ill-disposed to any question of his supreme authority, and all too ready to kill anyone who was deemed a threat to his rule. Others saw in him the strong hand that was necessary to restore and to maintain order. The Kubrick *Spartacus* film of 1960 plays on something of Sulla's complexity in certain aspects of its presentation both of historical events and in creative licence. When Crassus is reminded at one point that he could bring his soldiers into Rome, with Sulla cited as precedent, he is horrified and notes that Sulla had achieved infamy and 'the utter damnation of his line' by violating Rome's traditions against entering the city at the head of armed soldiers. But by the end of the film, Crassus is presented as if he were Sulla in late 82, arguing that what he was doing was not dictatorship, but order, and preparing proscription lists to maintain said order.

As the year drew to a close, Carbo was still alive, but his consular year had been an unmitigated disaster, and he knew that his head was wanted alongside those of Carrinas, Censorinus, Marius, and so many others. The ex-consul Norbanus had managed to escape Italy, heading to the island of Rhodes. He would not survive the year, committing suicide after he was named prominently among the proscribed. The Rhodians had to decide whether to hand him to Sulla, debating between the honourable practise of hospitality and sanctuary, and the consequence of incurring Sulla's displeasure. In the end Norbanus saved his hosts the trouble of having to decide his fate.

Pompey had little if any time to waste: no doubt he wanted to take his place among the leading figures in the prosecution of what promised to be the difficult next phases of the war. But the accession of Sulla to the dictatorship brought changes to Pompey's life beyond assignments in the ongoing civil conflict. Pompey was also to be joined to Sulla by a marriage alliance, one of the time-honoured ways to secure the increased power of families in republican life.[33] The fact that Pompey already had a wife was irrelevant; Antistia had been the price for Pompey's legal acquittal in his troubles after the death of Strabo, and now Aemilia would be the spouse of a political union with the dictator.[34] Pompey's social standing had risen appreciably, and he had been rewarded for his efforts and achievements in 83–2 BC. Aemilia was a stepdaughter of Sulla, and just as it did not matter that Pompey had a wife he would now need to divorce, so it did not matter that Aemilia was also married, and indeed pregnant with her husband's child. Political considerations meant far more to the Roman republican mind than any scruples about expeditious divorces.

The situation, however, was more than usually fraught with complications, and would end in tragedy. The tale of Pompey's second marriage is where Plutarch resumes the narrative of his life after glossing over the events of the civil war in Italy.[35] Antistia's father was apparently among those who were slain by the Marians on account of Sullan sympathies, and her mother had committed suicide in the wake of her husband's assassination. Despite the clear sufferings of the family on account of their loyalty to Sulla, the dictator judged it necessary for Pompey to be allied with him by marriage, and if Pompey objected, it was either left unstated or overruled. Fate, however, was not to look kindly on Sulla's machinations. Aemilia would die soon after, in childbirth. Pompey's second marriage ended, as it were, before the ink was dry on the certificate.

Pompey was not the only Roman who was expected to alter his marital status at Sulla's demand. Caesar was ordered to divorce Cinna's daughter Cornelia.[36] Famously, he refused: later critics (especially those partial to Caesar) would be quick to note that unlike Pompey, the even younger Caesar was willing to show independence to Sulla. Needless to say, romantic, quasi-mythic stories emerged from this period. Students of the period sometimes hear the claim that while Sulla claimed that there was many a Marius in the young Caesar, what is certain is that Caesar survived the proscriptions. Certainly it worked in his favour that he was a fellow patrician. Caesar would leave Italy, ready to take up an assignment with the governor of Asia. It is fairly clear that Italy had become an unhealthy place for Caesar to remain. He was closely associated with the Marian cause (though he had never taken up arms against Sulla, surely one of the decisive factors that ensured his survival), and arguably he was fortunate to have survived the year 82. Asia would be a place for him to commence a career, and to avoid any tensions in the capital.

Interestingly, the one appointment that had been selected for the young Caesar before the rise of Sulla was the religious and ceremonial role of *flamen Dialis*. The *flamen* was not able to enjoy a military career: there were strict prohibitions on behaviour that greatly constrained the priest from being able to do such common things as ride a horse or spend extended periods outside of Rome. When Sulla took power, Caesar was relieved of his appointment, and soon sent off to Asia. Clearly there was some interest in depriving the youth of a prestigious position, but in point of fact it might have been better in hindsight to have left the bold young man in his flamenate, were one worried about his potential on the battlefield.

Meanwhile, for Sulla and his allies there was the priority of dealing with the surviving consul. It is impossible to know exactly what Carbo was thinking or planning at this deadly juncture. 81 BC would by no means be a normal year; there would be consuls, to be sure, but the principal reason why the consulship of Marcus Tullius Decula and Gnaeus Cornelius Dolabella is not particularly remembered is because they were essentially consuls only in name, with Sulla as dictator and the only power that really mattered. Carbo was clearly on borrowed time, and interestingly for our story, it would be Pompey who would be sent to deal with the fallen consul. Appian tells a harrowing story.[37] Carbo had gone from Africa to Sicily, and then to the island of Cossyra (the modern Pantelleria). Pompey secured his capture along with that of many other Marians in his entourage. The orders given were that the lesser targets could all be killed without being brought before Pompey; Sulla's agent wanted to see Carbo personally. The ex-consul was brought to Pompey in chains, and treated to a tongue-lashing and harangue as the twenty-four year old commander insulted and condemned him. Finally Pompey killed him, and sent his head to Sulla to add to the roster of assassinated enemies of the new order of affairs. Livy says he died crying in womanly fashion.[38]

It is possible that here we find the first hint of a crueller, more savage side of Pompey. Plutarch offers one of his characteristic appraisals of the praetor's behaviour. We learn, for instance, that Pompey was generous to the cities of Sicily, which had suffered much under the administrations of the Marians.[39] But the Mamertines in Messana objected that they were protected by longstanding treaty and agreement with Rome to maintain a modicum of independence over internal affairs, to which Pompey is said to have retorted that laws should not be quoted to men who were armed with swords. As for Carbo, Plutarch makes the observation that had he been slain at once upon capture, it would have been added to the deeds of Sulla, the man who ordered his death. But Pompey's decision to harangue the prisoner and to subject him to the degradation of insult and invective made it Pompey's deed. Still, Plutarch notes that when stories about Pompey's alleged coldhearted, bloodthirsty nature are reported, one should be careful about lending easy credence when the sources were friends of Caesar, the young man's ultimate rival: Sulla was hardly the only victor to have an effective propaganda machine.

Certainly the Carbo episode adds a striking nuance to the developing portrait of the young man.[40] It was a violent age, and from the viewpoint of the Sullans, at least, Carbo was to blame for much of the chaos and destruction of the last two years. The truth, as often, lies somewhere between the extremes. Pompey was no saint, but neither was Carbo. The now ex-consul had been responsible for the elimination of many a Sullan sympathizer, and as Plutarch admits, nobody was arguing that Carbo should have been spared.

Fetching Carbo's head qualified as a mopping up operation, but it was an important one: he was the principal Marian at large, first on the list to be hunted down. The only other significant Marian supporter was Sertorius in Spain, who was preparing to hunker down in his western theatre, taking advantage of time and geography to strengthen his position. We cannot be certain if Carbo intended to head to Spain to take refuge with him; at any rate, Sulla would soon enough deal with the Sertorius problem.

At the time just before Carbo's assassination, the map was actually not so bleak for the Marians. Africa and Sicily were theirs, as well as a significant part of Spain. But appearances were deceiving: Pompey would not need to engage in any fighting to take Sicily, its Marian governor Marcus Perperna Veiento fleeing as soon as he could. One important detail of Pompey's mission to Sicily was that the dictator invested his young friend with authority as propraetor. We do well to remember that this was actually Pompey's first legally sanctioned, official position in government; everything he had done up to this point had been on his own initiative, or by unofficial assignment from Sulla. How exactly Carbo fell into Pompey's hands is unknown, but there is no question that if there was going to be a continued Marian resistance to Sulla, it would be not be based in Sicily.[41]

82 BC had been a highly successful one for Sulla, but the new dictator faced immense problems. The Marians in both Spain and Africa needed to be dealt with expeditiously, and the troublesome Mithridates was not exactly observing peaceful, good behaviour toward Roman interests in this period, either justifiably or not. Sulla had secured Italy, and that was rightly his priority. But wars would still need to be waged on three continents. We may mention briefly the immediate Asian situation, in which Pompey would play no part. One of the undeniable consequences of Sulla's swift conclusion of the First Mithridatic War was that affairs with Pontus were not truly resolved, at least not in any lasting, definitive sense. Even an unseasoned student of foreign policy could have foretold that conflict was likely to erupt again. As usual in such situations, both sides would complain that they were the aggrieved party. While Sulla was busy securing Italy, matters quickly turned critical in Asia. All things considered, the Roman side was probably to blame for much of the mess. Certainly what history knows as the Second Mithridatic War was not one authorized by Sulla, the Roman senate, or indeed anyone in Italy. It was probably the inevitable consequence of both the haste with which the Treaty of Dardanos had been ratified, and of the speed with which Sulla needed to see to business in Italy.

Lucius Licinius Murena could fairly be labelled the catalyst for the renewal of hostilities with Mithridates.[42] There is no question that the Sullans in Italy had far more pressing concerns than what was happening in the east; this is why Sulla had officials there. Likewise, said officials had been left hurriedly, probably without extensive guidance. The truth for the blame for the 'second war' likely deserves to be spread between several Romans as well as Mithridates. It was in Sulla's interest for there to be peace; one could argue that Murena wanted war, if only to secure a name for himself. Murena could also argue with some reason that Mithridates was a threat so long as he remained alive. When Murena would eventually complain to Mithridates that he had no written text of the Treaty of Dardanos, he was no doubt telling the truth. Sulla had been hasty in departing for Italy, and he was arguably in no position to be making treaties. Certainly the senate had never ratified Dardanos. Mithridates unquestionably faced uprisings in his territory, but he was also slow in evacuating territory he had promised to demilitarize, and Murena would have been blamed for incompetence had he ignored Mithridates' military buildup and suffered a Pontic first strike. The fact that Mithridates complained to the senate and Sulla that Murena decided to hit first, in clear violation of the treaty, has been interpreted variously. Mithridates did have legitimate grievances; on the other hand, it is not entirely clear that his ultimate intentions were altogether pacific. Murena would ultimately be defeated by Mithridates and forced to flee; in the end he would be honoured for his rather less than impressive, even hollow unopposed victories over the king, while Pontus would be granted new concessions and the overall situation in the east left arguably in a far more unstable position than after the first war. It would be no surprise to the judicious observer that conflict would be renewed relatively soon.

In the end, the Second Mithridatic War of 83–2 BC would end principally because of Sulla's diplomatic interventions. No doubt he was annoyed at having to resolve eastern business yet again, with so much work left to be done. He had far larger immediate concerns, in Africa and Spain. His young colleague Pompey had succeeded impressively in the civil war campaigns in Italy, and he had proven himself competent at handling his first official mission, though it would be in consequence of Sicily and subsequent events that Pompey's critics would conjure the unflattering nickname *adulescentulus carnifex* – 'adolescent butcher.' Only twenty-four, Pompey had acquired a reputation for bloodthirsty efficiency. It is no surprise that he would be entrusted with the more challenging mission of proceeding to Africa to deal with the remaining Marians there. It would be his first chance at overseas combat, a prelude to the great role he would play both in Spain and, ultimately and especially, in the east.

Chapter Four

Africa and Triumph

Sicily had not been a particularly difficult or challenging assignment, all things considered. Africa would be Pompey's first chance at a major overseas campaign.[1] The African campaign would be Pompey's first opportunity to navigate the perils of foreign affairs, given that much of his work would involve dealing with the complicated state of affairs in the Numidian realms that bordered Roman territory. Pompey's principal commission was to secure Roman Africa for Sulla; in this his main foe would be the Marian partisan Gnaeus Domitius Ahenobarbus, who had fled to the continent when his name appeared prominently on the lists of men to die. Numidia was a realm also contested and fought over by rivals for power, and whether to support Domitius or Pompey was the question of the hour for those that aspired to Numidian rule.

Pompey was well equipped for his voyage to Africa. The Sullans had naval capabilities not least on account of having had to ferry forces from Greece to Italy in 83. Recruitment was no doubt aided by the thus far victorious campaigns that Sulla's forces had waged in Italy; Africa promised to be a lucrative adventure. In imitation of how Sulla had landed at both Brundisium and Tarentum, Pompey's expedition would land at Utica and Carthage, following classic amphibious operations tactics. Not surprisingly, there were defections to Pompey's cause not long after he landed. Likely the Sullan force arrived sooner than some might have expected, and certainly there were plenty of Romans who had no stomach for continued civil war. If we can believe that the number of defectors was around 7,000, then there is no surprise that the Marians sought to defeat Pompey as soon as possible: initiative was on the Sullan side, and the Marians were running out of places to seek refuge.

Plutarch records an intriguing anecdote from this period soon after Pompey's arrival.[2] Allegedly, some of his men found a significant quantity of treasure, and the word spread that the Carthaginians of yore had buried riches that were simply waiting to be discovered. The whole tale is reminiscent of how in a later age, the emperor Nero would be dazzled by ludicrous stories of the hidden gold of Elissa or Dido, the Tyrian queen and traditional founder of Carthage.[3] Needless to say, there was no gold to be excavated, and Plutarch notes that after the soldiers spent days futilely digging for nothing, Pompey simply laughed at them, enjoying a moment of levity at the pointless hunt for wealth.

The Battle of Utica would be Pompey's first chance at military glory on distant shores. Here there was no allied army ready to aid him if disaster struck; he had been sent with praetorial authority to Africa, and whether the Sullan cause succeeded or failed here would be solely his responsibility.

The story goes that Domitius arrayed his force in front of a ravine that was difficult to cross, a good example of the use of natural terrain to aid one's defensive preparations and to try to compel one's enemy to fight in disadvantageous circumstances. There was a violent storm, and given the seeming impossibility of fighting that day, Domitius eventually withdrew his forces: where the ravine would not defend him, the rain and hail would. The problem with such a strategy is that Domitius thereby gave the initiative to Pompey. Where a less daring commander might have done the expected and waited for improved weather conditions, Pompey was master of the unexpected. He realized that if he crossed the ravine, he could launch a surprise attack on Domitius' forces.

Utica constituted a classic example of a battle that was won by knowing when to be daring, and how to press home an advantage. Domitius was taken by surprise. Plutarch says that the bad weather hampered everyone, even if the wind managed to work in Pompey's favour by blowing rain in the face of the enemy.[4] Still, the biographer notes that in the tempestuous chaos, Pompey was almost slain by friendly fire when he was not recognized on account of the downpour. No doubt breathless between wind and the onslaught of war, he was slow to give the password to the man who nearly killed him.

Luck once again saved Pompey for another day. What emerges from the description of Utica is of a piece with what we have seen elsewhere of Pompey's battlefield behaviour. He had an exceptionally good sense of timing, and he was willing to take calculated risks. Still, his audacity was enough to expose him to the risk of death, but that was true even for cowards in war. On the whole, Pompey was a brilliant commander, especially given his age. There is no question that the image of Alexander the Great was on his mind: he had much to do to try to rival the legendary Macedonian.

Extraordinary casualty figures once again prevail. Domitius is said to have had 22,000 men, of whom only 3,000 escaped the rout. Pompey was hailed by his men as *Imperator*, but before the commander allowed any celebration of the tremendous victory, he ordered that his men destroy the enemy camp: this would not be another occasion where weather or any other expedient allowed his foe a chance to regroup.[5] Domitius was slain in the subsequent attack; Plutarch adds the detail that for this phase of the war, Pompey fought without a helmet, not wishing any chance for a repeat of his being mistaken for the enemy in the fog of battle.

This was an auspicious commencement of Pompey's overseas career. While he had benefits from the men willing to defect to his side, he had also proven himself yet again on the battlefield. It is in these early years that we see clearly the significance of the age difference between Pompey and Caesar. Pompey had enormous experience at a time when Caesar was but finding his way amid the chaos of the republic's wars both at home and abroad.

Pompey still faced the problem of the Numidian complication. Numidia was one of those classic cases of a client kingdom, one that had posed significant challenges for Rome in past decades, and that like many such realms was riven by its own dissensions. Hiarbas is an obscure figure. Some have seen in him an inspiration for Virgil's characterization of Dido's suitor Iarbas in the fourth book of Virgil's *Aeneid*. The basic situation with Hiarbas was an all too familiar one. Hiempsal II had inherited eastern Numidia as his kingdom, but Hiarbas had revolted against him. In the game of diplomacy with Rome, the Marians found an ally in Hiarbas, which meant that whatever his prior inclinations, Hiempsal would find a ready friend in the Sullans. What complicates our knowledge of the exact state of affairs with regard to Numidia (both eastern and western) and its neighbours (especially the Gaetulians, from whose number the rebel Hiarbas likely hailed) is that we do not know exactly what the existing disposition of affairs was from the Roman perspective before the arrival of Pompey. What is clear is that Hiarbas was forced to flee from Pompey's pursuit, and that he was captured and slain. Hiempsal was restored to power; he would enjoy another twenty years.

It took Pompey about forty days to defeat Domitius, to destroy the hopes of the Marian cause in Africa, to end the problem posed by Hiarbas, and to pacify Numidia. Plutarch makes a point not only of the speed of Pompey's actions, but of the fact that he managed so much so swiftly at only the age of twenty-four.[6] We can readily believe the story that Plutarch tells of how Pompey commented that the very wild animals of Africa should also feel Roman power, deciding at once to make time for hunting and other traditional gentlemanly exploits. Once again we are reminded that Pompey likely knew well his Xenophon.

Plutarch highlights an important incident of the aftermath of Pompey's African campaign, one that is revealing both of his nature and of Sulla's.[7] The dictator wrote to Pompey, instructing him that he was to send the bulk of his army to Italy, remaining in Africa with one legion while he awaited the commander who would succeed him. Plutarch makes clear that Pompey was not remotely pleased with these orders, but that he concealed his displeasure.[8] His men, however, began to express contempt for Sulla, complaining that he was a tyrant and that they would stand by their *imperator*. Pompey begged them not to revolt, arguing in favour of obedience to the dictator. When the soldiers persisted in their near riotous behaviour, the lachrymose Pompey retired to his tent. Dragged out and reinstalled on his seat, the arguments continued to go back and forth. Pompey announced that he would commit suicide before he would countenance a revolt; still, his army persisted to remonstrate with him.

Sulla is said first to have received word that Pompey was in revolt, and to have lamented that like Marius, he was forced in his advancing years to deal with young upstarts. Then he learned the truth, and when he saw the adoration and adulation with which people in Rome looked forward to the arrival of so honourable and noble a young man, Sulla sought to rival them in displays of honour to welcome Pompey home. He had the perfect gift for his loyal mentee: he would award him the title *Magnus*, so that in his twenty-fifth year and thereafter Pompey would be Pompey the Great.

What are we to make of this dramatic story, this theatrical episode after the African campaign? A possible clue to what is going on may come from Plutarch himself, who notes that some said that the title *Magnus* was applied first to Pompey by his men in Africa, and that Sulla ratified the name by using it himself. We may recall the manner in which Pompey had greeted Sulla as *Imperator*, only to be saluted as the same in turn. Likely what we have in all this is deliberate artifice and the purposeful, artful crafting of a legend. Certainly there were likely voices in protest at the idea that the brilliantly successful general should send off most of his army and go off to some new task of which they at least were not privy. But Pompey no doubt realized that there was more to do than hunt wild game in North Africa; there was a long list of additional tasks that needed to be completed, in Spain and elsewhere. The story of what allegedly happened at Utica was designed to emphasize the loyalty of Pompey to the new order; it was meant to show that there would be no incident of some powerful commander deciding to revolt from central authority, no matter how successful or powerful. In short, Sulla was doing what he claimed to want: he was restoring republican order, and the era of the civil wars was being put to rest under his management. If said management were harsh, it was a natural consequence of the demands of the times, of trouble that he had not started, in his estimation at least.

Plutarch notes that the last man of all to use the title *Magnus* was Pompey himself.[9] Once again we see how the whole story may have been composed for the benefit of both Pompey and Sulla. A man who was able and willing to stand up to the temptation of succumbing to the appeals of his men was also loathe to use a potentially invidious title. The biographer further notes that the Romans bestow such titles not merely to those who manage to be successful in battle, but on those who are virtuous and distinguished for their honourable qualities. Again, we are reminded that whatever theatre was commissioned in the process of Pompey's transference to Italy to accept his new mission, it was good theatre: this young man was destined to do even more and better things as an agent of Sulla's thus far highly successful dictatorship.

Why did mutually beneficial stories need to be spread abroad? It was natural that there would be jealousies and tensions between ambitious men. The envy between rivals of the same age is different from that between men with significant age differences, but in all cases jealousy is an omnipresent reality and threat to good order. Pompey may have been willing to forego a grandiose title like 'the Great'; he had not, after all, done nearly what Alexander had accomplished to earn the same honourific. But there was one traditional Roman honour that he was inclined to insist upon: a triumph. A successful military commander and potential statesman needs to know when to practise humility, and when to be ready to assert one's justly earned prerogatives. A triumph was by no means an unreasonable request on the merits alone; one could argue that it would have been a sign of weakness or lack of assertive character for Pompey not to demand one.

But there was one glaring problem. Tradition demanded that a consul or praetor could earn a triumph, not one with propraetorial commission who was too young even to serve in the senate. Sulla had a good point, though of course one of his critics could note that tradition also said things like one should not march armed soldiers into Rome. Sulla's argument was that for Pompey to receive a triumph would be to the odium of both the dictator's regime and the young man himself; people would note the impropriety and would be inclined to note the traditional prohibition.

Allegedly, Pompey's response to this was that people paid more attention to the rising sun than to the setting.[10] Sulla is said not to have heard the response clearly; when it was repeated to him more distinctly, he called for Pompey to receive his triumph, which came either in 81 or 80 (we cannot be certain given the surviving evidence). In Plutarch's rendition of this anecdote, we may be tempted to wonder how much mythology had been composed around Pompey. Certainly the legend of Pompey was well underway, even at this relatively early stage of his career. We are told that when men objected to the triumph (just as Sulla had correctly predicted), the young honouree decided to annoy them even more by using elephants instead of the customary horses, in the end only resorting to horses when it was logistically impossible to navigate the gates with the pachyderms.[11] On the reverse hand, when there were supporters of Pompey who wanted to make him a senator despite his age, he refused with the note that he was seeking a different sort of reputation indeed. Pompey preferred to enjoy a triumph without being a senator, more than he wanted to be a senator before the traditional age. He wanted the triumph to precede any senatorial rank by a significant duration, all for the sake of accruing more renown. There is great significance in Plutarch's note that the people were delighted to have an *eques* and not one of senatorial rank celebrate a triumph, and no doubt popular praise factored into Pompey's decision.[12]

It is noteworthy, however, that Pompey's triumph was marred by one fact that likely gnawed at his sense of pride. For he was not the only man to enjoy a triumph in that period. Lucius Licinius Murena celebrated one as well, for his victories – such as they were – over Mithridates. Gaius Valerius Flaccus also earned a triumph, another decision that must have rankled with Pompey. Flaccus had been one of those who had studiously tried to maintain a balanced approach to dealing with the Roman civil war. To be sure, Flaccus had more than earned his Sullan credentials by being the man who officially sponsored the law by which Sulla was named dictator. But as with Murena, there was no comparison of Flaccus to Pompey in terms of the tradition of earning a triumph, whatever Flaccus achievements *ex Celtiberia et Gallia*. And Sulla himself marked a triumph for his defeat of Mithridates.

In short, there were either four triumphs in the year 81, or between 81 and 80. This was an extraordinary number in so short a sequence. Possibly there was a conscious effort on Sulla's part to add legitimacy to the dictatorship by public spectacle. There may well have been an effort to steal some of Pompey's thunder, as it were, by forcing the ambitious young man to share a crowded stage. In the pantheon of new heroes, Sulla and Pompey stood out far above Murena and Flaccus, and the point was likely deliberate and polyvalent. It was a surprisingly democratic roster for a dictator to put forward, perhaps a calculated bit of deflection from any invidious reaction to the thinly veiled tyranny. The tradition, in any case, may have been difficult to break. There would be many triumphs in the coming years, a clear mark of the jockeying for notice and achievement by a steady stream of ambitious men.

The chronology of this period has been debated; the available evidence does not permit definitive calendar to be reconstructed. Hence the confusion even on so important a matter as when Pompey had his triumph.[13] 82 BC was a busy year, and so was 81. Surviving sources dispute the age of Pompey, which is the source of the problem: the late author Eutropius in his abridgement of Roman history (5.9) states that Pompey was only twenty-three; an age of twenty-six can be cited, let alone twenty-four or twenty-five. Most everyone would agree that 82 was too early, and 79 almost certainly too late, but between 81 and 80 it is more difficult to choose.

Besides triumphs, Pompey had another matter that needed to be addressed. His wife Aemilia had died all too soon, and there was a pressing question as to who would be the hero's third spouse.[14] Mucia Tertia, the daughter of Quintus Mucius Scaevola, would remain Pompey's wife for the better part some twenty years. The exact year of their marriage is unknown; 79 is a likely year, but it may have been earlier. She would be the mother of all of Pompey's children of whom we are aware. It is possible that her first husband was Marius the Younger.

Mucia's father had become a legendary figure in the iconography of the Sullan cause. He had been killed in the violent uprising against Sullans and suspected Sullans in the chaotic period before Sulla's arrival in Rome, sacrilegiously slain on the very vestibule of the temple of Vesta while serving as *pontifex maximus*. Like many others, he had been in the ranks of those who sought ways to avoid civil war; his failure and sorry end made him an easy martyr for the new pantheon of heroes.

Plutarch barely mentions Mucia, for reasons that we shall soon enough explore.[15] Roman marriages were contracted principally for political and economic concerns, not for romance or passion; in the present instance, Mucia was a young widow and Pompey a young widower, and Sulla approved of the match; there were probably few other concerns for either man, both of whom were no doubt preoccupied with the immense list of tasks at hand.

The consuls for 80 BC were Sulla and Metellus. This was Sulla's second consulship (the first was in 88). This was an interesting instance given that Sulla was simultaneously dictator; once again there was a continuing pretence of republican government, but there was no question as to who was in authority. No doubt considerable time needed to expended on management of affairs in Italy after the years of the Social War and the war against the Marians. Africa had been pacified by Pompey, but Spain was a looming problem in the west, not to mention the all too unresolved difficulties looming in the east. Metellus had more than earned his consulship by his devotion to the regime and his generally good reputation, not least for *pietas*; he served as a good example of the close relationship between Sulla and his peer colleagues.

We do not have detailed information about Pompey's activities in Rome in this period. One man who was certainly active simultaneously has more than merited the attention that his life has attracted: Sertorius. Arguably he was at present the greatest threat internally to the stability of the Sullan dictatorship. Sertorius, if anything, was his own man. In some ways he would be a precursor to those would-be breakaway emperors of a chaotic later age of Roman history. At various points in his checkered career he was a thorn as much to his fellow Marians as to the Sullans. Sertorius had a dubious personal connection to Pompey: he had once faced Strabo in battle. Sertorius had been a restraining influence on the Marians in certain of their more violent moments, to be sure. But the serious conflict between Sertorius and his allies had come when Marius the Younger was consul in the fateful year of 82. Sertorius certainly coveted the office, and the fact that he had become disenchanted with Marius in his declining years added to his jealousy about the rise of his son. The Marians did not want to see Sertorius as consul, preferring instead that he serve as governor in Spain.

As far as Sertorius was concerned, the disasters that were steadily increasing for his faction were principally the consequence of the incompetence of the men put in power. His departure for Spain had two benefits: it removed him from conflict with his colleagues in Italy, and it meant that Spain would be secure for the Marian cause. It also meant that he was not present for the crises that continued in Italy; he was spared either the blame or the potential consequences of being at the heart of the maelstrom.

When Sertorius arrived in Spain with his army, Flaccus was governor of the two Spanish provinces, Hispania Ulterior and Hispania Citerior. Flaccus was a real problem for the Marians. He was highly suspect as a potential ally of Sulla; when Crassus had come looking for potential reinforcements in his territory, Flaccus had not stopped him. Sertorius was not sent to Spain with instructions to try to replace Flaccus; it was more a case of keeping an eye on Marian interests, and making sure that the governor did not try to move openly in favour of backing Sulla. When Sertorius arrived, Flaccus was not interested in a war; he was a master of diplomacy and of keeping his potential adversaries unaware of what he intended to do.

But Sertorius replaced Flaccus in Spain, apparently without much argument. We do not know the exact details of how this occurred. Sertorius had an army with him, to be sure. Flaccus had served a long time, and it was perfectly normal for him to be relieved after so extended a term of office. We do not know the particulars of another, related problem in the chronology of Flaccus' career. At some point he was also made governor of the two Gauls, Cisalpine and Transalpine. The main debate here is whether he was actually governing four provinces at once, or whether he took over in Gaul after he left Sertorius in Spain. Some would question whether Flaccus was really in control simultaneously of two, let alone four provinces. But these were difficult times given the Social War and how it was almost immediately succeeded by the conflict between the *optimates* and the *populares*. The triumph he enjoyed in 81, as we have noted, was over Celtiberia and Gaul. Certainly when later, far more famous Romans like Caesar (not to mention Pompey and Crassus) enjoyed extended terms of office, there were precedents like Flaccus.

When Sertorius first arrived with his army in Spain, Flaccus was placed in a difficult position. No doubt he was not interested in trying to go to war with Sertorius; he had already exceeded a normal term of office as governor, and he was studiously trying to avoid doing anything that would involve an open break with the consuls. Further, neither the consuls nor Sertorius were interested in starting a war with him. And there was Gaul to govern. Soon enough, Flaccus would be able to bring Gaul over to Sulla without much difficulty; Spain was a far harder place to govern anyway, and it is possible that Flaccus was ready to let someone else manage it.

Sertorius seems to have adapted well at first into the role of governing Spain. Increasingly, it is clear that he came to view it as his personal preserve. Sertorius' priority was to defend Spain, to which end he began to recruit both native Celtiberians and Romans. He was devoted to excellent, unimpeachable management of local affairs, intending to win over as many of the locals as he could to buttress his army. He had no delusions about his situation; there was no possibility (even if he were so inclined) of joining Sulla, and so the immediate plan was to try to make Spain as impregnable as possible.

81 BC saw the first Sullan efforts to deal with a problem that could not safely be ignored for long. Gaius Annius Luscus was sent westward to deal with Sertorius, a difficult task the execution of which would provide a good instance of the vicissitudes of war.[16] Sertorius sent a force to defend the natural border of the Pyrenees. Annius was unable to force his way through, exactly as Sertorius had hoped. But Sertorius' commander was assassinated, and his men withdrew from the passes, allowing Annius to invade.

So commences the exciting and colourful wanderings of the wily survivor Sertorius. He left Spain in that fateful and dramatic year, clearly thinking that he was not yet prepared for a full-scale engagement with Sulla's agent Annius. He did not leave the Iberian peninsula alone, taking with him as he did some 3,000 men in what amounted to a *de facto* private army: these men were loyal first and foremost to their no doubt charismatic and competent commander. Leaving Spain, even temporarily, must have seemed like a defeat to some of them. But staying would have meant war sooner rather than later, and the lure of adventure elsewhere and possibly the easy securing of plunder may have been an irresistible attraction. Further, it seems that Sertorius found it impossible in the immediate crisis to convince the native Iberian tribes to rise up and join him in a major war, and he did not have a lot of time to try to change their minds.

In consequence, Sertorius decided to make the short and easy crossing to Africa. It made sense, given that he was so outnumbered for the moment that resistance and confrontation would have been perilous if not foolhardy for any commander. At the very least, Sertorius would be able to stir up trouble for the Sullans in another corner of the map, and perhaps he was already thinking that Tingis, the modern Tangier in Morocco, was as good a place as any for just that sort of troublemaking. But matters would prove to be more adventurous and complicated than he expected.

We are reminded again and again in the study of ancient history that it was impossible to maintain complete control of a vast coastline. There was no easy system to monitor landings and departures, no modern contrivances of keeping shores defended and under surveillance. Certainly once one landed somewhere, their presence was likely soon to be detected. But the initial landing was difficult if not impossible to guard against, except for some all too obvious points of embarkation and harbour.

Sertorius could leave Spain and land in Africa, but his reception was not warm. Just as the Spaniards had made it clear that they were not interested in providing him with men to fight the Sullans, so in Africa he was repulsed. But there was one group operating in the vicinity with whom Sertorius no doubt soon discovered he had a strong affinity: the powerful and equally adventurous Cilician pirates. In an age in which the Romans were not yet able to exercise naval supremacy over the vast expanses of the Mediterranean, the Cilicians were a real threat on the high seas and in unprotected coastal areas. Sertorius and the Cilicians were natural allies in the immediate time and place. With their mutual assistance, it would be possible to start seizing territory, in this case a potential base in the Balearic Islands. It was an obvious enough strategy, and it would be the sort of naval ingenuity that Pompey's own son Sextus would appreciate in the civil wars of a later age.

Annius Luscus had his hands full, like Sulla and his other commanders. The Balearic base could not be allowed to remain unmolested, especially given that Spain was already a hotbed of problems both from restive locals and pirate incursions on the coasts. Luscus launched successful attacks on the would-be Sertorian/pirate operation, which drove the pirates off to Africa, where they were inadvertently instrumental in providing Sertorius with what he needed and perhaps had always intended: the beginnings of a takeover in the vicinity of Tingis.

Civil wars are always complicated, and the presence of free-wheeling mercenaries and raiders adds to the chaos. The pirates were clearly concerned that Sertorius was not a smashing success against Annius Luscus, but above all they were interested in the most profitable bottom line to benefit their coffers. Sertorius was not to be underestimated, for all of the setbacks and defeats he had incurred. A survivor of hardship, he took full advantage of the scenario that unfolded. The pirates helped to install a tyrant in Tingis; the word spread all too quickly that he was a mere puppet of Sulla. That was all that Sertorius needed to convince the locals that they should resist his rule, with the aid of Sertorius and his men. Sertorius' first African adventure had failed, but evidently he had learned from his mistakes. Sertorius succeeded in gaining control of Tingis, even defeating a Sullan commander who had been sent to assist in the installation of the pro-Sullan tyrant. At last, Sertorius had proven that not only could he succeed, he could win in the face of serious handicaps and prior losses.

This victory in Tingis was the catalyst for what would follow with Sertorius in Spain. In consequence of Sertorius' victory, and his consistently resolute attention to making sure that local populations were treated with exactly the behaviour most likely to secure their assistance, envoys were soon bringing the news that the Lusitanians of western Iberia were interested in Sertorius' help in Spain. Having proven himself, Sertorius was suddenly faced with the prospect of enjoying what he had most lacked: local support to fight the Sullans. To some extent, Sertorius had been the beneficiary of an extraordinary set of circumstances and good fortune. He probably also realized that it would be easier to achieve his possible ultimate aim of controlling Spain if he was able to succeed in the Balearics and Tingis, valuable areas from which to develop naval support for holding Iberia. We do not know for sure exactly what his thinking was in this period, however. He may have been exceptionally good at responding to the vicissitudes of fate, with no particular goal other than successful survival in some secure realm. Stories are told, for example, that before he settled in with the Cilicians as allies, he had heard reports from sailors of lands to the west, probably the modern Madeira or the Canary Islands, and that he had considered retreating there. Certainly he was possessed of a romantic, adventurous spirit that found ready expression in brushing the edges of the Roman world.[17]

Sertorius returned to Spain in 80 BC, having agreed with the Lusitanians that he would cooperate with them, in exchange for their support in his being recognized as Roman governor.[18] Such was the start of one of the most extraordinary episodes in Roman republican history. There is no question that Sertorius was competent and charismatic. He came to know Iberia and its peoples well, and he was widely admired and respected. From the start he won victories against Sullan forces, growing his pool of powerful reinforcements from the native population, and by something especially valuable: the increasing reports that Sertorius' Spain was the best place for disaffected Romans and Marian sympathizers to take refuge. As time progressed, Sertorius' available military power grew ever more impressive. He had abundant natural resources, as well as significant geographical barriers to build up his turtle shell defence, his Iberian bulwark that would pose an ever more perilous threat to the stability of the republic under Sulla's dictatorship.

Sertorius would manage to survive through several changes of fortune for some seven years. Pompey would eventually be instrumental in settling the Spanish problem, but he was not involved in any of the military events of the first years of the so-called Sertorian War. We have noted that the surviving evidence does not permit us to reconstruct a detailed chronology of Pompey's career in the period immediately after his arrival in Rome in the wake of his impressive achievements in Africa. Turning only twenty-five in 81 BC, there were many other Sullans jockeying for position and promotion, of more experience if not of superior acumen and competence. Pompey had already been treated with significant favour by Sulla, and we may accept Plutarch's judgment that Sulla was beginning to become annoyed with the popularity and great reputation that his young ally was accruing, even if he remained quiet. If Pompey had any serious impediment in this period, it was his youth and the barriers that posed to advancement in the traditional magistracies. Much of what he had achieved thus far had been thanks to the extraordinary conditions of first the Social War and then the civil war in Italy. After his Sicilian and African mission, it is not entirely surprising that he was not immediately given another overseas commission by Sulla. At the very least, the dictator may have wanted to keep a closer eye on the clearly quite ambitious and popular young man, lest civil war emerge from a different direction.

But the real mystery in this period is the enigma of Sulla, and in him we may find an answer to any lack of immediate dramatic actions by Pompey to follow his African achievements. His personality and decisions were debated and questioned even in his own day. The dictatorship that he had assumed was of indefinite duration, and his detractors were fond of pointing out that he was a tyrant in all but name. At the start of the consular year 80 he would assume office with Metellus.[19] We do not know how many men even in his inner circle were surprised when he announced that he was resigning the dictatorship, thus marking the resumption of normal republican processes: step one, give up the office of *dictator*, step two, serve a term as *consul*. The close of the calendar year 81 BC would thus be a momentous one.[20]

When Sulla resigned as dictator, Rome had immense unfinished business. Spain was a mess of challenges. Mithridates continued to loom large in the east. The whole experience of the devastating wars both with the Italian allies and the Marians was all too recent. There were those who criticized Sulla, even among the critics of his quasi-tyranny, the idea being that if you are going to seize authoritarian power, you cannot leave the mission you started incomplete.

A defender of Sulla could argue that history would prove him to be the last true republican, someone who genuinely believed that Rome should not remain an indefinite dictatorship. If he were a model for anyone in a future era of Roman history, one might think of Diocletian, even if the comparison is inexact. Certainly Sulla would offer an example to later generations of Roman leaders of the ability to step away from the allure of supreme power. He disbanded his legions, and once his term as consul was concluded, he left Rome. Officially, he was allocated the province of Cisalpine Gaul.

Africa and Triumph   61

Sulla was a mass of contradictions, and his retirement generated its own abundant stream of press. Close to sixty years of age when he retired, he was destined to live only until 78, not having long to enjoy his freedom from political and military life. We are told that he spent significant time living a dissolute life, consorting with actresses and the lower classes of Roman society, indulging heavily in alcohol and sensual pleasures. How much of this was the negative propaganda of his enemies is impossible to know for sure.

Pompey did not entirely benefit from Sulla's retirement; the end of the dictatorship would bring both problems and new opportunities to the young man. One thing was clear: he was indelibly marked by the Sullan dictatorship; he could never plausibly claim that he was one of the many who had prevaricated or looked for conciliation with the supporters of Marius and Cinna. He laboured under that notorious identification as a *adolescentulus carnifex*, which contrasted with the admitted high reputation he enjoyed in some circles. He was also, it would seem, not entirely in the best favour of his mentor Sulla in the last period of the dictatorship and in his retirement. Plutarch makes the point that he was not even mentioned in Sulla's will when the end came in 78 BC, though he notes also that Pompey did not respond negatively to any slights, indeed defending Sulla's right to be buried with honour in the Campus Martius, in the face of serious opposition.[21] After all, it was to Pompey's advantage to maintain the image of *pietas*; the honour and deference that he showed to Sulla would win him all the more credit if it were known that he had not been in the dictator's favour in the last years.

Here is a likely analysis. After his impressive work in Africa, Pompey and others like him needed to shore up the questionable foundations of Sulla's dictatorship, including what would happen after any resignation from the office. Pompey and his partners in supporting the regime depended on its legitimacy for their own reputations. To the degree that Pompey personally had faced criticism for being exceptionally zealous, coldly and cruelly inefficient in his execution of Sulla's dictates, he especially needed to have the Sullan regime firmly established as constitutionally legitimate in light of the immense crises that beset the republic. These domestic political considerations were just as important as resolving overseas problems both foreign and domestic. Just as many men had quietly been sympathetic to Sulla during the ascendancy of Marius and Cinna, so there were many who held their silence during the dictatorship, ready to pounce at the right moment against both Sulla's memory and those who were most instrumental in maintaining the regime.[22]

The consuls for 79 BC were Publius Servilius Vatia and Appius Claudius Pulcher.[23] Metellus was given a busy task as his post-consular mission: he was assigned to deal with Sertorius. The year would prove to be a momentous one, both in Spain and domestically. Pompey is said to have become open in his support for Marcus Aemilius Lepidus to stand for consul in 78.[24] No doubt it is significant that Lepidus had served under Pompey's father during the Social War; there had been a longstanding close connection that tied Lepidus to Pompey's family. During the civil war, Lepidus had impeccable Sullan credentials. What emerges, however, in Plutarch's account is that Sulla was not completely trusting of Lepidus, at least when the question came as to whether he should be a consul. Plutarch depicts Sulla as chastising Pompey for his support of Lepidus, though it is difficult to determine exactly why the retired dictator had problems with Lepidus, and the degree to which Pompey devoted himself to supporting the candidacy. Certainly Lepidus' service under Strabo is a noteworthy detail. Subsequent events may have influenced historical hindsight. For if Pompey had indeed made an effort to support the consulship of Lepidus for 78, he would soon regret it.

Chapter Five

From Consul to Rebel: Lepidus, 78–77 BC

Lepidus' homonymous son, the Caesarian and member of the Second Triumvirate, would be far more famous than his father. In some ways the Lepidus episode was a footnote to the Sulla-Marius civil war, an addendum to the dramatic events in Italy that accompanied the dictator's rise to power.[1] But Lepidus is a fascinating figure in his own right, not least for the aura of mystery that surrounds some of his actions in light of our surviving evidence. For our story he is of particular importance for the role he played inadvertently in Pompey's life at a critical juncture, as the Age of Sulla gave way to uncertainty as to the stability of the wobbly republic. Lepidus' eventual rebellion would also pose an opportunity for the young Caesar to think about involving himself in internecine republican squabbles, a chance that the wise future commander declined.

Lepidus served as consul with Quintus Lutatius Catulus. Other than the aforementioned story of how Pompey allegedly supported Lepidus' candidacy notwithstanding the warnings of Sulla, we know relatively little about the election season. What we do know for certain is that there was controversy soon enough as to the legacy of Sulla, who was in retirement and was destined to die of natural causes during Lepidus' consulate.[2] Lepidus and Catulus were certainly at odds as to the question of Sulla's constitutional and other reforms; it seems that Lepidus was interested in modifying if not annulling some of the retired dictator's initiatives, in a direction that would certainly have appealed to those who were either rather Marian in their inclinations, or who were displeased with Sulla for whatever reason. Sulla was meanwhile busy devoting significant time to his memoirs, a work that we would give much to have; they would be dedicated to his loyal colleague Lucius Licinius Lucullus.[3]

Lepidus was apparently more than willing to criticize Sulla publicly; he was certainly capable of employing rhetoric to denounce what he considered to be the excesses of Sulla's rule. If Pompey had privately shared his own concerns and criticisms of Sulla with Lepidus, we might imagine that Lepidus was speaking for those supporters of Sulla who had developed misgivings about some aspects of the dictator's rule. But we have no evidence for this, and are rather in the dark as to the initial reception of Lepidus' rhetoric among Sulla's closest partisans.

The real debate emerged when Sulla died, and decisions had to be made about the funeral and the disposition of the body. Lepidus was in favour of showing Sulla no honours whatsoever, quite the contrary: there was talk of *damnatio memoriae*. There may well have been Sullans of the view that whatever the rightness of Sulla's intentions for the republic, it was beyond the pale that he should do such things as march on Rome and assume a dictatorship. Sulla may have been in need of significant public relations help; indeed his reputation may have been unsalvageable, even for the most eloquent of apologists. He had been associated with some of the most shocking episodes in republican history. Much of what he had done in the name of the restoration of order provided the blueprint for the prosecution of similar atrocities in future civil wars. Sulla's behaviour had in fact made it all the easier to envisage internecine violence, all the easier to tolerate civil war as a means to achieve political change.

Catulus and Pompey were the prominent voices in demanding that Sulla should receive due honours. They were well aware, no doubt, that their own reputations were inextricably linked to that of Sulla. They may have felt that the republic would be well on the way either to renewed civil war, or to a worsening domestic political situation if the memory of Sulla were to be tarnished. All of them owed much of their current standing and political/military power to the now deceased Sulla. Honouring his memory seemed to be both the appropriate thing to do by virtue of *pietas*, as well as the expedient course in a world that was still all too unstable between Spain and the east. Metellus, for example, was having a difficult time trying to deal with Sertorius, and matters would become worse before there was any appreciable improvement; by the end of the following year, Sertorius would be at the zenith of his power.

What was Lepidus' thought process in seeking to denigrate Sulla's memory, and in attempting to revisit his legislation? He may simply have calculated that the resentment of Sulla was strong enough that it was in his best interests to cultivate the more or less silent opposition. He may have wagered that the future would bring a pendulum swing, and that ardent devotion to Sulla's memory and programme were not in his best interests. Tension was rife in the cities of the republic: Sulla had been responsible for numerous exiles, for instance, and the question of their fate loomed large, as did the exposure and liability of those who might face legal suits from disgruntled, arguably falsely accused victims of the darker days of the proscriptions.

One quick result of Lepidus' open criticism of Sulla may well have been the uprising that took place at Faesulae in Etruria, when local residents attacked Sullan veterans who had settled in the vicinity.[4] This was factional violence yet again, the renewed threat of civil strife. Lepidus was commissioned together with his consular colleague Catulus to restore order. Here we see something of the complex, even ambivalent nature of much of Roman republican political history. The senate assigned both consuls to deal with the crisis; this was, after all, the typical province of the consuls. Lepidus and Catulus were hardly on the same page with respect to most issues having to do with the Sullan dictatorship, but they were not necessarily at odds as to the need to maintain civil order.

Was Lepidus aware that when he arrived in the north, he would be acclaimed with pleasure and honour by the anti-Sullan faction? Probably. Did he know that they would choose the moment they did to attack the Sullan veterans? Doubtfully. Matters sometime move all too easily out of control in such discordant political circumstances. Lepidus clearly cultivated the support of whose who had a grievance with Sulla, but this did not necessarily mean either that he could control the opposition, or that anything up to this point that he had done was illicit as far as his rights as a consul. The senate trusted him enough to entrust him together with Catulus to resolve a problem; likely no one could have predicted with assurance what would happen.

The reception of Lepidus in Etruria was not unlike when Pompey was said to have been acclaimed by his loyal troops in Africa, men who were willing to denounce Sulla out of devotion to their beloved commander. Lepidus was hailed as the hero of those who were frustrated at living still under the burdens imposed by the now dead Sulla. Lepidus responded by siding openly with the rebels, a development that the senate does not seem to have reacted to with any particular displeasure. Likely we see in all of this that continuing disdain for civil war; the senate was well aware that there was significant resentment of Sulla, and no one seemed interested in renewing civil war over what seemed to be relatively minor provocations and incidents. The problem with this approach is that at some point a red line will be crossed, and this is what would precipitate the so-called Lepidus rebellion.[5]

Roman republican politics was an exceedingly perilous game. While we cannot know exactly what Lepidus was thinking, we do know that when he was ordered by the senate to return to Rome to manage the usual consular elections (for 77 BC), he made one of those classic impossible demands: he wanted a second consecutive consulship, and indeed without returning to Rome for the elections.[6] The stage was now set for what would be yet another civil war, albeit a relatively minor one in terms of scope and geographical sway.

It is difficult to determine what exactly Lepidus intended to accomplish. He certainly tried to amass powerful figures who would ally with him, and in this he found some success. It is no surprise that Lucius Cornelius Cinna the Younger was among them, representing the ghost, as it were, of his father Cinna. Marcus Junius Brutus joined him; his son, one of Caesar's assassins, would be far more famous. Speaking of Caesar, he was not interested in joining the rebellion; the fact that he was invited to do so speaks to his Marian credentials, not least the fact that he had resisted Sulla.[7] Ultimately, men like Lepidus were trying to exercise political power by the force of arms; the idea was that if he could not secure a desired second consulship by peaceful means (either constitutionally legitimate, or bribery), then he would resort to violence. This threat loomed over the republic as a quintessential feature of its decline and fall. Lepidus gambled and lost.

One of the key agenda items for the senate in 77 BC would be to deal with the burgeoning crisis and resurgence of republican dissension.[8] Pompey turned twenty-eight in September of 78, and he would receive the senate's commission as *legatus* with propraetorial powers to respond. If Pompey had supported Lepidus' candidacy for the consulate, Sulla had been proven correct in his warnings. To the degree that Pompey had backed Lepidus, he might have been all too eager to deal with the man who had so disappointed him by turning against the Sullan programme and the preservation of constitutional order that had been the ostensible reason for the dictator's extreme measures. Pompey was sent to raise troops, just as he had done some years earlier on his own initiative to support Sulla. It is possible that Pompey would ultimately be able to coordinate with Catulus: the latter engaged Lepidus not far north of Rome, and won a victory, and then Pompey moved from Lepidus' rear, catching him in a vise. Before this decisive confrontation, Pompey had a successful engagement with Brutus at Mutina, preventing him from being able to link up his men with Lepidus if that were his ultimate intention, or from maintaining his stronghold.[9] While conceivably Catulus handled his front alone, there is no question that Pompey had succeeded yet again in demonstrating his competence as a commander.

Lepidus was able to slip away from his scene of defeat. He fled to Sardinia, where he died soon after, though not before suffering the ignominy of additional defeats.[10] In his life of Pompey, Plutarch asserts that Lepidus became depressed and despondent, though not so much on account of his failed rebellion, as from learning that his wife had committed adultery.[11] Suicide was his desperate solution. Whatever the true story of his end, he took his place on the roster of Roman failures. Plutarch makes the explicit comparison that while Lepidus was a disaster as a commander, Sertorius in Spain was splendidly successful, continuing to dominate the scene in the face of Metellus' failures to resolve the crisis.

The fate of Brutus would prove to be more notorious and problematic for Pompey; indeed, it carried with it shades of the memory of the fate of Carbo. It seems that after Brutus had been forced to abandon his fortress at Mutina, he was allowed to depart in peace, only to be killed soon after at Regium Lepidi, by Pompey's friend and ardent supporter Geminius, clearly at his behest.[12]

The incident offered another occasion to witness the vicissitudes of republican government. The execution of Brutus was clearly extrajudicial; Pompey duly informed the senate of what had happened, and the reaction in Rome was that Pompey had behaved inappropriately with respect to Brutus' death. For those who thought the young man had a savage streak, the whole matter served as further evidence of what they had already concluded. Others both then and now would argue that Brutus remained a threat, and that the rebellion needed to be put down definitively, which meant that his death was a political imperative.

The exact details of how Pompey defeated Brutus are unclear. Plutarch was not certain whether Brutus' army betrayed him, or vice versa. Whichever the case, the biographer notes that the resultant problem for Pompey came when one letter to the senate announced the defeat of Brutus without bloodshed, followed by a second report that the rebel commander had been slain.[13] Again, it is most probable that whatever the details of the actual defeat at Mutina (and history offers ample examples of armies suddenly being unwilling to fight once the actual moment arrives), Pompey had reasoned that Brutus was too dangerous to keep alive.[14]

By this point Pompey was well aware of the danger that Sertorius posed, and that he was in fact a far more serious threat to the security and stability of the republic than anything put forth by Lepidus and his supporters. At some point he clearly conceived the ambition to be the one who would resolve the problem once and for all, especially as the reports continued to arrive with news of Metellus' failures. Sertorius had become a master of guerrilla tactics, learning from the most effective insurgency tactics of the Iberian natives.

Once the crisis with Lepidus was averted, it is telling that the consuls who were elected for 77 BC were Decimus Junius Brutus and Mamercus Aemilius Lepidus Livianus, almost as if the point were trying to be driven home that the growing crisis was not to be blamed on entire families, rather on the individuals who were siding with the rebellion.

One of the recurring problems in the tumultuous days of the decline of the republic was the question of commanders disbanding their armies once their senatorial mission was completed. Pompey had played this game with Sulla after his African achievements, when he had obediently surrendered his command even when he lacked a new commission. He was not interested in repeating the same act of dutiful submission without some strong effort at retaining his men for the sake of playing a key role in dealing with Sertorius. It was possible to play a delaying game for at least a while, though such prevarication would not work indefinitely. Clearly he had a plan that would circumvent certain challenges.

Pompey had still not held a magistracy, and so the legal and constitutional impediments to his command of an army remained. But he also had maintained and cultivated his network of powerful political allies, and he had senators willing to support the idea that he should be allowed to proceed to Spain. Lucius Marcius Philippus was among the most prominent of Pompey's associates. Philippus had proven to be one of the most ardent adversaries of Lepidus, after a distinguished career in which he had been one of the many eminent Romans who tried to maintain equanimity in the early period of conflict between the *optimates* and the *populares*, only to side decisively and openly with Sulla. Philippus was a noted orator, and he lent the skill of his golden tongue to the cause of Pompey being invested with proconsular authority for a Spanish expedition, notwithstanding the lack of traditional or constitutional authority for the appointment.[15] Pompey was twenty-eight, and thus far he had made it clear that his principal concern was for military glory, with political life a distant second.

Pompey was now free to recruit even more men, which was a *sine qua non* for a successful Spanish mission: this would be by far the most difficult of the tasks that Pompey had yet attempted. It would be a chance for the young man to achieve distinction in yet another corner of the Roman world. Metellus was to have the help he desperately needed, as two ardent, veteran Sullans were supposed to work cooperatively to destroy Sertorius. Plutarch vividly says that it was as if the spirit of civil war had poured forth all of its venom into this one man, who had become the most serious thorn in the republic's side.

One figure we have not mentioned for some time is Marcus Perperna Veiento. The reason for the silence is simple: he was among those who were fortunate enough to escape the Sullan proscriptions and flee into exile. Perperna was exactly the sort of man Lepidus was interested in seeing rehabilitated, the kind of figure who was to be summoned back for the rebellion of 78. Perperna had every reason to throw his lot in with Lepidus, and he was there for the defeat of the would-be second-time consul, and for the inglorious flight to Sardinia after Catulus and possibly Pompey had vanquished them. Lepidus may have found his answers in suicide, but Perperna had no such interest in giving up just yet. He gathered what force he could from the remnants that had escaped to the island, and he sailed for Liguria. After he learned that Pompey was recruiting a large force and was on his way to Spain to deal with Sertorius, he decided (not unreasonably) that the best thing for him to do would be to throw in his lot with the thus far highly successful de facto breakaway republic in Spain.[16]

The exact process by which Perperna transferred his men to Sertorius is not known. It seems that Perperna's men were not entirely satisfied with his skills as a leader; indeed in the whole matter of retreating from Liguria down toward the Pyrenees and Spain, there would have been a certain admission that Perperna could not stand up to Pompey; the fact that he had legitimate reason to fear being seriously outnumbered would not have altered the fact that it always looks bad for a commander to have to retreat. Perperna's men insisted that they wanted to be put under Sertorius' command, since he had amply proven that he was capable of protecting his men, unlike Perperna (and Lepidus, for that matter). Perperna was compelled to accede to their demands.

In all of this we see the clear contrast between the Lepidus rebellion and the efforts of the schismatic Sertorius. The former uprising had been arguably little more than a glorified episode of mob violence, while what was happening in Spain was a true breakup of the republic: Sertorius had even set up his own senate.

The consuls for 76 BC were to be Gnaeus Octavius and Gaius Scribonius Curio. Of the two men, Curio would become the more celebrated and better known to history. A friend to Cicero, he would also use his excellent command of Latin prose composition and oratory to inveigh against Caesar. The year was to be marked by the return of Pompey to what he seemed to do best, namely command troops in difficult overseas struggles. He could not have known that in some sense everything he was doing was prolegomena to his own involvement in a major civil war; Spain would be a major theatre of the later war with Caesar. Likely Pompey felt impatient: Sertorius had been more or less doing what he wanted in Spain, and winning appreciable victories, for some four years. This was another civil war, though the presence of significant numbers of hostile Iberians, and the fact that the peninsula had never been fully pacified by Rome, gave the war a welcome air of respectability, devoid of at least some of the usual ugly odor of civil war.

Pompey probably had around 30,000 infantry and 1,000 cavalry when he made his way toward the Alps in 77 BC.[17] Coincidentally, he would be in the far west while his future rival Caesar was continuing to make a name for himself in the east, albeit in far more modest, yet still noteworthy ways. He had saved the life of a fellow Roman during the siege of Mytilene in 81, thus earning the coveted *corona civica*, the first of what would be many honours for Caesar, and a clear demonstration of his bravery under fire. He had returned to Rome after Sulla's death, where he made a name for himself in the lawcourts by attempting to prosecute certain members of the Sullan aristocracy on various charges related to alleged malfeasance and corruption. He soon returned to the east, travelling to Rhodes to study rhetoric. We have noted the irresistible appeal of comparing the two lives of the future rivals in parallel. Pompey had had a busier earlier period in life, benefitting no doubt from the fact that he was a natural ally of the winning side in the civil war, while Caesar had close connections to the Marians that made it next to impossible to do much other than try to survive for a more opportune day. By the time he was twenty-three, Caesar had done less than Pompey at the same age, but he had already displayed signs of exceptional ability, not least in the matter of knowing exactly how far he could skirt the line between audacity and prudence.

The key year of 76 would see Pompey continue his storied career in the field, and it would offer the celebrated episode of Caesar and the pirates, where the captured hostage, once released, would gather his own first private army, as it were, to hunt down the brigands and dispense summary justice.[18] A striking anecdote, it is often taken as one of the most revealing, exemplary episodes in the life of the young Caesar.[19] There would be other noteworthy events in the Roman world involving the characters in our story, but the most attention would be fixed on the Iberian peninsula. It would be in Spain that Pompey would surpass all his past accomplishments, and help to set the stage for still greater and more extraordinary victories as he pursued his passion for rivalling Alexander the Great.

Chapter Six

Pompey in Spain

Crossing the Alps was a momentous military gesture since the days when Hannibal had orchestrated his bold invasion of Italy during the Second Punic War. Pompey took his place in history leading a large force northwest out of Italy in 77 BC. It was the year he would turn thirty, not so long before the age at which Alexander had died after having conquered so much, so quickly. Considerations of the calendar and of his own place in history may have weighed on the commander as he proceeded to commence his part at last in the Sertorian War.

All was not quiet and easy as Pompey proceeded through Transalpine Gaul toward the Pyrenees. We do not have much knowledge of the rebellions that he quelled on his way to Spain;[1] we are far better informed about the course of his activities for the next five years, the extended period when he would remain focused on the Sertorian campaign. The sheer length of time involved is a testament to the difficulty of the task; in hindsight it is easy to think that matters could have been resolved more easily if Pompey had been sent to Iberia sooner, but the reasons for the delay were not insignificant. Time was certainly on Sertorius' side, allowing him to solidify his hold on the peninsula and to shore up his defences. But the delay also permitted Pompey to move in with a huge force, with the peace of mind that Italy was in a more stable position than it had been two or three years before.

Spain would be the locale of Pompey's first reversals and defeats; if any myth had developed that the young hero from Picenum was invincible, it would be shattered by Sertorius.[2] Devotees of alternative histories might ponder how well Caesar would have fared against the same opponent. Plutarch reports that Sertorius insulted Pompey to his men, sarcastically referring to Pompey as an errant schoolboy who needed whip and cane to discipline him, while deriding Metellus as being little more than an old woman.[3] Interestingly, the same biographer records that Metellus had also developed a reputation for luxurious living, contrary to the pattern of his earlier life; Pompey, in contrast, was abstemious and more rigorous in his daily habits, thus inspiring greater devotion from his men.[4] There is no question that his arrival buoyed the spirits of the Romans; his youth and reputation alone marked the start of a new chapter.

The city of Lauron on the eastern coast of Spain was the first significant target of operations once Pompey was ensconced in the peninsula.[5] Lauron was a strategic point between the newly arrived 30,000 plus men with Pompey, and Metellus' main body. Lauron was destined to be a less than pleasant experience for Pompey. There is every reason to believe that he was overconfident, perhaps guilty of underestimating his opponent. Sertorius arrived at Lauron first, laying siege to the city; he was clearly irritated that Lauron was willing to go over to Pompey. When Pompey arrived, he was of the impression that he had succeeded in trapping Sertorius between the city and his own forces, so that the besieger was in effect besieged. For those wondering why Pompey was allowed to proceed as far as Lauron without trouble, we may note that Perperna was supposed to try to lure him into an ambush. It would not be the only time that Sertorius would learn that Perperna could not be trusted to execute significant tasks; Pompey was able to arrive unmolested in the vicinity of the city.

Sertorius, we are told, considered this to be the right moment to give a lesson to the youth he insulted as being Sulla's student.[6] The tactics that Sertorius employed were the classic techniques of guerilla warfare, in which he and his men had come to excel. The plan was simple in conception, and relatively easy in execution, especially if the enemy took the bait. One would seek to harass the reconnaissance and foraging parties of one's foe, pestering them again and again like a mosquito. Over time, the goal was to annoy Pompey to the degree that he made a mistake, which is exactly what happened. Tired of seeing his scouts and foragers constantly harassed, Pompey had them sent out to more distant areas, which allowed Sertorius to arrange for his subordinate commanders to lay an ambush for the now dangerously exposed Pompeian units, which were far from their main body and vulnerable to a surprise attack.

Striking against foraging parties at the right moment means that your enemy is laden down with spoils from the hunt; you also benefit from far greater knowledge of the terrain. It seems that the operation was meticulously crafted and executed, essentially in three phases. The first strike would be with light-armed forces, which were designed to provoke the Pompeian foragers into assuming the customary battle line of defence. Then there would be a devastating strike by heavy infantry. Lastly, at the very beginning of the operation, cavalry units would be deployed toward Pompey's camp, so that if and when the foraging party tried to flee for the safety of the base, the Sertorian horse would be waiting to intercept them.

The plan worked brilliantly, exactly as Sertorius had hoped. It was a massacre, a heavy defeat that Pompey was responsible for like any commander, even if he was not on the scene.[7] Once he was aware of what was happening, he sent out his officer Decimus Laelius with his men to try to break through the cavalry in the rear of the foragers, to rescue the routed men.

This was a dangerous operation, one fraught with potential pitfalls. Sertorius clearly anticipated that this would be exactly what any general in Pompey's position would do, and it is obvious that he warned his cavalry to expect just such an attack. The cavalry was given instructions: when you are pressed on and forced to fall back, flee and wheel around, so that you will entrap the Pompeian infantry just as you encircled the fleeing foragers. Laelius would then find himself caught between the Sertorian heavy infantry, and the wily equestrian units.

In short, the goal was to create a scenario where the Pompeians took the bait and were cut down by expert horsemanship and meticulously executed manouevres of combined arms. Sertorius would prove at the Battle of Lauron that he was an exceptionally competent strategist and tactician. Without question, the situation that unfolded for the twenty-nine year old Pompey was the most difficult that he had faced in his thus far glorious military career.

It was now time for Pompey to lead out his force to respond to the disaster unfolding both for his foragers and for Laelius' legion. Sertorius would have expected this; no commander could simply sit in his camp and allow a massacre to continue. This was, tragically, the moment when Pompey would demonstrate that he was no fool, and that luck and fortune were not the reasons for his career to date. To rush in and engage the enemy that was slaughtering his men would be to expose himself to an attack from Sertorius: in other words, to continue to take the bait. To engage Sertorius directly would mean that Laelius' men and the others would be destroyed, and Pompey would face a challenging engagement in which Sertorius' ambushers would be able to fall on him while he took on Sertorius' main body.

Patience is one of the hardest of virtues, and we may remember how Perperna's men complained that they wanted to serve under a man like Sertorius, a commander who knew how to protect his soldiers. What Pompey needed to do was to stand at the ready, prepared for any assault against his own force, but not to move either against Sertorius or his subunits of ambushers. The price of this patience was that Pompey would have to accept dreadfully high casualty figures, and that his men would have to understand why they were to resist the natural impulse to rush in to try to help their beleaguered fellows. It was one of the most difficult skills to learn as a commander, and if anything positive emerged from the Battle of Lauron for Pompey, it was the demonstration of his skill at knowing how to avoid falling into an all too natural trap.

Once the trap was sprung at Lauron, it is difficult to know what else Pompey could have done. On the whole, he made the correct decision in the immediate crisis. More problematic is to analyse what he could have managed differently to avoid Sertorius' trap. In the end, Pompey may have fallen prey to carelessness occasioned at least in part by impatience at how long it took him to be sent to Spain in the first place. While he was able to exercise patience when it counted in the heat of battle, arguably he could have easily avoided taking the initial bait from the harassing, opportunistic raids on his foragers.

Metellus, in the end, was a key figure in saving the day. Sertorius realized that if he were overly confident in the face of his tremendous victory, he might easily find himself trapped between two armies. Metellus' advance toward Lauron meant that this was not the opportune moment to consider a siege of Pompey's camp, or even a major engagement with Pompey. Sertorius correctly weighed the risks, and in a battle that had so hinged on the question of taking bait, the daring rebel commander avoided the temptation of going after Pompey. What he could do was destroy Lauron, and the city was burned as much out of revenge as anything else. It would serve as a warning for those who sided with the republic, and it worked well as a means of humiliating Pompey in the sight of his demoralized men. Whether or not we believe that Pompey lost 10,000 men, the damage to his reputation had been done.

Sertorius obviously would have preferred to have destroyed Pompey, but it was probably unrealistic to think that so large a force could be annihilated in one engagement. Pompey had made mistakes, but not of the sort that would have cost him his entire army, especially with Metellus as a significant threat. Sertorius had to have been worried in the aftermath of Lauron, for all he had achieved. If he knew anything about his adversary, he would be aware that the already determined Pompey would now be relentless in finishing the war. It is interesting, and not entirely surprising, to note that Perperna was not much use to Sertorius at this critical juncture, just as he had failed in any effort to try to ambush Pompey before he could reach Lauron. His principal task was to make sure that Metellus was kept occupied while Sertorius dealt with Pompey, and in this he failed.

Plutarch is no doubt correct when he judges that Lauron was the most difficult of days for Pompey in the Sertorian War.[8] Certainly he would never know such a defeat for the rest of the long months and years ahead. Once again Pompey would be compelled, however, to spend significant time reconstituting and reinforcing his army. It is a testament to the seriousness of the crisis that Pompey did little else in 76 BC after his defeat other than tend to preparations to renew hostilities. The winter would be spent among hostile natives.[9]

The consuls who were elected for the year 75 were Lucius Octavius and Gaius Aurelius Cotta. Coincidentally, both of them would die not long after their term of office had expired, the one of natural causes, the other in consequence of an old wound.

The campaign season of the new spring promised to be a significant one, if not decisive. In one sense, both Pompey and Sertorius laboured under the handicap of not having partners in command who were as talented, though Metellus had already amply proven himself to be more reliable than Perperna. It is interesting that Sertorius seems to have decided that he would turn to deal with Metellus, leaving Perperna and others to finish Pompey. His analysis may have been that Pompey had sustained such a major blow with respect to men, material, and morale, and that Metellus was actually the greater threat. This would have been an erroneous assumption, notwithstanding the events of Lauron. Perperna had already illustrated that in critical moments he was often a disappointment. Pompey and Metellus, to be sure, had a difficult challenge: any advance deep into the peninsula risked engaging with hostile natives, and while Metellus had had ample opportunity to become acquainted with the terrain, Sertorius had the advantage of more extensive experience. Pompey and Metellus decided to separate, which made sense given the vast scope of operations that were needed; Sertorius faced the same necessity, fraught as it was with peril. Whatever he thought of Perperna's abilities (especially relative to his own), like Pompey he could not be everywhere at once.

Perperna and Gaius Herennius were certainly eager to prove that they were capable of great actions. Nothing in the repertoire of military actions matched victory in a pitched, fair battle. Ambushes and subterfuge could win the day, and one could achieve glory for outfoxing the enemy. But a victory devoid of any hint of trickery and deceit was the best of wins.

The plains near Valentia offered just such the geography for a fair contest. In the aftermath of Lauron, Valentia was the obvious target on the map. Pompey could not be expected to resort to guerilla tactics; especially after his shocking losses, he needed the same thing that Perperna did: to vanquish his foe on the open field.

It is unfortunate that we do not know much about the details of the battle that unfolded. What is certain is that Pompey redeemed himself. The Battle of Valentia in 75 BC was a striking victory, one in which Pompey is said to have inflicted 10,000 casualties on the enemy, or an even number to the losses he had suffered at Lauron.[10] Herennius was slain in the battle. Perperna had proven yet again that he could not be counted on to deliver in time of crisis, even with preparation. Probably Valentia was a classic instance of being outclassed: Perperna and Herennius were simply not up to the challenge of facing Pompey, especially given the anger and fury after Lauron.

The fact that Sertorius decided to go after Pompey at this point draws attention to the mistake he made in leaving Valentia to his second-string commanders. It was arguably a colossal blunder to take charge of operations against Metellus. Certainly he was in a difficult position, since he had already experienced being let down by his subordinates when he needed them, and so whatever he decided, his Achilles heel was not being able to rely on his colleagues. Both sides had now suffered a smashing loss, and if Sertorius had any advantage, it was that he had not yet been defeated. Sertorius' desire to face Pompey was a mutual one. The last thing that Pompey wanted was for Metellus to defeat the enemy leader and to take glory for winning the campaign.

One important figure in this chess game has not been mentioned, in part because we know so little of his early life. Lucius Hirtuleius was part of the old guard of the Marius-Cinna faction, and a veteran of helping Sertorius in Spain. He had come to be trusted as one of Sertorius' best commanders, and it is not entirely clear why Perperna was given so much to do at junctures where Hirtuleius may have been the better choice; probably the answer lies in how for all the relative lack of faith in him that his men had, Perperna had been responsible for bringing significant reinforcements to the peninsula at a key moment.

Hirtuleius seems to have adapted well to military life in Spain, becoming a master of the terrain and of guerilla tactics. When Sertorius decided that he needed to deal with Pompey once and for all, it was Hirtuleius who would be commissioned to keep Metellus busy, if not to defeat him outright. Hirtuleius and Metellus would have a chance to perform their version of a dance of death, clashing like Perperna and Pompey in a classic pitched battle, the Battle of Italica, not far from the modern city of Seville.

We actually know somewhat more about Italica than about Valentia. Metellus is said to have executed one of the most famous and difficult manouevres in military science, namely the classic envelopment employed by Hannibal at Cannae, where one overwhelms the flanks and seeks to envelop the enemy.[11] Metellus may have already had something of the same idea that Pompey had: the man who defeated Sertorius would receive the lion's share of the praise, and the sooner Hirtuleius was finished, the sooner Metellus could proceed northeast to try to press on Sertorius' rear and to catch him in a vice with Pompey.

Italica would be another victory for the republican forces. 20,000 casualties are said to have been suffered by Hirtuleius, who was compelled to flee toward Sertorius: both the victor and the vanquished might well have thought that the conclusive showdown was soon to come. Italica was especially significant in that casualty figures and momentum now decisively leaned in favour of the republicans; Sertorius was in serious trouble, but he still had tremendous forces, and he had not yet been defeated since the game had changed with the advent of Pompey.

The combined victories at Valentia and Italica offered another of those moments in military history where overconfidence can be a serious handicap. We do well to remember again that the omnipresent problem for ancient commanders was the speed with which news travel. It is all too easy to look at maps and to read accounts the judgmental vantage point of a world where reports arrive instantly, and where surveillance allows ready access to the battlefield theatre as a whole. That said, the aftermath of the victories of Pompey and Metellus would present another instance where there was a temptation to succumb to reckless actions to press home what seemed to be an assured triumph.

The Battle of Sucro is a good example of one of those clashes where both sides do reasonably well and appreciably badly.[12] It qualifies as a draw, though the real loser was Sertorius. To be fair to both men, Plutarch is correct: neither Sertorius nor Pompey wanted Metellus involved. Pompey wanted all the glory, and Sertorius did not want to risk being trapped between two armies. Even if reports were not readily available or complete about Italica, there is no question that Pompey considered it his theatre and prerogative to deal with Sertorius alone, and it would have been inconceivable for him to act as if he needed Metellus' help to deal with his antagonist.

Pompey's trusted colleague in battle was Lucius Afranius. Afranius would prove to be one of the most loyal and competent of the clients of Pompey. On the day of the Battle of Sucro, Afranius had some thirty years ahead of him to fight for Pompey all over the Mediterranean, even after the death of his patron. He was one of the old guard from Picenum, likely a veteran of Strabo and the early days of the Pompeian pursuit of fame. At Sucro he commanded the left wing, with Pompey on the right; this meant that Afranius actually faced Sertorius (the commander of the Sertorian left wing is unknown).

Sucro was an extraordinarily challenging and hard-fought engagement, that much is certain. Pompey was able to push forward and threaten to overwhelm the opposing battle flank, which seems to have been forced to have made the difficult decision to try to relieve the position before it was lost.

The danger in such zigzagging manouevres in the fog of war is that when you go off to stabilize one wing, you run the risk that your own position will be overrun. Sertorius was highly successful in relieving his left and pushing back the Pompeians; indeed the situation became desperate, even life-threatening, for Pompey. The story is told that Pompey had a splendidly caparisoned horse, and that he abandoned it, thus inspiring such a tussle and fight as to which of Sertorius' men would seize the spoils that the fleeing republican commander was able to escape.[13] Whatever we make of the famous anecdote, Pompey's flank was in serious peril, but so was Sertorius' right: as one might have feared, once he went to shore up his left and even to counterattack, his own right was overrun, and Afranius was able to invade straight through to the baggage train. This is always a supremely risky venture, since while occupied in pillage and plunder one can always be pounced upon by the enemy. Afranius' invading wing was attacked by the timely intervention of Sertorius, who realized that chasing Pompey down to his camp was secondary to doing what he could to destroy Afranius' wing.

Sucro has been called a stalemate and a draw, and that is certainly a fair description. What are we to make of the respective management of the two armies? We must keep in mind that we are not sure what exactly Pompey knew about the achievements of Metellus at Italica. Even if he had reasonably complete knowledge, especially about the speed of Metellus' advance, most commanders in his position would not want to make it seem as if they needed two armies to deal with Sertorius. The story of the abandonment of the richly adorned horse fits in with the image of Pompey as not being addicted to luxury, to be sure. But more significant may be the fact that for whatever reason or reasons, Pompey and Sertorius were not in opposition at the start of the battle. When Pompey was winning on his flank and Sertorius came to save the day, it was all but assured that he would falter. Likewise it was guaranteed that Afranius would break through to the rear. Probably what was needed was for Afranius to attack Sertorius, rather than letting his men surrender to greed and the excitement of sacking the Sertorian camp. But such decisions are often difficult to execute in the heat and fog of battle.

The problem for Sertorius with a stalemate was that he needed to win at Sucro. He was in a good enough position to challenge Pompey to do battle the next day, but the news that Metellus was approaching invited exactly what neither Pompey nor Sertorius had wanted: a shared republican attack, and shared credit. Now Metellus would deserve thanks for his imminent arrival, since it quelled any fear that Sertorius might seek to exercise his initiative and destroy Pompey. Whether he could do that or not is uncertain, but what is clear is that his decision to withdraw rather than face both republican generals was hardly to his glory or emblematic of someone who was on the verge of victory. The comment in Plutarch's life of Sertorius is telling: he said that he would have dealt with the boy, had the old woman not arrived.[14] The bitter invective does not conceal the point that Sertorius should have been able to deal with both a boy and an old woman simultaneously, but of course his sarcastic rhetoric did not change the fact that he knew that his opponents – especially Pompey – were formidable.

Further, Sertorius had suffered appreciable losses, and Metellus' approaching force was drunk with victory at Italica and ready to take on whatever was arrayed against them. Terrain and the support of friendly locals meant that Sertorius could withdraw in relative safety, secure in the expectation that he would not be pursued aggressively in the immediate. Pompey and Afranius, after all, needed to recover from their casualties as well.

Another problem however was that withdrawal would mean that at least for the moment, Sertorius was ceding significant territory on the east coast of Spain to the republicans. This was ultimately the most consequential result of Sucro in some ways: it was an admission that Sertorius could not maintain control over the territory that he had already seized. It meant that he was now clearly on the defensive, having failed to defend a strategic and important part of his republic in miniature.

Withdrawal, however, does not seem to have happened right away. For a while, the two opposing sides remained relatively close together, moving toward the plains to the north, probably near the modern Sagunto. The so-called Battle of Segontia is difficult to explicate definitively. In his life of Sertorius, Plutarch asserts that the action was forced on the commander when his beleaguered opponents attempted to forage.[15] Sertorius once again fought Pompey, while Perperna and Hirtuleius engaged Metellus. Hirtuleius fell, and Sertorius exchanged places with Perperna; Metellus was wounded, but the wound shamed his own men into fighting more valiantly, and the tide of battle turned. Metellus however decided not to press home his advantage, preferring to allow his men (and himself) the chance to rest. Sertorius then launched a surprise attack on his camp, which was only halted when Pompey arrived and forced Sertorius to withdraw. Losses are said to have been frightful: Pompey suffered another 6,000 casualties, Perperna 5,000, and Sertorius 3,000. Metellus clearly lost many men of unknown number in addition. Besides Hirtuleius, Gaius Memmius was slain, the brother-in-law of Pompey.

Appian relates much the same story of an engagement after the draw at Sucro.[16] Battle was joined at noon and continued into the night. Sertorius defeats Pompey, and Metellus Perperna. As with Plutarch's account, one significant problem is that we do not know how close together the republican generals were operating. Sertorius subsequently attacks Metellus' camp, and Pompey rescues his colleague.

The problems and chronology of the battles with Sertorius have been the subjects of significant critical commentary, analysis that has tried to make sense of the surviving evidence. The Pompeian victory at Valentia and the stalemate at Sucro are the easiest of the engagements to study. The traditional view is that they were fought in 75 BC; some would prefer to date them to 76, arguing that the arrival of Pompey in Spain and the Battle of Lauro are to be dated to 77. Apart from the question of date, the Battle of Segovia (which we shall consider below) and the Battle of Segontia are murkier, especially the former. Segontia is traditionally dated to 75; again, some would prefer to assign it to

76.[17] Segontia, at any rate, was noteworthy for being the last time that Sertorius would ever fight a pitched battle.

With the benefit of hindsight, one could say that 75 BC marked a turning point in the long saga and geographical sideshow that was the Sertorian War. But just as Sertorius had failed to secure his goal of destroying Pompey and Metellus, so the republicans still had to deal with Sertorius, who in his own way was just as much a frustration and problem in the west as Mithridates was in the east.

Plutarch offers an interesting appendix to his account of the stalemate at Sucro.[18] He notes that when Metellus approached Pompey, the latter ordered his men to practise the customary deference shown to one who was superior in rank, as Metellus was. But Metellus insisted on treating Pompey as an equal. The anecdote, if true, reveals an honourable Metellus, who was sympathetic to what he would have realized was a difficult, even embarrassing moment for Pompey given the course of the battle. It also reflects the best of republican sentiments of respect for both precedent and authority.

Through all these events in the field Sertorius had managed to obtain an impressive reputation by his victories and his ability not only to survive, but to thrive. He was also something of a mystic, at least theatrically. Famously, he was said to have a white fawn that communicated messages to him from the hunting goddess Diana.[19] This was the sort of fraudulent, cultish behaviour that could not have possibly have impressed many of his Roman supporters; we have no way of knowing the extent to which the fawn story is credible. But given the setbacks of Valentia and Italica, one concern for the would-be favourite of Diana was the morale of his forces. For the moment, the most effective strategy was his familiar willingness to engage in guerilla action. Sertorius could always hope that the Romans would make a serious mistake, or that trouble elsewhere in the republic or simply time and the steady toll of heavy losses and expensive reinforcement and resupply would wear down the republicans. In theory, the rebels could last indefinitely, with homefield advantage and productive cultivation of the local tribes as allies.

The so-called Battle of Segovia in the busy year of 75 is a good example of the results of being forced into conflict despite an overarching strategy (for the moment at least) of hit and run raids. Segovia is one of the more mysterious campaigns of the year. Our sources are conflicted and difficult to entangle, and we do not have an abundance of information in any case. The problem is that there seems to be confusion between Metellus' clash with Hirtuleius at Italica Baetica (the so-called Battle of Italica), and a second engagement between the same two men. The narrative is further complicated by the question of when Hirtuleius died: was it at Segontia, or earlier? This much seems to be certain: Hirtuleius was slain in combat, because we do hear of how the news of his death was conveyed to Sertorius when he was preoccupied with another battle (possibly Segontia, possibly Sucro), and that he killed the messenger so that morale would not suffer among his men.[20]

How may we take stock of the violent clashes in no fewer than three major battles? Anyone who doubted the strength and resilience of Sertorius or the natural advantages of defending territory in Spain received an education. Sertorius was prepared, and on the whole he performed competently and on occasion brilliantly. Metellus and Pompey had an enormously taxing task, in which it is clear that the injection of Pompey into the equation dramatically raised the spirits of the republicans who had been fighting and suffering acutely in the long war. The cost in manpower was frightful, on both sides.

Sertorius had a strong retreat at Clunia, in the modern province of Burgos in north-central Spain.[21] The temptation is always for an attacker to take advantage of a defensive posture, and the republicans decided that the appropriate course of action was to try to lay siege to Sertorius. It would seem that the crafty rebel was successfully doing two things at once. He was buying himself time in a safe, fortified locale, and he was raising new troops elsewhere. To be fair to Metellus and Pompey, it is difficult to know how they could have prevented the new recruitment efforts; the territories in question where vast, and Sertorius very much had the homefield advantage in terms of knowledge as well as sympathy. The fact that Sertorius was able to break out of his siege and recommence his guerrilla actions is to the discredit of his opponents, who were clearly taken by surprise and no doubt rendered supremely frustrated.

By the time the campaign season of 75 drew to a close (or 76, for those inclined to accept that chronology), notwithstanding his successful ruse at Clunia, on the whole the balance had swung in favour of the republicans. Sertorius could expect to have a far harder time recouping his losses, provided that Rome was willing to keep Metellus and Pompey supplied. We are told that Sertorius was able to continue to raise more men in the immediate and to prove to be a major problem launching occasional surprise raids and harassing supply lines; guerrilla warfare is so effective in that it is cost effective and very difficult to suppress utterly. But the only real hope that Sertorius had was that his enemies would face more pressing problems elsewhere. This was a tedious exercise in civil war, and there was always the hope that Pompey or others would find other vocations more urgent.

Metellus and Pompey certainly would not be able to defeat Sertorius during the present season; the former apparently wintered in Gaul while his younger colleague remained in Spain.[22] It was also high time to make clear to the senate that still more men would be needed to solve the Spanish problem. At some point, possibly during this winter of reflection, the idea was probably first raised that perhaps someone should be convinced by bribery to assassinate Sertorius.[23] The problem with that strategy was that it was not exactly the sporting way or the traditional military manner of winning an honourable victory. One can well imagine that the winter after the experience of several pitched battles and other clashes against Sertorius was enough to render Pompey supremely frustrated. In some ways the Spanish campaign would prove to be the most difficult of his military endeavours, not least because he was compelled to share the credit for many achievements with Metellus, who had not had a notably distinguished career in the theatre before Pompey's arrival.

In his life of Sertorius, Plutarch notes that Metellus presented a contradictory face when it came to his rebel quarry.[24] On the one hand he insulted him, calling him a mere slave of Sulla. On the other hand, when he achieved a victory over him, he was so delighted with himself that he called for his men to celebrate him and to acclaim him as *Imperator*. Metellus had come to fear Sertorius, and Plutarch records that he was the one who sent out the word that any Roman who assassinated Sertorius would be lavishly rewarded for the deed.

Pompey's Spanish winter seems to have been spent in northwestern Spain, among the Vaccaei.[25] Here we learn of his communications with the senate, making it clear that more men and more supplies would be needed if they expected the campaign to continue into the new year. If any senators had expected the war would be finished by now, they had a poor grasp of the immensity of the problem. That said, there was probably no joy on having to consider making additional major expenditures at a time when the republic was still dealing with Cilician pirates and the need to maintain adequate defence against resurgence of trouble with Mithridates.

The consuls for 74 BC were Lucius Licinius Lucullus and Marcus Aurelius Cotta. It is no surprise that the senate did the only thing that was realistic given the circumstances, agreeing to send two fresh legions and more supplies and resources to Metellus and Pompey.[26] Lucullus, meanwhile, was faithful to his deceased benefactor Sulla, continuing to fight against populist sentiment and initiatives. Caesar was occupied wreaking his vengeance (or justice, one might better say) on the pirates who had kidnapped him, keeping his promise that he would hunt them down and crucify them for their brigandage.[27] And, beyond any shadow of a doubt, Mithridates was preparing to return to his place in the headline news of the republic. Part of the cause of the renewed troubles in the east was the fact that King Nicomedes IV of Bithynia died in 74, leaving his kingdom to Rome.[28]

It was perhaps inevitable that Sertorius and Mithridates would consider an alliance.[29] They were ensconced on opposite sides of the Roman world, and while it was not exactly logistically easy for them to aid or supply each other, it was all too simple a matter for them to keep the republic bogged down in both west and east simultaneously. The republic was literally caught in a vice between the two dogged and determined foes, and for the moment the great Pompey – easily recognized as one of the most competent commanders the Romans had – was more than busy in Spain, unable to be transferred elsewhere without risking the collapse of that front.

A good example of Sertorius' often successful adventurism came when Pompey tried to take Palantia by siege. While he was engaged in operations, Sertorius was able to launch a sudden strike and to disrupt the siege, forcing Pompey to retreat toward Metellus after trying to set fire to the walls.[30] Sertorius repaired the damage and rebuilt the fortifications, before resuming offensive raids. The siege of Calagurris is said likewise to have been interrupted, this time forcing Pompey to withdraw into Gaul, and Metellus into Hispania Ulterior.[31] History is replete with examples of this sort of deadly effective, seemingly nonstop raids. Plutarch in his life of Sertorius says that the rebel was not beyond reminding Pompey that he was willing to take up a quiet life in Rome in retirement, since he missed his homeland desperately.[32] Whether true or not, there was no way that the republic could come to terms with Sertorius after so much destruction and expense in lives and resources. Pompey, however, was not exactly the sort who liked being a policeman, responding now and again to this or that raid of Sertorius.

The citizens of the Roman Republic in 74 BC had every reason to feel exhausted. The Social War and the civil war between Marius and Sulla had been followed by continuing troubles in Spain and on the high seas, and in the unstable east, Mithridates would soon invade Bithynia and launch the Third Mithridatic War. Men like Pompey and Caesar had not known a republic that was ever truly at peace; violence both domestic and foreign was joined with perennial political squabbles and debates about this or that aspect of political and social life.

The consuls Lucullus and Cotta were to be the ones entrusted with the defence of Roman interests in the east, heading east to take control of the provinces of Cilicia and Bithynia (the latter of which needed to be organized as a new Roman territory). Caesar would also have his chance to take part in the response to Mithridates' newest military gambles. In Rome, Lucullus' younger brother Marcus would be elected consul for 73 BC, with Gaius Cassius Longinus as his colleague. If Pompey would have preferred the chance to take on Mithridates for the campaign season in 73, the question was a moot point; he had not finished dealing with Sertorius.

One thing is certain: honourable or not, from the moment that word spread that Metellus had offered a bounty on Sertorius' head, there was a slow and steady erosion of the rebel's trust in his Roman colleagues and staff. Some of this may have been due to the fact that the war was dragging on for so long, with no clear endgame other than the continuing life of raiders and brigands. Some may have been elated by the news of the outbreak of troubles in the east, but Pompey was clearly going nowhere until he finished his mission.

Sertorius was ultimately the victim of treachery and assassination.[33] In some regards, assassination was one of the best things that could happen to the legacy of Sertorius, all things considered: in death, he would receive sympathy and condolence for the duplicity of a man who owed him much: Perperna. The story goes that Sertorius was invited to a dinner that was supposed to honour him for a victory; in fact he was invited to meet his death. The news must have been received with a fair degree of revulsion, even among men who had become sick with the tedium of the war. Eerily, there would be parallels between the assassination of Sertorius and another day, in Egypt, over twenty years later.

The immediate aftermath of Sertorius' death could be expected. Some of his native allies quickly made their peace with Metellus and Pompey. They had been willing to fight under a commander they respected, but they had no interest in transferring their loyalty to his assassin whom they did not.

Perperna was not alone in his deed. He had Roman supporters. He was also no doubt aware of his own exceedingly perilous position. Did he expect that he would receive the rewards and bounty promised by Metellus? Did he expect to continue the war as the new Sertorius? Did Metellus ever seriously intend to reward anyone for so heinous a deed? Was Perperna a fool to think that he would long survive the aftermath of what was perversely his bravest and most daring deed?

The death of Sertorius came in either 73 or 72 BC; 73 is likelier. The end of the war was swift, and as ignominious for Perperna as he deserved.[34] Having tricked Sertorius, he would himself fall prey to the classic technique of subterfuge in battle: ambush. The story is simple: Pompey lured Perperna into an ambush by pretending to be in retreat. The resulting strike was devastating, and Perperna was captured. Coward to the end, he offered Sertorius' extensive correspondence and paperwork in exchange for his life. Pompey accepted the documents, which he promptly burned: he had no intention of allowing any of the revelations therein to be the catalyst for another civil war. Perperna was slain, his life ending in disgrace on account of having betrayed his commander and benefactor, and from the pusillanimous way in which he tried to save himself by provoking yet another civil war.

There were mopping up operations, to be sure. In some cases these minor conquests over holdout cities served one useful purpose: both Pompey and Metellus were eager for their achievements in Spain to be considered foreign rather than civil victories, so as to be eligible to enjoy a triumph without any of the invidious associations of having conquered one's fellow Romans. And yet few would have failed to appreciate that the Sertorian War was really the closing chapter of the Marian-Sullan civil war, fought to a conclusion years after both men were dead.

One important detail should be noted about the aftermath of Pompey's victories. While Perperna had no chance of being spared, the general attitude of Pompey toward the surviving Romans who had served under Sertorius and then his ill-fated, brief successor was magnanimous.[35] There would be no proscriptions, no more or less quiet elimination of enemies. The burning of Sertorius' correspondence was symbolic, but it reflected Pompey's policy. The man had grown up in a republic that had known nothing but civil strife for most of his life, and at this juncture, he was eager to put civil war and the Sertorian crisis in Spain behind him. Even if he were not naturally inclined to do so, no doubt he felt compelled to be clement and generous, given the work that remained to be done to stabilize the republic. Pompey is said to have erected a trophy in the Pyrenees to mark his victory and his departure from the peninsula.[36] One can well imagine the satisfaction and relief he felt as he took his leave of Spain.

The long Iberian nightmare was over. In theory the republic could breathe a little easier, able now to focus on the dramatic events unfolding in the east, and the renewal of war with Mithridates. But in the very heart of Italy, another crisis would burst forth in 73 BC, one that would threaten the very fabric of the social order and plunge Rome into yet another maelstrom of bloodshed and destruction.

Chapter Seven

Spartacus and the Third Servile War

The Spartacus slave revolt is one of those episodes of republican history that has long been a favourite object of study in the popular imagination. Our sources, as so often, are conflicted and incomplete, but enough information is extant to allow us to trace the fascinating and devastating course of the war.[1] It is not an exaggeration to say that the Spartacus war was the catalyst (both directly and indirectly) for much subsequent political and military history; the involvement of Crassus and Pompey would be the start of the clear sequence of events that led to the ultimate breakdown of the republic.

One problem that cannot be resolved in the absence of more evidence is what the intentions of the escaped slaves were at any given time during the war. It started at a gladiatorial school in Capua, where a plot was hatched to escape the *ludus*. Once the plot was uncovered, a force of some seventy gladiators fought their way out, a group that included Spartacus, Crixus, and Oenomaus. Of these the two less famous men were Gauls; Spartacus was probably a Thracian. Whether he had once served as an auxiliary in the Roman army, or was a captive is quite uncertain.

Escaped slaves, even a relatively large number of gladiators, probably did not constitute a matter that attracted much concern at first for the authorities in Rome. What seems to have happened immediately was that the gladiators were able to defeat the initial force sent out to them from Capua; between the school of Lentulus Batiatus from which they had fled and this first victory, they had a small supply of weapons and armour with which to defend themselves and, apparently, to plunder and raid the vicinity.

Their number increased. The crimes and banditry spread in Campania, and eventually the Roman senate authorized the dispatch of a force to deal with them. Having set up a camp on Mount Vesuvius as a defensive base, the slaves were almost certainly not viewed as a particularly serious challenge when Gaius Claudius Glaber led his force to destroy them.

Glaber seems to have had something of a militia force of 3,000 hastily recruited men; simply put, the slaves were able to surprise the besiegers at Vesuvius and annihilate them. Glaber disappears from the historical record after this; he may have been slain in the engagement.[2] The slaves also defeated a second Roman expedition, under Publius Varinius; while we are ignorant of all the details about his force (not least its size), by the winter of 73–2 BC, Spartacus and his co-commanders had a growing force, attracting increased numbers that swelled their ranks. They had more weapons after the two victories, and they had a relatively fertile territory for plunder and raids.

Certainly by this point, Spartacus had attracted Roman attention. Like Glaber, Oenomaus disappears from the extant record; he was probably a casualty of this early period of the rebellion. Spartacus and Crixus became the clear leaders. The truth is that we do not have any definitive evidence of what these men intended to do. Events had probably quickly advanced to a point that they had not anticipated. If they had intended simply to live as glorified highwaymen, they now had an army of significant size, and two victories over Roman forces to their credit.

There is some evidence that at least some of the slaves wanted to plan an escape from Italy over the Alps; others were clearly content to live on plunder. It is possible that there was disagreement between Spartacus and Crixus on this point, which led to a division. There was allegedly talk at one point of marching against Rome, but there is absolutely no evidence in the surviving sources to support the contention that Spartacus had some vision of ending the institution of slavery. Later movements in history would adopt Spartacus as a romantic, heroic freedom fighter, but this is far more indebted to dramatic fiction than to historical reality. The Spartacus revolt had more to do with unfinished business and inevitable consequences from the settlement of the Social War than any timeless aspiration for liberty.[3]

We do not know when Pompey heard reports for the first time about the disturbance in Italy.[4] After the deaths of Sertorius and Perperna, Pompey was occupied with the consolidation, administration, and restoration of affairs in Spain; it would have been a colossal blunder to try to leave immediately, given the enormity of the crisis that had finally been resolved.

The Spartacus war continued throughout 72 BC. This is the period in which the extant evidence is the most problematic. We have a fair amount of information, but no one coherent account of the events of the war. Pompey spent the year in Spain. The consuls for the year were Lucius Gellius and Gnaeus Cornelius Lentulus Clodianus, both of whom are remembered most in the historical record for the defeats they suffered at the hands of the slave army during their year in office. Again, the main mystery about the activities of the slaves in 72 is what they were intending to do, which amounts to a debate between escape from Italy and indefinite pillaging. Escape was the only realistic option to guarantee survival, but there is no question that managing the growing ragtag force must have been a herculean task, and there were clearly divisions and factions with different ideas about what to do.

One significant issue that probably worked to the advantage of Spartacus' force to an appreciable degree was the fact that if civil war was a distasteful way to earn military glory, fighting an army of escaped slaves and criminal brigands who happened to join up with it was an even less attractive prospect for ambitious commanders. Especially with a major war underway in Asia, chasing Spartacus was not viewed as the most glorious way to spend one's time. Reality, however, intruded on such dreams: the slave revolt was undeniably serious, a growing crisis that was engulfing much of southern and central Italy, perhaps even threatening Rome. One wonders how much later propaganda exaggerated certain aspects of the episode, especially to increase the renown of Crassus and Pompey, but there is no question that the problem was an immense one, not least because the slaves were just as capable of practicing guerilla warfare in the heart of the republic at exactly the same time Rome was preoccupied in Spain and Asia.

And there was the ongoing pirate threat. The Cilician pirates would play a role in the Spartacus revolt, though the slaves would be as much victim of pirate mendacity as anyone. It is a testament to the strength of the republic and the competence of men like Crassus, Pompey, Caesar, and the Lucullus brothers that the many crises of this period were circumvented, even if several of the saviours of the hour were doomed to fall prey to other, deadlier perils.

The consuls of 72 BC were not competent to confront the slave revolt, and ultimately Crassus was given the task of crushing Spartacus once and for all. The confusion in the historical record mostly applies to the period of consular management of the war, before the accession of Crassus. There do seem to have been initial successes: Crixus, for one, was killed with many of his followers, leaving Spartacus as the only survivor of the original three slave commanders. By the end of the year, it seems reasonably clear that Spartacus' army was in southern Italy; the question surrounds the movements of the force after the loss of Crixus in particular. If the slaves had a chance to make it to the Alps and escape into Cisalpine Gaul, they did not take it; arguably, there was probably an opportunity to do so, but the aforementioned difficulty of maintaining control over so large and likely unruly a force undoubtedly conspired against Spartacus was much as any successes of the consular armies.

Crassus was given six fresh legions in addition to control of the consular armies; as praetor, his commission was to strike Spartacus in the campaign season of 71 BC.[5] Crassus would have far greater success than his predecessors from the start; we hear of an initial major engagement in which some 6,000 rebels were slain, followed by a series of additional battles in which Crassus continued his relentless pursuit of the slaves. The Cilician pirates were apparently involved in a deal to rescue Spartacus and his men and transport them out of Italy; in Kubrick's film version of the story, the wealthy Crassus bribes the pirates so that they will betray Spartacus and not deprive the commander of his victory. In reality, Crassus did no such thing; the pirates simply cheated Spartacus on their own: there is no question that he must have been an easy mark for unscrupulous profiteers. There is some evidence that the slaves tried to fashion their own makeshift means of sailing away from Italy, aiming for the relatively easy journey to Sicily, but Crassus was able to circumvent such efforts. Spartacus was cornered, and neither pirates nor homemade rafts were going to save him.

In connection with Sicily, we may note one man who was deeply immersed in the worst sort of corruption that a republican magistrate could indulge in was making a notorious name for himself: Gaius Verres, the governor in Sicily. Ever attentive to using the current headlines to make a profit or to exercise authority, Verres – destined to be one of the most noteworthy of Cicero's defendants in the dock – was quick to accuse Roman citizens of having been escaped veterans of Sertorius' rebellion, and he was known for playing the despicable game by which he would accuse the slaves of particularly wealthy Romans of being involved in the Spartacus revolt, threatening to have them killed unless their owners paid him a substantial bribe. Profiting from the chaos of the servile war and sowing the seeds of his own downfall, Verres offers a case study in the problems of the republican system of managing government outside Italy, and a window into the means by which unscrupulous officials could abuse their office for personal aggrandizement.

Spartacus had by now retreated toward Rhegium, which made it easy for Crassus to blockade him. It is at this juncture that Pompey enters the story, together with Marcus Lucullus. The historical record is not clear on whether Crassus requested help to finish the slave war. One might think it unlikely that he would have given the impression that he needed any assistance, and in fact his forces were to be responsible for the overall prosecution of the war. If any Roman deserved credit for ending the Spartacus revolt, it was Crassus. That much is undeniable. Did he ask for help, or did the senate simply order Pompey to proceed south to shore up Roman defences and positions? All things considered, the latter seems likeliest. The Spartacus problem had already dragged on for some time, with significant economic disruption and embarrassment to the authorities.[6] Since the problem involved an escaped slave population, there was always the legitimate worry that defeated rebels would try to flee the scene of their defeat and blend back into the servile population, perhaps to rise up again another day. Pompey was due to return from Spain anyway, and he had an armed force ready and at his disposal.

Marcus Lucullus meanwhile landed at Brundisium. The 'Lucullus' cited in the historical record was Marcus, not his more famous older brother Lucius, who was busy fighting in the east. Marcus was proconsul of Macedonia at the time, and the report that he arrived at Brundisium with a force points to a call from the senate for reinforcements; again, it is difficult to believe that Crassus would have asked for help, especially from not one but two additional armies. Having Lucullus land at Brundisium as Pompey approached from the north made sense from a senatorial perspective, if the goal were both to extirpate the rebellion and to allow for the credit to be more or less shared.

Just as in Spain there was rivalry between Pompey and Metellus, so in southern Italy there would be a race to deal with the slaves. There is evidence that Spartacus was made aware that Pompey, at least, was approaching; he would have realized that he had no chance of withstanding both Crassus and Pompey. Any efforts to negotiate with Crassus were rejected: Spartacus could not realistically have expected that he was in any position to make a deal, and Crassus was in a hurry to finish the war himself.

It is a testament to the seriousness of the crisis that the war was still difficult. While Crassus clearly secured another victory, with units of his army falling on a body of Spartacus' force as it tried to break the blockade, killing over 12,000 rebels under the leadership of Gannicus and Castus, the Romans suffered losses of their own.[7] To the best of our knowledge, as the situation grew more desperate, elements of the slave army acted with increased independence, in some cases scoring appreciable victories on elements of Crassus' force.

The 'last stand' of Spartacus came at the Battle of the Silarius River.[8] This was the grand final engagement of the war for the slave leader, which (not surprisingly) is reported to have been a desperate, vicious struggle. Spartacus died in the battle, but it is reported that his body was never found, which certainly added to his mystique and contributed to the development of the legend of Spartacus. It is clear that there were heavy losses on both sides; thousands of rebels were killed in the battle, and we are told that Crassus had 6,000 of the survivors crucified as a grim warning to any who might think of taking up Spartacus' cause.

Pompey never actually engaged Spartacus. If many today think of Kubrick's film as reflecting historical reality, another of the errors to be noted is the depiction there of Pompey and Lucullus arriving in time to participate in the climactic battle. In reality, the only involvement that Pompey's forces had with the slave revolt was in encountering and massacring thousands of those who fled north. We do not know where exactly Pompey's men clashed with the fugitives, and our sources do not report any details of a significant military engagement.[9] Likely this was a mopping up operation, little more than a slaughter of defeated, demoralized, and disorganized survivors from Spartacus' forces.

The problem for Crassus was that Pompey was guilty, at least in his eyes, of stealing his thunder. Pompey informed the senate that indeed Crassus had defeated Spartacus, but that he, Pompey, had put the seal on the victory. Given our ignorance of the details of what happened, it is impossible to render a definitive verdict on just how unfair, if at all, Pompey's analysis was. It is likely that he faced no significant threat from the remnants of the slave army, but those with a memory of how small Spartacus' gladiator band had been at the start of the crisis might have been concerned about thousands of fugitives on the loose in the heart of Italy. The Third Servile War at its height may have involved figures as high as 120,000 with Spartacus, although that number may include women and children: one of the logistical problems that hampered Spartacus was that unlike a Roman legion, his mobile army included dependents and non-combatants.

The fact that we know so little about Pompey's final settlement of the slave war may reflect the general disdain for engaging in battle with the lowest social class in Roman society; Pompey would have preferred simply to say that he ended the uprising by killing a large number. If he did fight any actual battle, he probably would have preferred to have let its memory be obscured. One thing is certain: Crassus was not happy with Pompey's claims. That said, the two men were still able to cooperate moving forward, and in fact the coincidence of the Spartacus War set the stage for the two men to begin to work jointly in each other's shared interests.

What of Metellus? Like Pompey, he returned to Italy, and with his colleague, he would celebrate a triumph at the end of 71 BC.[10] The general sentiment seems to have been that he certainly deserved such an honour, though Pompey was clearly the man who received the lion's share of the credit, and fairly so, for ending the war in Spain. On the other hand, there was gossip and criticism that Pompey was a master of behaving like a vulture, swooping in and feasting on the kills of others; his achievements both in Spain and in the final stages of the slave war were derided by some as opportunistic. One of the perennial problems that ambitious and accomplished commanders faced was that they were always liable to be targets of carping and criticism from senators who, truth be told, would probably not have been able to do anything close to what their targets of opprobrium had wrought. It was impossible to survive republican politics without being able to tolerate either just or invidious attacks. It rarely seemed to occur to some senators that the more aggressively they criticized ambitious men, the more said men found it beneficial to make common cause.

There was one young participant who shared in Pompey's well-deserved triumph. His homonymous son was born probably in 75 BC, and was about four years old at the end of the Spartacus war. About eight years older than his more famous brother Sextus, we know next to nothing about little Gnaeus' early years, but there is numismatic evidence of his participation in his father's celebrations of his victories.

The consuls during this year of 71 where Publius Cornelius Lentulus Sura and Gnaeus Aufidius Orestes. Lentulus was destined to fall in the Catilinarian conspiracy of 63 BC., while his colleague disappears from the surviving record, not having taken up any office after his consulship. The real debate would ensue for the next election, where the leading candidates would be Pompey and Crassus.

We have no idea when the two men – rivals, at least after a fashion, in the last stages of the slave war – decided to stand for election.[11] Pompey in particular had serious handicaps to such political aspirations. He was both too young and too inexperienced, not having held the prerequisite magistracies for the office. There is no surprise, however, that Pompey settled on seeking the consulship for 70 BC. At some point the republican system demanded that he enter political life, and both Crassus and he were of the old guard of loyal Sullan colleagues. Both men enjoyed immense popularity in the immediate, having settled the Spartacus business and being able to claim that they had pacified Italy, protecting civil and economic interests. Pompey had the additional glory of Spain to his credit, and Crassus was exceedingly wealthy. Money, power, influence, popularity, and at least a general agreement on political and social issues made them likely candidates.[12]

Agreement, however, would prove to be more true in theory than in practise. Given their histories, it seemed likely that the two men would support a common policy; reality would prove more complicated. We regret not knowing more about how the two men reached their initial political accommodation; both were shrewd and sensible, and no doubt they saw mutual benefit from collaboration.

The crisis that remained abroad in this period was the war with Mithridates. The Roman most associated with the initial prosecution of this third war with Pontus is Lucius Licinius Lucullus. He would be the man who would most vociferously complain that Pompey was a vulture, incensed when the day would come that he would not be allowed to finish the war that he had spent years fighting boldly and resolutely. Pompey would enter his consular year at the age of thirty-five, now older than Alexander had been when he died after so many brilliant victories in Asia. For a man of military inclination who was insatiable in his hunger for victories and triumphs, Asia must have been the goal of Pompey, not least because of his memory of how he had been called an Alexander so early in life. As fate would have it, Pompey would be destined to enjoy some of his most impressive accomplishments in the east, even if for the moment the business of his consulship with Crassus was his priority.

Chapter Eight

First Consulship and Pirate War

One interesting and not entirely unexpected development accompanied the seeming transition of Pompey from military to civilian life: it did not really happen. Neither Crassus nor Pompey was particularly interested in disbanding their legions in the wake of the victory over the slave army. There was clearly significant prevarication by both men, excuses offered for why the legions should be maintained. Many people would have remembered how Sulla had been willing to march on Rome. There was no such crisis now, to be sure. But there were legionary encampments outside the city. The tradition and rule that Sulla had violated was to bring his men into the city; Crassus and Pompey did not violate that sanction, but they also did not make any move to disband their men. Certainly neither one was interested in surrendering such a trump card before the other. The inescapable fact was that the presence of the legions outside the city was a silent, powerful warning: civil war was an all too palpable memory.

Some of this, to be sure, may have been very good theatre. We hear that the people were frightened of the possibility of renewed internecine strife, and that they compelled the two would-be consular colleagues to have a public reconciliation and affirmation of their being together on the same page, for the good of the republic.[1] Such a demonstration would have improved the already high standing of both men appreciably, and it is possible that there was never any real danger of war, simply the recognition that it was to their mutual benefit to make it seem as if they needed to be reconciled.

Certainly Pompey was in a delicate position in the later part of 71 and into 70 BC. We recall that he had a reputation as a 'teenage butcher,' and even after the comparatively mild and generous resolution of the Spanish war, there were probably loud voices that considered him to be capable of the worst actions of a Sulla. But Pompey was complicated, no doubt both genuinely and in the public face he presented to both senate and people. For one thing, he was open to the idea of restoring authority to the tribunes of the plebs, something that had been anathema to Sulla and the *optimates* at the height of the controversies and conflict with the Marians. In other words, Pompey was suspect both for being a product of the Sullan dictatorship, and for seeming to court popular adulation by being open to abandoning some of the most controversial dictates of Sulla's rule.

A sympathetic critic of Pompey might say that he had come to decide (or, even, had finally become willing to admit) that Sulla's prescriptions, even if seemingly necessary and understandable in time of crisis, were in need of revision and adjustment. Perhaps the long experience of the Sertorian War in Spain had influenced his judgment, let alone having seen firsthand the devastation wrought in Italy both in consequence of the Social and the civil wars, and the Spartacus revolt. Being a republican politician was an exceedingly difficult enterprise to conduct successfully; criticism was inevitable. To some extent Pompey was not sufficiently conservative for the *optimates*, and certainly not sufficiently liberal for the *populares*. And, too, he may have been greatly affected by how opinion had turned against Sulla so strongly.

Plutarch is certainly right in his verdict that as the calendar turned from 71 to 70, the new consuls would have opposite wells of support.[2] The older Crassus was more experienced and trusted by the senate, while Pompey enjoyed the greater popular support.[3] This was not exactly a case where there was a serious risk of a resurgence of civil war, with Crassus and Pompey becoming the new Sulla and Marius. But it was a recipe for dissension, since it is clear that the devil was in the details: even if both men had broadly similar outlooks, it soon became apparent that they did not agree on how exactly to move from point A to point B.

Plutarch further asserts that men were not inclined to respect Pompey principally on account of his triumph in Spain or his first (and extraordinary) consulship, but because Crassus was so willing to respect and honour him.[4] If one can believe the biographer, Pompey was held in such regard by colleagues and people alike, that despite the serious differences that developed between the two consular colleagues, by the end of their term Crassus was willing to take the initiative and to express his affection and respect for Pompey, citing his tremendous accomplishments from his youth.

Likely in the events of 70 BC we see evidence of the natural revulsion to civil war that now and again was on display, notwithstanding the many occasions on which such revulsion did not succeed in averting conflict. There would be the normal elections for the consuls of 69, who were Quintus Hortensius Hortalus and Quintus Caecilius Metellus Creticus. Hortensius was a famous orator and rival of Cicero; he would be the defender of Verres when he was prosecuted for his behaviour in Sicily.

While war continued to rage in the east under Lucullus' ongoing management, the old problem of the pirate menace was worsening. The pirates had become bold; they were now making opportunistic raids not only in the Aegean Sea, but even against the Italian coast: Caieta, Ostia, and Misemum were all struck.[5] The Romans had no effective supremacy on the Mediterranean. The famous Mark Antony's homonymous father had been assigned the extraordinary commission of dealing with the pirate menace; it had been something of a family avocation, since his own father had been given the same task.[6] He was unquestionably incompetent; the job of clearing the seas was immensely challenging even for the best of men, but his failures were glaring and indisputable. His son, the future triumvir and rival of Octavian, was born in January of 83; Marcus Antonius Creticus died in 72 or 71, distinguished more by what he had not accomplished than by any achievement of merit.

The year 69 is noteworthy for being the year in which Cleopatra was born; Caesar, meanwhile, was awarded his quaestorship, which was to be served in Spain. Contrary to some fictionalized versions of events, there is no evidence that Caesar played any part in the settlement of the Spartacus revolt, though he had returned from Asia in time to participate. The year would be significant for Caesar for many reasons: not only was his future mistress born, but he lost both his aunt Julia (for whom he delivered the funeral oration), and his wife Cornelia, who died not long after his only legitimate child was born (a chance for a second oration).[7] His daughter Julia was destined to be a wife to Pompey.

Pompey and Caesar enjoyed good relations in this period. To the degree that Pompey was the darling of the masses and was willing to support such populist goals as restoring the power of the tribunate, Caesar was a natural ally.

Officially, Pompey had no job in the wake of his consulship. He had pledged that he would not take a province in the aftermath, and he kept his word; this was one of the ways in which he had secured a broad consensus for his technically illegal aspiration to the office. He had handed over control of his legions once he had no need for them (that is, as a cynic would say, once he had won his office with Crassus).

Plutarch says that in this period, Pompey rarely showed himself in public, with a reflection on the psychology of those who have enjoyed great success in the field and are now supposed to live in republican peace.[8] When he did appear, he was difficult to approach, because he always went out with a large retinue, evidently designed to maintain something of the mystique of his larger than life persona. Once again we see the enigma of the man on display: he had courted and received popular favour, but he preferred to be detached from the common throngs, a remote figure and object of reverential mystery.

The consuls for 68 BC were Lucius Caecilius Metellus and Quintus Marcius Rex. The former was destined to die in office, leaving Marcius as sole consul after his elected replacement Servilius Vatia died before he could assume office. This would be the year when Caesar was quaestor in Spain, where he is said to have seen a statue of Alexander the Great and to have been moved to tears: he was now, after all, approaching the age when Alexander had died, and he had no appreciable successes to measure up to the Macedonian.[9] Pompey must have felt something of the same sentiments in this period, indeed to a greater degree: he was older than Caesar, and he had been called an Alexander in his youth. Both men were in a sense waiting in the wings (Caesar now literally); it was another year that saw Lucullus battling in the east, fighting in Armenia and mulling an attack into Parthia. If anyone was playing Alexander, it was Lucullus, though he was also making enemies along the way, not least because the war was ongoing, seemed unlikely to be resolved anytime soon, was frightfully expensive, and was arguably expanding in ways that no one had seriously envisaged.

I have refrained from engaging in much overview, let alone detail, on Lucullus' prosecution of war with Mithridates of Pontus and Tigranes of Armenia; my views on the man have not changed since the publication of my study of his life. I remain of the opinion that Lucullus is something of an underappreciated republican figure, an exceptionally talented military man who on the whole performed well in one of the most challenging foreign policy crises that Rome had faced to date. Arguably he was far more skilled in military affairs than in politics; his ultimate failures were more the result of losing the political contest for the support of his peers than any of his defeats in the field. Ultimately Pompey was the greater success both on the field and in the equally challenging world of Roman politics; the same could be said of Caesar. In some ways Lucullus was the last true inheritor of the best of Sulla; in some regards at least, the republic breathed its last with Lucullus.

Lucullus could not do everything at once; in this he was like any would-be commander of republican armies. In any time and place where chaos reigns, piracy is prone to run amok. Mithridates supported it; so did Sertorius. Whether or not we believe Plutarch that the Cilician pirates had 1,000 ships and captured 400 cities, there is no question that while wars both foreign and domestic waged across the Mediterranean, the pirate threat worsened; this was part of the discontent with Lucullus that festered in some quarters.[10] The pirates had personally wronged Caesar; their stock in trade was making money from hostage taking, alongside general acts of pillage and rapine.

Mockery and insult toward the Romans was also one of their characteristic acts of insolence, an attitude that increased as the years went by and the republic seemed utterly unable to resolve the problem. Ships are expensive, and in an age without adequate meteorological prognostication, one could lose as many ships from storms and poor weather as from enemy attacks. The economic devastation wrought by the pirates was breathtaking; the blow to Roman pride was perhaps even worse. This was not exactly a slave war, but it was little better in terms of republican prestige.

Throughout 69 and 68 BC, Pompey remained widely popular in Rome, at least among the people. In some ways, it must have been one of the happier periods in his life, even if he was eager for a new assignment and challenge. If he wanted to be sent east to replace Lucullus, it was something being discussed privately, without any overt move as yet to offend the commander. Taking charge of the pirate problem would be attractive for two reasons. One, it would allow Pompey the chance to prove competence in naval combat: not many Romans could boast that they were capable of impressive results on both land and sea. Second, it was an obvious stepping stone to taking over the wars in the east: there was no way to extirpate the pirate threat without becoming ensconced in the eastern Mediterranean. For an ambitious Roman in Pompey's position (especially one with dreams of rivalling Alexander), it was an obvious enough choice of assignment.

The year 67 BC would see the fulfillment of Pompey's wishes for an extraordinary commission. The immense challenge that confronted Pompey in the period after his consulship was that for all his success in winning the hearts and minds of the masses, the *optimates* remained deeply suspicious of him. He seemed to be a Sullan who was shifting too much toward the *populares*; his actions as consul had done him no favours in quelling the development of any such feelings. The consuls of 67 were Gaius Calpurnius Piso and Manius Acilius Glabrio. Piso was a classic example of the old school *optimates*; he was deeply opposed to the idea of giving some special commission to Pompey. His colleague would be the man given the job of replacing Lucullus: he would be assigned to follow up his consulship with a proconsular appointment to Cilicia, with control over the prosecution of the war against Mithridates.[11]

The man most responsible for helping Pompey achieve his goals in the face of strong opposition was Aulus Gabinius.[12] Gabinius was one of Pompey's most devoted clients, and would play an interesting role in many significant subsequent political and military events, for some twenty years. He was tribune of the plebs in 67 BC, which allowed him to sponsor what history knows as the *lex Gabinia* or the Gabinian Law, the commission by which Pompey would be given extraordinary powers to combat the pirate threat.[13]

The basic problem here was that on the one hand, there was anxiety that no one man should have such power that he would be tempted to assume dictatorial airs, a new Sulla. Pompey had exactly the sort of *curriculum vitae* that made him an easy target for such fears. The pirate commission in particular seemed to be a threatening one, because the only way one could solve the problem was by having wide-ranging authority over the entire Mediterranean Sea, including its coastline.

On the other hand, the pirates were running wild. Probably the successful attack on the harbour at Ostia was the point of no return for some people: theoretical concerns about the threat of a new Sulla did not seem so important to people whose economic livelihood and personal safety were imperilled by the Cilician pirates.

In the end, political machinations were probably not the most important factor in securing Pompey's commission. Immediate, inescapable reality seems to have trumped any consideration, however wise, legitimate, and sober, for potential perils. Certainly those who feared Pompey's ambitions could claim that he had exercised political manipulation by co-opting the tribunate to further his own wishes. The argument was valid. But the pirates were more to blame than Gabinius for the anxiety that weighed on the *optimates*.

Plutarch says that one of the people who spoke in support of Gabinius' proposal was none other than Caesar.[14] The biographer is careful to note that the principal motivation for this act of solidarity was not favouritism for Pompey, but support for what the people clearly desired (likely he was also mindful of his own experience with pirates). Pompey was warned that if he tried to act like Romulus, he might end up torn to pieces like Romulus; it was clear warning to avoid that most hated of republican bugbears, monarchy. There was even an attempt to sway support away from Pompey by false flattery, using the argument that if the young man were so beloved, he should not be sent forth to risk life and limb.

In the end, Pompey won; he would be given his extraordinary commission. The commission was for three years; in the end, Pompey would not even need three months to finish the job of clearing the sea lanes. How do you win the day when your suspicious political opponents have tried to hinder your command? By surpassing every expectation, and then some.[15]

Pompey was given men, money, ships, and the advance word to all coastal areas that he was to be granted whatever he needed. Appian says that he had a force of 120,000 infantry, 4,000 cavalry, and 270 ships.[16] He had twenty-five assistants, who were parcelled out to maintain control over different regions of the Mediterranean; Appian gives the list of areas of responsibility of the sub-commanders, who were given propraetorial authority.[17] With each man strictly enjoined to stay in his area, the point was to avoid any possibility that pirates would be pointlessly chased too far, thus allowing other areas to open up for pillaging. Pompey himself embarked on a tour of every zone: this was a chance for the commander to expand his firsthand knowledge of the Roman world, travelling for the first time to distant corners of the Mediterranean.[18]

Plutarch's figures are similar in part to Appian's: he gives Pompey the same number of infantry, with 5,000 cavalry and 500 ships.[19] And he notes that even as soon as the commission was given and the extensive preparations were afoot, prices fell: such was the confidence that people had in Pompey, and he was praised as a victor even before he had cleared the seas.

For Plutarch, the pirates were like a swarm of bees: he says that they sought their home refuge in Cilicia, as the noose tightened. In every one of the districts of naval control, Pompey's ships engaged the pirate vessels, destroying some, forcing some to go ashore and be seized there, while others fled in increasing desperation for their eastern bases.

Stage one of the pirate war was to secure economic intercourse by the opening of the trade routes; this was accomplished, we are told, in some forty days. That left the second stage, the attack on the pirate strongholds in Cilicia, for which Pompey organized a fleet of sixty of his best warships. Stage one was not something that could be done by one man owing to the need to clear the entire Mediterranean, but Pompey was the vigourous organizer and relentless traveller, spending over a month in nonstop naval operations.[20] This was the chance he wanted to show that he could be a master of combat at sea, and he performed marvellously.

We are told that Piso as consul and leader of the suspicious opposition to Pompey was active in trying as best as he could to hinder the progress of the war. This could be done by seeking to delay the distribution of supplies and the money and material needed for an exceptionally expensive campaign. Pompey was forced at one point to return to Rome, where he was greeted with exceptional joy by the people for one simple reason: the markets were swiftly refilling, indeed overflowing with goods, because trade and commerce resumed almost instantly as the sea lanes were cleared.

Plutarch notes that there were agitations against Piso on account of his actions, but that Pompey suppressed them all and urged his supporters to abandon any attempts to punish the consul.[21] The narrative reflects the political skill of the man, and also his ambition: the focus was on the naval operations, not any tedious republican squabbling. At the same time, it would have galled the consul to be defended by Pompey.

On departing from Italy from the port of Brundisium, Pompey is said to have made time on his way to the front to stop in Athens, where he sacrificed to the gods and addressed the people. It was probably his first visit to the storied city.[22] In Rhodes he seems to have heard a lecture by the great philosopher Posidonius.[23]

Just as he had done after the Sertorian War, so now, even before the pirates had been fully eradicated, he displayed clemency to those who came to him and surrendered; as word spread that he was not slaughtering those who threw themselves at his mercy, more followed suit. It was a quick and convenient way to help solve the problem, while also attempting to disprove the charges of those who accused him of bloodthirstiness.

The climax of the pirate war would come when he faced those ready to give battle, having dispersed their families in strongholds near the Taurus mountain range. The pirate capital, so to speak, was at Coracesium in Cilicia. The terrain of the Cilician coast is exceptionally rough and difficult of access, which was exactly the point. Today the modern Alanya is a popular vacation area on the Turkish coast; for Pompey it was the scene of a naval battle that he won ably, followed by the commencement of a siege of their citadels. The pirates had neither the ability nor the stomach for a siege; they were ready to try to negotiate a surrender. Once again, clemency would be the watchword of the hour. Pompey was not interested in a mass slaughter of the defeated brigands, for all their crimes and bad behaviour. In the response of Pompey to the aftermath of the pirate war, we see a clear contrast with the actions of the same man (not to mention Crassus) after the servile war. The pirates were not slain or enslaved; they were, however, to be settled in various areas with a new occupation: the onetime brigands of the sea were to learn how to be humble farmers and herders. All things considered, Pompey was credited with a humane and practical solution to the problem. There were objections from those who wanted to see the pirates massacred; there were probably criticisms that he was once again currying popular favour, this time with a dangerous overseas population. But manpower shortages also meant that cultivation of crops and other menial tasks on which the republic depended were at risk, and the pirate prisoners and their families provided a ready population of labourers. They would not be slaves, but their lifestyle would completely change.

Details of the final naval engagement have not been preserved. Appian says that Pompey prepared enormous siege engines and other battle implements in anticipation of having to assault the pirate's mountain citadels, but that they surrendered in the hope of his mercy, with no final battle on land or sea.[24] Plutarch mentions the manning of ships by the pirates and the battle followed by a siege, but with no information on the actual combat.[25] Velleius also mentions a final battle, again with no specifics.[26] What likely happened is that at least some units of the pirate fleet engaged the Romans, but that whatever combat ensued was finished quickly, with most of the enemy surrendering at once, followed by a brief siege. This is more or less what Florus records; he says that the pirates did not refuse battle initially (their honour would have demanded something), but that as soon as they saw how they were enveloped by so immense a Roman force, they surrendered.[27] Florus is probably correct when he says that the Romans had never achieved so bloodless a victory, nor one in which the vanquished were rendered more loyal to the victor. Pliny cites a figure of 846 pirate ships captured.[28]

Pompey had done what nobody else had managed to achieve, albeit with tremendous resources at his disposal in men and material. He had cleared the Mediterranean of the Cilician pirates, and managed to put an end to their home base fortresses and to distribute them as useful labourers, with little chance that they would be rising up again to resume their life of plunder. He had done all of this in more like three months than three years. This was not Spain, which took years and the experience of several serious setbacks. This was also a win that showed immediate consequences for the population of Italy: the economy was almost immediately put back on a profitable footing by the protection of navigation. Florus says that Pompey managed to win without losing a single ship.[29] Even if this were not true, an argument could be made that Pompey's prosecution of the pirate war resulted in the most enduring of his achievements.

There was one significant event connected to Pompey's prosecution of the pirate campaign that did not go entirely well. Quintus Caecilius Metellus Creticus earned his honourific name 'Cretan' because of his assignment after his consulship of 69 BC: he was busy dealing with the pirates on Crete. Metellus was the perfect example of a prominent figure who would be discomfited by Pompey's broad command on account of the Gabinian Law. Clearly not as competent as Pompey, he nonetheless had no intention of abandoning his work subjugating Crete until he was finished. He was also not interested either in sharing credit for anything with Pompey, let alone in letting Pompey take over his work. Questions of exactly where Metellus' authority ended and Pompey's began in light of the latter's commission were a highly sensitive subject, to be sure. It was probably inevitable that there would be some sort of clash between the two men. Metellus' consular colleague Hortensius had not been interested in the Cretan assignment; he would emerge as the wiser of the two.

Metellus was not a particularly incompetent commander; he was simply not of the capability and reputation of Pompey, and no doubt jealousy was rife. Metellus had the ancient city of Knossos under siege, and the Cretans sent word that they were willing to surrender – to Pompey. Pompey's reputation for clemency toward defeated pirates had spread swiftly, and the Cretans correctly judged that they would have a far better lot handing themselves over to Pompey instead of Metellus.

This was exactly the sort of development that would incense Metellus. For any of the *optimates* inclined to mistrust Pompey on account of his cultivation of popular favour, this was evidence of exactly what they feared.

According to Plutarch, what happened next was beyond the pale.[30] Pompey accepted the request of the Cretans, first notifying Metellus that he was to cease offensive operations, and then writing to the cities of Crete, telling them not to pay heed to the dictates of Metellus. He sent Lucius Octavius as his legate; Octavius went so far as to fight on the same side as the pirates in defence against Metellus. The biographer notes that not even Achilles behaved this way with respect to the Trojans. Metellus is said to have defeated the pirates, sending Octavius back to Pompey with insults and public invective.

What really took place on Crete? Velleius simply says that Pompey envied Metellus his glory for his deeds on the island, without any details of what he did in consequence of his envy.[31] Florus mentions Pompey's sending someone to the island, but with none of Plutarch's dramatic details.[32] Appian has Pompey writing to Metellus and telling him to halt operations so that he could later go and receive the surrender, with the request/order being ignored.[33] Dio Cassius has the story of Octavius going to Crete, with an appreciably different analysis of what he did from that in Plutarch, characterizing the activity of Pompey's legate as being taken in defence of Cretans who were the objects of intolerable mistreatment at Metellus' hands.[34] Dio presents Octavius as having come to Crete not with men, but with orders from Pompey to take control of the cities; Lucius Cornelius Sisenna is said to have arrived and to have urged Metellus to spare the locales willing to surrender, but he was ignored.[35] Metellus seized one place notwithstanding Octavius' presence; he killed the Cilicians who were with him. At that point Octavius took over the soldiers of Sisenna, who in the meantime had fallen ill and died. He then undertook the defence of those who were being unjustly attacked and killed by Metellus.

Sisenna, we may note, is a fascinating and mysterious figure.[36] We know very little about his political career. He is best known for having authored a celebrated history of the Social War and the civil war between Sulla and Marius, which survives only in fragments. The great historian Sallust is essentially a continuation of Sisenna. In terms of the life of Pompey, he figures only as a resolute Sullan who played a minor role in the Cretan episode, before dying on the island in 67 BC.

Metellus clearly won in the contest of wills with Pompey. Pompey was not about to start a civil war over Crete. His assertion of his rights to command had been disregarded; before circumstances on the ground made it a moot point, there was not much he could do, short of outright hostilities. There were, however, consequences that he could implement moving forward: Metellus would be a target for all of Pompey's friends, who could, for example, do everything in their power to delay the award of honours for the conquest of Crete.

The Cretan episode must have been an exceptionally difficult one for Pompey. Legally, he did have something of a case about his extraordinary authority. That said, asserting that authority in the face of Metellus' ongoing operation unavoidably played into the hands of those who were already criticizing Pompey for being a dictator in training. Pompey's proposed policy toward the Cretans was the wiser one, but few of the *optimates* were likely to be sympathetic to the plight of the islanders given that Crete was basically the second pirate capital after Cilicia.

The year 67 also saw the marriage of Caesar to Pompeia, the daughter of Quintus Pompeius Rufus and Cornelia, the daughter of Sulla.[37] But it was Pompey who was the man of the hour; the Metellus episode reinforced the suspicions of those who were already hostile to Pompey, but popular support was greater than ever. The fact that Lucullus was increasingly unpopular with his men, and that Mithridates was still running amok, with no end to war in Asia in sight, made Pompey even more popular. The hour was drawing near when the vanquisher of the pirate peril would have his chance to assume the mantle of Alexander.[38]

Chapter Nine

Pompey in Asia, Part I

The year 67 BC was one in which Pompey met the expectations of both his supporters and his detractors. The pirate war was of a markedly different nature from the Sertorian rebellion in Spain, but the speed and comprehensiveness of Pompey's achievements, not least with its swift dividends for the economically beleaguered republic, offered a news story that needed little or no embellishment to offer in his praise. Conversely, his adversaries were more than convinced that he was infected with the same spirit as Sulla, aiming ultimately for dictatorial power and control of the machinery of government. The fact that he was by no means the only ambitious young republican meant that it was all too easy to try to play one prominent man against another, or to flatter the ambitions of one to try to keep another in check.

Lucullus did masterful work in Asia, but there is no denying that circumstances were dire by the time Pompey was finalizing his operations against the pirates. Lucullus had not come close to putting the finishing touches on the war (or, one might argue, wars). It is open to question whether another man could have done much better in the same time and with the same resources. The Asian crisis was more serious than the Iberian, and even Pompey had suffered considerable setbacks as Metellus and he struggled to pacify the peninsula. Lucullus, we have argued, was better at the military manouevres and strategical thinking than he was at political machinations. He was also not particularly gifted in the area of popularity with one's troops, an arena in which both Pompey and Caesar would distinguish themselves. Crassus was notorious for resurrecting such legendary harsh punishments as decimation to deal with poor performance in the ranks, but that was also during the Spartacus War, which was of relatively brief duration so far as concerned his involvement.[1] Lucullus would probably have been assassinated had he tried the same tactic with any recalcitrant men in Asia, even if he were so inclined to practise so marked a degree of discipline. One of the leading figures in the troubles that Lucullus suffered was his own brother-in-law, Publius Clodius Pulcher.[2] One of the most colourful and notorious figures of his age, Clodius seems to have had a perpetual problem with feeling disrespected; his self-esteem, one imagines, was easily bruised. Lucullus was one of the leading targets of his claims of being unappreciated and poorly treated, and backbiting among the commander's subordinates became one of Clodius' favourite hobbies. If Lucullus came to blame any one man for the mutinies he endured, it was Clodius. The charge that Clodius was having an incestuous affair with his sister, Lucullus' (soon to be divorced) wife, added to the scurrilous, scandalous nature of the whole controversy.[3]

The consuls elected for 66 BC were Manius Aemilius Lepidus and Lucius Volcatius Tullus.[4] Lepidus was one of those relatively obscure figures, for all his high office; he attained that obscurity by being one of those men who would refrain from becoming overtly involved when relations broke down between Pompey and Caesar in the late 40s. Neither of the consuls of the year would be as remembered as the tribune Gaius Manilius, who like Aulus Gabinius before him would distinguish himself as a partisan of Pompey and promoter of his cause. The *lex Manilia* or 'Manilian Law' called for exactly what some must have been musing over for some time before it was proposed, namely entrusting the prosecution of the Third Mithridatic War to the popular, thus far highly successful Pompey.[5] Needless to say, this was exactly the sort of thing that would cause some *optimates* to argue that Pompey was a populist manipulator, using (or abusing) the tribunate to secure his dictatorial ambitions. Lucullus, needless to say, was being set up to be deeply resentful of Pompey.[6] Those who had objected to the extraordinary commission of Pompey to manage the pirate war now had reason to feel even more convinced that they were right, and to think that they had been vindicated in their suspicions. How convenient it was that Pompey was already on the spot, in the east, with a sizable military.

Generations of Latin students are familiar with the events of 66 BC because of Cicero's great speech *De imperio Gnaei Pompeii* (also commonly known as the *Pro lege Manilia*), in which the gifted orator exercised his craft in defence of Pompey's ambition. If one reads, for example, the account of this crucial period in Velleius, one finds the analysis that Manilius was a man of venal character, while Lucullus, too, was so greedy for money that while he could have successfully brought the fighting in Asia to a conclusion, it seemed more profitable to him to continue his command quasi-indefinitely. Velleius notes that Pompey charged Lucullus with unbridled avarice, while Lucullus retorted with the insult that his would-be successor was insatiably greedy for military conquests and glory.[7] We may recall that Pompey had a reputation for being relatively abstemious in his personal habits, and it is true that Lucullus became renowned as a luxury-obsessed gourmand, given over to the pleasures of the stomach. If we remember the anecdote about the doctor prescribing a diet of thrush for a sick Pompey, a meal that could only be obtained out of season from Lucullus' aviary, we can appreciate the extent of the claims of decadence.[8]

Velleius admits that both Lucullus and Pompey were right, and surely the truth lies somewhere between the arguments of the two, overlapping and intertwining. We should not dismiss the powerful allure of the east for Pompey, and not only because of any race to match the ambitions and achievements of Alexander. By 66 BC, the thirty-nine year old Pompey had done much of note and high renown in Italy, Africa, Iberia, and on the sea. Asia was the only theatre missing from his geographical sweep from east to west. Asia was a far more pressing arena for potential glory in 66 than Gaul and the mysterious lands to the north and west, Britain and the theatres in which Caesar would find fame in the following decade. Asia was the obvious missing piece to give Pompey something of a complete roster of military conquests. And, after all, for whatever reasons (justifiable and less so), Lucullus had not finished the job despite years in the field, even without counting his extensive experience with Sulla.

Velleius further argues that a defining trait of Pompey was that he could not stand having an equal or a colleague in these endeavours.[9] The closest he had come to having to share appreciable credit and glory for a victory had been in Spain with Metellus, where he had suffered significant reversals, and where the war would likely have proven longer and more arduous if he had been managing it alone. But in the end, in Pompey's estimation Lucullus was the Roman Xerxes, and it was clear that he wanted to live up to his youthful reputation as a budding Alexander. He coveted Lucullus' command with a palpable intensity, and short of a new civil war that was little that Lucullus could do to avoid the changing of the guard. And Lucullus was neither inclined to start a new civil war, nor in anything approaching a position of favour and popularity with his soldiers even to entertain such a thought.

Metellus, meanwhile, was occupied in the reduction of Crete into a Roman province.[10] Not even a man of Pompey's ambition and ability to do everything at once, Metellus quickly was able to cement his position as the man responsible for the aftermath of the pirate war on that island.

Plutarch relates the anecdote that when the word was brought to Pompey that the Manilian proposal had passed, he lamented that he was always being compelled to solve one problem after another, not even able to spend time in the country with his wife.[11] He expressed regret that he was not able to live the life of an unknown, average man. His friends and associates had no patience for this; they knew, Plutarch says, that he was being insincere, and that his ambition and personal dislike of Lucullus was motivating him, and that he wanted nothing more than to be in command in Asia. We may wonder at this juncture whether it is true that Pompey had enmity toward Lucullus. In temperament they were very different, but probably if Lucullus had lived to see the subsequent divisions that emerged between Pompey and Caesar, it may well have been that he would have seen that he and his old rival had more in common than not. Lucullus had something that Pompey craved intensely, and part of the very craving was the fact that despite several years in the field, his rival had failed to finish the war. Something similar had been the case with Metellus in Spain, though not on quite the grand scale as the seemingly interminable eastern war.

Plutarch makes clear that when Pompey began traversing Asia Minor, he made a point to reverse the policies of Lucullus.[12] If Lucullus had excused someone for some fault, Pompey sought to punish them; conversely, he was sympathetic to those who had been condemned or felt slighted. If true, probably there was a conscious effort to make it clear that there was a new administration. Certainly if he blamed Lucullus for the failure to finish the job, he would have been eager to show that there was a new commander, and he would have been eager to show in every way possible that there was a new order of affairs. His priority was certainly not sparing Lucullus' feelings; there was, after all, little he could do to assuage his predecessor's bitterness.

The intensity of such resentment, and the omnipresent audience of those ready to see signs of slights and insult, can be appreciated from a seemingly trivial incident that is emblematic of Roman pride and decorum. Pompey and Lucullus were scheduled to meet at Galatia, for one of those always awkward encounters in military history where the old commander greets the new one as the page of history turns after a period of seeming failure and disappointment.[13] Because Pompey had been travelling through desert regions, the laurels that festooned his lictors' rods were withered and faded. Lucullus' lictors took some of their own, fresh laurels to share with Pompey. It was a gesture of magnanimity and respect, but it was taken to be a tangible sign that Pompey was coming to steal some of Lucullus' glory. It fed the narrative that like Metellus in Spain, Lucullus had done all the hard work, and Pompey was here to claim the victory and the spoils.

The charge was inevitable, even if it was not entirely fair. The meeting between the two commanders was as cordial as could be expected, up to a point; the tension, however, was clearly thick in the air, and before long the two men were snapping at each other, uttering critical barbs back and forth. Eventually their respective entourages and friends had to call an end to the meeting; it had proven fruitless if the goal was any sort of reconciliation.

The immediate aftermath seemed to bring more of the same. Pompey would do what he could to undo whatever orders Lucullus gave in his waning days. The only soldiers Pompey was not interested in taking over from his predecessor were those who, as Plutarch describes it, were so infected with a mutinous spirit that Pompey felt they were no good to him, useful only because they were hostile to Lucullus.[14] Pompey allegedly was free with his criticisms of Lucullus' administration of the war, while Lucullus recited the history from the Sertorian War, the rebellion of Lepidus, and the Spartacus rebellion, all as evidence that his successor was the consummate vulture. The Spartacus campaign seems to have been a favourite subject of Lucullus' insults: it was a war against mere slaves and gladiators, a conflict that seemed to offer nothing of the usual trappings of glory, and yet even there, Pompey could not refrain from seeking to seize some of the glory. It is possible that Lucullus felt particular animus and contempt for Pompey in this regard given that his brother had been one of the commanders involved in trying to put an end to the crisis.

Dio reports that Lucullus emphasized to Pompey that in fact the war was basically finished.[15] This argument would accord with the charge that Pompey was insatiable for military glory, and that he was interested in winning it on the carrion left by others. Certainly the war was not over, even if obviously anyone who prosecuted it now was finishing what Lucullus had both laid the groundwork for and had seen through to advanced stages of resolution.

When the historical record notes that on his return, Lucullus brought back a new fruit to Rome – cherries from Cerisus, whence the name – we see the strong influence, however much deserved, of the tradition of Lucullus as gourmand, almost as if Lucullus would have done better had he been as zealous for fame on the battlefield as for tracking down new and delectable dishes.[16] Pompey, meanwhile, had a war to wage.

In one key sense, the new commander was in a supremely advantageous position: he had an exceptionally well-outfitted naval force in the vicinity. There would no longer be any help to Mithridates from Cilician pirates, and the entire coastland could easily be blockaded from, as Plutarch notes, Phoenicia straight to the Cimmerian Bosporus.[17] On the Euxine, at least, Pompey would have naval supremacy.[18]

On land, Mithridates wished to take advantage of a time-honoured method of frustrating one's foe: constant retreat and unwillingness to engage in open, pitched battles. The idea was to wear down the enemy, who would eventually feel the want of provisions if lured into a pattern of constant hide and go seek. There was also the chance that sooner or later, one's adversary would make a fatal blunder. Mithridates had the homefield advantage, with far greater knowledge of terrain and local populations. The familiar dictum about avoiding land wars in Asia was at hand: Mithridates could retreat and retreat, circling and rounding back there, causing immense irritation, especially to someone impatient to achieve glory and renown.

The problem with such a strategy is that one must likewise always be on the move; destroying crops and provisions along the way harmed one's enemy, but it also incurred a loss to one's own territory. Nor could such a plan be maintained indefinitely, especially if one cared about large tracts of empire.

Plutarch says that at this point Mithridates had a force of some 30,000 infantry and 2,000 cavalry.[19] Mithridates took full advantage of mountainous terrain and areas of difficult access, again always with the intention to delay as long as possible from engaging in a direct clash. But there was one major diplomatic problem that the Pontic king faced, one that Pompey would exploit to the utmost.

The Parthian Empire was currently ruled by Phraates III. He was an uneasy neighbour both to Mithridates, and to Mithridates' son-in-law Tigranes II in Armenia. There had been a time when the Parthians were the clear dominant power in the Near East; those days had seemingly evaporated as Mithridates in particular proved to be so competent and resilient. Phraates was by all accounts wise in one major regard: he saw no reason to help Pontus and Armenia fight Rome, preferring instead to see what would unfold while he remained more or less neutral and on the sidelines. Triangular diplomacy seemed to him to be the safest course, and in this the argument could be made that he was correct, at least for the time being. His intention was that when the time was right, he would strike where it seemed most opportune and beneficial for Parthia.

One of the key provisions of the Manilian Law is sometimes unappreciated by those who focus overmuch on the matter of Pompey's being sent to replace Lucullus. Pompey enjoyed something far more significant than anything Lucullus had enjoyed: he was authorized to establish and to break treaties as he deemed fit, without the usual recourse for approval from the senate. This was the issue that most rankled the *optimates* who were worried that Pompey was a new Sulla in training: they saw the commission he received as something entirely contrary to the spirit of republican governance, and the point was not an unreasonable one. For some, the matter was one of practicality: the war needed to be concluded satisfactorily, and Pompey had demonstrated that he was able to do just that sort of thing, and to the economic, political, and military benefit of the republic. The only question for some sceptics and critics was what honours and rights he would demand in exchange for the next miracle he would work to dazzle his adoring devotees.

Diplomacy and the power to make treaties was exactly the expedient that Pompey was going to try to use to end the war quickly and on excellent terms. We are not entirely certain of every detail of Pompey's negotiations with Phraates in 66 BC, let alone the progress of subsequent diplomatic intercourse. The subject is of immense interest and importance, because it offers a priceless window into the relationship between Rome and Parthia at a crucial, relatively early stage of their serious mutual engagement. One of the thorny issues for scholars is the question of what agreements Pompey struck with Phraates as to spheres of influence, for example, the question of Roman acknowledgment that the Parthians were to be masters of Mesopotamia and Adiabene, or whether the Euphrates was to be the acknowledged, easily delineated border between the two powers.[20] Part of the reason for confusion in these matters is that subsequent breakdowns in relations were clearly rooted in the respective perceptions of what was agreed to in this significant year; the fact that Phraates was not to enjoy a long and prosperous life would add to the problems.

It seems that Pompey opened immediate negotiations with Phraates in Parthia, possibly with the simple suggestion: Parthia should invade Armenia, which would prevent Tigranes from assisting Mithridates while he was preoccupied with Phraates. It was triangulation at its best, and Phraates welcomed the idea. Next, there was a direct negotiation with Mithridates; it is not clear which man contacted the other first, but both were no doubt eager to communicate, since the king had no idea if his new Roman adversary would be willing to discuss terms that would never have been raised by Lucullus. Pompey was willing to make peace, but he would be the one to assert the terms of the peace treaty, and he was above all particularly interested in having Mithridates turn over all the Romans who had deserted to serve as mercenaries over the years in the Pontic military. Mithridates refused these terms; it is difficult to imagine that anyone could easily have accepted them. Pompey was probably quite honest in suggesting them: he was above all a pragmatist when it came to war, and in his estimation he was being generous. Mithridates could either submit to Pompey's clemency and humanity, or be destroyed.

Phraates was not exactly the most competent or skilled of allies. He launched his invasion of Armenia, striking at Artaxata and besieging it. But his campaign succeeded only in distracting Tigranes, which was enough to satisfy Pompey. If anything, it was beneficial to him that the Parthians were exposed as being weak, and they were not in a position to invade Armenia successfully. All of this worked to Rome's advantage.

One could summarize the general thrust of events as this: when Pompey first arrived in Asia, Armenia was closely associated with helping Mithridates, and Parthia was not; therefore, Armenia was a target of Roman aggression. Once the Armenian situation was more or less resolved to Pompey's satisfaction, relations with Parthia were decidedly colder, and Pompey was more inclined to force negotiation on both his new client kingdom, and his neighbouring rival power.

What is not entirely clear is the exact chronology, or the matter of who first decided that Phraates should strike Tigranes the Great. Two issues overlapped. Pompey had to deal with three monarchs and one prince, as it were: Mithridates of Pontus, Tigranes of Armenia, Phraates of Parthia, and Tigranes' rebellious, homonymous son, Mithridates' grandson. The players in this complex diplomatic dance were by no means equally matched; the quasi-superpowers were Rome and Parthia, with Pontus and Armenia essentially buffer states between them. Tigranes had helped Mithridates, and was facing an internal crisis with his son. Parthia clearly viewed Armenia as within their sphere of interest. Mithridates was in reality interested mostly in survival, preferably with his kingdom at least in some way left intact, rump or not.

The overlapping issues of Tigranes' bad relationship with his son and Pompey's interest in having Armenia not assist Mithridates came to a head. Dio presents the case that Pompey simply succeeded in anticipating Mithridates in securing favourable arrangements with Phraates, persuading the Parthians to strike Armenia.[21] Later, while Pompey was engaged with Mithridates, Tigranes the Younger fled to Phraates for help in his disputes with his father.[22] Phraates was hesitant to aid the rebellious son because of his treaty with the Romans, but he was persuaded to help the prince by attacking Armenia.

Our analysis is this. Pompey clearly was busy with diplomacy almost as soon as he was able to initiate communication with various powers. For Mithridates, the message was simply to surrender on Pompey's terms. For Phraates (who mattered far more in the game of practical politics than the squabbling father and son in Armenia), the communication was likely to feel free to exercise a more or less free hand; Rome was clearly after Mithridates.

What of the business of Pompey's early and decisive engagements with Mithridates? Initially, Pompey exercised a style of fighting that reflected both his own experience in Iberia, and his knowledge of what Mithridates himself was fond of trying to do. He began to launch seemingly desultory raids on the king's forces, pricking here and there with annoying, mosquito-like cavalry strikes that were designed both to harass the enemy and to try to lure him into carefully arranged ambushes. The guerrilla tactic of striking and retreating rapidly was a constant irritation to the Pontic forces, and Mithridates was also unable to prevent the devastation of his land. The Romans suffered from privations for want to supplies, but the king was also in increasingly grievous straits. At some point it must have occurred to him all too clearly that there was a very different commander in the field; likely he had heard about Pompey's great reputation, but he may not have expected the storied general to practise the same sort of guerrilla warfare that he had perfected in recent years. There was also a major difference between the privations the Romans suffered, and those of the king's men: Pompey was supremely competent when it came to logistics, and he strove to have supplies funnelled to his units, wherever he manouevred them. It was not a perfect system, and conditions could be immensely challenging. But he had supply lines that Mithridates could only dream of, and he was able to devastate crops and burn supplies wherever he found them, since he was not dependent on local produce to feed his men. Pompey also began to establish small forts and armed positions wherever the terrain seemed to call for it, in a sense imitating his strategy from the pirate war, only now on land: it was all about circumvallation and drawing the noose ever tighter.

Our sources do not offer a comprehensive account of the next stages of the campaign that agree in all details. The basic story is reasonably clear: Mithridates was harassed and pursued, and he was forced to flee. How many more or less major engagements there were is a matter of question: likely two. Certainly Mithridates withdrew into Lesser Armenia, where he seems to have hoped to try to ensconce himself in the fortress of Dasteira, probably at what would later be Pompey's foundation of Nicopolis or the City of Victory, the modern Koyulhasir in Turkey.[23] Plutarch reports that Mithridates abandoned his foundation when he judged that it lacked sufficient water; when Pompey arrived, he had a different view based on his consideration of the vegetation, and he ordered his men to dig wells.[24] The Romans thus took advantage of what was an excellent base, and Pompey commenced a siege of Mithridates' nearby new camp that lasted forty-five days. Mithridates finally escaped with his best soldiers, after killing his sick and wounded.

Pompey was hot on the trail of the wily king; he knew that Mithridates was a master of disappearing and living to fight well another day. The resultant engagement that would follow is usually known as the Battle of the Lycus. According to Plutarch, Pompey was worried that the king might move to cross the Euphrates, and so even though it was midnight he prepared his men in battle array, as if he were intending to do what ancient armies were usually loathe or at least hesitant to attempt: a night battle.[25] Mithridates actually had to be roused from sleep by his men, who informed him of the imminent strike. When the king prepared his forces, Pompey began to reconsider his plan to attack; the king seemed to have a force sufficiently large to make him hesitate to try the perilous gamble of a night engagement.

Pompey's men, however, reminded him of the moon: not only was there still some light sufficient to see persons in the field, but the moonlight was also at the backs of the Romans, with the light close to the horizon such that the shadows they cast would confuse the enemy and make the Romans seem closer than they were. Thus the threat of missile weapons would be seriously reduced: the king's men would at least in some cases hurl weapons at phantom targets.

Everything worked as planned, and Pompey led a successful night attack on Mithridates' camp, with a loss of allegedly 10,000 men for the enemy, and a capture of the camp. Mithridates is said to have charged through the Romans with an initial force of 800 companion cavalry, which was reduced to the improbable figure of three, one of them his concubine Hypsicrateia, who was said to have especially daring and reckless, such that the king called her by the masculine form of her name, Hypsicrates.[26] The king and these three survivors of his retinue made a successful escape; if there were anything that Mithridates was renowned for, it was his ability so survive the deadliest of calamities.

Appian also tells of the loss of a camp with 10,000 slain, although the details are significantly different from Plutarch's.[27] After initial operations that see Pompey setting up his forts and devastating the king's territory, Mithridates is said to have been in a state of hesitancy and even paralysis as to what to do. He took up a fortified hill position. There were skirmishes, and some of the king's cavalry made the mistake of rushing out to help their advance guard, without their horses. When they decided to race back to retrieve them so that they could take on Pompey's cavalry, they succeeded mostly in misleading their fellows into thinking that they had been routed. The forces on the hilltop began to try to escape for their lives, and they were cut down by Pompey's men, with heavy losses. Appian makes clear that the blame for the disaster rested with those who had rashly rushed into battle without being prepared. The whole question, in other words, hinged on the hazards of taking the bait. It was then easy for Pompey to finish off the bulk of the force that was left, again with an alleged casualty toll of 10,000.

Dio's version is also unique, though he has much in common with Plutarch.[28] He offers the more plausible conclusion that many of the king's men were killed and fewer were taken prisoner, but that a significant number accompanied Mithridates in flight. Dio also has the king seeking a fortified height, with the hope that he could exhaust Pompey while relying on provisions from friendly locals; he also launched periodic cavalry raids, which resulted in an increase of his population of Roman army deserters. Pompey was not interested in falling into the trap of trying to launch a difficult uphill attack; he withdrew a short distance, and purposely constructed a wooded forest camp so that he would be able both to be protected from cavalry attacks and to set up ambushes. Appian says that he then took a small force and approached the Pontic camp, throwing it into disorder and leading them exactly where he wanted to make use of his ambush strategy, with great success.[29] He was then able to seek provisions without constant harassment. Mithridates realized that he was in a losing position as long as he stayed on his hilltop; he fled toward Armenia. Pompey hastily pursued him, but the king was sedulous about not giving battle by day, and the Romans were worried about a night attack because of their relative unfamiliarity with the locale. Finally Pompey had no choice: it was either strike by night, or let the king escape deep into Armenia. The Romans are said to have been able to lay an ambush, which allowed them to attack Mithridates in the dead of night. The Romans were swift and sudden in their surprise attack, and the reverberation of the sound of their shouts and the clash of their weapons in the mountainous locale added to the quasi-supernatural nature of the attack. Mithridates was completely unprepared, and so his baggage was exposed and his men not prepared in order of battle. Once again we hear of the advantage that the Romans had with the moonlight behind them, resulting in a confusing cast of shadows. Festus in his *Breviarium* of Roman history knows about a night assault on the king's camp, and claims that some 42,000 were slain: implausible even for Pompey's deadly efficiency.[30]

What really happened? While our sources do not agree on the details, the common threads include Mithridates trying to take refuge in a fortified hill position, the evocative story of the moonlight battle, and both sides trying to use cavalry to goad their enemy and to lure their adversaries into ambush. Mithridates was in a losing position principally because he was dealing with an aggressive, ambitious commander who was fresh to the field and eager to prove that after the long years of Lucullus, the Romans now had a general who was going to put an end once and for all to the myth of Mithridates. There is no question that the real change in the equation of the war was Pompey. His ability to simplify the map at least temporarily by having Parthia invade Armenia was a brilliant use of diplomacy to aid his attack; it also served the valuable purpose of demonstrating to the Romans why it made sense to allow the commander on scene to have the power to initiate treaties and to strike bargains with foreign powers without the long and impractical business of consulting the senate. It was not at all republican government, but it was efficient in resolving the crisis.

Mithridates had failed in his initial clashes with Pompey. It is unlikely that he harboured any serious hopes of being able to defeat his new adversary swiftly. A major part of his strategy was wearing down the enemy, and he could plausibly argue that just as he had outlasted Lucullus, so he would Pompey. But the price of this approach was that he was always in fear that his allies and subordinates would grow weary, and certainly there was no glory in almost constantly being in retreat.

Mithridates was probably not happy about it (to say the least), but realistically his best option at this juncture (other than trying to come to terms with Pompey) was to seek what support he could from Tigranes in Armenia. That kingdom, however, had had just about enough of Mithridates and his war. The real issue was not that Pontus was fighting Rome. Tigranes was not only having trouble with Parthia on account of Pompey's diplomatic coup. He was also in conflict with his own son, who was in rebellion allegedly with the support of Mithridates. Tigranes the Younger was ambitious and opportunistic, to say the least. He had fled to Phraates in Parthia and had connived to put an end to the Armenian conflict.

We have noted the question of confusion as to who exactly had first suggested that Parthia should strike Armenia. Once Mithridates was on the run, the fact that he was rebuffed from Armenia was no surprise. Tigranes the Great blamed him more than anyone for the behaviour of his son, and Phraates had no interest in propping up or sheltering the defeated king. Tigranes the Younger was hardly in a position to do anything for his grandfather; his plate was more than full with his own difficulties, and he was certainly not about to join Mithridates' remaining forces in some continuing game of increasingly ignominious flight.

The situation in Asia would now focus mostly on Parthia and the pursuit of Mithridates. Parthia was eager for a renewal and confirmation of a state of peace with Rome. The winter of 65–4 BC would be spent by Pompey mostly in dealing with the problems between Parthia and Armenia; it was one of his more arduous diplomatic enterprises, as it would be for many a Roman to come. It meant a delay in the prosecution of the war against Mithridates, but it was a necessary one, and in the meantime a sea blockade would support the endeavour to keep the elusive king in check. Pompey had granted peace a second time to the Albanians, and had also accepted the voluntary surrender of other tribes on the Caspian Sea and the nearby ranges of the Caucasus.

Plutarch says that after Mithridates realized he had no chance of seeking shelter or aid in Armenia, he proceeded south toward Colchis.[31] Pompey certainly needed to pursue him, but it was also not exactly in the best interest of Rome to leave a powder keg like Armenia in a state of turbulence and uncertainty; the risk was too great. Plutarch has Tigranes the Younger inviting Pompey to invade Armenia, with the two men proceeding forth as town after town was willing to submit to the Romans once they saw Pompey leading troops in their territory.[32]

Tigranes the Great had no stomach for being defeated by Pompey the way he had suffered losses to Lucullus; in Plutarch's account, he had heard convincing accounts of how reasonable Pompey could be, and so he set out to negotiate. Pompey and the beleaguered met, and just as Tigranes had been led to expect, the new Roman commander was exceedingly generous; he was willing to propose that Tigranes should remain in power, as a Roman client king. Tigranes the Younger was to be expected to respect his father's authority; in short order, the Armenian civil discord was to be resolved immediately, by Roman order.

Tigranes the Younger was in no mood to be given commands by Pompey; according to Plutarch, when invited to dinner by the general, he is said to have made the insolent remark that he needed no honours from Pompey, since he could find them from another Roman.[33] The sarcasm and contempt earned him chains and the assurance that he would be a leading exhibit in Pompey's next triumph. Phraates responded to all of this by proposing border negotiations, with the Euphrates as a suggested demarcation line; he also wanted Tigranes the Younger to be sent to him. Pompey refused the request for the young man, and seems to have prevaricated on the treaty question. Appian says that the arrogant prince was supposed to rule Gordyene and Sophene (i.e., Lesser Armenia), with right of succession to his father.[34] According to his version, the son attempted to kill his father, which put an end to any consideration for him in Pompey's plans of organization. Appian records that Tigranes the Younger lived to be exhibited in Pompey's triumph, and was subsequently slain.[35] 'Nicopolis' was soon after founded as the tangible symbol of the commander's victory.

Dio has a broadly similar account in Books 36–37 of his history as he discusses the events of 66–5 BC, with some interesting additional clarifications and details. Mithridates wanted to come to terms with Phraates, but Pompey anticipated him, succeeding even in convincing the Parthians to invade Tigranes' Armenia.[36] Mithridates panicked and made his own move toward the kingdom, thus setting the stage for Pompey's attempt to intercept him and the resultant night battle.[37] Mithridates fled to Tigranes, though the reception was less than warm given that the king blamed him for his son's turning against him.[38] After relations soured between Tigranes and his offspring, Phraates was placed in the knotty position of having to respond to the overtures of Tigranes the Younger about attacking Armenia. Though worried at first about offending Pompey given the treaty he had made with the Romans, his hesitation was brief; he agreed to help son against father, only to decide to leave behind some of his force and to retreat back home once it became clear that Tigranes the Great was going to withdraw and force a protracted siege – fickle Phraates indeed.[39] Father then defeated son in this account; son decided to try to flee to Mithridates, but learned that he was also on the run, and only then sought to try his luck with the Romans. From there the story converges largely with Plutarch; Pompey tried to settle Armenian affairs, but before long he became thoroughly irritated with the rebel prince because of his insolent behaviour. In Book 37, he has an interesting account in detail of the vicissitudes in the relationship between Pompey, Phraates, and the Armenian question, of immense value for studying Roman-Parthian relations.

Phraates was eager to make peace with Pompey, but his problem was that both his record and Roman loyalty to their client Tigranes the Great made him less than favoured in the general's eyes. Phraates had proven that he was less than fearsome when it came to military endeavours, and his squabbles with Tigranes were an obvious source of irritation to Pompey. Parthia had invaded Corduene (i.e., Gordyene, in what is today eastern Turkey).[40] According to Plutarch, Pompey's loyal subordinate Lucius Afranius drove the Parthians out of the area, and pursued them even as far as Arbela, or present-day Erbil in Iraq.[41] Dio says that Corduene was occupied without a battle; the truth cannot be determined with certainty given surviving evidence, but what is clear in all of this is that Parthia had no interest or ability to wage full-scale war with Pompey. Dio also notes that Afranius operated in violation of agreements made with Phraates; if true, again, we may see an element of contempt for Parthia's king. Dio concludes with the sentiment that might makes right: Pompey was clearly militarily superior to Phraates, and so he could violate Parthian territory in any way he wished.[42] Parthia's kings gloried in the honourific 'King of Kings,' but Pompey always addressed Phraates only as 'king.'[43] Phraates is said to have taken this as a sign that the Roman commander was going so far as to assert that Parthia had been taken over. The king urged peace, and made it clear that the Euphrates was the inviolate border. This made sense: it was all too easy for there to be debate about less easily defined borders, especially with a major client kingdom like Armenia between the great empires. But the Euphrates was a line of demarcation that no could plead confusion or error about violating.

Pompey had been given repeated overtures from Parthia that peace was desirable. The fact that he seems to have been slow to respond makes sense in context. The longer Pompey delayed from making clear his plans or intention, the more Phraates was left to worry and to be in doubt. There were risks to such a psychological strategy, namely that the Parthians would feel obliged to strike first somewhere.

The problem in the immediate was that Parthia was not exactly exhibiting friendly behaviour toward Tigranes the Great in Armenia; Phraates was engaged in plundering of Tigranes' subjects in Gordyene in Mesopotamia. This was a classic instance where buffer states lead to conflicts between superpowers. For the moment, Pompey could rest assured that he faced no appreciable threat of warfare from the northeast; he had soundly defeated the Albanians, and he had Iberian royal hostages. There was time to deal with Phraates, especially since he was displaying an attitude not unfamiliar to Roman experience in the east: while unwilling to confront Rome directly, he was more than happy to try to bully Tigranes (at least from the Roman perspective). Parthia no doubt considered areas like Gordyene and Adiabene to be clearly within its sphere of influence, and we may recall that Pompey was not necessarily crystal clear as to Roman views on imperial buffer zones. Borders are one thing, and here too there may have been studied, purposeful neglect by Pompey of exact demarcations. In part this reflected the fact that what really needed to be discussed and well-defined was a neutral zone, one in which neither party was supposed to be conducting military operations. Such diplomatic affairs also involved Armenia, which would need to agree to where its national interests extended. Mithridates was still alive and a potential threat to Rome, but the clock would not stop ticking on the tinderbox that was relations with Parthia.

Tigranes the Younger clearly overestimated his ability to manipulate far more competent and, in some cases, cautious elders. Ultimately Pompey had an eye to finishing the war with Pontus, to settling the disposition of Mithridates' former territories, and to dealing with the eastern powerhouse, not with the petty concerns of Armenian royal family politics. Tigranes the Great was willing to accede to Pompey's wishes, and that was enough for the Roman conqueror, who had no patience or interest in hearing complaints from the disaffected son.

Tigranes was also a valuable ally to have: he would now be in a position to be called upon to provide Pompey with supplies and resources to continue the war, and to secure Roman interests along the Parthian border. In short, the idea was that Armenia would be a classic instance of a client kingdom, in this case one of the most strategic and significant that Rome ever secured.

Despite questions over exact chronology and the initial motivation of Phraates' invasion of Armenia with Tigranes the Younger, Dio is surely correct when he offers this summation of the feelings of the Armenian and Parthian kings: both men knew all too well that if either of them succeeded in conquering the other, they would only be hastening the conquering of the winner by Rome.[44] Phraates, Dio says, ultimately wanted Armenia to survive as a potential ally against Rome; Tigranes, for his part, was not thrilled that Rome did not defend him to the extent of being willing to engage in a full-scale war with Parthia. Dio's Pompey argued – for once? – that he had no senatorial commission to launch a Parthian war, and that in any case, the conflict with Mithridates was still not finished. Some of Pompey's associates urged him to reconsider, and to deal with Phraates decisively; they were overruled.

It is likely that Pompey felt that a Parthian campaign would run the risk of failure if an incensed senate decided to cut off his supplies/reinforcements, or even to recall him. The point about Mithridates was valid, and the consolidation of the east that had already been conquered was a pressing task. If the memory of Alexander pressed on him, it would be tempered with eminently practical concerns.

Some might be tempted to think conversely that Pompey no doubt had reached the conclusion that Phraates' Parthia was not a particularly fearsome foe. The Parthians had not been particularly successful or impressive in their efforts to cooperate with Tigranes the Younger in Armenia, or, when they had been so inclined, to vanquish him, and they had displayed no appetite for challenging the Romans. But we may remember again the aforementioned wisdom of Dio: neither Parthia nor Armenia wanted to see the other destroyed.[45] That said, clearly if Phraates thought that Rome could be handled, he would have been aggressive. Pompey wanted Armenia as a buffer to Parthia, and in the meantime at least, there were more pressing issues than launching what would be the greatest war Rome had fought in living memory. For now, in the delicate game of diplomacy with Rome's greatest rival in the Near East, Pompey was in the ascendant. When it came to the Elymaeans and the Medes, Plutarch reports that Pompey was inclined to extend an amicable response to their overtures.[46] Parthia gave him greater pause, but in the end, he could say that he had struck a deal to maintain the uneasy trinity in the distant Roman east.

But what of Pompey's so-called Caucasian campaign in the busy year of 65?[47] The inevitable problem of expansion is that one must always deal with new powers, new forces that become one's fresh borders. The area of modern day Azerbaijan and Georgia in the Caucasus was now a border area of the Roman sphere of influence, one that would pose interesting challenges for Pompey as he approached the winter of 66–5 BC. There must have been a heady mix of excitement and frustration for the would-be Roman Alexander. Mithridates was still alive, like Hannibal a constant threat as long as he was able to dream of fighting another day. To chase after him, however, especially with the approach of winter in an area known for harsh conditions, was next to impossible; Mithridates, to be sure, knew this and took comfort in the cooperation of nature with his escape. Further, while the Kingdom of Armenia had proven relatively easy to secure as an ally on paper, at least, threats abounded from the Caucasus. If Pompey had decided simply to pursue Mithridates at all costs, he would have risked serious disturbances from that theatre, not least because the area was known for its sympathies toward Mithridates and the ample aid the Caucasians had provided to Pontus in recent years.

A winter campaign against them, however, was also not Pompey's preferred strategy; ideally, there would be a chance at diplomatic resolution of the restive Armenian border area. The two major peoples Pompey dealt with that winter are known to us as the Caucasian Albanians and the Caucasian Iberians, to distinguish them from their better known western analogues (in point of fact, these Caucasians have nothing to do with modern day Albania or the Iberian peninsula). Plutarch has an account of how Pompey's December Saturnalia holiday was interrupted by an attack from the Albanians, who dwelled in the eastern Caucasus toward the Caspian Sea.[48] Allegedly they strove to strike the hopefully unsuspecting Romans with as many as 40,000 men, crossing the River Cyrnus in force. Pompey is said not to have opposed the crossing, allowing them to come over and to face his army, which annihilated the attackers in a pitched battle.

In the aftermath, the Albanian king threw himself on the mercy of Pompey, who secured the alliance of another monarch, again taking advantage of his powers to make treaties. Rome at least on paper had another client kingdom ready at the least to refrain from attacking Roman interests, and at best to provide supplies and resources as needed, men and material to aid Pompey's enterprise.

Dio provides more details of the Albanian action.[49] King Oroeses is said to have been motivated by his sympathy for Tigranes the Younger, as well as simply by anxiety that his kingdom would be next on Pompey's dinner menu. He expected that winter would aid his attack plans, not to mention the Romans' lack of familiarity with the area. Oroeses succeeded in bringing none of his war plans to successful completion; he was able to secure a treaty. Pompey was willing to agree to this, despite a desire to invade Albania out of revenge (and, we might think, out of a spirit of adventure, since he was now in a position to travel to corners of the world where no Roman had campaigned), but it was after all winter, and the list of tasks on his agenda was long.

Our sources are not in complete agreement as to all the details of the causes for this small war. We hear of Pompey being denied the right of passage through territory controlled by the Albanians and the Iberians. Whatever the exact list of grievances, the resolution of the Saturnalia campaign offered another chance for Pompey to dream of future triumphs; another king in a distant land had submitted to his authority. He was well on his way to his dream of emulating Alexander.

Orosius briefly mentions a total of three engagements between Pompey/his subordinates and the Albanians;[50] this accords with Dio's account that King Oroeses sent out three detachments, one against Pompey and the other two against other commanders, with the aim of trying to catch the Romans off guard and to leave them unable to help each other.[51] Pompey's sub-commanders were able to defend themselves ably, and once Pompey heard word of what was going on in other quarters, he proceeded out in time to anticipate the Albanian force that was heading for him. He destroyed that contingent of Oroeses' forces so efficiently and swiftly that he was able then to proceed to help his associates.

The Iberians presented a second problem. Plutarch claims that they took special pride in having always escaped foreign domination, since Alexander the Great had not spent enough time in their environs to subjugate them.[52] They were also quite well disposed toward Mithridates, and wished to prove that they were capable, loyal allies of that beleaguered king. Certainly they were not interested in signing any treaties with Pompey without a fight.

Plutarch is vague in his account here.[53] He mentions a major battle, with no details beyond a claim of 9,000 enemy dead and 10,000 prisoners; once finished, Pompey felt free to resume his pursuit of Mithridates.

Dio provides a fuller narrative of the campaigns in which Pompey was occupied as the new year of 65 dawned, and of the Battle of the Pelorus in the spring.[54]

He has King Artoces of the Iberians pretending to be interested in establishing a peace treaty, when in fact he was preparing for a treacherous surprise attack. Pompey was made aware of the planned duplicity, and struck first. Artoces was taken completely by surprise, and was reduced to such a state that his men surrendered after suffering a defeat in battle (of which Dio provides no details). Pompey left a garrison behind as he moved on to continue his Iberian invasion. Artoces sent word once again asking for a peace treaty. It seems that this king was being honest about his intentions, but that he was also extremely skittish by this point and not entirely trusting of Pompey; he fled, and probably out of genuine fear rather than some hope of catching the Romans in an ambush. Pompey caught up to him and won another victory, this time by making sure that his forces charged the Iberians so quickly and resolutely that they neutralized the enemy archers. Artoces fled again; some of his archer units tried to climb tall trees to fire on the Romans, but Pompey simply had the trees cut down to eliminate the threat. Artoces yet again made an appeal for peace, this time sending lavish presents. Pompey insisted on hostages from the royal family in light of all the frustration and the time that had been wasted. The king delayed for some time, until he realized that Pompey was pursuing him as earnestly as ever; he granted the hostages and signed the treaty. The Iberian campaign had concluded with another king on the list of Pompey's client monarchs, and another kingdom that was at least on paper if not in heart and mind a loyal ally of Rome. At this point, Pompey felt prepared to resume his hunting down of Mithridates.

Pelorus was unquestionably one of Pompey's greatest victories, even if it took place as something of a sideshow to the main events of the Asian wars. The use of a stunning, indeed brilliant infantry charge against enemy archers was inspired by the achievements of the Athenians against the Persians at Marathon, and no doubt Pompey was eager to be able to duplicate something so classic and celebrated as that engagement. It would serve as a paradigmatic example of Pompey's competence as a military commander, and a textbook instance of the use of infantry in offensive operations.

Meanwhile the Pontic king had fled toward Colchis, a legendary land associated with the story of Jason and the Argonauts, of the sorceress Medea and the quest for the Golden Fleece. According to Appian, Pompey sought to explore Colchis in large part on account of its mythological associations, and there is no reason to doubt this.[55] Dreams of legend and lore must have filled his mind. Prometheus had allegedly been chained somewhere in this vicinity, and Pompey was eager to see all the sites associated with epic and tragic tales.

Mithridates apparently had the intention of advancing to the Bosporus, eager to renew battle on land and sea to the utmost extent of his ability. Pompey proceeded as far as Phasis, where he intended to effect a linkage between his land forces and naval units that were stationed there.

The thus far victorious commander was no doubt eager to take on Mithridates, but as Alexander the Great himself had experienced, sometimes one is compelled to pay for the same real estate twice. That spring of 65 BC would see a renewed effort by Oroeses and his Albanians to strike the Romans. The reasoning behind the attack is not easy to discern. Oroeses may have felt that if he could surprise Pompey, he would be able to win a smashing victory and to further the cause of Mithridates, besides avenging the mistreatment of Tigranes the Younger. Oroeses must have been exceptionally confident in his chances of success, and rather unconcerned with any consequences of having betrayed his treaty.

When Pompey learned that Oroeses was ready to try to engage him, he decided to endeavour to conceal his numbers by shielding his infantry with cavalry. According to Dio, he placed his horses as a shield in front of his foot soldiers, ordering them to crouch down to give the impression that Oroeses had caught a detachment of Pompey's cavalry. The Albanians were to be tricked into thinking that they could easily rout this force. Pompey's goal here, Dio indicates, was not to try to win a victory by deceit and subterfuge, but to try to prevent Oroeses from retreating when he saw the Roman force. In other words, now that he knew that Oroeses was a mendacious, treacherous ally, the last thing he wanted was to have another king to chase around Asia. Eerily, Pompey would face something of his own medicine in the last battle of his life, when Caesar would use a similar trick for concealing one's forces as part of his tactics at Pharsalus.

Oroeses took the bait, and he fell on the Roman cavalry. The horsemen pretended to play along with the narrative that they had been caught by surprise and without infantry support, and they fell back in feigned flight for their lives. When the Albanians pursued them, thinking that they had won an easy victory, the Roman infantry was able to come forth, enveloping Oroeses' men as they made their reckless charge.

Now it was the turn of the Albanians to think about flight. Pompey's forces chased them down relentlessly, with all the zeal and vigour of men who have been wronged and are in search of swift vengeance. Dio includes the memorable note that as the Romans fell on the forest-bound Albanians, they cried out with the traditional holiday greeting *Io, Saturnalia!* – 'Hail, the Saturnalia!' It was a reminder to the terrified Albanians of how some months before, they had struck the Romans at exactly that holiday.

Plutarch also records the rebellion of the Albanians, noting the wrath of Pompey as he turned back to deal with the new crisis.[56] He records how the force of some 60,000 Albanian infantry and 12,000 cavalry was led by the king's brother Cosis, who during battle aimed straight for Pompey, striking his armour with a javelin. Pompey ran him through and killed him, thus earning distinction in single combat. Plutarch adds the romantic detail that Pompey must have fought Amazons in this engagement, as if he were Theseus or indeed a Heracles or Alexander, since after the battle the Romans found Amazonian lunate shields and buskins, though no corpse of a woman.[57] It is the sort of mythological colour that adds to the splendid narrative of the fighting of Pompey at the veritable edge of the Roman world. Appian also alludes to this episode, in more sober and less fantastic terms; he claims that there were female prisoners who bore wounds just like the men, women who had clearly fought in the battle.[58] He notes that it is uncertain if they were simply warrior women from among the Albanians, or actual Amazons, a distinct neighbouring people famous from legend and lore. What is certain is that among the intriguing tidbits of evidence for women in combat from the ancient world, we may cite the Caucasian Albanian engagement with Pompey's forces at the Battle of the Abas.

Pompey may have been enraged with the Albanians, but he also had Mithridates to deal with, a far better agenda to pursue than continuing to tarry among Oroeses' people. He made peace again, and also began to receive embassies from other monarchs, the Elymaeans and the Medes, who were interested in commencing negotiations. Notably, at this juncture King Phraates was also among those eager to make peace, in this case to renew his treaty. Pompey had already accomplished much, and was well on his way to surpassing Lucullus' record in the region. That said, he was deeply immersed in a complex and chaotic region. Despite the many challenges and perils that beset him, the would-be Roman Alexander was in his element. It was his good fortune not to be in the maelstrom that was Rome in this period.

Chapter Ten

Pompey in Asia, Part II

Events meanwhile in the capital were not without controversy and dissension, to say the least. The consuls for 65 BC were Lucius Aurelius Cotta and Lucius Manlius Torquatus. These two magistrates are best known today for being the targets of the so-called First Catilinarian Conspiracy, a political episode mired in myth, legend, and perhaps a kernel of truth in some regards. The consuls had been elected after the first pair of winners, Publius Autronius Paetus and Publius Cornelius Sulla, had faced legal prosecution in a corruption and bribery scandal. One would-be candidate in the same election cycle was Lucius Sergius Catiline, soon to be infamous for an all-too certain, well-documented, serious conspiracy. The scenario just outlined offers an obvious canvas for political and civil turmoil and potential if not actual violence. The stories that emerge from various ancient sources are dramatic; in Suetonius' life of Caesar, we even hear of claims and allegations that Caesar and Crassus were conspiring to take control of the state, with Autronius and Sulla as cover for the real plans of the two powerful men to seize the republic.[1] There has been much speculation and analysis with respect to the argument that what was really afoot in the election cycle of 66–5 was reaction to the man who was currently deep in Asia, Pompey the Great. By this line of reasoning, the ousted consul designates were the favourites of the *optimates*, while the ultimate winning consuls were clearly the candidates of the *populares*, the pro-Pompeian election ticket.

It is perhaps no surprise in light of later events that Cicero can be cited in support of the idea that there was a real plot afoot in 66–5, one that allegedly involved Catiline and Gnaeus Calpurnius Piso conniving to start assassinating senators, or Catiline alone. The extant evidence in Cicero is not conclusive, in large part because nowhere do we find a coherent, straightforward narrative of what is said to have happened. Sallust and Dio make allusion to conspiratorial events, and literary sources can be cited to note how the whole matter was hushed up in the face of attempted investigations.[2] Almost as if it never happened.

The consensus of modern scholars that there never was an actual conspiracy is right.[3] What is likely is surely that Cicero, at least, would have had ample reason to raise the suggestion that Catiline had been guilty of earlier conspiratorial behaviour when the time came to accuse him on account of an all too real threat later from the disgruntled rebel. There is also every reason to believe that the ongoing political squabbles and infighting in Rome involved a clash between the partisans of Pompey and those who were inclined to distrust him, especially as reports must have steadily arrived of his successful prosecution of the great campaigns in Asia. The return of Lucullus, disgruntled and offended, would likely also have contributed to an atmosphere of conflict and acrimony.

Plutarch also notes at this juncture that Pompey was exemplary in his conduct of avoiding the temptations of luxury.[4] Presented with the opportunity to take possession of exquisite wealth both from plunder and from the tribute paid by conquered and newly allied potentates, not to mention concubines seized from the stronghold and other properties seized from Mithridates' immense wealth, Pompey was resolute in not succumbing to the trappings and lure of luxury. He took only what was able to adorn Roman temples and public places; women were returned to their families. Some of this behaviour may have been a deliberate attempt to distinguish himself from the alleged decadence of Lucullus; even if the stories of his abstemiousness are exaggerated, they may have developed out of a conscious effort in the tradition to contrast the old and the new commander. There may have also have been a purposeful intention (again, either Pompey's or his biographer) to remind one of Macedonian Alexander, and to highlight how his Roman counterpart was not one to fall prey to creature comforts. One especially noteworthy companion of Mithridates, Stratonice, handed over the king's stronghold at Coenum, asking of Pompey only that he save her son Xiphares.[5] The Roman was unable to honour the request, however, given that Mithridates had him in his power, and killed him in revenge for Stratonice's perceived betrayal, leaving his body unburied as a further insult to satisfy his vengeance.

Plutarch also records how Pompey seized hordes of documents of the king from the fortress of Caenum, which he read avidly in an interest to learn more about his adversary and his history.[6] He learned, allegedly, of both the vicious and the libidinous nature of the monarch, and gained insight into the early stages of his wars with Rome.

Xiphares would not be the only son of Mithridates to run afoul of his father. His son Machares had years before made his peace with Lucullus; he had been made king of the Cimmerian Bosporus by his father, and now he faced the prospect that Mithridates was coming straight for him, no doubt eager to avenge himself. Machares fled to Chersonesus in the Crimea, where he committed suicide;[7] according to the version in Dio, the king pretended to want to make peace with his son, and invited him to a meeting under a promise of security, only to have him killed on arrival.[8]

Not all went well for Pompey's army, to be sure. Strabo reports that a savage tribe known as the Heptacometae slaughtered three maniples of his army (clearly a detachment from his main body) as they travelled from Colchis to Pontus; we are sadly ignorant of the details of so significant a disaster.[9]

Plutarch's life of Pompey records an interesting shift in his subject's attitude and mood at this juncture. Though Mithridates was now ensconced in the Cimmerian Bosporus, ready to start reconstituting what he could of his power and force, Pompey was motivated to explore the regions of Syria and Arabia, eager to reach the Red Sea and to take his chance while he could of finishing a complete circuit of the Roman world to the east.[10] He thought that a naval blockade of the Euxine ports would be sufficient to reduce Mithridates to famine and ruin; he was loathe to keep chasing him when there was the lure of so much to see and to do, and so easy an opportunity to use his effective naval units to enforce his will on the king's would-be harbours. The truth was that there was also a practical reason to visit the vast regions of Syria in particular: the long eastern campaigns had brought much disorder to Asia Minor, and reorganization and consolidation was a pressing matter, even if Mithridates had not finally been vanquished. Arguably this was a mistake, one might well think. Was Pompey thinking that nothing would so insult the king and demoralize him as to think that he was not so important now? This is probably part of the explanation for Pompey's actions, together with what may very well have been his own succumbing to the lure of the east: not its treasures or wealth, but its exotic venues for glory and renown, as well as firsthand knowledge. Even more than Caesar, Pompey was an inveterate traveller, a lover of seeing as much of the world as he could. And among the celebrated Romans of his age, few had seen so much of it.

If it seems odd that Pompey for the moment did not prioritize finishing off Mithridates, the subsequent narrative demonstrates just how much other business was pressing throughout the Roman east. It was not an exercise of psychological warfare to say that Mithridates was no longer the priority: it was fact. The clock was ticking in any case on Pompey's time in the east; he intended to try to do far more than anyone could ever dream of crediting Lucullus with, and faster. His critics would still be able to claim that he was feeding off the eastern carcass left by his predecessor, a vulture. But the more he accomplished swiftly, the more the invidious accusation would ring hollow.

If 65 BC had been exceptionally busy, 64 may seem calmer, but only on account of our having relatively less information about events. In reality it was a year packed with work. The consuls were Lucius Julius Caesar and Gaius Marcius Figulus; the former was the cousin of the future dictator. One man who was certainly feeling ambitious in 64 was Mithridates, who was allegedly entertaining grandiose designs of advancing through Scythia to the Hister (i.e., the Danube), and from there launching an invasion of Italy. One wonders sometimes if Mithridates was trying to convince himself, or to impress and/or terrify others, with visions of such schemes. Dio explains it by saying that Mithridates believed in exerting oneself to the utmost, in the most breathtakingly absurd yet nobly grand enterprises, preferring to die while reaching for the heights than to remain alive in disgrace, waiting to be eliminated one way or the other.[11] His health was allegedly weakening, while his mind remained firm and vigourous. But it is in this period that we begin to hear of growing dissatisfaction with him from his inner circle, a fact that Pompey may have predicted. He would have remembered how Sertorius met his end; there would be no dishonourable call for an assassination as Metellus had done in Spain, but the longer the king was essentially boxed in, the greater the chance that someone might decide that the future rested with Rome and not the all but vanquished king. Then again, for the meantime the longer Mithridates lived, the longer Pompey had legitimately to exercise his extraordinary prerogatives.

Students of this period are often curious as to why Pompey did not swiftly track down Mithridates. The likeliest answer lies in the matter of enjoying his essentially supreme power in the east. In Spain he shared credit with Metellus as well as subordinates; in the east it is sometimes easy not to appreciate the extent of work done by men like the loyal Afranius, but there was no one of the stature of a Metellus on the scene. The east was for all intent and purpose Pompey's arena, and he intended to make the most of the opportunity. Further, Pompey did not have merely superficial, perfunctory duties in the matter of reconstruction and organization. Pontus, for example, was not to remain a kingdom: a significant portion of its land would be attached to its onetime rival Bithynia, as part of a combined province of Bithynia and Pontus.[12] This territory along the Euxine coast of modern Turkey was one of the wealthiest and most valuable regions of the republic's growing empire, and even while Mithridates was still alive and worried about assassins and his ever more tenuous grip on provisions, Pompey could enjoy pride and credit for its pacification and reorganization as a Roman territory.

On the southern coast of today's Turkey, Pompey saw the new arrangement of the province of Cilicia. Once the home of the pirate peril, it was now reorganized in light of the addition of lands from Pompey's conquests, with Tarsus to serve as its capital. The governing principle that Pompey seems to have applied to the Roman east was twofold. On the one hand, there would be a strong bulwark of freshly constituted provinces. On the other, there would be a number of more or less important client kingdoms left nominally independent (that is, responsible mostly for internal affairs), which would serve as buffers against Parthia. Armenia was the jewel of this system; one smaller example was the little realm of King Tarcondimotus I in Cilicia, who was allowed to maintain his rule. He would be personally committed to Pompey in consequence, and would be among those who aided him in his war with Caesar.

What Pompey was occupied with in worrying about borders, taxes, and other administration matters in this period was all being done largely independently; in consequence of the *Lex Manilia* (especially a very broad reading of the spirit thereof), Pompey was acting more or less without senatorial oversight. The advantage of this was that much was able to be done swiftly and efficiently, and critics of Pompey's reorganization have generally admitted that what he was doing displayed foresight and common sense. The drawback was that he was also doing exactly what his enemies predicted. This was the behaviour of a monarch, and even if only out of spite, the day would come when senators were loath to give rapid seals of approval to what he had done. It is undeniable that Pompey's actions in this period had consequences in both the nearer long term and for the more distant future. The seeds were being sown for what would become the politically convenient alliance of Pompey, Crassus, and Caesar in the First Triumvirate, and the arrangements that Pompey was making on the ground in Asia would long outlive their founder.[13]

Mithridates meanwhile was in what is today the eastern Crimea. Ensconced in the city of Panticapaeum, he was somewhat limited in his options, most notably because Pompey dominated the Euxine coasts. He began to send envoys to Pompey, indicating that he was open to peace negotiations to come to some sort of terms; secretly, however, he was planning for renewed war.[14] Pompey did what was probably the best thing in such a situation: he responded that Mithridates should do what other kings had done, namely make arrangements to come to him in person. He was inviting the defeated king to become a suppliant, essentially to admit that he had lost his latest war against Rome, and that he should be grateful that the Romans were so magnanimous that they would let him live, perhaps even let him maintain a small client kingdom somewhere. Appian says that he was sick with some sort of ulceration of the face.[15] Whatever he was suffering from, no doubt it was in consequence of or exacerbated by long years of living either at war or on the run, and indulging in gluttony and decadent living.

Panticapaeum was a strategic place if you wanted to aim to control the straits that guard what we know as the Sea of Avoz (for the ancients, Lake Maeotis). Having slain his son Machares, Mithridates was now lord of the small kingdom of the Cimmerian Bosporus, and he had no intention of leaving it to arrange some meeting with Pompey to discuss terms. The problem that Mithridates faced was that he was not exactly the most secure lord of his newly acquired kingdom. His underlings faced two equally grim prospects: they could read the signs of the times as favouring Rome, and so they were hesitant to become involved in a renewed war. Second, in consequence of his difficult straits, Mithridates was displaying increasingly harsh behaviour toward suspected plotters and traitors. Pompey was every day looking like a more reasonable man to come to terms with, a fact that did not escape Mithridates, and thus exacerbated his tense and suspicious relations with his subordinates.

Mithridates, we have noted, entertained vain hopes of inspiring others to join him in a vision of invading Italy. Appian says that he reflected on the recent experience of Spartacus, a mere slave who had been able to wage war so long and so successfully in the heart of Italy.[16] He dreamed of inspiring the Gauls to join him, or perhaps the Italians who had been defeated in the Social War. He hoped to be the rallying point for anyone who was tired of Roman domination. And yet he found it difficult even to maintain or expand control on either side of the Cimmerian Bosporus. Our ancient sources do not agree on exactly how Mithridates planned to map his invasion route into Italy (i.e., whether he aimed at moving through Thrace, Macedonia, and Greece, or the more northerly route through Scythia); the confusion is partly due to the fact that neither scheme was realistic.[17]

The man who would be instrumental in finally sealing the fate of Mithridates was his youngest son, Pharnaces II. In the end, this was probably exactly in accord with the sort of fate that Pompey had decided would be best for his interests. Pompey would be able to report to the senate that the infamous king had met an ignominious end, dead as a result of the ultimate form of civil war, fatal dissension in the royal family. Perhaps the ideal would have been for the king to surrender to Pompey and to allow the Romans to display clemency, but that carried with it the danger that Mithridates would live to practise treachery: if the relatively insignificant Caucasian Albanians could do it, so could Mithridates. No, let it be murderous plots from within; then it would be easier to reorganize and manage the aftermath, and Mithridates' final chapter in history would not be a glorious one. There would be no Pontic banner around which ambitious future upstarts would rally. Pharnaces had his own dreams of receiving his father's kingdom from the Romans; he had had ample time to witness other family members and close associates of Mithridates dispensed with more or less summarily, and so it is no surprise that he began to think of how to eliminate his father. Dio notes that there were those who knew well what Pharnaces was starting to plot, but that they were hesitant to say anything because they had no particular affection for Mithridates at this point.[18] In Dio's estimation, the lesson is that even wealth and military might are of no use in the absence of friends; Mithridates' ties to those on whom he depended most were not the bonds of amity.

In the meantime, Pompey had other concerns. Another of the little kingdoms of the Near East (part of the remains of the Seleucid Empire) was Commagene, on the veritable crossroads between Hellenic and Iranian culture. The king was one of Mithridates' sons, Antiochus I. Commagene was another relatively minor realm, but strategically located in that contentious border zone between the competing Roman and Parthian spheres of influence. Appian says that Pompey marched into his realm and prosecuted a war that resulted in the king's surrender and acceptance of good relations with Rome and status as another of the smaller buffer states.[19] Abgarus of Osroëne is said to have made a similar deal with Pompey to keep the peace.

In 64 BC Pompey also visited the site of the Battle of Zela from three years earlier, where large numbers of unburied dead Romans had been left bereft of requiem rites and due honour. This was the sort of task that Pompey considered imperative, a key part of the successful ending of the long Asian wars. He proceeded to Cappadocia, where he settled the lands of King Ariobarzanes I, who had had a checkered career both with the Romans and Mithridates.[20] Ariobarzanes profited well from his dealings with Pompey; his kingdom's borders were enriched and secured, and succession plans were ratified to ensure that his son, the future Ariobarzanes II, would take over in due course. Pompey invested significant wealth in Cappadocia as part of his settlement of the realm; this was personal money that he was willing to pour into the kingdom as a means of stabilizing it, to be sure, but also to ensure the personal loyalty of the client king and the other beneficiaries of the grant. One could call this bribery, whether magnanimous or not. But it was effective both for pacifying the region and for guaranteeing as far as possible its loyalty to Rome, even if 'Rome' in this case meant Pompey.

As autumn and winter loomed, Pompey proceeded to Antioch in Syria, where he was received warmly.[21] Again he was deeply immersed in the problems of the remnants of the Seleucid Empire.[22] Antiochus XIII Asiaticus had been in power for some time; he had been confirmed as a client king of Rome during the heyday of Lucullus' rule. Pompey could not ignore visiting him, given that by all accounts Antiochus was by no means one of the more effective rulers of his strategically located and economically vital realm. It seems that he was bad at border security and bad at internal management; even if Pompeian propaganda would have exaggerated his weaknesses, he was a poor ally in an area that was historically prone to troubles.

Pompey did not confirm his continued rule.[23] Pompey seems to have connived with a Syrian tribal chieftain, Sampsiceramus, to eliminate Antiochus. 64 BC would be the year of the establishment of the Roman province of Syria. Sometimes Antiochus is considered the last of the Seleucid monarchs, though technically the dubious honour goes to Philip II Philoromaeus. Philip apparently briefly ruled some areas as a client king of Pompey; he was essentially in competition with Antiochus, his second cousin. We know that Antiochus was killed; we do not know the ultimate fate of Philip. There is some slender evidence that may indicate his survival, but certainly he fades out of the historical record, his greatest achievement being his status as the last of a much celebrated, storied line of Hellenistic monarchs.[24] Sampsiceramus was rewarded for his role in the whole somewhat distasteful business by being allowed to remain as a petty monarch, a client king who owed everything to Pompey.

Pompey wintered in Antioch in 64–3 BC. With the coming of spring, he would advance toward Damascus; throughout this period, his mailbox was full, as it were, indeed overflowing with contacts from the various petty potentates and would-be minor power brokers of the region.[25] The new year was to be one of the most important not only in his own career, but in the history of the republic. The consuls were Marcus Tullius Cicero and Gaius Antonius Hybrida; it would be a year that would be remembered (in no small part thanks to Cicero's mellifluous prose) for the Catilinarian Conspiracy. For Pompey, it would be the year that he would be immersed in problems in Judaea, and in which he would receive the welcome report that Mithridates was finally dead.[26]

For there was a significant conflict to be resolved in another hinterland, one that would prove to be inextricably tied to troubles erupting in Judaea: King Aretas III of the Nabataean Arabs, who made his capital at the famous city of Petra in modern Jordan.[27] The Nabataeans were Bedouin, and they dominated trade and economic intercourse in their region. They had at one time extended their influence as far north as Damascus, in part taking advantage of the general instability of the region in the declining years of the Seleucid Empire and the long period of conflicts between Mithridates and Rome.

Aretas III had established himself as one of the most outstanding of the Nabataean kings by the time Pompey had arrived in the Near East. His control of spice and incense trade routes alone made him a serious force to be contended with, besides his significant military might. And there was another problem at the moment of brewing concern: the Kingdom of Judaea, and its capital at Jerusalem.

The problems in Judaea before Pompey's attention focused on the region were in one sense a very old story: dissension in a ruling family, and the threat of civil war. Judaea was another friendly client state of Rome, at least in principle; Rome would eventually be involved, as so often elsewhere, in having to intervene in disputes about rightful rule. The Nabataean question would add a significant level of additional complication to the brewing problem.

Hyrcanus II and his brother Aristobulus were the discordant siblings for this new theatre of war and civil strife. Aretas would become involved when the day came that Hyrcanus would be compelled to take refuge with him. Pompey's legate Marcus Aemilius Scaurus had been named the first governor of the new province of Syria, and he would be responsible for overseeing the first Roman efforts to solve the crisis; needless to say, both brothers were eager to make the case to him as to who should win the throne of Judaea.

The crisis that confronted Scaurus was already ugly by the time it reached his desk in Damascus. Hyrcanus had taken power in 67; after only a few months his brother had launched a rebellion. They met in battle at the famous city of Jericho, and Aristobulus had won largely because many of Hyrcanus' men were happy to defect. Hyrcanus took refuge in Jerusalem, which his brother besieged; the two siblings actually came to a peaceful settlement, but (probably wisely), Hyrcanus mistrusted Aristobulus, and so he turned to Aretas, the closest power broker in the region at the moment. Aretas is said to have had some 50,000 men, and they advanced on Jerusalem.

Scaurus decided in favour of Aristobulus; he was allegedly and probably induced to do this by bribery, but there was another factor that likely weighed more than any talents of wealth: Hyrcanus had already made the decision to take refuge with Aretas. The argument could be made that if you felt the need to flee to the Arabians, clearly you needed no help from the Romans. Aristobulus' bribes may have helped, but the political equation was a simple one: by siding with Aristobulus, the Romans would be in the position to tell Aretas to withdraw the forces that he had sent into Judaea.

Hyrcanus, however, was the older brother and was arguably likelier in the long term to be a good ally of Rome. The great historian Josephus leaves no doubt as to his judgment on the matter when he says that the 300 talents offered by Aristobulus to Scaurus overruled any consideration of justice.[28] If we remember how Pompey had once told Phraates that the Romans would draw the border between their kingdoms with Justice as the demarcation line, not necessarily the Euphrates, we may imagine that he was not necessarily in favour of Scaurus' action, though it is arguably likely that at least for the moment, it was better to side with Aristobulus so as to effect the withdrawal of the Arabians. The fact that Aretas was willing to exit Judaea just based on threats from Scaurus was a clear signal to Rome that the Nabataean Arabs could be defeated.

Matters became more complicated when the Arabians agreed to withdraw from Jerusalem, only to be attacked by Aristobulus with heavy losses. For Josephus, this was further evidence of Aristobulus' character; he was not satisfied with what he had already achieved by virtue of his bribery of Scaurus. Josephus relates that ultimately the youth's arrogance is what doomed him with Pompey.²⁹ When he heard that Hyrcanus was going as a suppliant to the Roman commander, he knew that he needed to make his own appeal as well. He went with regal opulence and haughty airs, but seems to have decided at the last moment that it was not in accord with the dignity of a would-be king to start begging Pompey for favours. Probably he was also incensed at the fact that the sum he had deposited with Scaurus seemed to have no effect on Pompey's decision making.

A cynical way to read the situation is to imagine that Pompey knew full well what Scaurus was doing, and that the plan was to secure not only wealth from the upstart, rebellious brother (which would significantly reduce his ability to fund any war, either against his brother or Rome), and to remove the Arabians from the equation. Aristobulus had a reputation as a hothead, and the fact that he attacked Aretas and inflicted serious losses on him also worked to Roman advantage. We hear of deference that Pompey exercised toward Aristobulus at one point, in an effort to reduce the risk of full-scale rebellion. But there was to be no coming to terms with the brash young man.

Aristobulus fled into Judaea, and began to embark on a perilously provocative programme of entering fortresses and seeming to challenge Pompey to launch operations to evict him, alternating with appeals to come to terms. Word had no doubt preceded Pompey that the new Roman commander in the east was clement; this reputation combined with the young man's arrogance and willingness to take bold risks would prove a poor combination for achieving his rebel aims.

Pompey's message was simple: evacuate your fortresses, and send personal instructions to your subordinates that they are also to demilitarize. Aristobulus' response was to depart for Jerusalem, there to prepare to test his skill against Pompey.

This period was not occupied only with these weighty crises involving the question of the Judaean monarchy. There were other smaller powers in the region, petty monarchs who now faced the new Roman order. Ptolemy the son of Mennaeus was an Ituraean ruler who had tried through the years to expand his power in the region; in fact one of the reasons why Aristobulus was so popular in some quarters was because he had fought on behalf of the Jews against Ptolemy's encroachment on their land. Ptolemy was a good example of a minor potentate capable of causing appreciable problems in his relatively small theatre, and in the Roman view incorrigible. Pompey devastated his territory, thus reducing him to offering 1,000 talents to avoid further punishment. Pompey had overnight found a way to pay his men. Ptolemy's relative by marriage Dionysius of Tripolis was decapitated on Pompey's orders; he was apparently either not in a position to pay for his life, and/or he had succeeded in annoying the Romans even more than Ptolemy.

Pompey is said to have been engaged in dealing with Aristobulus when the word arrived one fine day that Mithridates was dead. We can only hazard guesses as to the immediate reaction of Pompey. Pompey had no doubt hoped for the king's own people to eliminate him; we cannot be sure if he expected this so relatively quickly. Mithridates had been dreaming of renewed war preparations, but those efforts only succeeded in angering his supporters and ever fewer subjects, combined with the fact that he was increasingly unstable as he saw conspiracy behind every door.

We have noted that the key figure in the king's downfall would ultimately be his youngest son, Pharnaces.[30] He was able to commence plans for a conspiracy, but the hyper-suspicious Mithridates was able to uncover it. For reasons that are not entirely clear, the king was persuaded not to kill another son; perhaps he thought that such an action would only result in even further rebellion from his obviously unhappy subjects. Pharnaces had no intention of reconciling with his father. He began to press the Roman deserters and others in Mithridates' army to defect; soon enough he succeeded in orchestrating a dangerous uprising.

Mithridates tried to flee; he sent envoys to his son, no doubt hoping that he could come to terms with the relative he had so recently spared. They never returned, and so the king who had spent years trying to build immunity to poisons now faced the problem that suicide in that manner was exceedingly difficult.[31] He succeeded finally in having a subordinate kill him, and now Pharnaces was in a position dutifully to send a report to Pompey. He arranged to send the body, together with hostages and tokens of complete submission to Roman authority.

Pharnaces would be rewarded for his actions: he was now to be confirmed by Pompey as client king, ruler of the Cimmerian Bosporus, friend and ally of the Romans. We are told that the territory of Phanagoria was the only portion of his prospective kingdom that was to be removed from his rule: that region had attracted Pompey's notice as being the first to rebel from Mithridates, and so Pompey decided to reward it with a grant of independence, as another smaller client state. It was a good way both to weaken Pharnaces, and to show that the Romans knew how to grant rewards.

Indeed, Plutarch's summation of this period is that Pompey principally made a name for himself by his relatively easygoing nature both with friends and suppliants.[32] He was generally willing to overlook the transgressions of those to whom he was attached by some bond of amity, or of those who appealed to his mercy and clemency. For Plutarch, this meant that those who had dealings with him were willing even to overlook the greed and harshness of his friends, because they knew that they could depend on him ultimately to make things right if called upon in time of need. It is easy to imagine that this was the period in his life when Pompey was engaged in exactly what he was most suited to do: maintain affairs both judicially and militarily, a new Alexander who was able to act largely independently of any external authority.

Plutarch has the receipt of the news of the death of Mithridates coming after the capture of Jerusalem.[33] He has Pompey deciding to move toward Petra in a show of force against Aretas III; the Arabian king had contacted the Romans with an offer of being willing to come to terms, and Pompey wanted to confirm everything in person. The biographer notes that some in his entourage were beginning to complain that Pompey needed to deal with Mithridates once and for all; this was in fact almost certainly something that had been said consistently for some time now. In this account, Pompey receives the momentous news and announces it to his men; there is tremendous rejoicing and celebration, no doubt in large part for some at least because they sensed that soon they would be homeward bound. And indeed Pompey immediately made plans to exit Arabian territory, and to proceed to Amisus, where the aforementioned gifts from Pharnaces were awaiting him, as well as the embalmed corpse of his famous foe. Recognizable by its scars, Pompey was assured that it was the body; he was not willing to see it, but had it sent to Sinope for honourable burial, eager, Plutarch notes, to avoid any divine displeasure.

The death of Mithridates did, of course, introduce some complications into the equation. The original reason for his extraordinary commission was now gone. But, for the moment at least, he was embroiled in active problems with his reorganization and settlement of the east, and no one realistically could start clamouring that he should be recalled. In less than three years, he had definitively ended the Mithridates crisis, and had achieved impressive results, indeed to an astonishing degree. And now he has deep in resolving yet another such crisis, as Aristobulus seemed eager for war.

'Seemed' is the appropriate word, because while Pompey was near Jericho, he received envoys from Aristobulus who indicated that the would-be king wanted to negotiate, and that Jerusalem was open to Pompey. Whether Pompey believed him or not, he dutifully sent his trustworthy legate Aulus Gabinius, who proceeded to the Jewish capital, only to find that the Romans were not, in fact, welcome in the city.

Aristobulus had apparently been quite honest in his rapprochement with Pompey, but he misjudged or misinterpreted the feelings of his men. For they were by no means interested in submitting to Pompey, and wanted to go to war. To complicate matters still further, there was dissension in the city; as one might expect, there were those who were in support of surrender to Rome, seeing the future all too clearly: destruction, death, and subjugation.

Pompey was irritated at any rate. He arrested Aristobulus, probably in truth both because he did not trust the young man, and also because he was frustrated at what he saw as the incompetence of a would-be king who could not even manage his people while he tried to negotiate a truce and a surrender.[34] As one might have expected (and Pompey likely understood this point), Aristobulus' friends in Jerusalem were not pleased at the arrest of their king, so that now there were more voices in support of going to war.

Pompey no doubt realized that Jerusalem was seriously divided, not to say unprepared for a siege. Clearly there were those who counted too much on the famous clemency of the Roman commander; current events were exactly the sort of thing that taxed the patience of generals, and Pompey may have remembered that Alexander had faced similar issues at Tyre and Gaza when those cities thought to resist him by forcing a siege.

The Siege of Jerusalem in 63 BC might have been a far more difficult undertaking for Pompey if the city did not have factions so opposed to each other that while some sought to seize the temple and to hold it as a fortified citadel, others were willing to open the city and to let Pompey and his forces enter.

Jerusalem's temple was destined to fall; Hyrcanus would be helping the Romans in the prosecution of what for him was the climactic episode of a civil war.[35] Josephus provides the most detailed surviving account of Pompey's operations in the city.[36] The 1961 film *King of Kings* commences with a vivid, violent depiction of the final stages of the campaign, including the entry of Pompey even into the Holy of Holies of the temple. In the film, the sonorous narrative of Orson Welles notes that Pompey was aflame with passion for gold and precious metals, but was disappointed only to find the Torah. Exiting the temple, Pompey is importuned for the sacred scrolls, which he hands over. Josephus conversely records that Pompey did find gold and other valuables, but that in accord with his noted virtue, he did not plunder the sanctuary.[37] The film reflects something of his much vaunted humanity, but depicts him as full of greed for gold.

What happened to Jerusalem was inevitable; the city had no real hope of withstanding the siege, especially not after it was a question of defending the temple precinct alone. Josephus notes that the Jewish defenders were dutiful in their piety in observing the Sabbath: they were allowed to defend themselves even on the sacred day of rest from direct attacks, but they were not lawfully supposed to engage in such actions as hampering the Romans while they were constructing siege works and preparing to launch strikes.[38] The Romans are said to have taken full advantage of the religious scruples of their enemy, and to have maximized their Sabbath work in such preparations.

Josephus further depicts Pompey as having ordered the cleansing of the temple and the resumption of sacrifices and normal religious rites; Hyrcanus was reinstated to his formerly held office as high priest, but was given no political office.[39] Judaea was to be reconstituted as one of the many vassal states of the east. Its fortunes and status would change multiple times in coming years, until Judaea would be made a province in its own right. For now it was to be under the sphere of responsibility of the Syrian governor; Hyrcanus was severely limited in his authority, a mere figurehead and little more.[40]

Josephus speaks of decapitations of those who were responsible for the rebellion and the decision to force a siege of the temple;[41] Aristobulus was kept under arrest with members of his family, taken into custody by Pompey as he prepared to think of his future triumph. The Jewish historian is clear in his analysis and estimation: the fault, he says, for the doom and trials that befell his people was the squabbling between the brothers, and the price of their civil war was loss of independence as well as of territory that had been conquered in Syria. Plutarch is characteristically brief: Pompey subdued Judaea, and he took Aristobulus prisoner.[42]

It is no surprise that the operations in Judaea and Arabia put the finishing touches on Pompey's Asian campaigns. In the space of some three years, he had definitely defeated Mithridates' Pontus, settled the problems on the Parthian border, established several client kingdoms as regional buffers (most notably Armenia), resolved the question of what was to become of the remnants of the long dying Seleucid Empire, organized what would be one of the important provinces of the empire in Syria, had campaigned from the Crimea to Jerusalem, in the Caucasus and throughout what is today Turkey. He had brought enormous wealth into the coffers of the republic, and had asserted Roman dominance over a large swath of the Near and Middle East and beyond. Peace and/or conquest had prevailed over territory extending from modern Russia and Ukraine through Georgia, Azerbaijan, Armenia, Turkey, Syria, and as far as northwest Saudi Arabia. It was a remarkable achievement, with exceedingly few setbacks and an overall grand display of Roman power.

Pompey had not yet reached the zenith of the power that he would enjoy in the republic, but in many regards he was at the height of his prestige, glory, and just satisfaction in work well done. This Alexander would not die in Babylon; he was destined to return to his home in triumph, there to face a new set of challenges. By the age of forty-three, he could claim that he had led armies with success on three continents, from Spain to Arabia, Africa and though Italy. Had his career ended in Jerusalem, his place in history would be assured. The future would be difficult, both on account of the equally strong ambitions of powerful peers, and the critical carping of little men. But as he planned to take his leave of the east, he did so content in the knowledge that he had done more in less time than any of his predecessors.

Chapter Eleven

Toward the 'Triumvirate'

Rome was a dramatic place in 63 BC. It was the year Cicero would become famous with his stirring response to the conspiracy of Lucius Sergius Catiline, a conspiracy familiar to generations of students of Latin on account of Cicero's speeches, as well as from Sallust's work on the so-called *Bellum Catilinae*. Catiline was from an old patrician family; readers of Virgil's epic *Aeneid* will encounter Sergestus, one of Aeneas' Trojan companions on the voyage to Latium and the settlement in central Italy. Sergestus was thought to be the progenitor of the *gens Sergia*, at least according to the cherished myth-history of the patricians' clans. He was roughly the same age as Pompey, born perhaps in 108 BC, maybe in 106.[1] He served in the Social War under Pompey's father Strabo. He was on the Sullan side in the civil war. One can cite surviving sources to paint a picture of Catiline as a bloodthirsty, enthusiastic participant in the Sullan proscriptions; care must be taken to remember that the historical record may be biased strongly against him (much of our knowledge about the man has been filtered through Cicero's vision, as well as Sallust's), but there is good reason to believe that he was by no means the most savoury sort, to put it mildly.

Catiline served as governor in Africa, where he was accused of bad behaviour; there is some evidence of adultery with a Vestal virgin. We have mentioned the alleged 'First Catilinarian Conspiracy' of 65 BC, which is probably fictitious, an early example of the exaggerated bad press that surrounded the young man in light of later events. Catiline was prosecuted for corruption in his gubernatorial administration in the same year; his prosecutor was Publius Clodius Pulcher, whom some have concluded was actually trying to help the defendant, not to convict him. Whatever the case, Catiline was always a complicated figure in the web of republican politics, and by 64, he was a candidate for the consulship in 63, with support from Crassus and Caesar. This was the year that was to be Cicero's; the famous orator would take pride in being what the Romans called a *novus homo* or 'new man,' the first in his family to be a consul.

Catiline wanted to win the consulship with Gaius Antonius Hybrida; the man to defeat was Cicero. The plan failed, however; Cicero won easily, and Antonius secured just enough votes to make Catiline the loser.[2] Catiline also seems to have faced legal troubles after the elections, related to his aforementioned behaviour during the Sullan proscriptions. Caesar – ever the man in this period to make sure that he was malleable and able to look at situations afresh, without regard for what he had decided on some previous occasion regarding the man – was ready to oppose Catiline, as was another senator who would play a great role in the history of the republic's decline, Marcus Porcius Cato (better known as Cato Minor or Cato the Younger).[3]

Antonius was now consul with Cicero, and Cicero was a more profitable partner than the loser Catiline. Happy to strike deals with Cicero, Antonius abandoned his alliance with Catiline.[4] The year was filled with the usual contentious politics, and Catiline intended to try again for the consulship. The rivals this time included Decimus Iunius Silanus, Lucius Licinius Murena, and Servius Sulpicius Rufus. Silanus and Murena won, in an election that was marred by reports not only of Catiline's bribes (that was by no means something unique to him in Roman electoral history), but by rumours that he was stirring up the poor, threatening wealth redistribution and even violence against the rich. The consul Cicero started using a bodyguard and armour; this was likely theatre on his part, but it was an effective stage performance.

At some point in the course of that fateful autumn of 63 BC, Crassus and Caesar decided that they were done with Catiline. Again, it is very difficult to gain a clear and unprejudiced view of the man, given that Sallust and Cicero have left so powerful an indictment against him. Brash and bold, reckless and ambitious, frustration must have been a constant companion of Catiline, and clearly he came to loathe Cicero, a sentiment in which he was by no means alone. Crassus and Caesar are said to have warned Cicero that Catiline was planning assassinations of the leading men of the state, including Cicero; it would have been something of a decapitation strike, one that would have constituted the quickest means to a coup: civil war without civil war, so to speak. Reports soon arrived that Catiline's supporters had raised a private army in Etruria to back the planned actions of their hero; these October developments prompted the senate to issue a *senatus consultum ultimum*, an emergency decree to allow the consuls to take whatever measures they deemed necessary to preserve the state.

One problem in our analysis of the unfolding scenario is that one could question whether there was one coordinated planned conspiracy, or a convergence of circumstances. The Etrurian force was apparently under the direction of one Gaius Manlius, a centurion and supporter of Catiline. By one way of looking at the picture, Manlius acted in support of Catiline without the other's awareness, and once Catiline was driven from Rome, Manlius was an obvious refuge and bulwark. We cannot be certain, but it seems likelier that Catiline was certain of Manlius' military backing before he launched whatever coup plans he had envisioned.

Cicero moved to see to the defence of the city; we hear reports of rumours of slave rebellions in southern Italy (the memory of Spartacus would have been fresh).[5] Catiline was in Rome at the time, and by early November was said to be moving toward zero hour: fires in the city, the assassination of Cicero, and departure from Rome to join Manlius' army. Cicero had his house barred and under guard; on 7 November, he convened the senate and delivered the first of his Catilinarian orations, exposing the plot and dramatically calling for the defeat of the rebel.[6] Catiline was there, and denounced Cicero; he offered to leave Rome for the sake of avoiding civil strife.

Catiline claimed that he was heading for Massilia, but in fact he went to Manlius; soon thereafter he was adopting the trappings of a consul, and claiming power. The senate then declared both Catiline and Manlius public enemies, and authorized the consul Antonius to go after them.

Meanwhile, Cicero oversaw the ferreting out and arrest of those who had conspired with Catiline. For some, it would always be a black mark on Cicero's record that they were executed without a trial on 5 December, after a noteworthy debate in the senate. The killing of the conspirators seems to have struck a blow to the morale of the Catilinarians in Etruria; a number of the men who had been willing to serve with Manlius now more or less quietly abandoned him. The force with Catiline and Manlius was carefully surrounded by republican forces, and by early January the forces met in the Battle of Pistoria.[7] Catiline did not survive the battle; he and his leading supporters were slain in a desperate fight.

We may step back and consider two interrelated problems. The republic was clearly a fragile construct, one that by no means had fully recovered from the immense drain on men and resources occasioned by the long wars both in Italy and abroad, in particular the civil conflict between the Sullan and Marian factions and all the sub-groups related to one or the other major banner. The senate was divided on such basic questions as land redistribution; consular and other elections were regularly marked by financial malfeasance, and occasionally violence. Slavery as an institution was a further source of significant instability; the Spartacus revolt had been a catastrophe both economically and in lives lost, and the threat of a new rebellion was an omnipresent fear.

And then there was Pompey. His enemies worried that he was a new Sulla in the making, an aspiring dictator whose accomplishments in the east would lead to a renewed civil war if he tried to seize extraordinary powers when he made his return to Italy. Sulla had come from the east and launched a war that was fresh in the memory; Pompey had a larger force, and his intentions seemed unclear, at least to his enemies and opponents. In reality, to the extent that

Pompey was kept aware and followed political news and domestic headlines, he was probably regretful that his time in the east was drawing to a close. He was always more inclined to be in the field, pursuing military glory and having a more or less free hand to manage his armies and to work on the organization and restoration of provinces and client kingdoms. He was a soldier and a diplomat, and consummate at both arts. His political interests had thus far been a distant second to these military and foreign policy concerns. The republic he had known for all his life was a disorderly, sometimes wild and violent place when it came to political life. As a soldier and diplomat he was a master of efficiency, and there was nothing efficient about the senatorial and judicial world of Rome. His adversaries feared his return, and likely he did, too.

In Rome, as the news of Pompey's momentous, astonishing achievements was made clear to the senate, Caesar was among those in favour of honouring him in every way possible. Cato was a leading voice in opposition, expressing those aforementioned concerns and fears about what price would be sought for such victories.

The mood at the start of the year 62 BC was incredibly tense. Silanus and Murena entered their consulship, and the name on everyone's lips was Pompey: it was known that he was on his way back to Italy. We have some evidence of his experiences on the long journey back. He stopped in various locales of the Greek world, including a return visit to Athens, where he was generous in financial expenditures on public works and as a display of munificence. He also visited Mytilene, where he witnessed artistic competitions and is said by Plutarch to have started taking notes for a theatre he wished to see designed in Rome for poetic and dramatic performances.[8] He went to Rhodes, ever attentive through his slow and stately progress to the philosophical and intellectual climate of the cities and towns he traversed. He appears to have cultivated a bearing of serenity and stateliness, as befitting his great achievements; he affected being in no great hurry to return back, which was probably designed in part to increase his mystique, perhaps with a hint of impishness toward his enemies (who were convinced of his nefarious intentions), and probably with a healthy dose of regret that he was leaving the east. Early in 62 was when Pompey began his almost leisurely return; before he commenced his long voyages, he rewarded his soldiers generously, as was customary. Cicero made sure to send him a letter that described in detail the dramatic events of his consulship; the new man never missed an opportunity to boast about what he had achieved while in office, not least in saving the state, as he would say, from Catiline.[9]

We hear that before he was on his way past Egypt, he was invited to Alexandria by Ptolemy XII.[10] Indeed in 63 BC, Ptolemy had sent him a golden crown as a sign of respect and honour. Egypt was a sensitive place in the Roman mind.

Ptolemy X had left his Hellenistic kingdom to Rome in the event that he had no heirs. The Romans had not been zealous about trying to involve themselves in Egypt, but the kingdom was clearly a strong client state of the republic. Ptolemy XII was a staunch Roman ally, at least in terms of maintaining respect and careful measures of deference.

There were, to be sure, prominent men in Rome (Crassus, notably) who wanted the economic powerhouse and breadbasket of the Mediterranean to be taken fully under Roman control. Ptolemy was no fool in terms of realizing that his grip on independent power was tenuous, and he was more than happy to try to shower this or that Roman with bribes and help where needed. In the case of Pompey, it was generous aid in the Judaean and Arabian operations. And, also, there was a request.

Ptolemy invited Pompey to Alexandria, deferentially indicating that he wanted help in dealing with certain internal problems. It must have been both a flattering and a tempting offer to Pompey: this was one of the most legendary realms in the Mediterranean, connected intimately to the deeds and lore of Alexander the Great, whose tomb was at its capital. And yet Pompey declined the invitation. It seems that he reached the conclusion that to go to Egypt and to become embroiled in Ptolemaic intrigues would only play into the hands of his enemies. He had no reason to go to Egypt by senatorial commission or the Manilian Law; he had no reason to do anything with his army other than to return to Italy. In light of later history, there is something eerie about the Egypt episode in the waning months of Pompey's eastern career; there would come a day when he would go to Alexandria as a suppliant, only to lose his head.

Pompey was a realist, perhaps a bit of a cynic. But he must have been annoyed at some level when his refusal to go to Egypt won him no praise nor even grudging respect from his Roman adversaries. He had in fact made an appreciable gesture of not aspiring to dictatorial power, but for his foes, no such deed would ever be properly acknowledged, let alone rewarded.

We have not said much about Pompey's personal life in this period, because he was consumed with his foreign military and diplomatic affairs. Affairs of a different sort had become gossip in Rome. Pompey's wife Mucia was the subject of reports of adultery; according to Plutarch, when the commander first started receiving such news, he dismissed it as false and worthy of contempt.[11] But as he drew nearer to Italy, he drew up an order of divorce, without providing any explicit reasons. The biographer says that the reasons are given in Cicero's letters, but if so, the letters in question do not survive; all that we have is a citation in his correspondence to Atticus that the divorce was wholeheartedly approved. Mucia was the mother of his children, his sons Gnaeus and Sextus, and his daughter Pompeia. Gnaeus had been born around 67, just before Pompey embarked on his eastern campaigns; he was but a young boy as he waited to meet the father he did not know.

Did Mucia have a prominent affair with Caesar? Suetonius says that Pompey referred to Caesar as 'Aegisthus,' a clever and biting mythological insult referring to Clytemnestra's illicit affair in Mycenae when her husband Agamemnon was off in the east fighting the Trojan War.[12] We cannot be sure of the veracity of the scurrilous rumour, but it is clear that nobody was inclined to question or to criticize Pompey for his decision to be done with Mucia. She would play a minor role in later history, in particular with respect to her son Sextus. For the immediate, she was destined to be the wife of Scaurus, Pompey's subordinate.

In this period, the three future colleagues Pompey, Caesar, and Crassus were by no means all on the same page, even apart from vicious gossip about marital indiscretions. Crassus had a longstanding rivalry with Pompey, and events such as those of the final stages of the Spartacus rebellion still rankled. Caesar had a different sort of problem, and one for which the exceedingly wealthy Crassus had an easy solution. Caesar had managed to accumulate a frightful number of creditors and high debts by the lavish way in which he lived beyond his means in the pursuit of popular support. During these crucial years of Pompey's return and what would be the slow and steady march to the first triumvirate, Crassus realized that he could secure Caesar's support and loyalty by helping to make his debts disappear temporarily: Crassus would extend credit to Caesar by giving surety to his largest and most aggressive creditors, thus buying Caesar time to come up with the money. Jockeying for power and political alliances never ceased in the ongoing, occasionally deadly game that was the republic.

Caesar had made a name for himself, at any rate, as a reasonable man of compromise, especially in contrast to Cato. He had argued against executing the Catilinarian conspirators, though he had supported confiscating their property; Cato, in contrast, was fully in agreement with Cicero about killing them. He served as praetor and was appointed later as proconsular governor of Hispania Ulterior; much of his racking up of serious debts had come from the inevitable bribes that had to be paid to ensure electoral victories and votes.

One thing Caesar did not have on his resumé was anything that could rival Pompey for military experience. Spain would be an arena for that, since there was still a lot to be done to pacify the restive native tribes; Caesar's campaigns in Spain would bring him to the Atlantic coast, as he began to hone his skills and reputation as a highly competent field commander. Under Caesar, the Romans would win territory in what is today both Spain and Portugal, and the commander would make more money to help to satisfy his creditors, whom Crassus was meanwhile holding at bay. All things considered, it was a prosperous time for Caesar, one in which his reputation was markedly on the ascendant.

We have noted that Rome was rife with stories about what would happen once Pompey stepped foot back in Italy.[13] He landed at the great Adriatic port of Brundisium in December of 62, the moment of truth for those who feared him. Plutarch says that in the anxious time before his arrival, Crassus took his children and his money and withdrew from Rome; the biographer gives what we might call the weighted alternative: either he was really fearful, or (more likely), he was trying to stir up sentiment against Pompey.[14] No such ruses or psychological tricks would matter. Pompey won enormous good will on his landing, because not only was he returning as a tremendously successful conqueror, but he also disbanded his army on arrival. There would be no march on Rome; Pompey was no Sulla. It was another hour that could claim to be the zenith of his power; he was beloved for his republican devotion as he voluntarily followed law, custom, tradition and precedent by surrendering his power.

Pompey had thanked his men before he sent them home, well paid and exceedingly grateful to their generous commander. He asked them to come back for his triumph. Plutarch notes that as Pompey travelled through Italy on his way to Rome, he was treated with even more respect because he did not appear at the head of an army, or with some armed retinue as if he needed bodyguards or swords to achieve his goals.[15] He was accessible and undefended, and his popularity soared in consequence. He had orchestrated and choreographed his return to Rome so as to hit the perfect notes; his enemies must have seethed to hear of the thunderous popular reception that he received wherever he passed.

A more complicated issue that soon surfaced, however, was a request that Pompey made with respect to the consular elections to be held for 61 BC. One might have anticipated that Pompey was eager to stand for office, but in fact he wanted to canvass votes for Marcus Pupius Piso Frugi Calpurnianus. Piso was one of those who had gone over to Sulla fairly early, despite having close early connections to Cinna; such men were always especially valued by the Sullan old guard. He served with Pompey in the east, and was sent ahead by his patron to stand for election; he was the desired and chosen candidate of the returning commander, who assumed that in light of all that had been achieved in the east, the very least that would happen would be successful canvassing for the future consul of his choice.

One of the reasons why Pompey needed to make this request in the first place was the fact that if one wanted to follow republican tradition and precedent, a returning victorious commander was not permitted to step foot in Rome before his triumph. Sulla had violated sacred custom and law by daring to bring armed men into the capital; Pompey was scrupulous about seeking to follow even the edict by which he was barred from entering prematurely, disbanded army or not. But Metellus had also sought to recall Pompey to Rome, allegedly to help with restoring order after the Catilinarian conspiracy; this was thought by many to be a thinly veiled attempt at establishing a dictatorship.[16] But what of merely wishing to canvass for votes for a consular candidate?

The senate was largely in agreement with what must have seemed like a reasonable aspiration (especially to anyone who had wondered if Pompey himself intended to seek the office). Cato was opposed, and he spoke so persuasively against the notion that the senate went along with him. Pompey was vexed at this rejection, and one could say reasonably so; given the realities of Roman republican life, he was playing within the system, even if here and there he was asking for some relatively minor concessions. His opponents, to be sure, would disagree, but Pompey had a ready response: now divorced, he explored a marriage alliance with Cato's family, looking to arrange something both for himself and for his son Gnaeus, in an effort to effect a strong political union in the classic, traditional Roman style.

Cato also refused this overture, sending a response back to Pompey saying that if the returning commander acted with justice and rectitude, in accord with republican sentiments, he would be happy to be his friend, and that such friendship founded on honour and honestly held intentions would be stronger than any nuptial bond of bartered wives. Here we see how Cato achieved his reputation, which was held as sacrosanct by some, and, on occasion, was considered to be a source of supreme irritation and frustration.

Plutarch makes the perceptive observation that Cato was acting in an extremely shortsighted manner, for all his undeniable high principles and exemplary traditional virtue.[17] Plutarch argues that the rebuff from Cato is exactly what impelled Pompey to seek an alliance elsewhere, and indeed there is a lot of truth in the analysis that the one thing that Pompey, Caesar, and Crassus all had in common was that they felt more or less not sufficiently appreciated by the state.[18] Cato, needless to say, would argue that the republic was not supposed to be in the business of seemingly endless indulgence of the whims and wishes even of those who had achieved impressive victories for her.

Plutarch notes that Pompey was willing to suggest the marriage tie to Cato in part because he respected his adversary for standing firm on principle.[19] Despite not succeeding in delaying the consular elections for 61 BC, Pompey's preferred candidate Piso won, and he served with Marcus Valerius Messalla Niger. We may well wonder how this happened absent the chance for Pompey to campaign for his favourite. The answer is both simple and classically republican: Pompey saw to it that bribes would be used, even if the briber could not actually distribute them in person. Plutarch says that the episode brought disrepute to Pompey; bribery was widely practised, but that did not mean that it was either legal or honourable. Cato is said to have commented on how he did the right thing in refusing the nuptial bond with Pompey, since otherwise his family's name, too, would have been sullied by the underhanded dealings.

The year 61 saw Pompey's forty-fifth birthday; he was about a dozen years older than Alexander had been at the time of his death. It would be the year in which he would enjoy the glory of a triumph. Scandals in the election season for 61 were a trivial matter compared to the lavish public show that would be offered for the enjoyment of the Roman crowds. The scale of the celebration was immense, as was the fact that Pompey had now amassed triumphs for three victories on the three continents of the known world: Africa, Europe, and Asia.[20]

Prisoners like Aristobulus adorned the triumphal procession; no doubt little Sextus Pompey would always remember the two days on which the father he barely knew enjoyed the thunderous applause of the adoring crowds. Plutarch says that those in his own day who were given over to comparisons of Pompey and Alexander claimed that he was less than thirty-four years old (i.e., in order to make the two men the same age), while in fact he was almost forty.[21] In fact he was forty-five going on forty-six. The age discrepancy issue aside, the biographer makes a reasonable case that this was the high point of the commander's life, and that never after did he enjoy the adulation that he did at his third triumph.[22] Plutarch argues that Pompey used his strength and power to make Caesar possible, and that then Caesar cast down the very man who had been so instrumental in his own coming to supremacy.[23] We shall take issue with this thesis, refining it and offering a somewhat more nuanced analysis. But Plutarch does not make an entirely unfair observation.

Scholars have noted that we find no evidence that the senate objected to Pompey's celebration of his triumph at the end of September (a birthday present to himself, in some regards) of 61. It would no doubt have stirred too much acrimony among the people, especially since several triumphs had been awarded for far less than what Pompey had done.

The historian Diodorus Siculus notes that Pompey recorded the achievements of his Asian expedition in an inscription, noting that he had freed all the coasts of the pirate menace, that he had extended the borders of Rome to the very ends of the world, maintained and in some cases increased revenue lines, and brought back immense treasures to be dedicated to a goddess (generally taken as Minerva, but perhaps Venus and in any case not definitively identifiable), all in addition to his extensive military campaigns on land through the Near East.[24] Significant scholarly debate has surrounded the evidence of Diodorus, hinging mostly on the question of whether the inscription should be dated to the time of Pompey's triumph in 61 BC. Ursula Vogel-Weidemann's offers a valuable analysis of not only Diodorus' passage, but also the larger question of Pompey's triumph and evidence thereof.[25] The conclusion reached is that what

Diodorus alludes to is actually an inscription set up at Ephesus to Artemis, before Pompey left Asia Minor; it would then date to 62; the argument is further made that the inscription offers a key piece of evidence in the development of the Pompey-as-Alexander equation, an obvious enough comparison, but one that was apparently zealously promoted by the clients and partisans of Pompey.

The year 61 BC is also when our surviving sources begin to record noteworthy problems in Gaul, matters that would soon allow Caesar to display his military acumen and abilities on a grander scale than that provided by western Iberia. Pompey, for his part, was active politically in helping one of his most loyal friends: Lucius Afranius would be consul in 60, together with Quintus Metellus Celer. The choice of Afranius in particular would have seemed an exercise of mere personal favour to Pompey's enemies, but then again they needed little incentive to find fault with him.

But in the political arena, the opponents and critics of Pompey were not cowed by grand triumphs and popular fawning over the victor of the east. Opposition to Pompey began to be centred around Lucullus, his predecessor, who had by all accounts entered into the late period of his life that is said to have been marked by overindulgence in luxuries and comfort. The main thing that Pompey needed from the senate was approval for all the arrangements that he had set up in the east, including what to do with his veterans: the many returned soldiers would need land allotments, and it was for the senate to start prioritizing honouring the men who had won so many victories over Rome's enemies.

Lucullus was certainly still resentful of Pompey, and neither he nor Pompey's other senatorial critics were above exhibiting what some would label jealous petulance. Pompey had annulled many of Lucullus' edicts, and so now he would suffer the ignominy of having to be as if a schoolboy before the senate with his lesson book, sometimes passing and sometimes failing, but always being in some way obstructed or delayed. None of this could have endeared the senate to the people; it must have all seemed like an exercise in resentment.

In brief, the question of the ratification of the arrangements made by Pompey would be the catalyst for the tensions and controversies that had long been stirring to burst forth anew. Lucullus, not surprisingly, would find an ally in Cato; Pompey would find a ready ally in Caesar after the ambitious Julian had returned from Spain. Much of what transpired in republican debate now was sadly predictable to anyone who had been paying attention to politics. Notably, Caesar had come back to Rome in the summer of 60 BC, and almost immediately there was another controversy with Cato. Caesar wanted to stand for consul in 59, but he also wanted a triumph for his deeds in Spain. Something of the same problem was at play as with Pompey when he wanted to canvas for Piso: Caesar was required to remain outside the city until he enjoyed any triumph.

In his case Pompey had asked for an extraordinary delay in holding elections; Caesar here asked that he be allowed to run for election in absentia, through the offices of proxies.

As before, so now, the ever-consistent Cato was firmly in opposition, while at first the senate was mostly in favour of granting the request. Cato was happy to filibuster and to do everything he could from the republican repertoire of delay to frustrate Caesar's wishes. In the end, Caesar abandoned the idea of having a triumph, which allowed him to enter the city. He had now experienced exactly the same sort of treatment as Pompey; the two men clearly disagreed on many issues and were of diverse temperaments, but they had a common foe, and they began to make common cause.

The stage was more than set for what would happen. And there was more afoot than the machinations and counter machinations of Lucullus, Cato, Pompey, and Caesar. Pompey found the senate a less than friendly place, and so it is not surprising that the plebeian tribunes seemed to offer an avenue to success. One of the key figures with whom he became more closely associated at this juncture was one of the more notorious figures in Roman republican history, a man to whose story we may now return: Publius Clodius Pulcher.

Clodius had lived more or less recklessly in the period up to and through the Catilinarian conspiracy, but ultimately his most notorious shenanigan would come in December of 62 BC, during the so-called rites of the Bona Dea. Caesar at the time was pontifex maximus, and his wife Pompeia was responsible for hosting the goddess' rituals, from participation in which men were barred.[26] Clodius showed up at the rites disguised as a woman; the rumour that spread was that he was having an affair with Pompeia.

The charge of profaning the rites was serious (indeed, a capital crime), and the gossip about adultery was a major embarrassment. Caesar divorced Pompeia, the occasion for what became the celebrated dictum that the wife of Caesar must be above even the suspicion of wrongdoing. Clodius perjured himself at his trial, lying that he was not even in the city at the time of the Bona Dea festival.

Various key political players had great stakes in the Clodius trial. Caesar, for his part, seems to have wanted to stay out of it all; given the issue of Pompeia, this was clearly the wise course. Lucullus was furious with Clodius ever since the aforementioned issue of Clodius having been accused of incest with his sister, Lucullus' wife. Cicero was desperate to make peace between Lucullus and Pompey, since he correctly foresaw the coming disasters if those two veterans of the east came to loggerheads. And so Cicero was happy to give evidence against Clodius as a favour to Lucullus.

Crassus may have played a spoiler's role in the whole drama. According to some reports, using his immense wealth, he was able by bribery and force of favour to convince jurors to acquit Clodius; the advantage to him would be that he then have secured a potentially valuable future ally. There is controversy here as to whether Crassus actually did participate in such schemes at this trial; certainly Clodius was guilty of bribery, and there is good reason to think that Crassus was willing to supplement the available funds from his vast resources. The scholar Maciej Piegdoń reaches the conclusion that Crassus did help Clodius, using the offices of go-betweens to provide him with the cover of plausible deniability.[27] The whole experience, at any rate, meant that Clodius would be indebted to Crassus, grateful to Caesar for remaining silent when he could easily have sought vengeance on him, furious with Cicero, and less than pleased with Pompey (to put it mildly) who had lifted no finger to help him.

Pompey's lack of interest in helping Clodius offers an interesting window into his personality and political attitude in this period. As with not being willing to enter Egypt when Ptolemy had invited him to arbitrate disputes, so now he was careful, one might well think, to avoid offending the *optimates*. He may have found it all the easier to do this because he did not think Clodius' stunt at the Bona Dea rites was the sort of misdeed he wanted to expend political capital excusing. Further, why should he waste finite and precious capital helping Clodius, when it was clear that others (his rival Crassus in particular) were taking the risk and making the expense? He may have concluded that merely avoiding being active in harming Clodius was all that honour may have demanded.

Clodius went to Sicily to serve as quaestor. At some point in the aftermath of his trial experience, and more generally given the political situation in Rome, Clodius conceived of an idea that somehow seems to accord with his personality, his proclivity for displaying few scruples, and his willingness to go to extreme lengths to attain his goals.

Students sometimes wonder why this member of the famous, patrician Claudian family is usually referred to as 'Clodius.' The seemingly odd orthography was something that Clodius himself began to affect after the success of one of the more significant decisions that he made in his career: giving up his patrician status by seeking adoption into a plebeian family. Clodius wanted to be a plebeian for one and only one reason: as a plebeian, he would be able to serve as tribune of the plebs, and he would have an easier time seeking his revenge on those he felt had done him wrong. First on the list of those targets of his ire was Cicero.

Where major problems would emerge was when competing efforts to seek vengeance converged: circumstances were aligning that would find Pompey willing to consider appealing to Clodius for help.

In this same period one interesting historical tidbit emerges that serves as a good illustration of the difficulties that could emerge as soon as a commander from a far distant realm was away from the battlefield. We noted that after

Mithridates died, his son Pharnaces took power in the Cimmerian Bosporus, and was confirmed by Pompey, while at the same time the region of Phanagoria was rewarded with independence for having been quick to rebel against Mithridates.[28]

Pharnaces invaded Phanagoria, though when resistance seemed futile, his victims were willing to surrender themselves and to give hostages, such that the king had asserted his power and recovered from the wound to his pride caused by losing that piece of his kingdom. It was a relatively small gesture, and not the sort of thing that in and of itself would attract much Roman concern. But it was a reminder of the fragility of foreign arrangements, even as in Rome debates were ongoing about the ratification of Pompey's settlement.[29] Matters were not exactly unravelling, but they may have seemed newly precarious.

The year 60 BC was also the occasion for a noteworthy event: the future Augustus' father, Gaius Octavius, was on his way to take up his new position in Macedonia as proconsul, but first he received a senatorial commission to deal with a problem of fugitive slaves in Thurii.[30] These slaves were survivors from both the time of the Spartacus rebellion, and of the Catilinarian disturbance; evidently they were living on plunder as bandits and brigands. Octavius quelled the revolt, and he was able to award his little son the title 'Thurinus' in commemoration. The boy had been born in September of 63; he would later be insulted by his enemies with the use of the name to remind him of his comparatively humble origins.[31] Octavius would be a serious prospect to stand for a consulship, but he died at Nola in 59 BC, before he could run.

Caesar, meanwhile, had given up a triumph to stand for the consulship for 59 BC; his colleague would be Marcus Calpurnius Bibulus.[32] Bibulus was one of the traditional senatorial old guard; if one wondered where he stood on matters, his wife was Porcia, the daughter of Cato. Caesar was the favoured candidate of Pompey and Crassus; Bibulus was the darling of the Catonians. Caesar wanted to serve with Lucius Lucceius, a learned man and orator who was a friend of Cicero.[33]

Lucceius seems to have been the perfect compromise candidate, at least according to the logic of the Caesarians. He was a friend of Cicero, which was thought to be a major gift to the opposition. The problem was that whatever chicanery or manipulation may have been afoot in the election season of 60, it was not enough: the *optimates* succeeded in securing the election of Bibulus, which seemed to bode poorly for getting much done.

Motum ex Metello consule civicum: so the poet Horace would commence the first poem in his second book of odes, addressing Asinius Pollio, who was endeavouring to write a history of the Roman civil wars.[34] It was a favourite activity then and now for historians to debate when exactly was the start of what would be a renewed period of civil discord. Pollio seems to have chosen the year 60, which certainly makes sense: it was the year in which the political interests of Pompey, Crassus, and Caesar coalesced.

Pompey and Crassus had a longstanding rivalry and opposition; we have noted Crassus' strong grudge against Pompey from the days of the slave war. We do not know exactly when or how the discussions commenced, let alone how the particulars of an informal agreement were finalized. Caesar was the reconciler of Pompey and Crassus. The wealthy Crassus had extensive business interests in the east; his principal reason for wanting the logjam in the senate to be resolved was economic. Caesar had to think about what he would do both during and after his consular year. Gaul, as we have noted, was already proving to be a problem, and at some point in the fateful summer of 60 or earlier, Caesar set his sights on commanding armies there and attaining a glory comparable to if not superior to Pompey's.

At the moment, Pompey had the military renown and tens of thousands of loyal veterans. Crassus had flowing streams of riches and revenues. Caesar was popular (in no small part due to his reckless spending), had a patrician family, evidently undeniable charisma, and a more than respectable record both in the field and in political life. If his resumé was thinner than that of the other two, he was also the youngest of the three, and Crassus, after all, could not compete with Pompey for military triumphs in the field.

In one sense, there was a real danger for Pompey that he was looking mostly toward the past, namely for the seal of approval and ratification of what he had already accomplished. Crassus was still actively involved in business dealings on a grand scale, and so he was acutely interested in what was happening financially today and tomorrow; his outlook was rooted in the present and the future. Caesar was in some sense the one with his eyes most resolutely focused on the future, which made sense given his age.

The political alliance that emerged from the three was all too real. Some scholars have enjoyed using the memorable reference of Varro to a 'three-headed monster' to describe it.[35] There was no official nomenclature for it: it is sometimes referred to as the First Triumvirate, a useful enough designation, as long as one realizes what the so-called triumvirate was not.[36] Pompey, Crassus, and Caesar did not hatch some scheme to overthrow the republic, the seeds of which may be found in the backroom deals made in 60 BC. There is no question that 60 was a turning point; Peter Greenhalgh is more than justified in marking it as the point where his life of Pompey as the 'Roman Alexander' (Volume I of his work) ends, with 59 as the commencement of his treatment of the 'Republican Prince' (Volume II).

I have no problem retaining 'traditional' terminology like 'First Triumvirate,' as long as there is no misunderstanding that it was some title that described an official effort by these three extraordinary men to manage the affairs of government. At its heart, it was deadly simple: three men of immense ambitious and talent saw tremendous mutual benefit and expanded opportunity in working together. All three (arguably, Pompey and Caesar in particular) had in one way or another encountered frustrating roadblocks in the normal progress and practise of republican government. Whether from a Cato or a Cicero, senatorial objections made it difficult to move forward expeditiously on such issues as the reorganization of the east, the question of land for veterans, or the political aspirations and, yes, vanity and ego stroking of larger than life men.

Was there some oath between Pompey, Crassus, and Caesar? There is some evidence that there was, but whatever was agreed to was clearly contingent on the personal honour of the three men. The agenda of what they had to do in the senate was long; Caesar was in some sense taking the most acute risk, since he would be the consul.

Psychologically, one can only speculate on what Pompey wanted for tomorrow other than the seal of approval on what he had already done. Later history would make it clear that in some sense he was in the vice of having done too much, too soon. Some have seen no greater long term intentions on Pompey's part than to be some highly respected senior statesman, a man looked to for counsel and advice that would be readily accepted by those who respected his authority and dignity. I suspect that Pompey was not quite ready to fade into a quasi-retirement. He may not have determined exactly where next he wanted to exercise his manifold talents. But a quiet, predominately political life does not seem likely to have been his preferred destiny. Gaul was not on his mind, chances are; Parthia might have been, since he knew better than anyone that trouble was likely to emerge from that quarter sooner rather than later. A modicum of respectful gratitude from the senate might have gone a long way, but certainly Pompey wanted more than honours and flattery. The day would come when Caesar would feel something of the same sentiments, more acutely than he thought he did as he struck his deal with his two allies.

Some astute observers of Roman political life late in 60 BC (if not earlier) might have said that many men on both sides of the political divide were playing with fire. They would be proven right, as events soon seemed to move in unpredictable and swiftly destructive ways, seemingly out of the hands of the men who were trying to maintain the reins of the republic's increasingly unstable chariot.

Chapter Twelve

The 'First Triumvirate' in Action, Part I

The great frustration for Pompey in the year 60 BC had been the question of the ratification of his eastern settlement. One can imagine the look on his face when first he learned that Lucullus wanted the senate to revisit his own arrangements, which had largely been abrogated by Pompey. The senate was full of men who believed that one should inspect every paragraph, as it were, of a document; every item needed to be carefully studied. This was especially true when the documents were the work of a man like Pompey, who was held in such suspicion by some, regardless of what he did. But there was more to it than that: for some senators, it was simply the job of a republican official to exercise oversight, bureaucratic or tedious as the job might be.

If you make a private pact with two of the most powerful men in the state, you have every right to expect that you will either achieve your goals, or you will plunge the state into chaos. The degree of fear of Caesar on the part of the *optimates* may be evidenced by the fact that despite what must have been serious efforts to keep Bibulus out of the senate, the 'triumvirs' lost a major victory when he narrowly secured election. Clearly the opposition had worked very hard, and their candidate was in office, obviously as an intended check to Caesar's power.

Caesar was conciliatory in his early interactions with the senate. He made it clear that Bibulus and he were colleagues, working together for the good of the republic. It must have been a classic performance on Caesar's part. Clearly it was an effective act of psychological warfare, because we hear of how Bibulus did not know how to respond. Amity seemed to drip from everything Caesar said. And yet, Appian reports, secretly Caesar was preparing the masses, raising an armed force that was designed not to act in some violent way, but merely available to show that they did, after all, have weapons.[1]

In fairness to Pompey, Crassus, and Caesar, if they had tried to proceed with republican business as usual, they might all have entered their dotage without seeing anything of their programme accomplished; the senate was intractable, and so were they. Rome had a relatively fresh memory of the cost and horror of civil war, and there was still that healthy revulsion to the idea that the state should be riven in violent upheaval. Threats were enough in some regards, even if the game being played was exceedingly risky.

Caesar made his land redistribution proposal, and as anyone could have expected, the senate was filled with voices in objection.[2] Caesar exited the senate, not trying to hide his disdain at being rebuffed. Likely enough he expected the resistance, but after his stage performance of being an irenic man of republican virtue and compromise, he now needed to shift to the role of one who is indignant at how impossible his colleagues are.

Caesar refused thereafter to summon the senate, and one consul could not do so without the agreement of the other. This could be interpreted as a game of taking one's ball home and refusing to play, except there were indeed ongoing games, of a potentially dangerous sort. Caesar began holding popular assemblies, where he presented his ideas and complained about the intractable senate; the people, for their part, always up with concealed weapons.

The senators, meanwhile, met at the house of Bibulus; it was not legal to have normal senatorial meetings, but there was nothing illicit about gathering together at a consul's house. There they decided on a plan: they would go out and confront Caesar, challenging him and presenting their views before the people, notwithstanding the hazards; the goal was to display sufficient courage and fortitude, so that the Caesarians would seem to be the supporters of legislating at the point of a blade.

There was disrespect and the threat of violence from the unruly crowd, which soon became nothing short of a mob. Bibulus was mocked and threatened. Appian depicts him baring his neck, as if ready to die a martyr for the republic; his friends pulled him away and removed him before there was a chance to test how far this might go.[3] Cato tried to speak, but he was forcibly evicted not once but twice by Caesar's thugs.

Dio has Caesar presenting his land reform plans to the senate, only to be challenged by Cato.[4] Cato, the historian notes, could not find anything specifically objectionable in the proposals, but invoked the traditional Roman disdain for innovation. Caesar is said to have threatened Cato with imprisonment, but Cato indicated he was ready to be jailed, and other senators stood with him; one of them memorably said that he preferred to be in prison with Cato than in the senate with Caesar. Caesar was embarrassed, at which point he adjourned the senate, and commenced his use of the popular assemblies. Nonetheless he wanted everything he proposed to have the support of Bibulus, only to learn that the answer was a resolute no.

Dio highlights how Pompey and Crassus, though private citizens, were happy to do their part to cooperate in the pact with Caesar; Pompey in particular spoke in support of the Caesarian proposals, and not without a threat of being willing to stand with those willing to fight if necessary.[5] Bibulus did show his face on the day that the law was to be passed by the people; he protested and tried his utmost to stop the travesty unfolding before him, only barely to escape with his life. For the rest of the year he did not leave his house, simply sending meticulously regular missives to his colleague about the illegality of this or that undertaking. There was talk among some tribunes about arresting him, but the idea was dismissed, and the consul was allowed to keep railing in traditional republican fashion, from his private residence.

Suetonius also references the speech of Pompey, deploring his willingness to go along with any acts of bloodshed; the people, however, apparently were delighted at the sight of their hero being willing to talk about standing with them, weapon in hand.[6] It is noteworthy that Pompey is said specifically to have promised that if anyone raised a sword, he would take up a shield. It was a powerful invocation of Pompey as defender, as guardian of the people; coming from the man who had returned from the east after astonishingly impressive victories, it must have struck an effective note.

This image accords with Plutarch's account of the whole business, where Caesar courts popular favour and clashes with Bibulus and especially Cato, only to bring Pompey before the people as a potent symbol.[7] The picture of Caesar asking Pompey if he would defend against any resistance the passage of his agrarian law, and Pompey responding in the affirmative, ready with shield and buckler, was vintage republican theatre. Plutarch considers it the most vulgar and arrogant thing that Pompey had said to date, so much so that even his clients and friends found themselves apologizing for it.

What exactly was going on here? What were the three 'triumvirs' doing? Nothing less than fulfilling the purpose of their informal, yet ruthlessly efficient and deadly consequential pact. They were playing no game here of 'win some, lose some'; they were determined to see their wishes ratified, one way or another. Were they willing to go to war? Probably their conclusion – rightly so, as it turned out – was that there would be no war. They were not intending to overthrow the republican system; they had no plan to transform Roman government into something that it was not. Confronted with the annoying and frustrating realities of that system, they simply wished to exert their collective will decisively, not without a marked undertone of 'the ends justify the means.'

These were also men who at some level probably thought, at least we are not emulating Sulla. This was a republic that within living memory had witnessed proscriptions, not to mention recent violence and conspiracy from the likes of a Catiline. Still, the violence reported in connection with Caesar and Bibulus cannot be discarded as anything approaching business as usual: it was not.

Two key figures we have not mentioned in connection to this ugly episode and worrying course of events were Lucullus and Cicero. Of the two, Cicero would prove to be the more formidable foe; Lucullus seems not to have had any interest in challenging Caesar and the others directly. Whether he was threatened into silence or not, to the best of our knowledge he would not play a significant role in the political drama. Suetonius says that Caesar openly spoke of prosecuting him as soon as Lucullus started to be a little too free in his objections to the brash young consul, even to the point of reducing the onetime Asian commander to pleading not to be attacked in the courts.[8] Whatever the truth of the embarrassing episode, Lucullus seems not to have taken any chances.

Cicero was a different story. If anyone had hoped that he would go along with the machinations of Caesar and his allies, he had woefully misjudged the situation. The instrument and agent of dealing with Cicero would be someone who had every reason to want to see him destroyed: Clodius.

We have mentioned that Clodius sought adoption into the ranks of the plebeians, so that he could serve as tribune. This scheme could serve abundant purposes, not least facilitating an attempt to strike a blow at Cicero. Clodius was not happy with Pompey, to be sure. But Cicero was the main object of his bile and lust for revenge. Crassus had helped him more than anyone in the Bona Dea scandal, and Caesar – who had all too personal reasons for hating Clodius – had discreetly stood aside. Any dislike Clodius had for Pompey could be overlooked, given the circumstances.

If Cicero had an Achilles heel that his enemies could target, it was the question of the execution of the Catilinarian conspirators without a trial in December of 63. Cato had spoken in favour of that action, and Caesar had opposed it: the perfect combination of contrasting responses to raise the issue in the current climate.

Clodius seems to have been increasingly obsessed with his scheme of plebeian adoption all through 60 BC, and finally in 59 he had the moment to see it come to fruition. We can be reasonably certain that Pompey was the least happy of the three partners about helping Clodius. Not only was he not especially inclined to like the man, he was also a friend of Cicero, more so than Crassus or Caesar. Clodius wanted to see passage of a law to send into exile those who ordered the execution of Roman citizens without trial. It was asking in some ways for Pompey to betray a friend. For Pompey, it was a chance to begin to reflect on the nature of what Varro would come to call the 'three-headed monster.' But he went along with it, to his discredit. Publius Fonteius would adopt Clodius; Claudius was now definitively Clodius, and the farce had been completed at last.

What happened? Clodius was not to be tribune in 58 simply to punish Cicero. Clodius would also be instrumental in furthering the agenda of the 'triumvirs.' It was also not as if Clodius alone could destroy Cicero; realistically, he would need the support of Pompey, Caesar, and Crassus. Allowing Clodius to become a plebeian created a climate in which Cicero had to live with a sword hanging over him, and for the moment, that was enough of a torture for Clodius to inflict. Pompey could rationalize the increasingly fast-moving situation by saying that Clodius' tribunate would allow passage of legislation he wanted; legislation he found distasteful (i.e., the Cicero issue) was not on today's agenda, and so for the moment was a hypothetical problem. Things were spiraling, even if for the moment it was all too easy to think that one could remain in control of events.

In April of 59, Pompey strengthened his relationship to Caesar by marrying his daughter.[9] The union of Pompey and Julia would have been a source of tremendous stress and anxiety to those who were worried about the ambitions and machinations of father-in-law and son-in-law. Pompey developed a reputation for being infatuated with Julia. Born around 79 BC, she was close to thirty years his junior, and noted both for loveliness and virtue. The day would come when people wondered if Pompey had decided to focus on family life and to retire more or less definitively from public affairs and administration. But in the spring of 59, the principal reaction in the senate would have been alarm at the firm bond that had been established between Pompey and Caesar.

Studying Pompey in this period almost invites thoughts of what Alexander would have been like, had he not died in Babylon at almost thirty-three. In some regards Pompey was always best suited for the life of a military commander, not that of a statesman; he was good at organization and logistics, even exceptional, but he had little patience for the mode and manner of senate operations. Some with that attitude would have preferred monarchy or dictatorship to republic government. Pompey was not of that inclination, for all the constant fear and anxiety he inspired (largely, in fairness, because the ghost of Sulla still haunted Rome). Pompey had no vision of overthrowing the republic, or of seeing Rome under a different form of political organization. But that did not mean that he was especially patient with its daily life, and it was his lot to have Cato and Cicero as leading men of the senate. It was an age of extraordinary men, some of whom were exasperating.

The joke arose that the year 59 saw the consulship not of Caesar and Bibulus, but of Julius and Caesar. Having married his daughter off to Pompey, Caesar began to think of a replacement for Pompeia. Sometime late in the year he would marry Calpurnia, the daughter of Lucius Calpurnius Piso, who was destined to be consul in 58. It is possible that Calpurnia was slightly younger than Julia; in reputation, she would emerge as a respected woman, somewhat shy and retiring it seems, and not inclined to object to the fact that her husband was notorious for his peccadilloes. One of the more notorious rumours that began to spread about Caesar's penchant for adultery was his involvement with Brutus' mother Servilia; Suetonius says that she was Caesar's favourite mistress by far, and claims that he bought her a pearl during his consulship that was worth six million sesterces.[10] According to Suetonius, there were even stories that Servilia prostituted her daughter to Caesar.

Certainly the marriage to Calpurnia was a political one, as one might expect. The plan was for Caesar not to have to worry overmuch about affairs in Rome once he was out of office; he had his sights set on going to Gaul and winning military glory, and in the interim he would not need the stress of having his initiatives undermined in Rome. Pompey's old friend Aulus Gabinius would also be consul, thus giving Pompey and Caesar both a handle on power in the next year, as the machinery of the republic continued to function, even if it was showing increasing strain. The marriages and the consular arrangements allowed for both men to keep an eye on the other.

Velleius argues that Caesar was interested in reducing the reputation of Pompey by having him take at least some of the odium for what was being done during his consulship.[11] Certainly all three men were ultimately interested in what was best for themselves; their marriage was one of convenience, not of affection. Crassus, Velleius notes, had been unable to satisfy himself independently with power and influence; he saw Caesar and Pompey as agents to achieving what he had failed to attain through his large wallet. Odium had to be expected in consequence of brazen acts like that with Bibulus; you could always count on the support and even adulation of those who were indebted to you, but again the loyalty was based on business. And the crowd could be fickle. The 'triumvirate' had the advantage of distributing the bad reputation, and as the spring wore on, the reputation was indeed worsening.

Cicero could at least boast (and he did) that he was not to be bribed by offers of appointment from Caesar. Caesar could claim that he had tried to be reasonable with Cicero, that he had been willing to reward the man with some high place in the system – but Cicero was resolute in refusing to deal. And his name would arise in conjunction with one of the more curious episodes of 59 BC.

Lucius Vettius was one of the old Sullan guard; he had served under Pompey's father, and he had made a name for himself among other things for being an informant during the Catilinarian conspiracy.[12] He had been one of Cicero's sources of information, and allegedly he had tried to implicate Caesar in the plots afoot that fateful autumn of 63. Caesar, needless to say, would have been less than pleased with Vettius the would-be professional informant.

In 59, Vettius' penchant for informing on alleged plots and schemes reached new levels of drama. We may begin by stating clearly that in light of the surviving evidence, it is impossible to determine with certainty what really happened. Could there have been a plot against the 'triumvirs' that spring? Certainly. 'Plot' is an ambiguous word. It is not hard to imagine that some voices began to be raised in support of eliminating Pompey, Caesar, and Crassus; such things often start simply with someone musing how better off the republic would be if these ambitious, quasi-dictators were gone. The main problem for such would-be conspirators was that unlike, say, the spring of 44, the spring of 59 presented three problems, not one (or even two, if one wanted to include Antony with Caesar). Any move to assassinate one, two, or three of the leading men of 59 would risk another civil war. It was easier to think of eliminating one, and of the three, Pompey was a likely choice. He was not consul, and he was seen by many (not without reason) as the real power behind Caesar.

But let us return to what we know. One of the wilder narratives is recorded by Dio.[13] He says that Cicero and Lucullus hatched a scheme to eliminate both Pompey and Caesar, and that they enlisted Vettius to help them. Vettius was exposed, and he denounced his two puppet masters, as well as Bibulus. The problem was that Bibulus had warned Pompey of a plot against his life, and so nobody trusted Vettius' accusations against Cicero and Lucullus. Vettius was killed in prison before there could be a full investigation, and whatever secrets or truths he had died with him. Cicero, however, was never again fully trusted by Pompey and Caesar.

Dio's narrative raises numerous questions, not least who arranged for the death of Vettius, and why Cicero and Lucullus would have ever trusted the unscrupulous, notorious informant as an agent for so bold and difficult a deed.

In his life of Lucullus, Plutarch says that clients of Pompey made use of Vettius, claiming that he was caught plotting against their patron.[14] Vettius was questioned, and he revealed that Lucullus was plotting to assassinate his old rival. Nobody believed the allegations, and a few days later, Vettius was found dead in prison; most people thought that he had been killed by the very same people who had bribed him to incriminate Lucullus. In consequence of the whole sordid business, Lucullus withdrew even more from public life, which is of course exactly what Pompey and his allies wanted.

In his life of Caesar, Suetonius says that Caesar was the puppet master, suborning perjury from Vettius to harm his adversaries; when the scheme failed because nobody believed Vettius, Caesar had him killed.[15]

Appian has his own dramatic version of events.[16] He has Vettius rushing forth with a dagger, claiming that Bibulus, Cicero, and Cato had sent him to kill Pompey and Caesar. Caesar used the episode to stir up popular resentment of his enemies; Vettius was imprisoned until there could be an investigation, and he was soon found dead. Caesar claimed that clearly his opponents had found a way to eliminate the man destined to turn state's evidence.

Cicero alludes to the episode in his speech against Publius Vatinius, who served as tribune of the plebs in 59.[17] Cicero's speech dates to about three years after the would-be plot; he references Vettius' public confession that he had armed himself to assassinate Pompey. Vatinius is said to have brought Vettius forth to make his admissions, an act that Cicero deplores as the introduction of some scoundrel to the sacred rostra, a scoundrel and informer who slandered the names of such leading men as Bibulus, Lucullus, and Curio the Younger. Cicero's remembrance of the episode makes it clear that in his judgment, Vettius was simply a stooge of the tribune, paid off to bear false witness against leading men of the state. Cicero has Vettius step down from the speaker's platform, only to converse openly with Vatinius as if receiving his instructions; Vettius then is asked if he could name any other purported conspirators, and he proceeds to make another report. Vatinius announces that there will be a full investigation; after it becomes clear that nobody was falling for the poorly directed farce, the tribune arranged for Vettius to be strangled in prison.

What really happened? One of the few uncontroversial, undisputed facts of the whole affair is that Vettius died under mysterious circumstances. One possible sequence of events is this. There was talk of assassinating at least Pompey, but such talk never rose to the level of actually resulting in a serious plot. Among those inclined not to mourn should any or all of the Big Three turn up dead, there would have been a broad spectrum of responses to the idea of actually moving forward with a plot akin to the famous one of the Ides of March in 44. Fear of civil war would have been palpable. In a plot of two men, only if both are dead can there be a guarantee of no leak of information. Pompey was in the unique position of being both the most respected head of the three-headed monster, and, in consequence, the one whose death would be arguably the most consequential. He was likely informed of plots afoot, if only as a potentially valuable warning shot across his bow.

Pompey, once informed of more or less vague threats being made against him and of nascent plots, goes to Caesar and Crassus. Caesar decides to have Vettius serve as he had done so often before: serve as informant. Vettius is then encouraged by Caesar to make the story as convincing as possible. The notorious informant need not have been commissioned to go undercover to try to uncover information by subterfuge; he may have thought of the idea on his own. The problem for Caesar was that Vettius was not exactly a reliable source of information. The point of having Vettius claim to be exposing some plot was primarily to build sympathy for the Big Three; it was a way a pull the rug out from underneath any all too real plots that were being contemplated. To try to prosecute successfully men like Lucullus, Cicero, Bibulus, Curio the Younger, and others would have been to risk chaos and civil war, and the risk would have been all the greater once it was abundantly clear that Vettius was the weakest of links in the chain, with nobody really inclined to believe anything he said. It was no problem to kill Vettius; his death eliminated a significant potential source of information, since once he was dead it was not likely that Caesar, Vatinius, or anyone else privy to the back room shenanigans was going to talk.

To summarize: there was at least talk of assassination; Pompey caught wind of it. Once learning about it, Caesar hired Vettius to help expose it. The plan succeeded insofar as at minimum, there would always be lingering doubt in people's minds about the veracity of his story of assassination plots. The plan would have worked even better had Vettius been more credible, but in the end killing him served its own coldly logical purpose: Caesar and friends could claim that Vettius had been slain in prison at the behest of men like Lucullus and Cicero, who feared an informant. And Caesar and friends would not have to worry about a day when Vettius talked and people actually believed him.

Caesar, in any case, had more important agenda items for his consular year: he secured both Cisalpine and Transalpine Gaul as his provinces for after his term of office expired.[18] Suetonius claims that he was so unscrupulous that he made sure to steal a large sum of gold from the Capitol, having it carefully replaced with gilded bronze. Money was no doubt a major preoccupation; everything he had been doing at least since Pompey's return to Italy was costing him frightful sums. Keeping the people entertained and eager to support your initiatives was a very expensive occupation.

We have noted how when Pompey was on his return to Italy, he had refused the invitation of Ptolemy XII to come to Egypt to assist in management of internal problems in Alexandria. Domestic affairs in Egypt were not going well for Ptolemy, and one of the costly measures he seems to have taken in this period was to make sure that bribes continued to flow to men like Pompey and Caesar to maintain the status of friend and ally of Rome. During Caesar's consulship, Ptolemy's daughter Cleopatra VII was ten years old; she was destined to become by far the most famous member of her father's family, which was poised at the moment on the precipice of disaster and upheaval. The money that flowed into Caesarian and Pompeian coffers helped to ensure how history would be written once those problems burst forth.

The coalition that had been born in 60 BC was informal, extraordinary, and by no means some official arm of republican government. It was also exceedingly formidable. It would last until 54 BC, when destiny ensured that one of its members would die. But its first year in action had netted its members appreciable rewards for their expenditure of effort and wealth. Pompey was able to see the ratification and settlement of his eastern achievements, Caesar won his consulship and his assignment to Gaul, and at the very least Crassus continued to profit impressively from both his firmly protected overseas as well as domestic business ventures, alongside his prideful satisfaction in clearly being one of the three most powerful men in the state, even if (especially given that he was the oldest), he must have been feeling increasing pressure to achieve more fame and renown in his own name.

The agreement and understanding that the three ambitious Romans had arrived at was a means of pursuing mutually beneficial goals. While very different in many aspects of both desired future plans and personal temperament and experience, Pompey, Caesar, and Crassus had much in common to bring them together. Eerily, and yet somehow not at all surprisingly, all three men would die by violence.

The year 58 would be a dramatic one in its own right, filled with momentous events both at home and abroad. The 'triumvirate' would hold together, even as significant challenges mounted. Their collaboration brought with it the important benefit of averting any resurgence of civil strife. Fraught with tensions and challenges (especially in its political context and relationship with the senate), in time it would become all too clear that the effort to avoid civil war can in its own way contribute to its likelihood.

Chapter Thirteen

'The First Triumvirate' in Action, Part II

The year 58 BC is famous to students of Latin as the first year Caesar was in Gaul, and the year in which the spring saw Cicero go into exile. Publius Clodius had his tribunate, and if anything he was a master of the use of the mob as an agent for social change. The consuls of the year were Lucius Calpurnius Piso and Aulus Gabinius; the latter had already made a name for himself like Afranius as a loyal subordinate of Pompey.[1] Piso was Caesar's father-in-law: it was a year in which both consuls could be expected to serve as agents of the 'triumvirs.' Piso is noteworthy to students of literature and philosophy for his connections to the author Philodemus, and to the circle of devotees of Epicureanism in Rome and in Campania.[2]

One of the most precious sources of information we have about many of the events of the so-called decline and fall of the republic is the treasure trove of Cicero's correspondence. While like all surviving sources, Cicero's letters need to be used judiciously and with an eye to historical criticism, surely we can trust the picture that emerges of Pompey as having an increasingly rough time of it in 59 and 58 BC. There was a price to pay for heavy-handedness, but beyond that general truism, there must have been an acute sense of fear that he had peaked in his life's career. Having conquered the east, he was now dealing with petty politics, and having to take extraordinary measures simply to see his own initiatives and settlements ratified. It was all somehow far less satisfying than his experiences and accomplishments in the field in distant lands. The Roman Alexander was living a very different life from his Macedonian counterpart, whom death had taken at an age that spared him an extended period of time in bureaucratic matters and domestic politics.

If Cicero hoped to drive a wedge between Pompey and the other two triumvirs, the events of 59 BC shattered any such dreams. The Vettius conspiracy, whatever the truth behind it, had reduced any vision of a rapprochement between Pompey and the *optimates* to naught. For better or worse, Pompey, Crassus, and Caesar would continue to work together, and the last of these was now off to Gaul.

Cicero went into exile in March of 58.[3] Clodius had had his way: adopted as a plebeian, he was tribune, and his law was passed as he wished, declaring punishment for those who had condemned Roman citizens to death without trial. It was all aimed at Cicero for the events of December of 63, and Pompey, for all his friendship and close bonds to the orator, was not going to do anything to intervene. The consuls were also not willing to intervene on behalf of Cicero (this was no surprise), and Cicero spared himself the embarrassment and the farce of a trial by simply going into exile.

Pompey was clearly embarrassed about the whole affair. Of the Big Three, he was the least connected to Clodius, whom he likely found utterly reprehensible and questionable. If he was not feeling sufficiently guilty about the treatment of Cicero in 58, he would soon have even more to regret, as he watched Clodius evolve fully into a creature beyond the effective control of the very men who had made him possible. Clodius was interested first and foremost in Clodius, and his orders ultimately came from his own passions and prejudices. His loyalty to Pompey was virtually nil.

Pompey found solace in his wife Julia, and we have mentioned the reputation he began to develop for uxorious living. This was by no means a Roman virtue; indeed, any appearance of being overly devoted to his young spouse opened a door to criticism for his invidious adversaries.

Marcus Antonius ('Mark Antony') meanwhile was one of those who at least temporarily found a ready friendship and camaraderie with Clodius.[4] Cicero had to leave Rome in 58 because of exile; Antony would leave to head east to indulge in study and leisure in Athens, where he honed what would become his lifelong passion for all things Hellenic. Antony's scholarly interests were likely subordinate to the fact that like his future mentor Caesar, he had amassed frightful debts; even if we may question Cicero's hostile reports of his youth, Antony seems to have devoted his early life to the pursuit of his pleasures, running up enormous bills and a list of creditors who would find it harder to collect in Athens than in Rome. But he did not leave for the east without serving his time, as it were, with Clodius.

It was thanks to Clodius that the consul Gabinius would be assigned the province of Syria for 57; this would be part of a convergence of events that would see Antony as part of his staff, and that would figure in the brewing developments and discord in Ptolemaic Egypt.

The immediate issue involving Egypt on Rome's agenda involved the younger brother of Ptolemy XII. 'Ptolemy of Cyprus' had made at least two fatal mistakes in his ill-starred career. One was that he seems to have thought that he would be able to survive on his eastern Mediterranean throne without having made any deals or agreements with Rome to confirm his kingdom. The second, and deadlier in the current climate, was that he had deeply offended Clodius when the latter had needed his help with ransom money from Cilician pirates: Ptolemy had helped the hostage, but with such a small sum of money that the pirates had felt sorry for Clodius, laughing at how little he was deemed to be worth. Clodius always found time to try to punish his personal enemies, either by the mechanism of his tribunate or by his street thugs. And so Clodius not surprisingly decided to push for Cyprus to become a Roman province, and to have Ptolemy deposed.[5]

Cato the Younger was assigned to deal with Cyprus; he recognized no doubt that this was all personal vendetta, and so he recommended to Ptolemy to give up power quietly and quickly, with a guarantee that he could live unmolested on a generous pension and a sinecure position. Ptolemy refused the concessions, and committed suicide.[6] Cato, meanwhile, had clearly been entrusted with his mission to Cyprus for one reason: it removed him from involvement in the daily affairs of Rome.[7]

The suicide of his brother and abrupt takeover of Cyprus were major factors in the weakening of the position of Ptolemy XII in Egypt. While his kingdom was guaranteed for the moment, there was always the looming threat of Roman annexation, and in the immediate the problem of internal strife and dissension in part occasioned by the seeming crippling weakness of the royal family.

Ptolemy was increasingly unpopular in part because he had spent so much money bribing Romans that could otherwise have been spent on the needs and wants of his Alexandrians. Beyond looking intolerably weak by not lifting a finger to help his deposed brother, he had not even spoken out against the Romans. By living in fear of what the republic might do to him, he had succeeded in making his own people the real immediate threat. Ptolemy constituted the perfect example of the client king caught trying to serve two masters, and failing miserably.

Ptolemy went to Rome, complaining of his lot. Our sources present a not altogether clear picture of what happened. Certainly he was beleaguered, under threat, afraid, and seemingly (at least in his own estimation) without the means to defend himself. Was he driven out? Quite possibly, though exactly how is uncertain. Was he deposed as soon as he left for Rome? This is also possible. His successor was his eldest daughter, Berenice IV.[8] We do not know if she was in sole power; matters are so confused and uncertain that it is possible that she was ruling with her mother, Cleopatra V.

What likely happened is that when Ptolemy went to Rome to make it clear that he needed help if his throne was to be secure, the Alexandrians revolted and chose his daughter as figurehead ruler, probably with her mother. This much is beyond question: the departure of Ptolemy for Rome was to be followed by a period of supreme instability in Alexandria. The handwriting had long been on the wall that the Romans were going to annex Egypt; arguably the only reason that it had not happened already was the huge flood of money that Ptolemy had poured into Roman coffers. Now he was in Italy, personally safe but finding himself without a throne to return to in Alexandria; the only way that he could regain that throne was by Roman arms. This would require more money to persuade the republic to make sure that Rome's economic and other interests in Egypt were maintained. Meanwhile, Berenice was in an exceptionally perilous position. The history of the Ptolemaic monarchy was about to become exceptionally violent and chaotic, all paving the way for the dramatic developments that would lead to the accession and power of the ruler destined to be the last of the long dynasty, the Cleopatra VII who was at present an adolescent girl.

Caesar, meanwhile, was occupied on the other side of the Roman world with his storied adventures in Gaul. For Latin students, the relatively simple, clear and elegant prose of his *commentarii* on the *Bellum Gallicum* constitute a traditional first major text for reading comprehension; we are able to read about Caesar's deeds from the pen of the commander himself. He would also compose *commentarii* on his experience of civil war; together, the two works provide an invaluable window into the life of the man.

In Rome, Clodius seemingly had checkmated Cicero and had sent off Cato to oversee the sideshow in Cyprus. Caesar was in Gaul. It was perhaps inevitable that the reckless, arrogant tribune would begin to take an increasingly hostile tone with Pompey. It seems that Pompey had become more and more concerned about Clodius' swaggering, brash attitude and heavy-handed management of his office, not least in how he persecuted Cicero so relentlessly. One could argue that Pompey should not have waited so long to stand up against the thuggish tribune, but whatever the reasons or justification for his hesitance, there was soon no question that Pompey had incurred the wrath of Clodius.

His street gangs were clearly under the impression by the late summer of 58 that Pompey could be a target for their violence; we hear of the onetime conqueror of the east being forced to remain in his house for fear of his life.[9] Clodius was increasingly thought incapable of such extreme plans without the backing of someone powerful, and that someone would have been Crassus, Pompey's old rival. Certainly republican politics was a deadly serious chess game, and for the moment, Caesar's presence in Gaul was a good reminder that the 'triumvirate' worked best when there were three men in the same city at the same time.

Clodius certainly needed little encouragement to do anything that seemed to give him more power and authority. One could argue that the three-headed monster had birthed a monster; Clodius had been useful in securing what the monster had wanted, but being so close to the centre of power had begun to give Clodius the little encouragement he needed to aspire to more and more pronounced assertions of authority. Cicero had left Rome before he could be brought to trial, and Clodius moved anyway to strike at him, destroying his house and seizing his property, as well as moving to formalize his punishments by legal act and censure. Acts of arrogance and vengeance were his stock in trade; he used the tribunate as his personal mechanism for pursuing his grievances, and his gangs of thugs as enforcers of his will.

Pompey and Caesar were still, it would seem, on reasonably good terms. They both supported Publius Cornelius Lentulus Spinther for a consulship in 57; he had assisted Cicero at the time of the Catilinarian conspiracy, and had enjoyed a more or less normal patrician career. His consular colleague was more of a problem for Pompey. Quintus Caecilius Metellus Nepos had served under Pompey in the campaigns against the pirates and in the east; only a few years younger than Pompey, for many years he would have been considered an ally and colleague of the commander, without question. Their relationship became strained after Pompey's return to Italy in 62. Nepos had left Asia to stand for the tribunate, clearly as a Pompeian ally. As tribune, he was one of the men who objected to Cicero's decision to have the Catilinarian conspirators executed; he was one of the louder voices in favour of prosecuting Cicero for murder. Nepos was then involved in political intrigues on behalf of Pompey that brought him into serious conflict with the *optimates*.

The cause for the falling out between Pompey and his hitherto loyal friend was a personal one. Nepos was a half-brother of Pompey's wife Mucia, who was divorced amid rumours of infidelity. Pompey's decision to present her with a bill of divorce, even without specific complaint or explanation as to why he was doing so, was enough of an admission to the gossip-laden city of Rome that Mucia was, indeed, guilty of adultery. Nepos was incensed at what he took to be an unforgivable slight to his relative's honour. From that point on, Nepos was inclined to block Pompey's political initiatives; indeed he became one of the reliable voices in opposition to the machinations of Pompey, Caesar, and Crassus.

57 BC would thus be another classic republican consular year, with potentially quarrelsome officials: Spinther was the candidate of Pompey and Caesar, but even 'triumvirs' cannot always secure everything they desire. Nepos won his consulship, against their efforts to block him.

To add to the political and personal turmoil, Nepos was a cousin to Clodius. Despite his efforts to stop Cicero in December of 63 BC, Nepos was all too aware that Clodius and the Big Three had succeeded in nothing so much as making Cicero a martyr to many. Voices were increasingly being raised in favour of recalling the orator from exile. Loyalty to his cousin, however, made Nepos' already complicated life and difficult position all the more problematic.

57 BC would also bring to the forefront a figure whose involvement in political life was destined to be memorable, to say the least. One thing both Pompey and the *optimates* were in agreement about was that the best candidate for tribune to replace Clodius would be one Titus Annius Milo. For those paying close attention to the ever fickle weathervane world of republican politics, Milo was being groomed to try to reverse some of the worst excesses of Clodius' term, including resolving the question of Cicero's exile.[10]

The term that Clodius had served from December of 58 to December of 57 had been one swing of the pendulum, and it was inevitable there would be a correction. Cicero had ended up in Thessalonica, and Clodius' gangs had been busy torching his property.[11] A shrine was built to the goddess Libertas on the site of Cicero's house; it must have all seemed ridiculous and unseemly, even for those who were happy to see Cicero in Greece.

But above all, Clodius had created an unhealthy climate in Italy by his hired enforcers. Milo would be encouraged to do the same; if Clodius could employ thugs, so could others. Gladiators made for effective persuaders.

Caesar, meanwhile, was being circumspect. He was willing, for example, to see a bill to recall Cicero; when Clodius vetoed efforts to restore the increasingly popular exile, Caesar indicated that he would support introducing a similar bill in 57, when Clodius would no longer be able to veto it. One of the reasons why Milo was encouraged to hire his own gangs was because Clodius assumed that if you no longer have a veto because your term as tribune is over, you still have thugs who can threaten, harass, and if necessary pummel anyone who challenges you. The key difference that Milo's supporters (Pompey prominent among them) succeeded in implementing was making sure that Milo's street gangs were led by quite talented gladiators, men who were masters at effective brawling. In early 57, street fights were not uncommon news items in the Roman press.

Cicero would return at last from exile, arriving in Brundisium in August. This was one of the high points of his career, if not its pinnacle. He was the darling of the crowds, a personification of victory over adversity. Clodius, to be sure, was not interested in coming to any sort of accommodation with his mortal enemy. When Cicero's house was to be rebuilt at public expense, Clodius managed to see to it that the workers were harassed by his gangs. The house of Cicero's brother Quintus was also set on fire.

A great victory had been won, however, by the determined and dogged friends of Cicero. Spinther had helped, as had Milo. Pompey was also influential in the process, but it is not especially surprising that he was not shown much in the way of gratitude from his usual adversaries in the senate; they were more inclined to ask where he had been when Cicero had needed him in the first place. Plutarch notes that while Cicero was in exile, when Clodius would openly mock and insult Pompey, senators who normally would be inclined to despise Clodius and his gangs were delighted with the attacks on a man they blamed for Cicero's misfortunes.

For those wondering about direct efforts to stop Clodius' outrageous behaviour, there were indeed attempts to prosecute him; as tribune, this was a major agenda item for Milo. Clodius' cousin Nepos, however, was a powerful, indeed consular force. He was more than willing to try to shield his relative from legal efforts to ruin him. Alliances occasionally shift and are more or less significantly altered and adjusted; Clodius should have realized that his list of enemies was a dangerous one, but for the moment, at least, it seemed to him that he was protected from any serious harm.

In Syria, Pompey's friend Aulus Gabinius was successfully managing the problems of his eastern realm, with revolts and uprisings that required military experience and acumen; we hear of Mark Antony making a name for himself in Gabinius' service, his reputation improving as he showed himself capable of being a competent soldier and loyal army man.[12] His reputation for heavy drinking and womanizing would dog him his whole life, but nobody doubted that he was a superb fighting man.

In Gaul, Caesar continued his impressive victories and work; he was winning a reputation for military valour that invited comparison with Pompey's record.

Ptolemy XII, meanwhile, spent the year 57 continuing his efforts to drum up money and support to regain his Egyptian throne. We hear that he arranged to have envoys to Rome from Alexandria assassinated. We have noted that there is uncertainty as to the number of queens in Egypt at this time; if Berenice IV had not been ruling alone before, she certainly commenced her monarchy in 57, after the death of her mother from unknown causes. One cannot avoid the suspicion that Alexandria was not the healthiest of environments.

Berenice was largely occupied in this period in the ongoing effort to determine who would be her husband. There were at least three candidates in quick succession; to give an indication of how arduous the process was, and how perilous it could be to aspire to be the consort of Egypt's queen, the first candidate died during negotiations, the second was not allowed to be considered by order of Gabinius, and the third was killed on the queen's orders after he proved to be insufferably boorish and vulgar. Needless to say, the situation in Alexandria was a disaster that was practically inviting a Roman takeover. Egypt was too important economically to let it be a mismanaged Ptolemaic client kingdom.

The fourth of Berenice's suitors was a Greek nobleman named Archelaus, who was possibly if not probably Macedonian. He had a distinguished family that had served in the army of Mithridates. Pompey had bestowed high office in Cappadocia on him in the great year of eastern settlement, 63 BC. Needless to say, Archelaus continued to maintain good relations with his Roman benefactors; he would endear himself to Gabinius in 56 by offering his support when the proconsul was contemplating war with Parthia. Archelaus would succeed in securing a marriage to Berenice, though in this case, marriage was destined to bring him death together with his bride.

The reason why Gabinius needed to think about war with Parthia was because that great Roman rival was facing its own crises and controversies. Simply put, Phraates III was assassinated in 57 BC, in a conspiracy involving his sons, Orodes II and Mithridates IV.[13] Mithridates was the elder brother; he had decided to seize power in the time-honoured Parthian manner by slaying his father. His younger sibling Orodes was certainly complicit in the patricide. There is of course no honour among thieves, and it is absolutely no surprise that the two murderous brothers would commence their own civil war. Mithridates was soon faced with rebellion from Orodes, and he would decide to flee to Gabinius for help.

Parthia had long been a Roman problem. Pompey had not exactly resolved the Parthian question to anyone's satisfaction, but he had secured a few years of stability and peace while Phraates remained on the throne. Empires in civil war are supremely unstable. What is interesting and clear in hindsight is that the Mithridates/Orodes civil war was a key moment for Rome to pounce. When a Parthian king comes seeking the help of the neighbouring Roman proconsul to regain his throne, the opportunity is there to shape the future of Roman-Parthian relations far more stably and securely than anyone had dreamed possible. It was a gift horse, but circumstances conspired against Gabinius. On his right he had Parthia, and on his left he had Egypt. The affairs of both realms were immensely consequential for Rome, but if one were forced to choose between them, Egypt was the more crucial one, both by dint of geography and by economic significance. Egypt would be where Gabinius would feel compelled to focus his priorities.

Indirectly, then, the unfolding and ongoing chaos in Ptolemaic Egypt would be directly consequential to Roman engagement with Parthia. Alternative history cannot be determined with certainty, but Mithridates would clearly have been in a better position if Egypt had been stable, and Gabinius free to devote his attention to the east. As it was, Mithridates was destined not to live so long, and the victorious Orodes, complicit in the death of his father and brother, would pose a significant problem for Rome.

One of the men who took particular interest in the ongoing problems in Egypt was a man who had decided to do what at the time he thought (correctly) was the proper course of action for a loyal republican. Pompey had been invited to resolve troubles in Alexandria, but he had declined; now he could connect the dots and a plethora of problems emerging from that fateful decision. Loyalty to the principle of republican government had proven costly. Pompey was not alone in this period in thinking that Ptolemy needed to be restored to power, and swiftly. Under such a scheme, Roman military might would back up a man who was ardent in his devotion to Rome on account of his owing his power to the republic.

Pompey, meanwhile, was kept busy not only by family life (which had brought him a fair amount of criticism, as we have seen), but also with the progress of work on his theatre, and with patronage of the arts. One thing Pompey does not seem to have been particularly given over to was writing. Sulla had composed memoirs, and Caesar had literary enterprises; Cicero could have passed many a year in exile with his authorial ambitions. Pompey was ultimately happiest and most content when he was immersed in military affairs; in this regard he was more single-minded, arguably, than Caesar.

If we seem to know less about Pompey's deeds in 58 and 57 BC, our sources bear some of the blame for our relative ignorance. Scholars have noted that Cicero's exile is partly responsible: he would have been our major source of information, and understandably he was more preoccupied with his own plight than with the affairs of Pompey.

We have noted the heavy price that Pompey paid with the *optimates* for his unwillingness to help Cicero in his time of need. One thing that Pompey did receive, however, was some support from Cicero after his return. This came in the wake of a crisis directly connected to the trouble in Egypt. Rome was suffering a grain supply programme, the result at least in part of the economic problems caused by the Egyptian upheaval. Cicero supported Pompey's being entrusted with a commission to oversee the critical matter of making sure that there was food security in Rome. There had already been violence in the city, in addition to the uneasy and dangerous climate caused by Clodius and his thugs. Managing grain sufficiency may not have seemed like a particularly glamorous job for someone who had conquered Rome's foes on three continents, but the problem was as grave as any other Rome faced.

Pompey would be *curator annonae*, a 'corn commission' that was similar to his pirate commission in that he was given a broad range of authority, with responsibility for the price and supply of grain across the Roman world.[14] He was suited for the job in that he had extensive experience of most of the Mediterranean, and he was still widely regarded by the public as a saviour of Rome. Now the saviour would save the republic from hunger.

Plutarch notes that Clodius was among those who objected sarcastically that the grain crisis had been manufactured for the sake of giving Pompey enormous power over harbours, trade routes, and the like, while others argued that Spinther was happy to support Pompey being entrusted with this job, so that he would be kept from being sent to deal with Egypt.

Cicero was barely back in Rome when he was helping Pompey secure this plum position. It must have been seen by some as a mark of the man's honour and good will that he was willing to help the man who had not done much for him; Cicero's critics, conversely, would carp that he was making a play for favour with the powerful man and his friends. Certainly by this point, Clodius was the target of many, and it was easier to forgive Pompey for any sins of omission now that Cicero was back.

We are not entirely certain of all the exact details of Pompey's commission, and we are not sure about what exactly Pompey wanted in view of the fact that there seems to have been some debate as to the extent of his powers. There were those who wanted Pompey to have more power, in essence, than any local authority when it came to matters connected to the grain issue; this was of course intolerable to those who feared the possible consequences of giving any one man too much authority. Pompey seems to have opted for the less extensive powers, likely clearly to avoid any new eruption of an old and familiar sort. Suspicious sorts (even if reasonable in their cynicism and suspicion) might have thought that Pompey had actually wanted the broadest possible commission, and that he had had the idea proposed to gauge reactions. But likely he needed to do no such thing; he knew that he was already fortunate to be enjoying the pendulum swinging back in a direction he favoured, and he knew the limits of what was realistic.

Dio comments on Pompey's new commission with an interesting summation of the current feelings between Cicero, Caesar, and Crassus.[15] Neither of Pompey's partners, he observes were particularly fond of Cicero, and the dislike was mutual, with Cicero mostly blaming those two for his exile. In other words, while Pompey had not helped him, Caesar and Crassus had been actively responsible for his exile. Dio includes a good example, though, of practical politics: Caesar and Crassus were happy to deal with Cicero now that he was back, since it was pointless to try to remove him again, even if they were so inclined.

Cicero was not forgiving in any way toward Clodius, and he went to the root of the problem by challenging the legality of his adoption into the ranks of the plebeians. While he was unable to do everything that he wanted, Cicero was able to be compensated fully for the losses that he had suffered at the hands of Clodius' goons.

The consuls for 56 BC were Gnaeus Cornelius Lentulus Marcellinus and Lucius Marcius Philippus. Marcellinus' career is not entirely traceable, but he was certainly a subordinate of Pompey at one stage. He served as governor in Syria before Gabinius. Philippus was also a former Syrian governor.

Marcellinus and Philippus were willing to go after Clodius; the list of his friends must have been growing shorter by this point. But they were also by no means supporters of Pompey and Caesar. One problem that had emerged was Pompey's difficulty in lending his voice in support of the appeals of Ptolemy XII to be restored to his throne. Supported by Spinther, Pompey failed to gain senatorial acquiescence with the Egyptian intervention plan. By January of 56, it seemed that the deposed king was at the nadir of his fortunes. Before too long, he was departing for Ephesus, seemingly having exhausted his hope for a change of fortune in Rome. Cato, meanwhile, returned from what had once been the island of Ptolemy's homonymous brother, laden down with gold and treasures plundered from Cyprus.

Clodius, meanwhile, moved to prosecute Milo for forming his band of gladiatorial thugs to counteract his own. It was the height of hypocrisy, in other words, the very essence of Clodius. He was under no misapprehensions as to his realistic abilities, no vain dreams that he would succeed in his prosecution. His goal was simply, it seems, to be annoying and to have a chance to harass and to insult those who supported Milo, among them both Cicero and Pompey.

Cato would play his own part in the Clodius drama. It was a good example of where Cato would exasperate his friends and allies. We have noted that Cicero had tried to have Clodius' acts as tribute annulled, and had not met with anything approaching complete success. Cato played his role in the ongoing debates, resolutely arguing that even where deplorable or regrettable, Clodius' actions were legal. Of course Cato had a personal reason for this position: he had no wish for his own commission in Cyprus to be questioned. Legally, he was probably on sure footing; morally he was arguably not. One thing is certain: Cato's interventions on behalf of Cato resulted in a severe strain on his friendship with Cicero. It would be some time before the two men would be reconciled. Dio emphasizes the argument that Cato's real reason for supporting Clodius was that he had a grudge against Cicero, but his desire not to have his work in Cyprus called into question was reason enough.[16]

Cato's assistance to Clodius proved to be thankless; soon the two of them were quarrelling about Cato's management of affairs in Cyprus, and Clodius was once again providing ample illustration of why many were growing tired of him. Caesar was in Gaul and did not have to deal with him in person, and so there was no potential strain on whatever continuing, behind the scenes support he bestowed on the rascal. To the extent that Caesar was hostile to Cato or at least interested in annoying him, Clodius was eminently useful.

Dio argues that in this same period, Pompey was feeling once again especially slighted by Caesar and Crassus in particular, convinced that he had done more than either of them and was not remotely appreciated in any way commensurate with his achievements.[17] Resentment may have spurred him on to doing an especially determined job as *curator annonae*, though it was very much in keeping with his usual practise to try to do everything he undertook well. Plutarch tells an interesting, characteristic anecdote about Pompey in connection to his exercise of the grain commission.[18] He was enthusiastic, zealous, and efficient in conducting his work. He went to Sicily, Sardinia, and Africa to gather grain. At one point, there was a particularly violent storm, and the ship captains were hesitant to sail, wisely fearing the tempest. Pompey insisted that they weigh anchor and proceed, noting that sailing was a necessity, living was not. According to the biographer, the result of comments like that was that before long, the sea was filled with ships transporting grain and seeing to the lowering of prices and importation of a surfeit of commodities. Just as Pompey had secured economic relief for Rome with his prosecution of the pirate commission, so once again he was helping to improve the markets and to bring prosperity and relief to Rome. It may not have been a glamorous or exciting post, but it brought immense popularity and appreciable earned credit to the commissioner.

Plutarch is suspicious in this period of Caesar, arguing from the benefit of hindsight that the war in Gaul was being used as a pretext by Caesar to train an army for eventual domination of the state.[19] This is to impugn Caesar unfairly; the day would come when he would merit serious criticism, but at this juncture in his career he was trying to play something of a game of catch-up with Pompey. His victories were designed to give him a resumé of accomplishments in the field to compare with his storied colleague. The same impulse would drive Crassus soon enough to his doom.

By the end of 57 BC, Caesar had conquered much of Gaul, and he was experiencing something of a vindication of his troubled consulship. He had been condemned widely as heavy-handed, a veritable bully with Bibulus. Now, however, after some two years of brawls in the streets and significant civil turmoil, Caesar was in higher favour. The three 'triumvirs' had serious strains in their relationship, and yet they were miraculously still functioning more or less as a team, if more often than not a quite dysfunctional one. There was major distrust afoot; Pompey was often convinced that Crassus simply wanted him conveniently murdered, but Crassus was as jealous and worried about the rise of Caesar as Pompey.

56 BC would be the year the three men would finally try to meet once again in person to see about putting their problems to rest. The so-called Conference at Luca (modern Lucca) was held on Caesar's territory, at basically the very border of Cisalpine Gaul.[20] While we do not know for sure what happened at Luca in anything approaching definitive certainty, we do know about major agreements that emerged from the conference.[21]

For one thing, they agreed that Pompey and Crassus would stand for the consulate. Sick no doubt of the opposition that they had faced, this allowed them easier control. Caesar would be awarded another five years to exercise a free hand in Gaul. When the consulships were finished, Pompey would have Spain and Crassus would have Syria – no doubt he had already decided on Parthia was a venue for his own chance at military glory.

Much has been written in analysis of Luca and the results thereof.[22] Crassus was a big winner, to be sure. He had been the odd man of the three in terms of having no appreciable military glory, and the promise of Syria seemed to bode well for rectifying that deficiency in his career. Caesar had the boon of almost half a dozen more years doing what he seemed to enjoy and certainly what he was having tremendous success managing. He would have armies and more opportunities for military victories.

But what of Pompey? Luca was positive for his colleagues if they wanted to confirm the membership of their colleague in their informal yet all too deadly serious pact. Some have argued that if Pompey had abandoned the agreement, he would have been in a worse position than he was, and this is surely right. Luca affirmed his connection to Caesar and Crassus, and solidified it with ties; it is clear that one of the agenda items must have been reining in critics of the three (Cicero prominent among them). Everyone at Luca knew that at various times, they all had been guilty of employing proxies to try to hinder or impede one or both of the others. Probably one of the points made was that Crassus, for example, would feel better about his position if he were finally able to pursue serious military glory; this would reduce the likelihood that he would resort to less reputable means of managing his relationship with his colleagues. We can speculate, but ultimately it seems reasonably clear that all three men exited Luca in a better state than they entered. And, at least in theory, the threat of civil war was to be averted for a few more years. It was a stressful and anxious way to live, but it was better than revisiting the dark days of the past.

Either in 57 or 56 BC, Lucullus died, allegedly in his dotage, far gone in mental and physical health.[23] He had never been vindicated, but he would be also be spared witnessing the slow unravelling of the republic he so cherished.

Chapter Fourteen

Consulship with Crassus

Pompey and Crassus each served their second consulship in 56 BC. That simple, declarative sentence reflects the will of the 'triumvirs' as sealed by their agreement at Luca, and the reality of their service. But the path from Luca to the consulship was not so simple or straightforward, as might be expected.

Previously Pompey and Crassus had denied that they intended to run; now they were open about it to their associates, even though they had supported the ambitions of other men. They were less forthcoming when asked directly by the consul Lentulus if they intended to be candidates. Pompey said maybe yes, maybe no; Crassus indicated that he would do whatever was for the good of the republic. To the extent that Lentulus had been a force in opposing the two men, it was the response he had earned, chilling as it was (especially Crassus') to any sense of how republican government is supposed to function. Plutarch says that Crassus was more politic in his reply than Pompey, but it is by no means clear that Lentulus would have agreed.[1]

Lentulus criticized Pompey, which prompted a more forceful answer once it became clear that the consul was making an eloquent speech against him. Pompey observed that Lentulus was ungrateful: Pompey had, after all, given a speechless man a reason to give a good address, and (alluding to his management of the grain crisis) he had allowed him to start vomiting instead of remaining famished.

There was, to be sure, a weighty constitutional problem: they entered their nominations too late, and Lentulus was among the least likely of men to support any sort of irregularity on their behalf. The response was to bribe a tribune to help to orchestrate a postponement of the elections until Lentulus' term expired; the use of an *interrex* would constitute another good example of manipulating the old republican system to achieve a desired end.

Clodius played acrobat yet again and supported Pompey in his electioneering. He had apparently come to the realization that he needed friends, badly, and helping Pompey seemed to be a good strategy that would also annoy eternal enemies of his like Cicero.

There was still some opposition, even to the end. Lucius Domitius Ahenobarbus continued to run for office right up to the last day; Cato is said to have encouraged the candidate to persist in the cause of liberty. Early one morning, however, the slave who was holding a torch to guide his way in the darkness was murdered, and Domitius received the message and gave up his quixotic quest. Cato is said to have been wounded in the arm when he tried to defend Domitius. Crassus is said to have brought soldiers to Rome with him to ensure that there would be no doubt as to election results. If true, he had remembered a tactic of his mentor Sulla, and had no compunction about employing it. As for Domitius, he would have his chance both to be consul, and to die in Pompey's service: it was a strange age, with almost constantly shifting alliances, or the threat thereof. There had been many gestures in defence of *libertas*: the senate in the late autumn had refused to participate in the *Feriae Latinae*, and had acted as if they were in mourning. Domitius and Cato had earned their mention in the annals of the history of freedom.

After the success of the new consuls in securing their election by such unscrupulous means, there was violence in the process of managing other elections that irregular season; we hear of street fights even to the point of Pompey being spattered with blood. Plutarch recalls this story as an incident that attested to how devoted Pompey's wife Julia was to her husband.[2] When he went home to change his bloody vesture, Julia fainted away at the sight, and suffered a miscarriage. Pompey continued to attract criticism for being overly devoted to her; she, for her part, was smitten with him in part because he was so faithful to her (a rarity in their circle), and he was exceedingly kind and restrained in all dealings with her.

In foreign affairs, the drama in Egypt and the theatres of the east was moving toward a critical, perilous juncture. Gabinius, as we have observed, was busy listening to appeals from Mithridates of Parthia about his brother Orodes and the hostile takeover of the throne that he himself had won by patricide. Gabinius' plans to move against the Parthians were interrupted by the ongoing machinations of Ptolemy, now back in the east after having been rebuffed by the senate in his efforts to regain his throne.

Pompey notified Gabinius that he should move to restore Ptolemy to his throne. According to Dio, one was motivated by kindness, while the other was driven by bribes.[3] Certainly Ptolemy felt indebted to Pompey, and likely he was convinced that it was better for the interests of the republic if he were on the throne instead of Berenice. There were problems, to be sure. Gabinius was the governor in Syria; it was a strict Roman tradition that a governor was not supposed to be launching military adventures beyond his border. Egypt was a client kingdom of Rome, and certainly not in Gabinius' purview.

If Dio can be trusted (and events seem to bear out his analysis), Berenice was afraid of the Romans, but she did little if anything to guard against them.[4] We have mentioned her husband Archelaus. Gabinius had had Archelaus on his radar, and indeed had arrested him on suspicion of having questionable dealings with the Egyptians. But he had released him (pretending that he had escaped) and let him go to Egypt to his prospective royal bride, having been bribed by his prisoner, and having calculated that he would benefit even more from letting him go to Alexandria. Archelaus went to Egypt, and was wedded to Berenice in the winter of 56–5. The honeymoon would not last long.

Once instructed to move against Berenice, Gabinius made short work of the Alexandrians: he is said to have invaded Egypt and to have vanquished the defensive forces in a day.[5] Archelaus was killed, and the kingdom was once again Ptolemy's. The death of the queen's consort seems to have come in battle; as for Berenice, once Ptolemy XII was restored to his throne, he had her slain.[6] Dio says that Ptolemy also had many of the wealthiest Alexandrians killed; the pretext would have been that they were complicit in his having been deposed, but the real reason was that regaining his throne had been extremely expensive, and he needed money desperately.[7]

In his life of Antony, Plutarch says that it was the future triumvir and lover of Cleopatra who persuaded Gabinius to intervene in Egypt.[8] But likely money and doing a favour to Pompey were more than enough to convince him. More importantly in light of later history, Antony would claim that this was the occasion when he first saw Cleopatra; she was fourteen when he was serving as Gabinius' cavalry commander.

The likeliest reason why Gabinius had been willing to dismiss Archelaus was indeed bribery; in the end, the queen's husband was an insignificant figure, a mere sideshow in what was one more stage in the steady march of Egypt toward its Roman future. Gabinius, meanwhile, knew all too well that he had played a dangerous game. He made no announcement of what he did to the senate, since it was, after all, illegal. But news of the deed became impossible to conceal.

Cicero, not surprisingly, would voice some of the loudest objections. Pompey was of course willing to excuse what he had ordered, while Crassus was also happy to back his 'triumviral' colleague, especially after he received his payment of a bribe from Gabinius. We hear of Pompey and Crassus going so far as to insult Cicero by making fun of how he had been exiled; they steadfastly blocked efforts to call Gabinius to account.

Pompey was more than willing to abuse the republican system in order to achieve what he considered to be an end expeditious for Rome, not to mention himself. In the present instance, he had every reason to believe that he had succeeded in securing the loyalty of Ptolemy, and indeed he had. Less than a decade later, he would learn that loyalty did not extend from one royal generation to another.

Gabinius left soldiers in Egypt; after all the troubles that Ptolemy had suffered in the past, there was every reason to believe that he would face renewed threats, and he needed Roman protection. On the other side of the Roman world, 55 BC was the year in which Caesar would briefly cross over to the east bank of the Rhine, and would land in Britain. His efforts in Britain constituted in a significant way the commencement of the long involvement with the island that would continue under such future Roman leaders as Claudius and Septimius Severus; while Caesar's undertaking on the mysterious front did not extend very far in time or space, and did not constitute a permanent occupation, it was a noteworthy start, and Caesar could boast that he was indeed going where no Roman commander had ever led an armed force.[9] Cato would try all he could to block honours and offerings of thanksgiving on behalf of Caesar, but there is no question that the general was scoring impressive successes. Winter was approaching, and Caesar did not have sufficient forces to launch a major invasion of Britain while also making sure that there were no disturbances erupting in Gaul; he was able to secure some hostages, apparently, but militarily little more. The ancient view generally is that nothing much practical was won by Caesar in his adventure to Britain; the general simply magnified his adventure into a dramatic event. But he did succeed in bringing Britain to the fore of the Roman imagination, and even if it was not on the must-do military agenda for some time, it never again fell from Roman memory.

In the east, Mithridates IV did not take the departure of Gabinius on his Egyptian adventure as an impetus to refrain from his own machinations. He returned to his lost kingdom, ready to fight his brother Orodes. Mithridates succeeded in winning appreciable victories in the Parthian civil war; Orodes was soon on the defensive, as Babylonia fell and the tide seemed to have turned. Orodes fled, becoming another example of a would-be Asian monarch who would take full advantage of the sheer extent of land to regroup and prepare to fight another day. Mithridates would not enjoy his regained crown for long.

Crassus, meanwhile, is said literally to have been counting his wealth, preparing for his own future in the east.[10] He was premature in his dreams of future riches, given that he was doomed to be the first of the 'triumvirs' to fall. All three men, perhaps not surprisingly, were destined to perish violently; Caesar would die as a casualty of civil assassination, while the other two would meet their deaths in the east. None of them would enjoy the solace of winning the death of a soldier in battle. In the case of Crassus, it would be said that he died in direct result of the curses that were heaped upon him by his enemies in Rome as he planned for his grand departure.

Crassus needed armed forces for his planned departure to take up his Syrian governorship; he had his sights set on major campaigns in Parthia to begin to rival the deeds of his colleagues, and that would take more money, materials, and men. The ancient estimation of the man is that his principal vice was avarice; the lust for wealth drove him to errors and miscalculations in other arenas. The curses allegedly uttered by the tribune Gaius Ateius Capito were not his only problem: the future Syrian governor was now about sixty years old, hardly the age generally considered suitable for a Roman general to aspire to a military command. Cicero alludes to the sorry sight of the man as he prepared to wind down the term of his second (and final) consulship, as he was engaged in settling his affairs before his long journey eastward.[11] In many ways he was chasing the legend of Pompey, and he would meet with no successes comparable to those of his younger colleague and rival.

The consuls who won the election season for service in 54 BC were Lucius Domitius Ahenobarbus and Appius Claudius Pulcher. Sometime students of this period are surprised to learn of the victory of Domitius; the man had seen a slave murdered before his eyes in the election cycle the previous year, and he had needed Cato to help defend him from street thugs and killers. The election of Domitius is a testament to how firmly established was the power of the 'triumvirs' by the autumn of 55. Again, despite their obvious stranglehold on political life, the republic was still functioning, if in an unhealthy and toxic way. In a sense it was a sign of the power of the three colleagues that they were not particularly concerned if Domitius served; Caesar, in particular, had secured his extension in the west, and Crassus was focused more or less single-mindedly on the east. Pompey was happy with his family life, and his new theatre was dedicated in August, complete with its temple in honour of Venus Victrix, the shrine of the victorious Venus.

The theatre of Pompey was one of the finest public works amenities that Rome had ever seen. Its dedication was accompanied by dramatic performances as well as wild beast hunts and other entertainments.[12] There were the usual criticisms from some quarters; the sight of elephant fights and other such exotic performances was not exactly sober and traditional in the old Roman estimation; one gets the impression from surviving evidence that Pompey himself was not necessarily a fan of the more excessive manifestations of Roman popular entertainment, but that he recognized the value of keeping the people amused. And amused they were, as by all accounts the August celebrations were well received by the majority of the population.

Pompey should not be thought of as not having a job comparable to Caesar and Crassus in this period. It is true that he had no prospects for military glory like those that could be attained by his colleagues. But he had Spain, and in a particularly appealing way: he would govern by legates. His trustworthy associate Afranius would go to Iberia together with Marcus Petreius; they would govern Spain as Pompey's ambassadors. Pompey, in other words, would be able to reap at least some of the benefits of overseas rule, while also remaining in Rome where he could both enjoy his family and be the 'triumvir' on site in the capital. It was a desirable arrangement for all parties concerned.

This is not to say that Pompey was enjoying popular favour without a heavy dose of recrimination. His efforts to levy monies to help to finance Crassus' proposed campaigns were met with much protest; there seem also to have been some rumours that the theatre complex was also the work of a freedman of Pompey, who put the name of the commander on the project so that there would be no criticism as to how a *libertus* managed to amass so much wealth.[13] While this later story is likely the product of gossip and the imagination of Pompey's adversaries, the reported negativity surrounding the Crassus initiatives is probably close to the truth, even if there must have been a fair amount of revisionism after he was killed, with people indulging in the time-honoured custom of claiming that there were 'signs' that doom was afoot.

Scholars and interested observers since antiquity have tried to make sense of what was happening in Rome in the second half of 55, at least with respect to the mood and attitude of various constituencies toward the actions of Pompey, Caesar, and Crassus. Cicero is a major player in this analysis, in no small part because of his voluminous correspondence and the windows it opens into the period.

It seems reasonably clear that the general mood was more positive in 55 than it had been in 59. Cicero seems open to admitting that perhaps the root of the problems had been that the *optimates* had been unfair to Pompey from the start. The situation in the east was a tinderbox in some regards (i.e., with respect to the Mithridates-Orodes civil war in Parthia), but in terms of what Gabinius had done both in Egypt and in Judaea, there was at least tacit admission in some quarters that Roman interests were being advanced. This is not to deny that there was major opposition to Pompey's agent: Gabinius would face serious problems as a result of his carrying out Pompey's will. Pompey had powerful opponents in Rome, both among the *optimates* and (less overtly) among those who were partisans of Caesar.

All things, considered, though, Pompey was not in a bad place as he prepared to leave consular office. Some have wondered if the election of Domitius were a sign of how Pompey's opponents constituted a formidable force. They did, but it was also a testament to Pompey's power that he was likely not particularly discomfited by the election. There is no greater evidence of power than when one is even-minded about seeing political and personal opponents in positions of authority.

A detached observer could still conclude with the same analysis as would have been valid in any recent year: Rome was at risk of another eruption of civil war. While relations between Pompey, Caesar, and Crassus seemed peaceful and probably were, all three men were in a position to disturb the equilibrium. Caesar's power was growing with every new victory in Gaul. Crassus was poised to achieve his own glory on the other side of the world. Pompey was both the most and the least dangerous of the three; he still had a name that roused significant applause and renown, and he had a powerful network of agents and clients ranging from Spain to the east, not least on account of his recent and lucrative grain commission.

The current situation was not one of long term stability; this had been true of Roman political life for some time. Few could remember a time in Roman life when there had been stability. Republican governance was not supposed to depend on the whims of a few men, but these same few men were also managing to keep the economy running successfully, to deal with foreign threats both real and perceived, and to avoid the renewed outbreak of civil war. Human nature being what it is, it is no surprise that all the players in the current drama wanted to be appreciated for what they perceived rightly to be deeds of outstanding service to the republic.

Major change also takes time and effort. Gabinius' deeds in the east were actually part of what Pompey had started when he received his Manilian commission. We have noted the longevity of many of Pompey's eastern initiatives; the durability of his settlement was founded on relentless and meticulous attention to detail. Pompey would have less power in the east once Gabinius was back in Rome, but he had also managed to secure Egypt, at least for the moment, as a major ally, personally indebted to him for the restoration of Ptolemy's crown.

The final months of 55 BC seemed to pass almost too quietly. Whatever the highhanded behaviour of Pompey and his colleagues at previous junctures, the election season for 54 passed quietly. Even in the worst day of the bullying and street violence practised by agents of this or that cause or strongman, there had been no proscriptions, no violence of the sort that was all too remembered from the days of Sulla. The consulship of Pompey and Crassus had also been a term that seemed focused less on governmental reform and memorable initiatives, and more on maintaining the line against the *optimates*, in particular Cato and his closest associates. Luca had been a conference about how to solidify authority and control through maintenance of republican machinery in 55, while preparing for the events to follow (this was especially true for Crassus in the field).

It is easy to overlook it, but the troubles in Spain in this period should not be underestimated. North-central Iberia in particular remained very much a frontier region of the republic's overseas territories; the situation there was at least intermittently just as violent as anywhere.[14] Pompey knew Spain better than most, but he had not pacified all of Iberia; the prosecution of the Sertorian War allowed for a significant degree of pacification to be imposed throughout the peninsula, but much remained to be done. It was a legitimate way to assign armies and resources to Pompey, even if the scene would be managed in large part through his aforementioned legates. Luca would have been a failure for Pompey had he not received armies, and in fact if anyone's military arrangements for 54 were questionable, it was Crassus': he was clearly preparing for war on the pretext of helping Mithridates, but the deposed Parthian king had been successful to an appreciable extent on his own, and it was not clear exactly what the endgame of Crassus' agenda was supposed to be, besides money and self-aggrandizement. Crassus owed thanks to Pompey: the same tribune (Gaius Trebonius) who oversaw the legal mechanism of approving Pompey's legions for Spain also managed to tack on, as it were, Crassus' commission.[15] One factor in the relative ease with which Crassus secured his fateful appointment was the fact that Parthia did represent a potent propaganda name to invoke to those worried about Roman business interests in the east: the border there had long been unstable, and overseeing Roman affairs there was a not entirely improbable enterprise by any means, even if Crassus was happy not to let any possible crisis go to waste.

Trebonius had faced the usual Catonian opposition. Pompey may very well have wished that he was the one being pushed through for a Parthian commission. That would probably have been better from a military perspective, though it was politically impossible. Crassus had waited too long without a chance to do more than oversee something like the Spartacus rebellion; he was too bitter at having had his glory even in initiatives like that threatened by the work of Pompey. Pompey may have wanted Parthia far more than Spain, but he had no realistic chance to insisting on such a point. His devotion to Julia in the period after her miscarriage should also not be underestimated. If any Roman potentate was ever devoted to his spouse, it was Pompey to Julia. It was more in accord with his uxorious temperament to manage Spain from afar than to commence a second eastern campaign.

It would be easy to look back later and to call the second half of 55 in particular a period of calm before the storm. It was miraculous the Pompey, Crassus, and Caesar had done all that they had done without a new war. For the moment, all eyes were focused on how the three would manage their respective affairs in the various corners of the Roman world.

Chapter Fifteen

54 BC

When Josephus says that Crassus plundered the temple in Jerusalem to raise more money for his eastern initiatives, it is easy to believe him.[1] The historian notes that he stole the treasure that Pompey had left undisturbed, thus drawing a clear contrast between the behaviour of the one 'triumvir' and that of his successor in the east. Crassus' reputation for greed preceded him, and while his avarice was likely being embellished by all commentators and writers on his life, his actions probably made their work all too easy.

Plutarch says that Crassus had been impatient to leave for the east.[2] Officially, his commission commenced with the new terms of office in December, at exactly the season of the year when sailing was generally avoided. Crassus was so eager to leave from Brundisium that he was heedless of the hazards of winter; he is said to have lost many ships in the crossing. When he met with King Deiotarus in Galatia, he made sarcastic remarks about the works the king was undertaking in the twilight of his years; the aged monarch is said to have retorted with a similar estimation of the sexagenarian Crassus. For Plutarch, the real blunder of Crassus was conceiving the idea that he could launch a major war in the east. While experienced in military affairs, what he was contemplating would have taxed the ingenuity and stamina of a Pompey or a Caesar, and Crassus had nothing approaching the veteran's record of either of his rivals in the field. Jealousy and a complex of inferiority, especially when added to his lust for ever more riches and treasure, would be more than enough to spell doom.

Caesar meanwhile was contemplating a second expedition to Britain after the less than impressive results of his first landing; this required constructing ships and supplementing his naval forces.[3] Before long he was destined to commence his long friendship with a man who would prove to be among the most loyal of his allies. Mark Antony had been serving in Alexandria, part of the military force left behind by Gabinius to protect the newly restored Ptolemy. Antony's next travels would bring him to Gaul, where he would continue his career under Caesar.[4] All things considered, it was all for the best that he did not venture east with Crassus; the day would come when Antony would have a chance to try his hand at visiting the Roman burial ground that Parthia became known for being.

Gabinius, for his part, was on his way back to Rome: his long and controversial service in Syria and, less legally, Egypt was at an end, and he must have known that he would face questions and judicial threats when he returned home; his solace would have been from knowing that his patron Pompey was exercising influence on the scene in the city.[5] Apparently when he first arrived back in Italy he was studious in trying to keep a low profile, which was exactly the smart thing to do in light of events.

The year 54 commenced as a relatively secure and happy one for Pompey, but it was destined to be marred by the greatest personal tragedy of his life.[6] Julia had already suffered a miscarriage, and we can only speculate on her health as the months passed. She became pregnant again, and died while in delivery or shortly thereafter. The child did not live long after her mother's death. Caesar thus lost a daughter in childbirth, and Pompey his beloved wife.[7]

Plutarch says that there was also immediately great travail in the city, for the eminently practical political reason that the death of Julia was interpreted as the end of the personal ties that were keeping Pompey and Caesar closely bound.[8] This is almost certainly another instance of reading too much into the event from the benefit of hindsight. Pompey and Caesar were rivals in 55–4, but they were in no serious danger of going to war with each other, with or without a marriage alliance. It would be easier to later think that 54–3 was the beginning of the end because of the deaths of both Julia in the one year and, more significantly, Crassus in the next. But Julia was a piece of the political puzzle, and not even the major one. Her death did not help the situation, especially when the day would come when her presence may well have helped to forestall a civil war. But the main consequence of the loss was a personal one for Pompey that cannot be underestimated. In many regards, he would never recover from the devastation he felt. That said, both Pompey and Caesar would acquire a no doubt well-deserved reputation for dealing well with grief; both men (especially Caesar in his campaigns) resumed their duties with alacrity, displaying traditional Roman values in how they continued in public life.

Pompey intended to have Julia buried at his Alban villa, but the people forcibly ensured that she would be buried in the Campus Martius.[9] It is unclear whether this was done at the instigation of Caesar's friends; Domitius is said to have opposed the deed, since it was forbidden to bury the woman in a sacred place without special sanction of law, but the force of the crowd would not stand for convention or precedent. Caesar had enjoyed some successes in Britain in his second campaign adventure there, but whatever joy he felt on account of having brought Roman arms successfully beyond where any predecessor had visited, it was shattered when he returned to Gaul and learned by letter of the death of his only legitimate child.

Julia's lost child was almost certainly a daughter, though there is some confusion in the tradition.[10] Pompey's two sons Gnaeus and Sextus remained a potent future source of pride for his family; Caesar, in contrast, had no such bulwark for a would-be dynasty. Crassus, for his part, had two sons. Publius Licinius Crassus had distinguished himself for service with Caesar in Gaul, before making the fateful transfer to go with his father to the east. Caesar, and indeed Cicero, seem to have thought quite highly of him. Crassus had another son of roughly the same age, Marcus; he also served under Caesar in the Gallic campaigns, and he would remain a loyal partisan of Caesar. Apparently less distinguished for military service than Publius, he was nonetheless a highly regarded member of Caesar's staff, and was certainly noteworthy for his constancy in devotion to Caesar as his patron.

Pompey's personal tragedy was exacerbated in 54 by the probably inevitable consequences of the work Gabinius had done for him. Pompey was no political amateur, no naïve practitioner of republican arts; he would have anticipated that Gabinius would face prosecution at least for Egypt, but he knew that he would be able to save his loyal legate from condemnation. He may have underestimated the degree of recrimination, however, that Gabinius would incur; in some ways the now returned governor would become the target for all the resentment that the 'triumvirs' had incurred. If anything, Gabinius' prosecution reminded anyone who needed the refresher that the actions of the Big Three could be more or less quietly resented, even in relatively quiet, successful times.

Gabinius was brought to trial for the illegal invasion of Egypt;[11] bribery from the offices of Pompey was able to secure an acquittal *in parte*: on the charge of *maiestas* or treason for having launched an illicit war, he escaped condemnation.[12] Gabinius' partial salvation in this regard may have been the result as much of his accomplishments as of anything else. There was legally no real question; he had acted *ultra vires* in bringing his forces to Alexandria (let alone leaving some of them there), and Pompey had had no authority to order Gabinius to restore Ptolemy. If Gabinius had incurred a significant defeat or loss, there is no question that he would have been in a position of far greater peril. He had succeeded in his mission with minimal losses, and so all was forgiven on this first charge once the republic continued to dispense justice with an eye to profit, not excluding bribery.

That said, Gabinius had amassed powerful enemies for other reasons. One of the problems was the simple matter that bilocation is impossible. When Gabinius had embarked on his Egyptian ventures, he was not in a position to oversee affairs in his actual province. There had been disturbances and losses of tax revenue; a governor is, after all, supposed to remain in oversight of his territory. One way of analyzing the situation was by the number of enemies one made on each charge. The treason charge was really an academic one, a philosophical question about how commanders are supposed to behave. Again, there had been no appreciable losses, and tremendous benefit.

The second charge that Gabinius faced was extortion: Ptolemy had, after all, paid his benefactors quite handsomely for his restoration. Here certainly Pompey pleaded for his friend just as strenuously as on the treason charge, and Cicero defended him as well. Some scholars have debated the question of why and how Cicero was induced to support Gabinius; there has even been the speculation that he was convicted for extortion because Cicero had deliberately sabotaged his defence by not doing a particularly good job on his behalf. The truth may be simpler: there was a strong undercurrent of desire to make sure that a message was sent to Pompey, not to mention Caesar and Crassus: what had happened in Egypt was outrageous in terms of republican sentiment and practise. Something had to give way, and there needed to be balance. And so the difference would be split, and Gabinius would be convicted on one charge at least.

There had also been a third accusation in the indictment, namely that Pompey's legate had engaged in illegal electoral activity in his canvassing for the consulship. This charge was dismissed; again, all three were deadly serious charges, and there was only need to punish him for one. Gabinius' property was confiscated, and he went into exile.

Gabinius' role in history was not at an end; he would be recalled one day, when civil war rendered his potential services useful once again. He must have been embittered by his experiences in 54, to say the least. He could not entirely blame Pompey, who tried very hard to save his loyal friend. One could argue that he had not paid enough attention to making sure that everything was secure in Syria while he was engaged in Egyptian affairs, though anyone would have found the task near impossible. Gabinius was a sacrifice, and a warning shot across the 'triumviral' bow.

The Romans were always quick to notice allegedly portentous happenings; omens and prodigies were dutifully reported. Pliny the Elder says that iron rained down from the sky in Lucania in the year before Crassus met his end in Parthia; the prodigy was taken as a harbinger of how Lucanian soldiers would perish with their ill-fated commander.[13] Even Gabinius is said to have faced troubles before he returned to Rome, because there had been one of the more severe of the Tiber's regular inundations, and people began to say that the heavens were furious at how the governor had behaved in restoring Ptolemy even when Sibylline oracles had warned that to do so would lead to trouble (in this case, at least for Pompey the Sibylline warnings, if accurately reported, were by no means incorrect).[14]

Even if one were inclined to put absolutely zero faith in such incredible reports, there was reason to worry about Crassus. He was overly eager, even to the point of hasty recklessness. Crassus' greed was actually not the real problem; merely being governor of Syria would have been enough to bring in rivers of money. The problem was that he was hungry to become a Pompey or a Caesar overnight.

For Pompey, 54 BC was a year to be reminded that where he was weakest was in the senate of Rome, and on the battlefields of Gaul. These reminders should not be taken to mean that Caesar was causing Pompey overmuch worry. There were sufficient problems with uprisings in Gaul to make Caesar think that he would need more soldiers sooner rather than later for the next year's campaign season, and when that day would come, he would call upon Pompey, and Pompey would respond graciously. The fact that Caesar felt that he could ask Pompey for help is noteworthy, as is Pompey's acquiescence; one could wonder if Caesar were trying to undermine Pompey by depriving him of new recruits who would otherwise go to him, or if he were merely seeking to balance out the forces between them insofar as possible. Certainly both men were keen to give the impression to friends and foes alike that they were united in the aspiration of doing what was best for the republic; all of Rome's field commanders were aware that foreign enemies were prone to slaughter all Romans, regardless of political affiliation or partisanship.

Rome continued to be a particularly violent place in the last months of 54. Plutarch mentions how the tribune Lucilius Hirrus eventually raised the suggestion that what was really needed was for Pompey to be granted dictatorial powers.[15] We cannot be sure of exactly when this would have been proposed; it would have had to have been either quite late in 54, or early in 53. The proposal was dead on arrival; there was the expected strong senatorial opposition, and we hear that even close associates of Pompey argued that he had no interest in such a position.

Likely this was no testing of the waters, but a genuine appeal for a restoration of order in the city. Recourse to street violence had been a consistent problem. The fact that it was a tribune who proposed the idea is likely key to understanding the proposal: even after the bad memory of Sulla as dictator, there was willingness from the unlikeliest of quarters for drastic solutions to the problem of civil disorder.

That said, there were reasons to suspect that Pompey had visions of a dictatorship. He had command in Spain, which he was exercising remotely. He had the authority of the grain commission, but his power within the city of Rome was constricted. This by no means suffices to support the claim that he wanted dictatorial powers. In time of growing instability, it is all too easy for people to start rumours about dictatorship.

More serious was the fact that the election season of 54 was a cesspool of intrigue and suspicious behaviour. Matters were destined to reach such a point of chaos and disorder that there would be no new consuls for the usual start of the terms of office in December. It seems that Gnaeus Domitius Calvinus and Gaius Memmius entered into a plot with the consuls of 54, by which via bribery there would be a deal struck to ensure that consulships would be awarded in exchange for the provinces and arrangements desired by the outgoing magistrates. Domitius Calvinus was destined to be a lucky man. By the time the dust would settle on the scandalous election season of 54, he would be a consul; he was also destined to be one of the most loyal of the partisans of Caesar and Octavian, thus guaranteeing that he would on the successful side of history.[16]

Memmius, his partner in electoral shenanigans (not to say crimes), is most famous today as the dedicatee of Lucretius' *De Rerum Natura* poem.[17] Exactly what happened in the attempted election manipulations, in particular the exact role of Memmius and his motivations at various junctures, is uncertain.

One economic consequence of the political troubles is certain: there were serious interest rate problems by the high summer of 54, because there was so much bribery afoot. Memmius seems to have been something of a fickle partisan; he was originally a close associate of Pompey, only to become more devoted to Caesar. Pompey was in favour of the consular candidacy of Marcus Aemilius Scaurus, his old colleague and his ex-wife Mucia's new husband. What seems to have happened is that Pompey found out about the bribery (it had to have been an open, or at least poorly guarded secret), and before long he was prevailing on Memmius to go to the senate to initiate the requisite investigations and legal manouevring to respond to the crisis.

So one mystery is how exactly Pompey managed to convince Memmius to betray the pact, and why. The idea that at least in part the whole thing was some scheme to pave the way for Pompey to become dictator is likely implausible. Consular elections were always fraught with potential problems, and both Caesar and Crassus were more than preoccupied with other problems; Pompey was in the best position to do something to see to the manipulation of elections. This was, in fact, probably one of the reasons it was appealing to the 'triumvirate' for him to stay in Rome; someone needed to be on the scene to see to triumviral interests. The fact that those interests were not always on the same page was part of what made the politics of the age so potentially explosive.

Memmius was Pompey's sister's nephew; the fact that he had gone from being more of a Pompeian to more of a Caesarian makes it easier to understand how he could go back to helping Pompey. Memmius, needless to say, incurred Caesar's displeasure by his willingness to expose the election plot; he would go to serve as prosecutor of Lucius Domitius Ahenobarbus. Domitius was also a Caesarian;

one of the problems of the age was that the most powerful men had multiple clients and partisans, and it was not always possible to keep them all satisfied.

54 BC was hardly to be the last year in which Memmius would be engaged in political and social scandals. All things considered, it is easy to imagine that the explanation for what was going on was that Pompey wanted supreme power. But this ultimately seems to be a facile analysis. Likelier is a combination of facts: Pompey was no friend to Domitius Ahenobarbus to be sure. As 'triumvir' on the spot in Rome, to have a major scandal under one's nose and not to do anything about it ran the risk of redounding to Pompey's discredit, a fact that was especially distasteful if Caesarians were to be the beneficiaries of the bad behaviour. In other words, forcing the exposure of the scandal gave Pompey some room to exercise moral *auctoritas*, and it allowed for the discomfiture of some friends of Caesar. The plot had been serious enough to cause high interest rates as early as July; by September, Pompey was probably convinced that it was time to put an end to the chicanery. It all ran the risk that he would be accused of aiming at supreme power, but that was an old charge with which he was all too familiar. And his friends were prepared to tell the truth: he does not want the job. Even when matters were so bad in Rome that tribunes were open to suggesting dictatorship for Pompey, the man of the hour was willing to increase his reputation by denying any interest in such an office. Perversely, Pompey's reputation would increase the longer the crisis dragged on; this should not, however, be taken as proof positive he orchestrated the mess.

There are mysteries, to be sure, about the political circumstances in Rome as the year drew to a close. The tribunes likely would have much to do in the immediate, but it is not entirely clear how the city would function. One gets the sense that Rome must have been a chaotic place as month after month progressed without consuls. Another problem is that we have no certainty as to what Pompey was due to be occupied with for the first months of the new year. It is entirely possible that he was busy with some duty related to the grain commission. Some have wondered if in fact he simply took some time away from public affairs: 54 was a difficult year for him personally in light of the loss of Julia, and the political blow of Gabinius in addition to the election scandals made for a stressful time. Likeliest is that Pompey was away on duties; whether this involved grain supplies or business in Iberia is uncertain. My personal suspicion is that he actually did visit Spain, at least briefly; it would have made sense for him to make an overseas visit to his provinces, even if in general his plan was to manage affairs from afar. He would be gone from Rome for the first half of the following year; Cicero, it seems, was at one point supposed to be away serving as his legate in some capacity. But it seems that in the end that never happened. Suspicious minds have taken Pompey's absence from Rome as further circumstantial evidence that he was the grandmaster behind the political chess game.

The Parthians, meanwhile, were aware soon enough of the foreign affairs news from the west; they knew that Crassus was coming, and that there were reports that he was hot for battle, ostensibly on behalf of Mithridates IV. It was the usual stuff of embassies and diplomatic communication to begin to send word that the position of Orodes II was simple: it would be best for the Romans not to become involved in the internal affairs of Parthia.

We may recall how Mithridates had been ousted from his kingdom, only to seek refuge with Gabinius. After the latter was on his way to Egypt, the deposed monarch did his best to launch strikes against his brother, even without Roman aid. He was able to make progress in Mesopotamia, conquering Babylonia. 55 BC had been the year of his victories, and there is numismatic evidence that he was still in authority in Seleucia in 54.

While our knowledge of the back and forth campaigns of the rival Parthian brothers is woefully incomplete (it was probably poorly grasped by the Romans of the time as well), it seems clear that Orodes was able to do reasonably well securing his position and launching counterattacks. Mithridates would eventually be besieged in Seleucia. On the west bank of the Tigris, Seleucia had been the first capital of the homonymous empire. Even after the capital was moved to Antioch, Seleucia had remained a major city.

Mithridates would not survive the year; captured by Orodes, he was slain, thus putting an end to the war between the brothers. The Tigris is the eastern of the two great rivers of the fertile crescent, its western counterpart, the Euphrates, had long been seen as the more or less understood line of demarcation between the Roman and the Parthian empires.

What went wrong for Crassus in the campaign season of 54?[18] He had struck successfully into Osroene, but while waiting for reinforcements to move into position so that he could proceed toward Seleucia, the Parthian commander Surena had enough time to dispense with Mithridates after his successful siege.

Crassus seems to have had a huge force of some seven legions.[19] His son Publius had come from Gaul with about a thousand Gallic cavalry; these figures do not include the initial help of some 6,000 cavalry from Armenia.

Scholars have poured much energy into debating and reflecting on the vicissitudes of the relationship between Rome and Parthia. There is little question that Crassus wanted a war; there was probably nothing that any Parthian monarch could have done to forestall it. What is less clear is what exactly were the limits of Crassus' intentions and plans. There had been a long and tedious history of border-related disputes, and the civil war had given a pretext for intervention of some kind.

Crassus was entering the east at a time when Pompey's settlement was still fresh news in the region. It seems fair to conclude that the Parthians had no interest in a war with Rome at least for the present. That said, one should not underestimate the violent intentions of Orodes, like Mithridates; both men were culpable for overthrowing their father Phraates, and Orodes was certainly not about to accept bullying from Crassus. The war that was about to commence could have been avoided in 54, and probably for some time thereafter; that said, a showdown between Rome and Parthia was in some ways inevitable.

Crassus moved quickly to bring significant forces into Mesopotamia. He was now clearly a potentially serious threat to Orodes, and emissaries were sent to remind him of the peace that had been agreed under Pompey. Our sources indicate that Crassus was quite dismissive of the delegates; we hear that he peremptorily told them that he would explain why he had entered Mesopotamia with an army in discussions at Seleucia – in other words, he made it crystal clear to the Parthian ambassadors that he intended not only a crossing of the Euphrates, but even to seize the city that not long before had been the final refuge of Mithridates IV.[20] This was nothing less than a declaration of war, and it is clear from our sources that the Parthians were outraged. We hear of one delegate showing the palm of his hand, and noting that hair would sooner grow on the palm than Crassus would arrive in Seleucia.

It was not a sporting or honourable way to do business militarily, but Crassus was insolent because he was both in a hurry and had no interest in negotiation. Probably the only thing that could have prevented a hot war was if the cold war had ended now, with Orodes making extensive concessions of territory and plunder.

The year 54 is in some respects one of the most mysterious and elusive in the period of the so-called First Triumvirate, and to a fair extent we know less about Pompey's doings in Rome (especially toward the end of the year) than we do about the dealings of Caesar in Gaul or Crassus on his eastern journey and after his arrival. The republic was in serious trouble, no doubt; this had been true for some time. There were no easy answers to the problems that did not involve ignoring human nature: there will always be men of extraordinary ambition and talent, and always a risk that such men will come into conflict with each other. For better or worse, the arrangements of Pompey, Caesar, and Crassus succeeded in keeping things relatively calm – emphasis on relatively. The patient seemed stable, with occasional bouts of serious relapse. Was Cicero correct when he mused that the *optimates* had made unnecessary trouble with Pompey in the past? Assuredly, though their fears were not entirely unreasonable in light of their experiences with his mentor Sulla, whose ghost had still not been exorcized by the tense close of 54.

Could anything have been done differently by any of the prominent men of 54, to improve the republic's overall health? Crassus could have given up his zeal for fighting, focusing more on determining a coherent national policy toward Parthia (in concert with his colleagues and the senate) that he would then go and implement, if necessary (as was likely) by force. Caesar could have done a better job of reining in the worst tendencies of his partisans in Rome, and could have cooperated on a British policy that could then open more lucrative economic opportunities in the west. Pompey could have focused entirely on the pacification of Iberia, and on managing the trade and economic routes in the Mediterranean, especially from Egypt; he could also have worked in close concert with other officials on public works and infrastructure. The senate could have taken the lead on promoting these efforts in particular, devoting itself primarily to helping to improve the mushrooming public network of roads, harbours, and other businesses that was inevitable with expanding borders. A healthier balance could have been sought between dividing responsibilities for certain spheres of influence, namely military and diplomatic endeavours on the one hand, and domestic and economic on the other. There was obviously significant overlap between these arenas of activity, but men like Pompey and Caesar demonstrated time and again that like Alexander the Great, they were better at foreign conquest and international affairs than they were when left with the comparatively tedious and even boring duties of civil administration. Crassus' problem was that he was a master at making money, but had never demonstrated any real acumen for the battlefield.

Certainly this is all oversimplified, and it may qualify as wilfully naïve given the aforementioned realities of human nature. The problem of ambitious commanders was the human equivalent of an ambitious republic that had never quite figured out the best way to try to run an empire in a republican fashion. Rome had sleepwalked into empire, and was soon to be in a nightmare from which she would find it difficult to awake.

Chapter Sixteen

The Three Become Two

The year 53 BC started out inauspiciously in Rome given the political uncertainty and turmoil. While the difficulties of the election season would be resolved, the answers to the problem would come so late in the year that it would be time to start a new election season, with more turmoil. In terms of the arrangements between Pompey, Crassus, and Caesar, 53 would be the year in which the so-called triumvirate would become a duumvirate. Crassus would be dead, which would allow for later critics (including artists like the poet Lucan) to claim that a significant element of restraint was removed from the equation: Crassus in this sense was viewed as a key factor in keeping Pompey and Caesar from clashing.

The relationship between the three constituted a classic case of triangular diplomacy; now three superpowers would be reduced to two, which carries with it a different set of problems, one no less deadly than when you had three.

Crassus' experience in Parthia has been the subject of frequent and detailed analyses, the conclusion of which is almost invariably that the commander was the victim principally of his own arrogance. We may commence the catalogue of his errors of judgment by considering the question of what should have been one of his most effective sources of help, namely the client kingdom of Armenia. Artavasdes II was in power, a son of Tigranes the Great who had assumed the throne in 55. Artavasdes was willing to help Crassus, in accord with the expectations of a client king. The new monarch had provided 6,000 cavalry for the initial attacks Crassus launched in Mesopotamia. Now he made a generous offer of some 10,000 cavalry and 30,000 infantry, though he had a condition, one that was effectively a recommendation: he wanted Crassus to launch his attack from Armenia.[1] His logic was that Armenia's mountainous terrain would render the Parthian's strong cavalry significantly weaker; they were trained and suited for desert warfare.

The problem with Artavasdes' plan was that an Armenian attack would take appreciably longer than a direct strike into Mesopotamia. Crassus had already launched such a strike across the Euphrates in 54, and his zeal for accomplishing his work expeditiously meant that he was not inclined to take some detour that would lead to a much extended campaign. Artavasdes, of course, knew exactly what he was talking about. He could do nothing to help Crassus with the problem of moving quickly, but then again no one could: the enemy was the Parthian Empire, and if Crassus hoped to win decisively and with lasting positive consequence for Rome, he could not hope to get the job done as if it could be done virtually overnight.

Crassus rejected the offer of help with such strings attached, and made plans to move directly against Parthia. Orodes II must have learned quickly enough what was going on with his enemies, and he would have been in a difficult position: he could not assume that Artavasdes would simply remain in Armenia. And so he developed a twofold plan of battle: he would send a strong force to Armenia to make sure, essentially, that Artavasdes would be no help to Crassus. And then he would have the main body of Surena's cavalry force to face the Romans.

Orodes was the superior strategist in this deadly game. Crassus seems to have assumed that the Armenians either would not be attacked, or that they would be able to handle any such strike on their own. Likely Orodes and Surena were not impressed with Crassus' actions in 54; he had not, after all, succeeded in saving Mithridates. It had actually been one of the rare occasions on which Crassus had been quite cautious about moving too far, too fast, and the commander deserves credit for not imperiling his army. But the price he would have paid was appearing less than formidable for his first appearance before the enemy. Crassus was no Pompey when it came to logistics; an argument could be made that he should have been better prepared for the campaign.

The Parthians were masters of desert cavalry warfare, and Orodes' commander Surena, like all qualified Parthian equestrian officers, was a master at harassment, of hit and run attacks. Surena did not have a force that was a match for Crassus in size; a major pitched battle was exactly what the Parthians were not interested in, at least for the moment. Indeed, Crassus probably had something like 40,000 men, mostly legionaries, alongside light infantry and cavalry. Surena only had about 10,000 men, of whom 9,000 were cavalry archers, and the rest cataphracts. This was an asymmetrical lineup, but it was also one that with extreme caution and care should have been in favour of the Romans.

Crassus had made a clear blunder in not listening to Artavasdes, and he made a second major mistake in choosing to listen to the man Dio identifies as King Abgarus II of Osroene.[2] Abgarus had been loyal to the Romans when Pompey's legate Afranius had been in northern Mesopotamia in 64 BC. Times were different, it seems. Allegedly, he was now working for Orodes. His game of switching sides was not destined to serve him well; ultimately he would be removed by Orodes when the Parthians decided to take over Osroene.

Plutarch refers to the same story, naming Ariamnes as the traitor, and identifying him as an Arab chieftain.[3] The basic trick was to lead Crassus into the desert, where he could be both deprived of supplies and water, and more easily surrounded on terrain where he would not be able to fight using the Euphrates as a defensive geographical feature (not to mention as a conduit of provisions). Festus blames 'Mazzarus' for the deception.[4] Few things are as dangerous as an untrustworthy guide; Abgarus/Ariamnes would play a major role in setting up the catastrophe.

June of 53 was to see the deaths of both Crassus and his son at the Battle of Carrhae.[5] It would be one of the most notorious and devastating defeats in Roman history. It would have been bad enough if Crassus had died in battle, but with either a victory or even a sustainable defeat. Carrhae was a smashing, decisive victory for Orodes; the Romans would lose some 20,000 men, with another 10,000 captured; thousands would manage to escape with their lives. Parthian losses are unknown, but it seems that they were quite minimal, all things considered.

By the time the dust settled, Crassus' quaestor Gaius Cassius would be in at least nominal charge of scattered survivor groups here and there, the militarily and economically strategic province of Syria defended by nothing more. One thing would be certain on the political stage: as soon as word of the defeat arrived in Rome, Pompey would be the inevitable comparand. He had spent years in the same general region, and he had never suffered anything remotely comparable. While it would not have been a fair comparison, some with long memories might have wondered if the Spartacus rebellion could have been solved even faster had Crassus not been involved in ending what had already been a campaign marred by failures. The reputations of both Pompey and Caesar rose appreciably once desert stories of defeat and disaster started trickling in to the Roman press.

Crassus' guide seems to have lied to him not only about directions/provisions, but also about the current state of preparedness of the Parthians. There was one final chance to change course: word reached Crassus' armies from Artavasdes, announcing the invasion of Armenia and asking for help.[6] This was Orodes' force that was intended to prevent any allied aid from assisting Crassus. Crassus did not move to assist the client king, since he was convinced that the Parthians could be smashed quickly and easily on his own front, and that then he could deal with the Armenian front.

Before long, Crassus had his wish: the Parthians were reported to be near. This was not exactly what the false report of disorganization had led him to believe would be the case, but it did fit with his plans to finish the war speedily. Two tactical errors followed: Crassus was urged by his general staff to follow classic Roman practise of infantry in the centre, cavalry on the wings. He was afraid, however, of being outflanked, and so he arrayed his men in a hollow square formation, which made it challenging to manouevre quickly. Given how outnumbered the Parthians were, even with cavalry better suited for the desert terrain, it is likely that the Parthians would have had trouble outflanking the Romans. The second error was timing: Crassus was advised to camp and to let his men rest; his son, however, pushed to strike hard and fast. Evidently he had come to share what must have been his father's disdain for the enemy, and/or the desire to move as quickly as possible.

Waiting would have run the risk of giving the Parthians the initiative, but again the relative sizes of the forces involved would have favoured the Romans. One cannot discount the possibility that Crassus did not have a good sense of just how significantly he outnumbered the enemy; in fairness to him, it is easy to criticize his penultimate decisions in hindsight; on the scene it may have seemed wiser to do as he did both in formation and in timing.

Surena, for his part, abandoned any plans for a frontal attack with his cataphracts, preferring to surround the hollow square and to use his cavalry archers as mosquitos. The trick was a classic Parthian tactic: you shoot, and when the harassed and irritated targets come too close to try to squat you, you fly away. Frustration and panic spread; the arrows keep falling. The Romans would have expected that eventually the arrows would run out, but if you know the area and have prepared for your campaign, camels start conveying a steady supply of arrows. The Romans literally found themselves caught in a shooting gallery, paralysed and unable to counter the horse archers. It was already a disaster, probably a fatal one. But graver problems loomed.

The classic Roman answer to nonstop, harassing missile fire was to 'send out a turtle,' the fierce, mobile armour trick of interlocking shields and forming a *testudo* of infantry. The problem is that the 'turtle' cannot deal effectively with close, melee combat; the Parthians had cataphracts as well as archers, and every time the Romans started engaging the one threat, the other could respond in a fine example of utilizing combined arms.

Eventually, Crassus realized the source of the arrows needed to be shut down. His son led a detachment of cavalry, including archers and infantry. Publius was supposed to deal aggressively with the horse archer problem and disrupt their rearming. It was, however, a case of sending a small force out to be separated and trapped. Before long, Crassus' son was cut off and without a chance against the combined threat of cataphracts and archers. While the sources indicate a brave stand, it must have quickly become apparent it was a last stand. Few would survive to be taken prisoner; Publius committed suicide by ordering his aide to slay him.[7]

Crassus apparently realized that his son's force needed help; perhaps the plan from the start had been to organize a two-front attack. He advanced his square as best he could, but the constant shower of arrows combined with the cataphract charges were impossible to combat. He fell back, hoping to regroup; he was near Carrhae, the modern Harran. Apparently the sight of his son's head on a spear hastened his retreat.

It is clear that the Parthians were shocked that they had won so decisive a victory; the fighting went on until nightfall. Crassus likely barely slept; the mood in the Roman camp must have been one of despair. The abandoned Roman wounded were killed as the Parthians advanced. And, the next day, the word came from Surena: he was ready to deal.

All things considered, the Parthians unquestionably made a reasonable proposal. They were prepared to make a settlement, with the Romans to cede all claim to lands east of the Euphrates. Crassus and his surviving force would be allowed to retreat to Syria unmolested. Crassus must have realized immediately that accepting such terms would in all likelihood have spelled the end of his career. He knew the extent of the disaster near Carrhae; in the span of less than thirty-six hours in the desert, he had destroyed Roman hopes of advancing to Seleucia, let alone to Ctesiphon. Cicero and others considered the war with Parthia worthy of denunciation, a war without cause. The war now seemed to have ended in total humiliation for the 'triumvir,' his dreams of rivalling Pompey and Caesar shattered.

Not surprisingly, Crassus seems to have resisted the call to negotiate with Surena. We hear of a threatened mutiny in his camp.[8] His men did not share his dreams of glory. They hoped to return to Italy; they had no interest in fighting and dying in the remote southeast of what is today Turkey. There were attempts at escape and a breakout; there were scenes of despondence and despair. But ultimately, the men saw no other palatable way to end the nightmare. They apparently forced Crassus to enter discussions with Surena.

What exactly happened as the crown and climax of all this is shrouded in some mystery. This much seems clear: there was a parley between Crassus and some of his officers and men on the one hand, and the enemy on the other. The Parthian side seemed to be pushing for a formal signing of a treaty, complaining (not without cause) that the Romans were not exactly trustworthy when it came to keeping agreements with the Parthians. Plutarch emphasizes that after a horse was brought for Crassus and he was mounted upon it, some of the groomsmen and other attendants were inciting the horse to move forward swiftly; evidently there was confusion on the Roman side as to what was happening, and attempts were made to stop them.[9] A scuffle ensued, not surprisingly; soon there was a skirmish between the small, even makeshift forces. Crassus was killed in the melee.

It was an ignominious end. Publius had died in battle as a suicide; his father was killed in what amounted to the confusion of a brawl in which it seemed as if the honour and dignity of the older Roman commander had been affronted. We hear stories of how molten gold was poured down his throat; we hear that his head furnished a prop for a performance of Euripides' *Bacchae*, in which Crassus starred as Pentheus.[10] Whether true or not, the oldest of the three 'triumvirs' had died in disgrace in the desert, his son with him.

One of the fortunate survivors of the Roman disaster was Cassius, Crassus' quaestor.[11] He seems to have been, at least for the moment, the ranking officer in Roman Syria. Carrhae would eerily echo Cannae in both name and scale of horror; Cassius, however, seems to have acquired a good reputation. There is some evidence that at the mutiny after Carrhae, voices were raised in support of replacing Crassus with his quaestor; Cassius silenced such cries, but his commander's death made the point moot. The Parthians, at least for the moment, had settled the question of whether the Euphrates was the border; they posed a threat (as usual) to Syria, which soon came under attack.

Cassius was the man of the hour in terms of rallying the routed Romans and restoring some sense of organization as he regrouped his forces. The Parthians had not expected to do as well as they did, and so they were not necessarily prepared to launch a full-scale invasion of Mesopotamia and beyond. And in future engagements, Cassius seems to have proven himself to be a more than capable commander. The Parthians are said to have regarded him as Crassus' superior in strategic and tactical skill, not without good reason.

Cassius would be busy after that fateful June of 53, working to defend Antioch and the province of the dead Crassus. He was destined to become far more famous for his involvement in the assassination of Caesar and the aftermath, but the name he made for himself came from his superlative conduct in singlehandedly saving the Roman situation in the east after Crassus' blundering had nearly paved the way for what some feared would be a complete collapse of the open fronts.

Parthia, it must be remembered, was not the most stable of empires. On paper and with the usual benefit of hindsight, it is all too easy to plot maps and strategies by which one could wargame Orodes to total victory in the east. Communications difficulties, internal dissensions, the inability of the Parthians to project power very well outside their borders, all conspired to make it clear that the Crassus defeat could be contained. There would be no great wave of Parthian power; there was a potential nightmare situation, but it could and would be contained. There was a disgrace to be avenged: the Parthians had Roman eagles, standards of the slaughtered armies serving as trophies of warning. But in some ways, an uneasy atmosphere of stalemate and draw slowly seemed to descend over the long front. There would be future reckonings, and the Parthian problem hovered as an omnipresent threat over Roman interests in the east. But fundamentally, things would remain relatively stable in the Roman east. The Parthians had illustrated that the Romans needed to try far harder to expand east of the Euphrates, and they had at least tacitly revealed again that they were not very good at projecting westward in any sustained way, or at the siege works needed to take cities.

The consuls who were eventually finally chosen for 53 were Gnaeus Domitius Calvinus and Marcus Valerius Messalla Rufus. These two officials would only be able to take office in July, and they would have a notably difficult time managing the elections for the following year. Chaos and disorder domestically had continued to prevail. Around the same time that order seemed to be restored, at least as evidenced by the belated accession of consuls and the renewed functioning of more or less normal republican political life, Pompey was back in Rome; he seems to have been a key factor in the amelioration of the situation, though exactly what he did or said is obscure. His enemies would continue to claim what they had alleged for years: he wanted to be dictator. The hollowness of their incessant accusations to this end would be remembered by some when Pompey would seem the best option to counter Caesar's dictatorial ambitions.

Plutarch's life of Pompey presents the picture of Cato essentially shaming Pompey into supporting normal governmental functioning, with the *optimates* in the position of compelling Pompey to allow for the resumption of normal constitutional life.[12] The questions raised by Pompey's behaviour in 54-3 have been endlessly debated. Certainly Pompey would have been annoyed if elections did not seem to be going the way he wanted, though if there were any notable manipulation afoot on Pompey's part, arguably it would have been to keep Memmius out of the consulship, and if this was indeed what was going on, he succeeded. Assuming the dictatorship would have invited immediate blowback from the Caesarians.

The fact that anarchy persisted even after the elections were finally held is no surprise; it was too late in the year, and people were already starting to worry about the offices for 52. As news reports arrived from the east, the Carrhae disaster would have caused even more unrest and disorder. Those enamoured of traditional republican order could reasonably claim that the fault for continued or renewed civil unrest lay with those who had delayed the elections; those who were inclined to highlight the problems with the current management of the machinery of republican government by the Catonians could note that even when they were given what they wanted, the *optimates* failed to quell disturbances. Both sides had legitimate arguments, and there were increasing calls for a public declaration that there was indeed an emergency, and that only a dictator could resolve the problems. Pompey, at any rate, was not interested in the job. Psychologically there must have been an element of *Schadenfreude* in at least some of his behaviour: as he watched the unfolding, multiplying travails of the republic both in Rome and in the east where once he had held sway as the Roman Alexander, he must have felt a certain understandable degree of smugness. Now they said that they needed him.

Some scholars of the late republic see one easy solution that had never been implemented thus far, at least not effectively or in anything other than a desultory fashion. Rome had no police force. The violence of the crowd, of the thugs hired by a Clodius or a Milo, were able to function essentially unchecked because there was no state-managed security force. No policemen made sure that you would not be murdered in the night. If you wanted bodyguards and physical protection, you hired them, making sure that your gladiators were ready to serve essentially as a private police patrol to safeguard your interests.

A police security apparatus would have improved the situation, but one of the glories of the republic also served to hamstring it. Innovation was looked upon with suspicion; there was an inherent distrust of anything that seemed novel. That said, policemen would not have solved all the problems of the day, and perhaps would have been easily bribed into becoming agents of this or that faction.

Caesar meanwhile was continuing to exercise his command with overall impressive results in Gaul. He crossed the Rhine for the second time, but was cautious about becoming literally entangled in forest warfare.[13] If there was a bright spot in foreign affairs news for 53, it was to come from the west; Caesar continued to be preoccupied with proving his military talent and organizational skills on a challenging front.

We have not spoken in some time of the notorious Clodius. His relationship with both Pompey and Caesar had deteriorated, largely due to his own behaviour and thuggish behaviour. When scholars speak of recourse to the aforementioned police solution to republican troubles, usually they are thinking about Clodius and his armed gangs. For the election season of 53, Clodius intended to stand for a praetorship, and his archenemy Milo planned to run for a consulship. Clodius had more or less avoided dramatic involvement in politics of late, probably in large part because for all his propensity for reckless behaviour, he was also staunchly devoted to self-preservation. Pompey's presence in Rome would have helped to keep him in check; when Pompey was out of the city for the first half of 53, it may have encouraged Clodius to feel more inclined to take a lead once again in urban politics.

Clodius' greatest strength was his ability to employ enforcers to work his will; it was also his greatest weakness, since as we have seen, it encouraged his opponents to play by the same rulebook. Clodius throughout had displayed exactly the worst sort of qualities of a republican politician; when we think today of similarities between certain aspects of Roman politics and the world of organized crime, Clodius' methods factor prominently in the equation. If the election season of 54 had proven anything, it was that if you could not guarantee a win, the next best thing was to delay the elections. If Clodius were not able to prevent Milo from securing a consulship, better that things be as delayed as possible; conversely, if Milo felt that the election would not go in his favour, the best thing he could do would be to replicate the chaos of the previous cycle.

Clodius tried every trick to keep Milo from having any chance at his electoral dreams. He raised the argument that his enemy was not allowed to run for office in the first place, given his serious debts; Cicero needed to defend Milo against the accusation. Mark Antony was a candidate for quaestor, and the future fervent opponent of Cicero was in the present circumstances on the same side as the orator: he assailed Clodius even to the point of violence, driving off the would-be praetor.

Milo's opponents for the consulship were Publius Plautius Hypsaeus and Quintus Metellus Scipio; needless to say, whatever differences they may have had, Clodius was doing all he could to support them: the enemy of my enemy is my friend.

As usual in Roman politics, matters were exceptionally complicated. The patron-client system had undeniable benefits, but we have noted that problems were prone to emerge when there were conflicts between men who had rival claims on one's patronage. Pompey had good reason to favour Milo. But he had other demands on his support, in part the result of the June disaster in the desert.

Crassus' son Publius had been married to Scipio's daughter, Cornelia. We are not sure of exactly when, but perhaps before the end of the year, Publius' widow was married to Pompey. Some would say that it is likelier that the union was after Pompey entered into what would be his extraordinary, 'sole' consulship in 52; the evidence is inconclusive. Certainly the marriage has been the topic of much analysis. Cornelia was young and reputedly lovely; she was also something of an intellectual, knowledgeable about music, geometry, and the arts.[14] Politics aside, nobody could have faulted Pompey for pursuing the marriage.

But politics were important, indeed even more so in the wake of the deaths of both Crassus and Julia. It seems that Caesar was eager for a renewal of a nuptial alliance between their families; he proposed that Pompey marry Octavia, his sister's granddaughter.[15] Pompey decided against that marriage offer, and chose Cornelia.[16] As always, we must be careful of reading too much into events from the benefit of hindsight, even as we must consider the events that preceded the breakdown in relations between Caesar and Pompey.[17] Further, we must consider another complication that made it difficult to accept a proposal to marry the Octavia who would prove to be so prominent in later history.

Born around 66 BC, she was the full sister of Octavian, the future Augustus. Her stepfather, Lucius Marcius Philippus, had overseen her marriage to Gaius Claudius Marcellus. Caesar's proposal that she marry Pompey would require a divorce, something that admittedly was not a particularly difficult problem in the heavily politicized world of prominent Roman marriages. But it seems that the happy couple did not want to divorce. Coupled with the likelihood that Pompey was attracted to Cornelia, it becomes easy to see why he would reject Caesar's plans.

One additional detail has been introduced into consideration of the Cornelia marriage: at some point, Pompey's older son Gnaeus was married to Claudia, the daughter of Appius Claudius Pulcher. Pompey was now linked with some of the most venerable of the old, aristocratic families of Rome.

What was he thinking? Roman marriages were almost always political first and anything else a more or less distant second. That said, Pompey had been noted, even seriously criticized, for his uxorious relationship with Julia. He was clearly devastated by her death, and we should not discount the possibility that Cornelia seemed to him to be the one girl who could distract him and provide solace in his depression. He may genuinely have preferred Cornelia to all others, and he may have decided that marriage alliances were not needed to maintain the peace with Caesar.

Further, to the degree that Pompey had long felt resentment at being unappreciated by the *optimates*, both his marriage and that of his son may have seemed all too natural in a period where some voices, at least, were calling for Pompey to be the man of the hour to save Rome from domestic (if not foreign) perils. Did Pompey crave approval from the old guard aristocracy? Certainly. Did he enjoy feeling needed, as if he were at last recognized as the reliable hero of the republic? Assuredly.

Pompey made his decision; he would marry Publius' widow. Cornelia would be Pompey's last wife; she would be destined to be remembered for how she would be all too privy to his sad end in Egypt. All things being equal, one should not read overmuch into the choice; Pompey was likely more interested in soothing his weary soul in the wake of the loss of Caesar's daughter, than in seeking to give a sign that he was distancing himself from Caesar.

Cornelia was born around 73; the significance of the fact that she was only about three years younger than Julia should not be discounted. Pompey may have been chasing the ghost of his lost wife. And even if a psychiatrist would not diagnose it so, he may simply not have wanted to marry a mere girl who was clearly a political pawn, rather than a lovely replacement for Julia who also brought him closer to aristocratic families whose favour and support he craved.

Whatever the romantic and wistful thoughts of the aging conqueror, the usual political (not to say battle) lines were being drawn, and certainly the greatest instability would have been felt from the armed gangs that regularly accompanied both the would-be praetor Clodius and the would-be consul Milo. It was a situation ripe for the intervention of fate.

Matters reached a head on 18 January, 52 BC.[18] The mood must have been tense: the city had been plunged for a second year in a row into electoral chaos. What happened on that January day was inevitable, some might say. One could well be surprised that nothing of the sort had happened years before.

Clodius seems to have been travelling along near Bovillae, a few miles outside of Rome. He was accompanied, as usual, by his entourage of gladiators and bodyguards, but he seems to have been more lightly defended than usual. At some point along the road, he encountered Milo, who was also accompanied by his gang of thugs. The two sides seem warily to have made their way past each other; certainly there must have been tense words, sarcasm and insult, threats and bluster.

Somehow, a scuffle erupted, and soon a violent melee. It was a street battle between the rival gangs; Clodius was injured and had to be taken away to a nearby inn to rest and be treated. It seems clear that Milo's gang had won the battle; Clodius' defenders were largely slain or forced to flee. We cannot be sure how serious Clodius' wounds were. If he had survived, he would have been able to tell dramatic stories about how he had been nearly murdered by the would-be consul. It would have been a political and propaganda nightmare for Milo. It seems that quickly (for time was obviously of the essence), he made the decision to send his gladiators to finish the job. Milo clearly decided that he was at risk either way; he was in legal jeopardy no matter what happened. The choice he settled on was to see to it that Clodius never gave another speech.

Milo was no fool; he realized that he now faced enormous challenges. Clodius' body was soon discovered, and news did not have far to travel. Clodius was now a martyr to his devotees; Milo could be denounced as a murderer.

The death of Clodius brought about the expected political turmoil. Pompey was no particular fan of Clodius, but he was also not a supporter of Milo's bid for a consulship. Clodius had many enemies, but he could still could on significant support, even beyond the grave; in some ways, death made him even more popular.

The situation for Pompey was a precarious one, whatever he chose to do. This was clear both to him and to partisans of both factions; everyone was eager to see Pompey lend his powerful support and sheer *gravitas* behind their cause, even apart from practical help he could provide. The tribunes had been stirring up the people, which one imagines did not take much effort; Milo, after all, had resorted to street thugs no less than Clodius, and there were those neutrals who would have been happy to hear that Milo was dead alongside his ardent enemy. The body of Clodius was burned in the senate house, and such was the eruption of anger, mob violence, and tribune-sanctioned chaos that the very building was allowed to catch fire, such that its smouldering wreck could serve as the macabre stage for the traditional requiem repast.[19] This was the Curia Hostilia, which was to be replaced by the Curia Cornelia.

Milo's house was an obvious target for the incendiaries, but the man who had ordered Clodius' killing had his own friends, and they defended his residence as street battles spread. Milo was forced into hiding, and increasingly the senate was full of voices calling on Pompey to take a prominent role in resolving the latest eruption of chaos.

A figure who emerges as a significant player in this period is Marcus Aemilius Lepidus, the future triumvir with Octavian and Antony.[20] Lepidus was elected as *interrex* by the senate, with the hope that he, the tribunes, and most of all Pompey could arrive at some plan to resolve the unrest in the city. Lepidus would prove to be one of the most interesting men of his age; in a sense it is fitting that he enters our historical consciousness at a time of near-anarchy. Like Milo, soon enough Lepidus would experience the threat of having his house burned down; it was one of the classic signs of the troubled times.

At some point amid the mess, Pompey must have realized that he was likely to be asked again to consider taking some office to help to fix things. Caesar had wintered in Cisalpine Gaul, and his military and organizational work was by no means at an end; he was in no realistic position to swoop in to the capital to help resolve things, even if he were so inclined. Pompey had rejected dictatorship; his enemies would continue to make the cynical argument that his refusal was actually aimed at instigating exactly the sort of chaos that had ensued.

Milo, needless to say, was no less busy than the partisans and clients of the dead Clodius. As soon as arrangements for his safety seemed stabilized, he began to work on restoring his reputation. One thing that seems to have helped him is the fact the burning of the Curia Hostilia did not go over well with public opinion at large; it was seen as an affront to the very republic even by those inclined to want to see Milo condemned. The word was spread, too, that a plot against Milo had been formed by Clodius; the man was said to be acting, in any case, legitimately in the face of mortal threat. Conversely, voices were raised on the Clodian side, going so far as to argue that the murderous Milo actually was plotting against even Pompey, who had after all proven quite unhelpful to him in the consular elections.

The senate seems to have taken control of the situation by ordering the *interrex*, the tribunes, and (above all, we might think) Pompey to respond to what was clearly a crisis that imperilled the safety of the republic. The *senatus consultum ultimum* gave the authority to raise troops for the restoration of order. Pompey was the obvious man to do this since he had proconsular authority, even if he was supposed to be in charge of Spain and not handling civil order and chaos in Italy.

What followed was in some ways a repeat of the past. First and foremost, Pompey was a master of levying soldiers. He was able to form a powerful personal bodyguard from the start, moving forward with raising an impressive 'peacekeeping' force. Pompey's name was enough to inspire men, especially when the mission could be advertised as something noble like the preservation of the republic from harm.

Pompey was able to meet with the senate; we are told that the senate met in the portico of his theatre so that the rule would not be broken about someone with proconsular authority entering Rome proper (no doubt the burning of the Cura Hostilia rendered senate meetings a more complicated affair anyway). Pompey took the side of those claiming that his life was in danger; whether he believed it or not is impossible to determine. Rome had proven to be an exceedingly dangerous place; there is no question that civil disorder and chaos had progressed to a frightful state of constant upheaval.

What began to be considered by the senate at this juncture was, at least from the start, more of the same: should Pompey be named dictator? That question was always followed by the matter of whether Pompey would accept the job; he had steadfastly refused it. We cannot underestimate the residual loathing of the title and the office on account of the experience of Sulla. Caesar in distant Gaul was a factor, no doubt, but the simple fact is that *dictator* was an odious, highly problematic word that gave its bearer tremendous authority, but at a high price. And that price was too high for Pompey to pay.

That said, Cornelia's new husband must have taken great satisfaction in being considered for such an office even by *optimates* who not so long before would never have permitted even discussion of the idea. The solution that would be arrived at was a clever one, even if like most clever ideas in this period it did not bode well for the health of the republic in the long term.

Pompey would serve as sole consul for 52 BC.

Chapter Seventeen

Consul a Third Time

Could anything be more emblematic of the dying of the republic? The whole reason why there were two consuls was to avoid monarchy. The kings of Rome had been replaced by consuls in 596 BC so that no one man would have supreme authority. The republic could envisage having a dictator in time of emergencies, but there was absolutely no provision for having one consul. This was a charade: clearly Pompey was the dictator, in all but name, some would say. It is proof positive of how bad the situation was in Italy that this was able to happen without another civil war.

Was Pompey given over to vanity? Did the idea of being sole consul appeal to him, given that it was a unique distinction? Perhaps, given human nature. Caesar would have enjoyed the same honour; few Romans could have honestly said otherwise about their own ambitions. But even the Catonians were willing to see Pompey as sole consul.[1] They could argue that the machinery of the republic was continuing to function, even if the motors were making telltale signs of terminal struggle.

The Caesarians were no doubt feeling all too aware of the trade-off of military glory. Were Pompey in the east fighting Parthia, and Caesar exercising a remote proconsulship from Rome, perhaps he would be the one levying troops and enjoying a unique office. Pompey, to be sure, enjoyed once again being called upon to save the state; this was like the grain commission, just on a grander scale. And he had armed forces.

There were other legal problems. Pompey was still proconsul, which made it impossible, strictly speaking, to be consul. He was also supposed to wait a decade after his last consulship; three years between terms was illegal. These matters were comparatively trivial; the real issue was serving alone. And yet that is exactly what happened.

Plutarch emphasizes some of the oddities of the process by which Pompey received his newest job.[2] Bibulus was the one who proposed it; he was by no means a Pompeian ally, but he is said to have argued that either Rome would be saved from its current anarchic state, or it would be a slave to its strongest citizen. It was a craftily worded proposal, one which was rendered all the more effective when Cato was willing to stand up and say that while he would not have been willing to be the one to suggest it, now that someone else had proposed that Pompey should serve alone, he would support it. The Catonian argument was that Rome had become a virtually antinomian society, and that Pompey was the one man who could probably fix things, if anyone could. It is possible that implicit in all of this was the conclusion that Pompey would be better than Caesar, if there had to be one person in charge.

Ultimately it was decided that the novel scheme would be approved, with the stipulation that Pompey could pick a colleague after two months. The 'two months' figure allowed for a hint of a reminder that the situation was not only urgent, but also extraordinary. Pompey was supposed to get the job done with his characteristic efficiency, and the message was being sent that this was not the 'new normal.' The idea that Pompey should pick his own colleague no doubt reflected how contentious the last two election cycles had been.

Having such immense power means that one needs to do the job, and Pompey did. He was able to put an end to mob violence by using his levied troops as policemen; they were allowed in Rome, after all, since they had been raised specifically for the purpose of maintaining the peace. And the courts and legal machinery were to be used to prosecute malefactors. Milo was, not surprisingly, at the head of the list of those to be charged.

We have Cicero's famous defence speech, the *Pro Milone*; it is a common choice for Latin students of his oratory, given its rhetorical splendour and fine display of the art of prose composition.[3] The speech was never actually delivered; when Cicero rose to make it, he was so incessantly and severely harangued by the crowd that he was unable to continue. In the end he would be consigned to sending a copy of the oration to Milo in exile.

Probably from the start, however, there was little realistic chance for Milo to escape condemnation; no doubt for some it seemed fair that on the one hand, Clodius should be dead, and on the other, Milo should go into exile. He was condemned, apparently by thirty-eight votes to thirteen. It was not exactly a close call, but it was a reminder both of the disdain for Clodius and the favour for Milo that prevailed in some quarters.

All things considered, Pompey handled the affairs of his latest commission with the same acumen and alacrity that characterized his earlier work, from dealing with Sertorius to evicting pirates. And there were no proscriptions, none of the ugliness from the Sullan dictatorship that had rendered many in Rome so fearful of the man still remembered as having been a 'teenage butcher.' 52 BC was a year that saw more than its fair share of legal cases and judicial processes, but people were not being executed with a show trial, if that. Pompey might have laboured long under the suspicion that he was a dictator at heart, but he was certainly going out of his way to prove that he was not his mentor Sulla.

Milo departed for exile in Massilia.[4] Marcus Saufeius was another of the noteworthy targets of the prosecutions of the period; he had been the one responsible for leading the attack on the tavern in Bovillae that resulted in Clodius' death.[5] Despite repeated effort to convict him, he was able to escape condemnation by the narrowest of margins. Milo's supporters were by no means the only men prosecuted during the legal actions of Pompey's third consulship; Sextus Clodius was charged. Clodius' son was blamed for the fiery disaster at the senate house; he was the one who had had his father's body brought there, and it was he who had stirred up the crowd and caused a riot. Gaius Memmius was successfully prosecuted for corruption.

It was inevitable that the Caesarians would be uncomfortable with Pompey's holding a sole consulship. Further, there were those just as suspicious of Pompey as of Caesar, or more so; even apart from such potential objectors and opponents, the price of sole power is that your every move is scrutinized.

Pompey was criticized for what was seen (not unreasonably) to be his heavy-handed interference in some legal cases, notably the prosecution of his new father-in-law, Quintus Caecilius Metellus Scipio. Plutarch mentions how hundreds of jurors were invited to a meeting with Pompey, in what amounted to a clear instance of interference in the judicial process; the prosecutors eventually gave up the case, when they saw Metellus being escorted by jurors.[6] The message had been given: Pompey's new marriage relation would not face trial for corruption.

Caesar, meanwhile, made the most of 52 BC in Gaul. His extensive work was continuing with impressive success, despite appreciable challenges from revolts and uprisings; Mark Antony was in his service as quaestor, and we can be sure that their friendship continued to develop as they worked closely together in making a name for Caesar on the field and in foreign diplomacy. The problems that Caesar faced with uprisings in Gaul were directly related to the chaos in Rome; while his holdings and achievements would likely have been at risk even without the anarchy in Rome, it is clear that the news that filtered in to the Gallic tribes about violence and disorder in Caesar's capital spurred them to greater provocations and more reckless acts.

In the east, Gaius Cassius continued to be occupied with keeping the Parthian threat at bay, and with managing Syria in the aftermath of the Crassus disaster. To be sure, Rome had problems enough between Gaul, Spain, and Italy; if Pompey would have preferred to go to the east to deal with Parthia, it was not realistic. This was especially true once it seemed clear that the Parthians were not planning a major invasion; they seemed content on consolidating their power east of the Euphrates. That situation could not be expected to last long, and there would be strikes into Syria. But it seems that the Parthians were now the ones who underestimated the Romans; they did not send nearly enough forces, clearly expecting that they would meet with only token resistance. Cassius was more than competent in driving them back; again, the day of reckoning seemed to loom, but for the moment, the Romans were maintaining a stable front.

Bibulus, meanwhile, was destined to be Crassus' gubernatorial replacement in Syria.[7] In 52, the ex-consul's most historically significant deed was that he had proposed the Pompey consulship. Bibulus would not be appointed to his new post, however, until 51. The reason for this relates directly to what would become one of the greatest sources of tension and trouble in the republic, a problem that would contribute directly to the eruption of civil war.

Essentially, Pompey and his supporters claimed that they were interested in eliminating major sources of election cycle corruption and bribery. Two major issues were at play here. There had long been a legal expectation that a man running for office should actually be present in the city to stand for election, as opposed, for example, to entering one's candidacy from Syria, Africa, Spain, or Gaul. Stricter enforcement of this law would qualify as a modest reform in the eyes of some; the republic was simply doing what it had always been supposed to be doing.

The other issue was the question of time limits on taking office. One of the major sources of scandal and bribery came from office holders like consuls, or consular candidates, seeking to guarantee securing proconsular appointments. The game was one of picking which province one wanted to secure when one's term in office expired. Provinces had become commodities, able to be bought and sold by ambitious consuls.

The law that had been proposed by the consuls of 53 and enacted in 52 centred on a five-year delay. If you were consul, you would need to wait five years before you could be appointed governor of Syria, for example. The idea was that no lender of money would be willing to help you with your bribery schemes if they knew that they would be waiting as long as six years; further, it meant that the appointment of provincial governors would now truly be a senatorial prerogative. The days of bartering for plum appointments were, in theory, to come to an end.

It was obvious that Caesar would be affected by these initiatives. Even in a world where Pompey was acting out of the purest of republican intentions, eager to see an end to the constant corruption and political turmoil, there was no way to avoid deeply offending Caesar, perhaps even risking a civil war. The cure could not be worse than the disease.

One name that would be weighing heavily on Caesar's mind was Aulus Gabinius. When he had returned from Syria, he faced prosecution for his management of his governorship. Now it was true that the main impetus for the charges was the Egypt intervention that Pompey had orchestrated; Caesar's situation in Gaul was very different from Gabinius' in Syria. That said, his enemies could have easily tried to trump up charges against him from his five-year commission. And, too, Caesar had the threat of charges stemming from his conduct in his first consulship, the so-called year of Julius and Caesar. Regardless of the validity of any of the charges, Caesar would then need to defend himself, and depending on the vicissitudes of Roman political and judicial life, he did run the risk of conviction and exile, which would spell the ignominious end to his career.[8]

The only way to avoid the risk of being prosecuted was not to return to Rome as a private citizen. Coming back to a consulship would shield him from any prosecution peril, but it was impossible given his absence from Rome during election season, not to mention the whole issue of waiting five years. Caesar was in serious jeopardy; he would be leaving a lot to uncertainty if he allowed matters to take their own course. There was much more, too, than simply the question of legal vulnerability. There was also the question of the ratification of Caesar's settlement in Gaul, just as Pompey's eastern initiatives had been the subject of legal delay, question, and controversy.

Caesar was busy dealing with Vercingetorix and the serious revolts that occupied so much of his time; news from Rome must have added to his anxiety.[9] While some students of this period have been convinced that Pompey was actively working against him, the record does not sustain the charge. The prejudice of hindsight is no friend to sober, dispassionate analysis of Pompey's actions. On the matter of running for office in absentia, Pompey actively sought to secure a specific exception to allow for Caesar; the idea was that the law would be honoured moving forward, unless a specific name were approved for an exception. Caesar would be able to run for consul even from outside Rome. In the meantime, his preoccupation with Gallic affairs was demanded by circumstance; September of 52 would see the great siege of Alesia, the last major campaign between Gauls and Romans.

The scenario would then be this: Caesar would stand for election as consul while still in his proconsular territory; he would be able to campaign in absentia. Then he would serve as consul, for the usual term of a year. At the end of that term, he would then be a private citizen, and subject to prosecution. Essentially, he would be buying himself a year of immunity from prosecution; the only way to extend the immunity would be to move immediately from his consulship to another provincial command.

That extraordinary concession was not envisaged by either Pompey or the *optimates*. In fairness, Pompey may well have been considering the comparison to his own situation when he had returned from the east. Pompey had not received any guarantee of anything comparable to what was being prepared for Caesar. One of the main reasons for Pompey's feeling discomfited, bitter, and resentful was that he felt he had been shabbily treated after he had done so much for the republic. Caesar was certainly being treated far better as he began to consider life after the Gallic campaigns.

Things were not so simple, however, even about the question of standing for office in absentia. Caesar had thought of this in time for his friends to make sure that the college of tribunes was supportive of his plan to stand for office from abroad.[10] When Pompey's legislation came forward, it was noted that the regulation did not accord with the previous legal manouevring on Caesar's behalf. And so Pompey added a hastily-composed codicil, so that the legislation would honour the exception made for Caesar. Now Rome was a highly litigious society; last minute alterations invited legal challenge, and it was not entirely clear that Pompey's addendum carried the force of law.

Let us take a step back, to review key dates and to try to discern where Pompey's mind was regarding Caesar. In 59 BC Caesar had been given his proconsular command (the *lex Vatinia*); the term was for five years, expiring in March of 54. The Luca conference was held in 56; in 55, Pompey and Crassus were consuls, to be followed by their own five-year commands in Spain and Syria respectively (the *lex Tribonia*). While serving as consuls, Pompey and Crassus extended Caesar's command (the *lex Licinia Pompeia*); presumably this would have taken Caesar through to 50 BC. No successor would be appointed by the senate before 1 March of that year. Crassus was killed in June of 53; Pompey is appointed sole consul in 52. That same year, the tribunes passed their law allowing Caesar to stand for consular election in absentia; that would allow him to stay in Gaul to finish his work, and still be able to move seamlessly into consular office. Pompey was willing to accept this exception to the usual policy about requiring candidates to run in person.

This breezy summary belies a serious problem that continues to arouse scholarly debate: the exact duration of Caesar's extension of his proconsular *imperium*. If the Kalends of March of 50 were the date after which it would be appropriate to consider a replacement, it makes sense that it was a five-year extension. You could in theory have a replacement selected after that date; then Caesar would leave office when the new governor arrived. If your first five-year term ran from 59 to 54, then any new five-year term would run from 54 to 49. The extension came in 55, and spoke of March of 50 as the date after a replacement would be made. The question came down to whether the second period commenced after the original expiration date, or after the renewal? One year would make a significant difference if you were worried about legal exposure.

To state matters more simply, ideally Caesar wanted to run for election in the autumn of 49, and he wanted no gap between Gaul and assuming his consulship.

Pompey clearly wanted to fix the Roman election/political corruption problem. Allowing Caesar to stand for office in absentia as an exception was not a problem for him. Was he at some point careless, having forgotten what the tribunes had already legislated for Caesar's benefit? Certainly this is possible. What makes Pompey's conduct more suspicious is that he made sure to see to it that his own proconsular authority in Spain would be extended, essentially giving himself another four- or five-year term (our sources disagree here). He was also to receive 1,000 talents annually, to help to support his overseas troops.

Pompey was in no mood to give up having legions while Caesar still maintained his. That said, he was clearly exposing himself to a charge of hypocrisy. Dio states that Pompey was hypocritical both in giving himself an extraordinary extension, and in allowing Caesar to run for consul in absentia.

In the background, Pompey the consul would have been hearing from angry Caesarians on the one hand, and bitter Catonians on the other. The Caesarians wanted their man to incur no risks; the Catonians wanted Caesar to be a private citizen for that vulnerable window. What was really going on in Pompey's mind? For years now, extraordinary arrangements had been made for Caesar and for Pompey, as for Crassus before his death. The unofficial 'triumvirate' had become an unofficial duumvirate. The republic was still functioning, though most would call it dysfunctional. Pompey was trying hard to change that, in cooperation with the senate. Still, extraordinary measures continued. Making sure that he would retain his proconsular *imperium* was extraordinary. Making sure that Caesar could stand for the consulship without being in Rome was extraordinary. There was always opposition to such measures. Giving Caesar the right to stand for office from abroad, *and* giving him a guarantee that he could leave office at the end of 49 and proceed to a province or provinces, was almost certainly a bridge too far for some; the Catonians would never have supported it.

We have noted that Pompey had known moments of uncertainty and vulnerability after major achievements and high office. Probably this fact has been underestimated in appreciating his mood in 52. As for Caesar, there was another thorny issue, though one that perhaps would have been among the easier problems to resolve. A man was supposed to wait ten years before serving again as consul; legally, Caesar needed to wait until 48. This question must have seemed an absurd one given Pompey's current status as someone who not only had not had to wait, but who did not even have to brook a colleague. Further, the calendar could work this way to Caesar's safety: if no replacement were appointed until after March of 50, given that the senate would appoint one of the consuls for 49, Caesar would be safe. That is, were it not for the law about a five-year waiting period between consulship and provincial appointment.

Politically as well as militarily, Caesar was still very much burdened by an overflowing agenda. The pacification of Gaul was not yet complete. Caesar had done very impressively, but the job was not finished. He would be in Gaul for all of 52 and 51, and at least into part of 50. If he then served as consul from December, he would remain in office until December of 49. To make a guarantee now would be a promise for well over three years in the future. Of course a Caesarian could claim that a four-year extension of Pompey's command in Spain would extend until 46, if it were calculated from its current expiration date. And what business had Pompey to serve simultaneously as sole consul and as proconsul? Already there were serious exceptional grants of privilege.

In July, probably, of 52 Pompey ended one of those anomalies, and restored 'normal' republican functioning, at least in theory. He took a consular colleague – his father-in-law.[11] No doubt there was annoyance if not more or less quiet seething from some; Pompey had defended Cornelia's father to an inappropriate degree in his hour of legal peril, and now he had been selected as consul. Forget elections and legalities of how to run for office; this was vintage nepotism.

Some may have thought that two consuls were still better than one. Some of Caesar's friends had suggested that he should serve with Pompey. This would have been exceedingly difficult, though given that so many exceptions to custom and law had already been made, the idea was not so crazy.

One thing is beyond doubt: by the high summer of 52, Pompey was in a very good position indeed in terms of Roman governmental life. This is not to say that he did not face opposition; in fact he was regularly criticized by those of more Catonian outlook. Caesar seems to have been relieved that things were calmer in the capital and elsewhere in Italy; this made his own difficult job in Gaul appreciably easier.

Were Pompey and Caesar drifting apart in 52? Probably yes. The marriage to Cornelia and not Octavia, the attempt to satisfy everyone and in the end please no one with the question of standing for office and assuming proconsular commissions, the fact that with Crassus and his son dead, and Pompey the father of two and Caesar the father of no one – all of this was a recipe for a growing lack of trust and the potential for serious crisis and conflict. Civil war was by no means inevitable in 52, and in some ways a lot had been done to avert the possibility of a decisive break between the 'duumvirs.' But the situation remained seriously unstable. Caesar had every reason to be stressed and anxious as the months passed.

The good news that Caesar could celebrate in September must have been one of the most gratifying of events: Vercingetorix making his personal surrender.[12]

The senate approved twenty days of celebration in thanksgiving; this was exactly the sort of honour designed to make sure that a commander did not feel unappreciated.[13] We hear of determined effort on his part to win popular acclaim and favour, whether by financing gladiatorial entertainments or by seeing to better pay for his soldiers.

Probably also in 52, there was some measure of vengeance for the death of Crassus. King Orodes had his general Surena slain, apparently out of concern that he was becoming too powerful.[14] The Parthian losses to Cassius could not have helped the mood in the empire. Still, the absence of immediate and dramatic threats from Parthia to Roman stability in the east was a double-edged sword. It became all too easy in the immediate to put Parthia lower on the agenda of crises to resolve.

Some would say that Pompey's decision to be based mainly in Rome while maintaining his Spanish command was a major source of trouble; others would say it brought much needed stability to the capital. As 52 progressed toward its end and the usual elections, it became ever clearer that even out of office, Pompey would remain a source of immense authority, carrying much weight in government affairs. One thing is clear in verdict on his third consulship: he had carried out his office in a manner utterly foreign to how Caesar had behaved when he served with Bibulus. If Caesar had reason to be worried that someone would want to see him prosecuted for his behaviour in office, Pompey provided an all too fresh and vivid example of a consul who actually worked with the senate. Both men could be heavy-handed, autocratic and dismissive. Both men benefited from and sought to engineer extraordinary concessions for their own advantage. But Pompey unquestionably had behaved in a different way from Caesar.

The consuls who would be elected for 51 were Servius Sulpicius Rufus and Marcus Claudius Marcellus. It was a victory for Sulpicius to balance the loss he had suffered to Lucius Licinius Murena in 63; students of Cicero's oratory know the *Pro Murena* that was written in his defence against Sulpicius' charge of bribery. Marcellus was an ardent Pompeian in his sympathies and loyalty; his consular colleague was as well, if not to quite the same degree of fervent devotion.

Tacitus in his *Annales* offers a harsh view of Pompey in his third term of office.[15] Chosen to reform society, Pompey fell into the aforementioned trap of concocting cures that were worse than the disease. He made laws that he himself broke. It is an indictment that comes with significant blame for what would soon come about; for Tacitus, Pompey incurred appreciable blame for what Caesar would do.

Tacitus is supremely critical; others have been warmer, even if they were to agree that the steady drumbeat to war commenced in 52. This is a bit earlier than I would prefer to argue for; the following year was to prove far more problematic and consequential in this regard. Caesar was still speaking well of Pompey, and when the tribunes pushed to let Caesar run for office in absentia, Pompey did not object.

Let it not be forgotten in all this that military men are inclined to have greater respect for each other than for those who have never known battle, or have never led men in the field. At some level, Pompey and Caesar spoke a language that neither Cato nor Cicero knew. Of the three 'triumvirs', Crassus was the odd one out in this regard; he was something of an amateur, at least in comparison to his two colleagues. Those exploring the decline and fall of the republic can consider what it means for republican government to maintain what for all intent and purpose is a professional army, with a professional officer corps. Beyond all these considerations, Pompey had given use of a legion to Caesar, a sure and abiding sign of amity.[16] That legion would become a point of contention, but not for the moment.

Pompey had attained significant power by 52, and without violence or war to secure his standing. Caesar's position was also relatively strong, for all his legitimate anxiety; both men, in fact, had reason to be worried about their situation, like anyone with high ambition in an inherently unstable environment.

Chapter Eighteen

A Republic Rife with Tension

The new consuls of 51 were not destined to be bringers of serenity or irenic managers of republican life. Marcellus in particular was no friend of Caesar, and he seems to have entered office with a particular animus toward the conqueror of Gaul when it came to questions like the hero's future and his legal standing.

Marcellus seems to have been determined to make his consular year focused on the agenda of reining in Caesar's interests. In the most positive and idealistic of analyses, Marcellus was a true republican who saw Caesar as a dire threat to the stability of Rome. While sentiments of this sort may have been at play, likelier is that Marcellus simply disliked Caesar and his associates, or men like Caesar: ambitious, larger than life figures who seemed more interested in meriting pages in military histories than in managing the business of a republic. Whatever his reasons, Marcellus went for the jugular.

Appian prefaces his consideration of the term of Marcellus by saying that when Caesar heard of the consul's intractable attitude toward his demands, he responded by handling the hilt of his sword and noting that if Marcellus were not going to accede to his wishes, then the sword would win what he wanted.[1]

A cynic might conclude that the bill was overdue after decades of pretending that there was a republic in all but name. Had the 'triumvirate' really weakened the cherished republic even to the point of death? Or rather, had the machinations of the Big Three saved the republic from another civil war?

Marcellus is infamous for his outrageous treatment of one of Caesar's beneficiaries. Caesar had built Novum Comum in Cisalpine Gaul, and he had inaugurated a system to reward the local magistrates with Roman citizenship; it was a smart plan, and one that would have been a good example of one of the initiatives that would need to be approved, like Pompey's in the east. Marcellus had a man from Novum Comum flogged; the man protested that he was a Roman citizen.[2] Marcellus said that the man should go and show his scars to Caesar, noting that they were the brand of a foreigner. In other words, this was a gratuitous insult, and with a savage and sadistic bent; it was of no benefit to checking Caesar's ambitions or dampening his ardour or ambition.

On the contrary, it was the sort of thing that was clearly likely to do nothing other than provoke the proconsul.

Marcellus also started arguing that if the war in Gaul were finished, then Caesar's commission should come to an end. This was a claim open to legitimate and strong rebuttal, and the continuing campaigns of the year would amply disprove it. Enemies of Caesar would be prone to claim that the proconsul was simply provoking further conflicts, but that was a challenging case to render persuasive to those not already unfailingly hostile to him.

Events in the Mediterranean for 51 BC include developments in the situation in Alexandria, where Ptolemy XII remained in power with Roman protection. Protection consisted of the 'Gabiniani', a force of some 2,000 legionaries and 500 cavalry. These men were not functioning in any officially sanctioned capacity; they were the legacy of the general after whom they were nicknamed. Over the years they became essentially mercenaries of Pompey; this process was accelerated by the fact that some of the force consisted of Gallic and Germanic auxiliaries, who felt no particular loyalty to Rome. And in time, the 'Gabiniani' were living with Alexandrian women, living more and more like Alexandrians than like Romans.

At some point, Ptolemy named his son Ptolemy XIII and his daughter Cleopatra VII as his heirs and co-rulers, with Rome to be the executor of his will, the undisputed guardian and protector of his kingdom.[3] Ptolemy XIII had been born around 62 BC, Cleopatra probably in 69. Their sister Arsinoe IV was born between 68 and 63; she was destined to play her own role in the family drama.

Ptolemy XII died in the spring of 51, probably of illness (though in late Ptolemaic Alexandria, the question was always worth asking).[4] Brother and sister succeeded as co-rulers and sibling spouses. The problem was that the new king was underage; it would not take long for the boy to acquire his own court of attendants, namely the eunuch Pothinus, the commander Achillas, and the rhetorician Theodotus of Chios. Those three men would take their dubious place in history; they were the closest guardians, associates, and managers of the young monarch.

Pompey meanwhile was still a proconsul, but Spain was not on his immediate itinerary.[5] He seems to have departed Rome as if he were heading there; this would have been in accord with the notion that the crisis that had given him a sole consulship a year before was now finished; there was every reason for him to leave the capital.

The significance of the fact that Pompey stayed in Italy in this period should not be underestimated. Pompey was well aware that the situation was tense; he knew that the conflict developing between Marcellus and Caesar was perilous and unpredictable. Did Pompey want Marcellus in office because he knew that he was more than capable of provoking trouble with Caesar? It can be easy to imagine that great men like Pompey and Caesar were prone to be masterminds overseeing a complex chessboard, where every act is calculated for some ulterior motive to secure power.

But a republic must be allowed to be a republic, and for all their seeming addiction to power, in 51 BC the two most formidable men in the state seem to have had a genuine desire to avoid monarchy. That said, they wanted above all security from harm (legal and judicial), and that was linked inextricably to military power. They were ambitious for glory, and that also came via infantry and cavalry. They were also witnesses to undeniably chaotic times, and they were convinced that if there were no immediate solutions to the root problems of the chaos, at the very least the most competent men should have a hand in keeping the situation as stable as possible. Stability, after all, led to the aforementioned matter of security.

Certainly Caesar and his supporters had their view of Marcellus as a threat to Caesar's security. He was developing a programme that hinged on the key date of the Kalends of March; he wanted the question of Caesar's replacement to be discussed at the earliest possible date, and to make sure that there was no seamless transition from office to office.

Bibulus, meanwhile, was an ex-consul who was already preparing to serve in his new province, Syria. Not long into his term, he managed to offend many of his soldiers. They were fiercely devoted to Cassius, whom they venerated as the man most responsible for having saved their lives in the wake of the nightmare at Carrhae.

With reference to Bibulus' arrival in Syria, an account by Cicero from his correspondence with Atticus makes a revealing remark about the problems brewing in Rome.[6] Pompey, Cicero says, could not be sent anywhere without fear of civil war, while at the same time the senate was paying no heed to the demands of Caesar. It is a precious window of insight into how one leading man at the heart of the crisis saw the situation. His analysis is surely right; it was the perhaps inevitable consequence of trying to pretend that a culture of tolerating exception after exception to precedent, custom, and law could continue indefinitely. A breaking point was inevitable.

Cicero himself was a busy man; he was on his way to Cilicia in 51, to take up his own provincial command. He spent time with Pompey in the late spring; the great veteran of the east could speak at length about Cicero's destination. The mood that we detect from Cicero's correspondence in this period is one of complete faith in Pompey, in particular with his ability to maintain order in Italy.[7] We have considered the possibility that what Rome needed was some sort of system on the one hand, managing domestic affairs, and on the other hand foreign affairs, with cooperative consuls or other officials with primary responsible for particular areas. Such a system could have been integrated into a more effective security apparatus (the police problem). Pompey should have been in Spain; when we hear that he was telling people that he was going there, only to remain in Italy, we can discern the psychological trait of a man who desperately wants to feel appreciated and valued. Reminders of this to flatter one's ego are free, but sometimes hard to obtain; Cicero, at any rate, was willing to shower Pompey with compliments.

Pompey had a more difficult time in high summer than in late spring. Cicero could be a voice of supreme reason, or a tremendous pain depending on the subject or his mood; probably he would have been helpful in the challenges posed by the senate as temperatures rose. Pompey needed to visit with his troop levies, to make sure that they were paid and all was well; they were essentially Rome's security apparatus.[8] The occasion was pounced on by many senators, who noted that Caesar had borrowed one of Pompey's legions, and that especially as the war in Gaul was winding down, it was high time for the legion to be returned.

Now in fairness, the legion had been borrowed, not given; it was always supposed to be turned back to Pompey. The men in it were loyal to Rome first and foremost; they were not supposed to be partisans of either Pompey or Caesar. Such are the idealistic fantasies that fall before rude awakening. No one could expect the legion to be demanded back now without some sense on Caesar's part that he was being mistreated or at mistrusted. On the other hand, it was not 'his' legion. Caesar's consistent position would have been that he planned to surrender it when he was finished. Pompey was now being pressured to agree with the senate position that it must come back now.

Pompey was in a difficult position, as usual of late. The price of staying in Rome or relatively close to the city was that he was the veritable ombudsman for senatorial complaints. He heard everything, and was constantly being judged and evaluated for his response. He seems to have settled on a policy of remaining as non-committal as he could, always speaking respectfully of Caesar, and at the same time always paying deference to republican institutions, first and foremost the senate. This policy of trying to please everyone can make peace for today, but it is not sustainable; between forces like Cato and Caesar, sooner or later there would be a clash.

If we can believe Suetonius' note that he was twelve at the time, then 51 was the year in which Octavian delivered the oration at the funeral of his grandmother, Caesar's sister Julia.[9] Traditionally this has been taken as the debut of the future Augustus in public life; the story would fit into the mythology and mystique that developed around the young man, especially after he was adopted into the Julian family.

Caesar, meanwhile, was moving rapidly and decisively to complete his pacification of Gaul. He was in a vice: he needed to show that he was performing stunning miracles in the field, but the sooner he finished, the sooner he needed to deal with his enemies demanding the end of his commission. And there was the aforementioned problem of having those same enemies claim that he was provoking unnecessary conflicts just to remain in the field.

There were, however, legitimate problems that were making life difficult for Caesar and potentially threatening to Italy. Caesar was focused on the situation in Gaul, but he was also responsible for Illyricum. Probably around this time, there were troubles among the natives of this restive area as well, as Dalmatians and other Illyrians struck against the city of Promona, a Liburnian stronghold in what is today Croatia. Appian mentions the capture of Promona by the Dalmatians, and how Caesar sent a warning that it should be returned to the Liburnians; when the demand was refused, he sent a strong force to help the beleaguered Roman allies.[10] The force was completely annihilated, but the situation could not be remedied at once, Appian notes, because of the conflict that developed between Caesar and Pompey. We cannot be sure of the date of the Illyrian attack, but it was probably just about now, when Caesar was otherwise finishing his work in Gaul.

Bibulus was in a calmer situation in Syria.[11] Thanks to the work of Cassius and a fortunate dose of Parthian disorganization and internal dissensions, he had inherited a situation that was mostly under control. The senate was willing to give him honours when he reported his alleged accomplishments; no doubt this increased the resentment that some felt for him. It cannot be underestimated how dangerous the situation remained. Orodes' son Pacorus had made it as far as Antioch before he had been defeated, with his commander Osaces slain. While the chronology cannot be certain, what is clear is that the work was largely done before Bibulus arrived. And this much seems clear: Bibulus realized that there was a danger that Parthia would strike again, and strike hard. He had no wish to be in command when that day arrived; he had no wish to be the next Crassus.

Could Parthia have been the key to avoiding civil war? Cicero in Cilicia was able to gain a better sense of what was going on in the east, and he was no fool; he quickly realized that Orodes was a tremendous threat. What should have happened is that Pompey and Caesar should have designed a plan to cooperate on how to resolve the Parthian problem once and for all. It would have given both men the chance to do what they did best, and to share credit and glory for securing the east for generations to come. Such is the stuff of dreams; while there would be talk of something akin to this proposal, it would never come to fruition.

Pompey's aforementioned visit to his troops was at Ariminum, the modern Rimini. We have no evidence of what happened there, but we do know that by the end of summer Pompey was back in Rome, urging the senate to be cautious about Marcellus' demands regarding the contentious issue of provinces. There was an important meeting on 29 September of 51; Pompey apparently reminded the senate that there were not to be any decisions about Gaul until after the Kalends of March.

We can only imagine the stress that both Pompey and Caesar were under that fall, the one from hearing what was being discussed in Rome, the other from dispatches that his friends were likely sending to him about the discussions and debates. We hear of how Pompey was asked probing questions, including what would happen (i.e., what would he do) if Caesar wanted to be consul and to retain his armies. Pompey famously is said to have responded with his own, rhetorical question, namely what would he do if his son struck him with a stick.[12] It was vintage Pompey: try to remain non-committal, try to continue to keep the peace and to avoid conflict wherever possible.

Did Pompey meet with Caesar at Ariminum, the way he did at Luca? Some have speculated that there must have been a second conference, but on the whole it seems likely that there was not. Caesar, for one thing, was more than preoccupied. Certainly there should have been another meeting, though it is hard to know how much leverage either man had over the other, and, more importantly, how much room there was for concession on either side.

Nothing, after all, had changed for Caesar. There was the possibility of remaining in Gaul until he won the consulship, and then seamlessly moving from provincial rule to Rome. The only other option he was willing even to consider was to stay in Gaul, in command of his provinces. What he would not tolerate was even a day as a private citizen, exposed to the wolves ready to prosecute him for past sins (real or alleged).

The consuls for 50 would be Lucius Aemilius Paullus Lepidus and Gaius Claudius Marcellus Minor. Marcellus was the second of three members of the family who would hold a consulship in these key years; he was a cousin of his predecessor. Paullus was the brother of Lepidus; earlier in his career he had been among those who supported Cicero in the Catilinarian conspiracy, but one person he had never shown much enthusiasm for was Pompey.[13]

The more remembered official of the year 50 was Gaius Scribonius Curio, who held a tribunate. Curio had a checkered career. Early in life he established a friendship with Mark Antony; enemies of the two were quick to charge the two with immorality. Later, Curio was a supporter of Clodius. His name was mentioned in connection to the mysterious Vettius conspiracy. He married Clodius' widow, Fulvia; she was destined to be a wife of Mark Antony.[14]

Over the years, Curio had acquired a reputation for being opposed to the 'triumvirs.'[15] Certainly he had not been inclined to help any of them. At some point, it seems that Caesar decided that Curio was exactly the sort of man who could be convinced to help him. Antony may have been a factor in this, but likely nothing would have been as persuasive as the right amount of bribery. Caesar, after all, had become wealthy in no small part from his long tenure in Gaul; he was at this time in what was even for him an especially generous mood. Worried about his vulnerabilities in Rome, he was eager to make sure that he had loyal troops, men who could count on good pay and a commander who was clearly devoted to their welfare. And someone like Curio might also prove to be quite useful to have on the payroll.

Curio has acquired a reputation for being one of the most culpable Roman politicians when it came to the blame game for the civil war soon to erupt. Like Antony (and, sometimes, Caesar), Curio had a problem with lavish spending; he was in serious debt as he entered office, and Caesar seems to have honed in on this weakness. Our sources indicate that Curio was by no means the only man Caesar tried to sway to his side; we hear that the busy campaign of increasing the number of his supporters extended even to the manipulation of the slaves of those whose votes and support Caesar craved.

Curio is said to have played a careful game of trying to conceal for as long as possible that he was converted to working on Caesar's behalf. Especially if he were prone to being fickle, Curio would have needed time to adjust to his changed outlook; as the money would have continued to pour in, he would have been more resolute in his new allegiance.

In late 51, the *optimates* had every reason to suspect that Curio would not be warm to Caesar; it seems that even his old friend Antony was not supportive of him, no doubt because by this point Antony was firmly in Caesar's camp. The usual explanation for Curio's change of heart is purely monetary; like so many of the more obscure issues of the age, the truth is probably more involved. Whatever happened, it happened quickly. Curio was by no means a scrupulous man: if anyone was corruptible, he was.

There is no question that Curio was doing more and more in early 50 BC to create problems, using the very mechanisms of republican government to create delays and to obstruct anything that might be to Caesar's discomfiture.[16] He failed in his proposal that an intercalary month be inserted into the year; in this he played on certain calendar peculiarities that had become more problematic in the years before Caesar's eventual calendar reforms in 46. Our sources make clear that Curio was livid about the rejection of his proposed insertion; it is hard to escape the conclusion that he wanted an extra month before the crucial date of 1 March arrived.[17]

We also hear of talk from Curio about proposing new ad hoc assignments, like the grain commission that Pompey had managed. There was an undeniable need for infrastructure repair and expansion, and some scholars think that Curio was fishing for a new post for Caesar. One thing that was never going to happen was an agreement that Caesar was immune from prosecution, and so the only solution was the same old conundrum: what job should he be allowed to have during any window of vulnerability?

It is easy to look at the late winter of 50 and to conclude that nobody was willing to compromise. Pompey had bought himself a reprieve until the fateful Kalends of March, but the calendar was crumbling (especially given the denial of an intercalary extension).

Curio could always try to stall come 1 March, and this he did; such stalling could not last long, and in the brief respite, tensions would only be exacerbated. Curio would be the proponent of a new idea: Caesar would give up his legions, at the same time that Pompey gave up his Spanish ones. Curio had clearly undertaken to be the mouthpiece of Caesar as to the idea of having both men surrender command of their legions simultaneously; at the very least, raising the proposal would compel some people to show their cards.

It had the advantage of seeming on the surface to be a fair deal. Pompey's extension of his own command had not exactly been the most straightforwardly appropriate, even legal of manoeuvres; the Caesarians were not entirely without a point in saying that both men should relinquish military command.

Here we see a clash between what was right for domestic politics, and what was right for foreign affairs. The ghost of Crassus loomed. Crassus' death is often said to have precipitated an inevitable clash between his surviving 'triumvirs,' as if Crassus were the staying power or the *sequester* that prevented his ambitious colleagues from going to war. In reality, what Crassus' death did was make trouble from Parthia a major factor in determining the future of Roman diplomacy and military affairs.

The senate was completely justified in planning contingencies for the possible renewal of full-scale war with Parthia. The main sources of men at the moment were from the large armies controlled by Pompey and Caesar, and discussions centred on having each man contribute to the needed expeditionary force. The Caesarians could argue that the situation was not entirely fair, given that Pompey could contribute the legion that he had loaned to Caesar for the Gallic campaigns, which in one way of looking at the account sheet meant that Caesar was losing more than Pompey. Pompey could rightly claim that the legion he loaned to Caesar was his own legion, not Caesar's; if it were sent to the east, it was going there as a Pompeian legion, not a Caesarian one.

Did Pompey want an eastern command at this point? There is good reason to suspect that he had long wanted another chance to rival Alexander. The main problem he faced was that leaving Italy and Rome meant inviting a return of chaos. After having seen firsthand how fragile things were in the city, likely he found it ever harder to envisage a new and long campaign cycle in Asia. If Caesar were with him, he would not need to worry about his ambitious rival. But realistically, leaving Rome behind ran the risk of hamstringing both men; civil unrest and perhaps even a return to the anarchy of the days of Clodius and Milo must have seemed likely.

What should have happened, arguably, is that Pompey and Caesar should have considered securing commissions for a joint expedition, with mutually selected agents and subordinates to maintain order in Italy (Antony would have been an obvious candidate for Caesar). This idea also carried risks, but for the moment, things were stymied on multiple fronts.

Curio managed to incur a fair amount of blame for the virtual paralysis of some aspects of governmental functioning in that dreary winter. If Pompey were annoyed or concerned about any of his proposals, he did not need to do much to oppose them; Curio was good at making enemies without much encouragement. The degree to which Fulvia was a strong force in motivating her husband is uncertain; some have seen an eager effort on her part (and, truth be told, on Caesar's as well) to resurrect Clodius.

The consul Paullus was supportive of Caesar's position, but he seems to have had serious problems with Curio. This was an old story for the republic, and especially for would-be quasi-dictators: your supporters did not always cooperate well together, and often to please one meant to annoy another.

Could there be more complications? Yes, and among them a major one. As the time drew nearer to start thinking about the consular elections to be held late in 50, Caesar needed to start evaluating his chances of winning. One of the problems with republican government and elections is that even if you practise bribery on a grand scale, even if you do everything you can to manipulate the election cycle, you still face the risk of losing. Short of going to war, you cannot guarantee how the season might end. Caesar could probably count on remaining safe from threat of prosecution until he could stand for election and win, but if he lost, he would have nothing to shield him from harm. His enemies would know this all too well, and they might be eager to do everything they could to see to it that the hero of Gaul suffered a humiliating defeat, which would be followed by his prosecution. And we may recall the questionable legal games by which Caesar had been granted the exception needed to let him stand for office in absentia. By no means could he count on that extraordinary concession;

it would have been one of the first things challenged when he made formal announcement of his candidacy.

Men entertaining such thoughts were playing with fire. Through it all, Pompey must have been feeling frustration on the side from the behaviour of men like Curio, and on the other hand from the expectation of Caesar that he should not have to face uncertainty: Pompey, after all, had spent plenty of time in his career at the mercy of fate, with no guarantees.

Alexandria meanwhile was once again in the news. Bibulus had sent his two sons to the court of Ptolemy XIII and Cleopatra VII (and the agents of the king) to secure the use of the 'Gabiniani' for defensive and other operations against Parthia. For the men of that quasi-mercenary force, the idea of going into normal legionary service was intolerable. Ptolemy's handlers were also in no mood to give up their private army.

The Gabiniani decided that one way to solve the problem was to kill Bibulus' sons, and this they did, early in 50 BC.[18] Cleopatra seems to have realized that assassinations of this sort were likely to bring down the vengeful wrath of Rome, no matter what. Cleopatra ordered the arrest of the murderers, and arranged for them to be sent to Bibulus.

What happened to the murderers is a matter of dispute. Bibulus is said to have sent them back to Alexandria, arguing that only the senate could decide what to do with Roman citizens.[19] In fact as proconsul, Bibulus could have handled the case; some have concluded that the assassins were, in all likelihood, killed on his orders.

What is certain is that Cleopatra's action solidified whatever likely resentment and discord already existed in the royal family. She had shown herself to be determined to remain on good terms with Rome, while Ptolemy's handlers were more inclined to take an independent approach to managing the kingdom. Certainly the 'Gabiniani' would now be inclined to support Ptolemy at all costs; his sister had proven that she was ready to see them slain. The seeds were being sown for the eventual breakdown of affairs in the realm, and the active intervention of Rome. Again we see the cost of inaction and neglect: men left behind by Gabinius should never have been allowed to enter such a state of anarchy that they were ready to kill official representatives of the republic.

At some point in the year, Pompey fell seriously ill while at Neapolis; the exact nature of his malady is unknown.[20] His recovery brought a tremendous outpouring of public support and thanksgiving. Plutarch claims that the reception Pompey enjoyed from his adoring fans in the wake of his first appearances in good health contributed directly to the impending civil war, because he became arrogant when he saw the popularity and adulation he commanded.[21] This is highly unlikely; if Pompey had any inclination toward arrogance, it did not need to be incited by cheering crowds. If anything, the bout of serious illness may have inspired some of his senatorial supporters to be more worried about a future in which he was dead and Caesar had no rival to restrain his own ambitions and hunger for power.

Pompey's illness seems to have lasted for weeks; the reports claim that he was at times in danger of death, but this may have been exaggerated. Appian offers different details from Plutarch.[22] He claims that while sick, Pompey wrote a letter in which he indicated that he would willingly surrender his powers if asked; he would not wait for anything like the expiration of his Spanish commission. He praised Caesar, while also praising himself. If Appian preserves an authentic bit of information, then one could come to the reasonable conclusion that Pompey was trying to make himself look good, and Caesar bad. The possibility cannot be discounted that a truly seriously ill man was simply exhausted, and ready to be done with saving Rome every day.

The prayers for Pompey's safety that were made by the cities of Campania would have seemed to some to be akin to treating their object like some eastern potentate, but probably too much should not be read into the gesture.[23] The late republic invites cynicism; no doubt there was genuine affection for the man who had brought so much peace to Italy after so many impressive deeds abroad.

Appius Claudius Pulcher meanwhile was responsible for bringing the borrowed forces from Gaul who were to be returned to Pompey as his contribution to the Parthian expedition, together with Caesar's own legion that would be sent with them. We hear that Pompey was given the clear message there was demoralization in Caesar's army, and that the true loyalties of the military rested with Pompey.[24] Appian claims that the men were bribed by Caesar to make these claims, all so as to lull Pompey into a false sense of security; this seems improbable.[25] Allegedly, when asked what he would do if Caesar ever marched on Rome, Pompey is said to have said that wherever he stomped his foot, legionaries and cavalry would spring forth to help him save the city.

What likely happened is that Pompey's own men were genuinely happy to be back in Italy, whatever the future might hold for them; as for Caesar's legion, if they had any fears about renewed revolts or trouble in Gaul, they would also be happy to be back on Italian soil, again come what may. Soldiers home from the battlefront need little cause to be enthusiastic. It is possible to be cynical about Caesar and to think that he was playing chess several moves ahead, already seeking to manipulate Pompey into feeling overly confident. But there are simpler explanations, including the possibility that certain voices in opposition to Caesar were making their opinions known loudly and persistently.

We have noted that there was a clear deadlock in Rome once Curio's proposal that Pompey and Caesar should surrender their armies simultaneously was rejected, and once it became clear that Curio was going to veto any attempt to replace Caesar. The compromise that was reached is one that brings its own element of mystery. Pompey seems to have settled on the date of 13 November as a proposal for when Caesar should vacate his provincial commands. We have no certainty as to why that date was selected. In one sense it did not matter, because Curio was not interested in the idea.

Curio, in fact, was interested in playing hardball. He took on the mantle of alleged republican defender, noting that if Caesar surrendered his provinces while Pompey still had his armies, then Pompey would be handed supreme power. If Pompey had no armies and Caesar did, then Caesar would be supreme. Since neither possibility was acceptable to a republic, it was necessary either for both men to keep their armies, or for both men to give them up at the same moment. A balance of terror was preferable to what would, in effect, be a dictatorship.

No doubt some people accepted what Curio was saying as a reasonable proposal. Others were convinced that Curio was speaking as Caesar's agent, clearly having been bribed by him. A key factor in all of this is that the senate was filled with men who were hostile to both Pompey and Caesar. The senate was home to the sentiment that it was highly problematic to have powerful men whose armies became more loyal to them than to the republic, men who were able to enforce their will by threat of force, just like Sulla when he marched on Rome.

Pompey's bluff had been called with respect to any letter he had sent while sick offering to resign his command responsibilities; Curio was certainly demanding that he do just that. By high summer, the situation was increasingly worrisome to many. Civil war was beginning to seem inevitable; there seemed to be no way out of the impasse. The question of who would be the more sympathetic in the eyes of, say, the senate was open. So was the matter of who would be more to blame for any outbreak of war.

There was tremendous confusion and uncertainty throughout the republic in the summer and early autumn of 50. That confusion is reflected centuries later in the vigourous debates about just what was going on in the minds of various parties. Were Pompey and Caesar seriously contemplating going to war? Where did various senators and those holding magistracies or running for office for 49 stand? What was the general sense as to the crisis in Parthia?

If we start from the position that neither Pompey nor Caesar intended to disarm, then we may consider the possibility that neither man saw war as inevitable. It was a dangerous game of brinksmanship, to be sure. But both men would have been aware that opinion could waver; the public could be counted on to be fickle. Someone would be blamed for the war, and the imputation of responsibility could change overnight for whatever reason.

There were many options short of war. The idea that Caesar could be persuaded to surrender his armies together with Pompey, only then to take his chances with prosecution, must have been utterly unrealistic, and understandably so. But Caesar could play a game of remaining outside the city, postponing his triumph until he could stand in absentia for a consulship. While unlikely, it was at least possible.

Pompey may have miscalculated in one area. He had been suspected of planning to return to Rome as a conquering dictator, ready to follow in the footsteps of his mentor Sulla and to march on Rome. Instead, he had disbanded his force as soon as he landed at Brundisium, inviting them to come to Rome for the triumph. Pompey may have felt that Caesar was also being unfairly maligned in some circles; the odds were that he was not going to do the unthinkable and take the city.

Throughout the history of the so-called triumvirate and now duumvirate, the real quest was that elusive status of *princeps*, or first citizen. It was not an official position. But it was a potent honourific, one craved palpably by all ambitious men of talent and acumen. By that fateful autumn, there was still a chance of salvaging the situation, of pulling back from the brink and of improving the stability and health of the republic. But the republic would prove to be hellbent on its own ruin.

Chapter Nineteen

Zero Hour

The election season for 49 BC saw consulships won by Gaius Claudius Marcellus and Lucius Lentulus Crus. The Claudii Marcelli thus saw their third successive consulship, after the terms of Gaius' brother Marcus in 51 and the cousin Gaius Claudius Marcellus Minor for 50. The consuls-elect were entering office at a time of extreme peril and tension; even before they commenced their terms, it was clear that difficult decisions would need to be made. It was no exaggeration to say that one wrong step could provoke a war, but it was also the case that there was a chance, even an ample one, to forestall any such nightmare.

The real problem, in the end, may have been that there was no real trust between certain factions and persons. Sadly, it seems that Pompey and Caesar were not in such a bleak situation, but that increasingly the actions of others had created a situation in which the unthinkable was ever likelier.

Caesar had been busy during the election season. Increasingly, he sent his soldiers back to Rome to participate in the process, which may well have included some degree of bribery, the time-honoured way to get certain things done.[1] Allegedly, a centurion from Caesar's army was standing near the senate-house one day, when he overheard that the senate was in no mood to grant any extensions of authority to Caesar. The centurion ominously tapped his sword, noting that if the senate did not award it, the blade would.

Various omens were reported in the city as the year 50 drew to a close; this was the stock report of troubles that preceded any crisis.[2] A noteworthy fire added to the climate of ominous foreboding.

The thirteenth of November had been proposed by Pompey as a significant day in the ongoing crisis of Caesar's surrender of his power. Nothing important seems to have happened as the day passed; Pompey's proposal, after all, had never been accepted in the first place. The senate met on the Kalends of December, where some important votes were taken to see where men stood at such a critical moment. The senate had a majority in favour of sending successors to Caesar's provinces, and a majority against asking Pompey to disarm.

Curio was correct, however, that few men wanted to see a civil war. And so he proposed a different question. Instead of splitting the issue, there was but one query. Should both men disarm? Here, there was a vote of 370 in favour, with only twenty-two opposed. The sizable but at the same time seriously outvoted minority bloc was, not surprisingly, the Catonians. In the ultimate display of brinkmanship, they were holding out for what they would have preferred to call respect for the expectations and traditions of republican government.

The Catonians were at the moment sick of Caesar, and eager to see him silenced one way or the other. If that meant war, they were prepared to see that happen in preference to what they viewed as indulging Caesar's whims, and letting him run roughshod over the republic. The Catonians were also not entirely trusting of Pompey; that issue would come to the fore in terms of how Pompey responded to the endgame that was drawing ever nearer.

Not surprisingly, when Curio announced the results of the vote on this question, there was rejoicing among the general public; they were convinced that war had been averted at the last hour. Their view contrasted dramatically with the reaction of Marcellus, who when he saw the lopsided result of the vote, sarcastically wished the majority well with their peace, with Caesar as their master. Marcellus had been a critic of Caesar throughout his term of office, and it seemed that the new consular year was not boding well for the conqueror of Gaul.

Indeed, the significance of the consular election results for 49 should not be underestimated. Both of them were arguably anti-Caesarians, although Lentulus seemed more conciliatory. He was deeply in debt, and at least for a while very eager to see war averted. But Lentulus was not destined to lift much of a finger for Caesar, any more than Caesar had been inclined to do anything for Lentulus in his canvassing for election.

Conversely, Caesar would be happier in the tribunate elections; he needed a new Curio, and Mark Antony was there to stand for office. Much has been said ever since the letters of Cicero about the idea that the disreputable were inclined to support Caesar; he was the popular champion against the elitist world of the senate-house. For some, the villain of the hour was not Pompey, but Cato and his allies in the senate; Pompey was popular, and so was Caesar, while the Catonians enjoyed significantly less widespread favour.

Cicero, for one, was eager to do whatever he could to effect some sort of reconciliation of the situation.[3] Reconciliation was urgently needed; while Curio was celebrating the fact that a clear majority wanted peace, Marcellus was calling for nothing less than a declaration that Caesar was a *hostis* or public enemy.[4] The claim that Caesar had already crossed the Alps with his forces was utilized to dramatize the urgency of the situation. Marcellus called Caesar a brigand, a robber who was approaching Rome with ten legions. Perhaps in his spittle-flecked denunciation of Caesar, he was alluding to the image of Hannibal crossing the Alps to invade Italy; it was insulting, and deliberately so.

Was Caesar willing to compromise at the last minute? We hear that in the end he was willing to accept Cisalpine Gaul and Illyricum, together with two legions, until he could stand for a consulship; everything else could be surrendered.[5] What is not clear is exactly when specific offers like this were made. Some sources point to the second half of December, others to January. The reason for the confusion may be a simple one: the discussions were ongoing, even somewhat repetitive (as often happens in tense and difficult debates). Pompey seemed open to the provincial command, but not to the retaining of legions. Cicero took his role as arbiter seriously, and seems to have argued for letting Caesar retain soldiers, just a smaller number than two legions; Pompey seemed willing to budge on that point, and was open possibly even to the two legions, if it would avert a war.[6]

Pompey and Cicero, however, were not in charge, any more than Caesar was. The senate hardliners were not alone in being implacable on the idea that Caesar could not overextend his term, let alone maintain armies. Velleius famously states straight out that Curio was more responsible than anyone for the nightmare that was soon to descend.[7] For Velleius, Curio was a man clever in his perversity, one who was incapable of satiety when it came to his wealth and appetite for pleasures. Certainly Pompey's mood was bleak in December; he was convinced that war was almost certainly unavoidable.

A letter of Cicero to Atticus that is often cited is from 26 December of 50; it gives insight into its author's impression of Pompey's mood and train of thought after they met for some hours on the previous day.[8] He says that Pompey thought that if Caesar became consul again, he would threaten the constitution, and that if Caesar went mad and attacked the republic, he was confident that the armies of the republic could defeat him. Cicero's spirits were buoyed hearing that Pompey was not open to peace at any price. Most interestingly, they considered together a speech of Mark Antony from 21 December, in which Antony had spoken very disparagingly about Pompey. Pompey's reaction was, if this is how his quaestor talks, how will Caesar behave?

The news announced by Marcellus that Caesar was invading Italy, however, was a false report. Caesar may well have been planning for war, but he had not yet struck. Curio challenged Marcellus on the quite reasonable grounds that the alleged provocation was untrue. Marcellus did not seem to mind; allegedly he retorted that if the senate did not allow him to act in defence of the republic, he would see to it himself as consul. This seems to be the juncture when he went to Pompey, who as commander of his own armies could not be within the city proper.

The moment we hear of in our sources was one of high drama and theatrical flourish; Marcellus handed over a sword, and said that his consular colleague and he were commissioning Pompey to march against Caesar for the security of the republic.[9] The reply credited to Pompey was another of his deliberately ambiguous, frustrating replies. He said that he would obey the consuls, unless a better way could be found.

In this vignette we see the portrait of a man zealous to remain officially loyal to the traditions and practise of the republic, but supremely uncomfortable with the current crisis. A fair critic of both Pompey and Caesar could say that much of what was happening was the inevitable result of years of extraordinary actions and manipulation of the system. Often the rules were followed selectively; all three 'triumvirs' were guilty of this, and they were by no means alone. The eradication of bribery and corruption seemed impossible. Rules were often followed more in letter than in spirit; the list of foreign problems was extensive, and the security of both the provinces and Italy/Rome was at risk. As a patient, the republic had been sick for some time, and the prognosis seemed grim if not terminal.

Many scholarly studies have explored the path to war. Much has also been done on a problem for which our ancient sources do not offer much help: how Pompey thought a war could be fought, especially one he may not have wanted to see fought. Pompey, like Caesar, was first and foremost a military man. The military situation in Italy at the end of 50 BC was this. There were forces in Italy, forces like those that had been employed for security duties; one could also count on quick levies of veteran forces. But even in the best case scenario, nothing in Italy could confront Caesar's legions; he would have the clear advantage.

Pompey had forces in Spain, and he had the resources of client kingdoms as well as a strong naval capability, the legacy of the war against the Cilician pirates.[10] The equation was quite simple: Caesar could invade and capture Italy, but he might find the rest of the Mediterranean basin quite hostile, with the threat of cutting off the grain supply from Egypt in particular, and the likelihood that the day would come when Pompey could strike at Italy from any number of directions. The Gauls and Illyricum strengthened Caesar's position, but the chessboard was at least equal, and in some ways could be seen as leaning toward Pompey.

We have often considered the point that there was a strong revulsion and detestation of civil war. The passage of the years certainly had reduced the number of those who felt particularly passionate on this point. It is likely that neither Pompey nor Caesar was enthusiastic to fight. But Caesar was quite enthusiastic when the subject was self-preservation, and both Pompey and his rival were devoted to the concept of being the first citizen, *princeps* as opposed to dictator or *rex*.[11]

Marcellus had gone to Pompey, who had to stay outside of Rome; Curio as tribune, meanwhile, was not allowed to leave the city. He sent out word that nobody should respond to any calls for a levy of troops for Pompey. But his term was nearly at an end, and his voice increasingly drowned out in Rome. Soon enough his mind was set on heading north to stay with Caesar, with whom he had now cast his lot.

Even at this late stage, war was not a foregone conclusion, perhaps in large part because it was imminent that new officials were about to enter their terms. Even if the consuls were known to be unsympathetic to Caesar, much could change when it was actually the responsibility of the office-holder to oversee a civil war. Sometimes in political life there is talk of a 'silent majority.' Such a plurality clearly favoured peace, but it was not clear how many were willing to stand up and to demand it, since a plurality was also not in favour of letting Caesar maintain his armies. A majority was not in favour of peace at any price. And so the Catonians had a wedge, and they were inclined to paint everything as a simple issue of republican freedom resisting thinly veiled monarchy. None of it, however, was simple.

Curio rendezvoused with Caesar in Ravenna, right on the cusp of Caesar's provincial border. Curio was thanked for his loyal efforts on Caesar's behalf. The advice Caesar received was not unexpected given the attitude of his fiery ally: strike at once to seize Rome.

Caesar indicated that he was open to continued negotiation. We have noted the terms that had been suggested in back and forth discussion and debate: could Caesar keep Cisalpine Gaul and Illyricum? Could he retain two legions? Could he keep the provinces, but with fewer men? Could there be a gentleman's agreement that he would be the leading candidate for a consulship?

This last point may have been the real sticking point for some people, and for that all the fault rested with Caesar. He had behaved autocratically, and was not above countenancing mob violence in practise if not in theory.

The fact that Pompey was willing to entertain compromises of this sort is no surprise; again, he understood Caesar better than anyone, especially the difference between a man of arms on the field and a man of words in the senate. The new consuls did not agree with the compromise proposal; this came as a shock to no one. Caesar sent Curio to Rome to deliver a letter to the senate; the bulk of it was a reminder of all that Caesar had done for the republic: shades of the same problem that Pompey knew all too well. The republic had a way of making its commanders feel less than appreciated, or at least the senate did. Caesar was still open to the idea of surrendering his armies, if Pompey did so at the same time.

There was not only more of the same now, however. Caesar also made clear that he was willing to avenge what he considered to be the wrongs that he had suffered. The fact that Curio read the letter must have made this key detail sound even worse, but it would have been a red line no matter who read it. It was all too easy to construe Caesar's threat as a declaration of war, and very hard to defend it. Perhaps Caesar was pushing brinksmanship to its very limit, banking on aversion to war, especially since he knew as well as Pompey that Rome would be exceedingly hard to defend. Were the Catonians and their allies ready to evacuate the city? Were they willing to roll the dice on the question of public support and mood?

There is some evidence that Curio made sure to bring forth the letter only when the consuls were at the senate-house, since he was worried that they would not read it, and that they did try to resist doing so. The new tribunes Mark Antony and Quintus Cassius Longinus demanded that they do so.[12] This was probably a case of fearing the uncertain; the consuls were not sure of all the contents. That said, if they wanted war, they had nothing to fear: the letter helped their cause with the part about Caesar's willingness to march on Rome. If Caesar had hoped to pin the blame for the war on Pompey, he was not necessarily displaying the deftest touch.

There was certainly a great debate; Caesar gives his own summary of it at the start of his commentaries on the civil war.[13] Pompey's father-in-law Metellus Scipio voiced the idea that a date should be set for Caesar finally to surrender his army, after which he would be declared a public enemy.

Antony did his job as tribune: his colleague and he refused to support any declaration against Caesar. Cato was a leading player, not surprisingly, in continuing to argue the anti-Caesarian case. Pompey seems to have been given the clear message that any accommodation with Caesar, any last minute concessions or compromise (for example, letting Caesar keep one legion instead of two, *vel sim.*), would result in the Catonians breaking with Pompey. The hardliners were exerting enormous pressure, but it is likely that Pompey had had his full of Caesar, or, perhaps more accurately, of Caesar's agents Curio and now Antony. Looming above all may have been the profound resentment of a man who had more than his share of experience of not being appreciated. This psychological issue meant that he was both less inclined to treat Caesar like a prima donna, and also more susceptible to finally being accepted as a favourite of the *optimates*. Some would argue that he was being cynically manipulated by Cato, whom they would blame for much of the deadly impasse. As in many moments in the long century of the dying republic, there was more than enough blame to be shared.

Clearly there were voices, and loud ones, eager to go any extra distance necessary to avert war – literally. Calls were heard for emergency gallop to Ravenna to meet with Caesar and to continue negotiating; these initiatives were not supported by a majority. In fairness, it is unlikely that such efforts would have changed minds on either side.

In the end, the Catonians had won the debate; a replacement was to be sent out for Caesar, as if republican life were normal and there was simply a change of command. Lucius Domitius Ahenobarbus was now Caesar's successor, at least on paper. Antony and his colleague Cassius exercised their veto, but Lentulus is said to have made clear to them again that life could be unpredictable if they remained in the vicinity. It was clear that mob violence could return; it was a threat, and not to the consul's credit. In fairness, Antony was more than capable of making his own threats; tensions were at a fever pitch, and Lentulus was probably correct that the tribunes were at risk, at least from some senators and their entourages. But Lentulus was playing into the hands of those in Caesar's camp who could then say that Caesar's friends were being driven from Rome, as if the city were once again mired in the mess of the days of Clodius and Milo, or even Sulla and his proscriptions.

That same night, Antony, Cassius, Curio, and Marcus Caelius Rufus all departed from Rome, heading north toward Caesar.[14] Caelius is perhaps best known today because of Cicero's speech on his behalf, the *Pro Caelio*. Caelius had been accused of murdering an Alexandrian ambassador; because of the bitter ending of an affair with the notorious Clodia, there were accusations that the murder charges were the result of Clodia's vengeful manipulation of the prosecutor and legal system. Crassus defended Clodius on the actual charges in the trial in April of 56 BC, while Cicero focused on attacking Clodia; Caelius was acquitted. Caelius later served as a tribune; having thrown in his lot with Caesar, he is said to have advised Cicero not to trust Pompey to save the republic.

The senate had issued its *consultum ultimum*; the republic was to suffer no harm, and all measures to ensure her security were to be taken. 'Poor, helpless Rome' is the sarcastic witticism uttered by Charles Laughton's fictional 'Gracchus' near the end of Kubrick's *Spartacus*. The republic had not exactly been sleepwalking as it entered a state of civil war, but she was now suffering a nightmare, one from which she would not awake for some twenty years.

Chapter Twenty

How to Start a Civil War

There was much to be done. For all the debate and negotiation about questions such as when armies would be given up or whether a candidate for election could run in absentia, one could easily develop the impression that there was not so much consideration of how a war would actually be prosecuted. Here we are probably victims of our sources. Both Pompey and Caesar must have devoted considerable thought and time to strategizing about war; Cicero was not the military men those two were, but he also had a strategic mind, both for the battlefield of politics and for war. Time was of the essence for both sides to begin to implement whatever had been brooded over in the tense weeks and months before the fateful January day.

One problem had likely occurred to Pompey already, and in some ways it was insurmountable. Caesar and his inner circle had far more freedom than Pompey did. To be the champion of the republic meant to be beholden to the senate; Pompey could not act like some proconsul on a distant battlefield, able to make every decision more or less independently. Nor was Pompey some lifelong darling or trusted member of the senate. The Catonian wing of the senate had a long history of mistrusting him just as much as they mistrusted Caesar, sometimes even more.

We have noted the main strategic problem that faced Pompey. He had ten legions, but seven of them were in Spain. Defending Italy would be a serious challenge; Caesar had the initiative there if he wanted to strike hard. Levying more troops for the defence of the peninsula and especially Rome would be paramount on the list of tasks. Provincial appointments would also matter, and not just Lucius Domitius Ahenobarbus and Transalpine Gaul. The east would need to be abuzz with war's alarms; the republic needed men, material, and money. Ships would be needed for blockades. The assumption was that the republic could call on every resource except Caesar and his armies.

Did Pompey think that even now, Caesar would avoid a struggle by giving up his provinces? This had been a game of brinksmanship, and in theory Caesar's bluff could be called. It is likely that Pompey knew Caesar well enough to know that even if the Rubicon had not been crossed, as it were, the time to turn back had now passed. It would have been fatal for Caesar to give up now, and Pompey would have known that. The seventh of January had been the decisive day; the *consultum ultimum* had been the instrument by which fate would exercise her will.

At least some of the senators seem to have thought that Caesar would be hesitant to move quickly into Italy. This was at variance with the argument made about a need for heightened alarm, the propaganda cries that Caesar was ready to pounce on the peninsula with little warning. More astute analysts (including Pompey) must have known that Caesar could indeed go for the Roman jugular, even if doing so exposed him to serious peril on other fronts, and ultimately in a besieged Rome.[1]

The crossing of the Rubicon has entered the lexicon even of those who know little about the ancient classics; it is recognized widely as one of those moments in history that matter.[2] Ariminum was the first town just across the border of the Rubicon that delineated Caesar's province of Cisalpine Gaul; it was illegal for Caesar to assume control or power south of the stream. To cross the river was nothing militarily; there was no defensive picket or force because only in a civil war would it be crossed. It was also a more or less indefensible spot; again, it was more an administrative border than any serious obstacle. Caesar's crossing it – complete with the story of the comment about casting the die of fortune and destiny – was monumental in part because it was physically so simple an act.[3] For the Neronian poet Lucan, it was a chance to depict goddess Roma rising up to ask her son why he was attacking her.[4] The senate had issued its decree, but the first act of the war was Caesar's. There could be little if any hope left now that matters could be resolved without bloodshed. The grim spectre of civil war had returned to Rome.[5]

It was perhaps the night of the tenth into the eleventh of January, maybe the next. We cannot be sure (and we should remember that the pre-reform calendar was about seven weeks or so behind the 'Julian' calendar of 46 BC). We hear that when Caesar crossed, he commented not only about throwing the die, but about how if he did not cross, he would suffer immense harm, while if he did, the world would.[6] Caesar was able to occupy Ariminum with basically no fight, or an exceedingly minimal one; as usual in a world with relatively poor communication and in a situation susceptible to widespread rumour, there was apparently a flood of refugees from the town, people frightened and uncertain about what would happen and what they might be caught in the middle of as Caesar's men invaded. Kindness was the order of the day from Caesar's military, except for those who resisted them.

Ariminum was no serious military victory; the town was not defensible on almost instant notice. But Ariminum was of immense psychological value to Caesar. Italy was now invaded, and Caesar occupied a town and was clearly in a position to strike fast and hard by land in any direction he wished, including

Rome. We hear of some voices now urging an accommodation; such men would have been those who were assuming that Caesar had been bluffing and that the Catonians had called him out. Now they had a war that they had never actually expected to see, since they had not been paying attention.

Rumours spread that Caesar had come with all his forces; this was untrue. He had come with a relatively small force so that he could gain the element of surprise and speed. Plutarch says that crossing the river was like hurling oneself from a precipice into some yawning abyss.[7] That metaphor may have entered the minds of some of those who went along with the *consultum ultimum*, but with respect to their own situation. If early reports were arriving that Caesar had come in force, then panic would be justified; if the truth had been revealed quickly, namely that the invading force was more modest, probably the alarms would not have been screeching quite to frightfully.

We simply do not know the full extent of what Pompey expected, let alone what Cato thought. We have no record of someone telling the senate that a vote essentially to go to war might well mean that Rome would need to be abandoned, and so the senators should think long and hard about whether they were ready to move to Greece or elsewhere to conduct a long and arduous war. Pompey may have been somewhat petulant; if the senate wanted to play hardball, then they would have to expect the consequences. Caesar was also a master of daring and reckless action; in the Alexandrine War, he would put his life at risk in a clash that was not, in the end, so hugely consequential militarily. While Pompey clearly did not think that Caesar was bluffing about his willingness to go to war, he would also not have extensive intelligence on what Caesar was doing. If anything, men like Antony and Curio were keeping Caesar better informed about what had been going on in Rome.

There was one man, however, who was destined to achieve at least a modicum of a hero's welcome by the republic, a bringer of inside information about Caesar. Titus Labienus had been a tribune in 63, and he was one of the most distinguished of Caesar's legates in Gaul. Labienus defected from Caesar at some point, probably in the second half of January, for reasons that are not entirely clear.[8] He seems to have acquired a certain sense of arrogance and haughtiness in his abilities, and certainly his relationship with Caesar suffered. Was he motivated by a genuine concern that Caesar was behaving rashly and utterly at variance with traditional republican principles? These are not mutually exclusive possibilities, and likely the truth is that his motives were complicated. But he did defect from Caesar, and he brought a small force with him. His greater value was in being able to provide intelligence about what Caesar had been doing; just how valuable his information was is unclear. But that intelligence likely was not available to Pompey and the senate when it was needed most, in the crucial opening days of the crisis.

Wars are always unpredictable, and the immediate consequences of the seizure of Ariminum were especially so, at least in the estimation of some. There seems to have been a serious recurrence of fear and revulsion about a revisiting of the worst days of Marius and Sulla. Again, we are left to conclude that many of the senators had been playing with fire; they should not have been surprised when a conflagration threatened to engulf them.

Those whose business was omens and portents were enjoying a booming business as refugees arrived south and rumours spread. There was apparently a delegation sent from Rome to Caesar around the fourteenth of January; the mere fact of the embassy would be an indication of the profound misgivings of some men at least about going to war. The Catonians could not entirely quell such sentiments; the more hawkish they seemed to be, the greater the odds that they would be blamed. Cato seems to have been more than a little self-righteous, convinced that he was defending the republic. But not everyone was so ardent to see the republic watered by the blood of martyrs.

Lucius Roscius Fabatus and Lucius Julius Caesar were the envoys sent to Ariminum.[9] Lucius' father was a cousin of Gaius Julius Caesar; he was clearly chosen because of the family relationship.[10] We do not know the exact contents of the message that they were sent; we hear that Pompey appended his own note to the communication from the senate, noting that he hoped that both men would act for the good of the republic, and expressing the point that he had no animus against Caesar; this was all about the republic. The contents of the message may be less important than the fact that the embassy illustrates the ongoing efforts to avoid a full-scale war.

This was clearly an 'unofficial' mission, the result more of Pompey's efforts than of anyone in the senate. The two men may have travelled together, or separately; we cannot be certain. Substantially they delivered the same message, and they received the same reply.

Caesar seems to have made clear to the delegates that he had been wronged by his enemies, but he indicated that he was eager to avoid war. Caesar once again voiced the view that Pompey should give up his armies at the same moment that he gave up his; he hoped that there could be a meeting between the two of them to resolve any problems, and that there would be a free, open and normal election cycle in 49 (whatever that meant in light of the experience of recent cycles).

Probably if decisions were solely in the hands of Caesar and Pompey, a war could have been avoided. But both men had to deal with the reality of the contentious and divided senate, as well as the more extreme partisans on both sides of the divide. Roscius and Lucius Caesar relayed the message back to Pompey and the consuls, who seemed to be of the view that Caesar should be told to leave Ariminum, to return to Gaul and to disband his armies, while Pompey would go to Spain, and in the meantime the raising of troops for the defence of Italy would continue, until Caesar pledged that he would keep his promises with respect to the proposed agreement.

If that was indeed the substance of the discussion, then exceedingly little progress had been made. Caesar could never be expected to give up his armies while Pompey had his; the fact that troop levies would continue across Italy would be viewed as a clear threat to his security. Was the detail about Pompey departing for Spain and Caesar going to Gaul subtle coded language for an agreement to meet to try to resolve the crisis without the din of the senate? Possibly, but if so it was not enough; the real sticking point had always been about Caesar having to give up his armies while Pompey still had his.

There was also the important propaganda war; both men needed to be worried about appearing innocent in the verdict of their peers and of history. And they were both not exactly in fighting shape: Caesar had struck hard and fast, but also recklessly. The main body of his army was not ready. Pompey and the senate needed time to assemble a credible force to defend Rome and Italy.

Because we do not know exactly what the message said that came from Pompey's pen to Caesar's desk, we cannot be sure whence certain details arose, but the bottom line remained that Caesar was supposed to give up his command. Where there was wiggle room for negotiation may have been on issues like Caesar being willing to come to Rome in person for elections. But such matters were sideshows compared to the army issue.

Further, once the consuls heard that Caesar was open to talking privately to Pompey somewhere, they became quite agitated. This is no surprise, especially given the strong undercurrent in the senate of suspicion of Pompey. Pompey was learning quickly (if he needed the lesson) that to cast oneself as a dutiful son of the republic and defender of traditional republican values means that one is a servant of the senate, even when in your estimation the senate is being intractable and unreasonable. At some level Pompey must have been sick of both Caesar and Cato.

We have spoken often of the problems of communication and the realities of infrastructure and travel times. There was nothing approaching the realities of early twenty-first century instant communication. Events moved quite swiftly in January of 49, and it was exceedingly difficult to keep informed of accurate information. Not only was there a communications issue, but every back and forth exchange required evaluation of reactions to new revelations; Pompey in particular needed to worry about the public attitude toward an imminent war, especially for those with memory or knowledge of the violent upheavals of the past.

If the envoys were sent on 14 January, they would need time to arrive, to have discussions, and to return. It seems that they returned with Caesar's peace proposal on 18 January. By 17 January, it seems that there was more ominous news, probably of no surprise to many: Caesar's men had occupied the towns of Pisaurum, Fanum, and Ancona, and Mark Antony was sent to Arretium. Probably as a direct consequence of the news received on the seventeenth, Pompey left the same night for Capua.

As the news filtered in to Rome with ever more confirmatory weight, there was clearly utter chaos and upheaval in the senate and beyond. Pompey was a recognized master of logistics and planning, but it is one thing to control an army in the field, and quite another to organize senators. We hear of insults and sarcasm directed toward Pompey; he was reminded of his comment about stomping his foot and having armies spring up on cue. He was blamed by Cato, noting that much of the responsibility for the crisis rested with him; Pompey must have wondered how any one man could possess so much gall.

Pompey quickly settled on the strategy of withdrawing from Rome.[11] From a military point of view, the decision was certainly understandable, even if debatable. Our sources do not permit us to have definitive insight into what Pompey was thinking; unlike Caesar, Pompey was not given to writing books, and even if he were, he would be dead the following year. It is possible (and here we should underscore the fact that we are speculating) that Pompey had an idea in his mind: if the senators and he (along with many others) were to appear to be fleeing Rome, the citizens of central and southern Italy would be likely to see Caesar as an invader, a brigand coming to capture the beloved, profoundly symbolic capital. The Gauls had famously captured Rome centuries before; now the Roman who had spent so long conquering Gaul had come to do exactly what the Gauls had once done. He had come over the Alps, like Hannibal. He was a robber, an enemy of the republic. And one could always recall his behaviour when he had held a consulship. Caesar did not play well with others according to the expectations of republican life, and now when he had not seen things go his way, he was the new Sulla, marching on Rome with an armed force.

It was brilliant propaganda, potent and persuasive at least to some. Others were deeply attached to Caesar, especially in the wake of his great victories; there was widespread empathy for his position. You could probably find many common people willing to die for Pompey or for Caesar; for Cato and his senatorial allies, no such deep reservoir of good will existed. But invading Rome was unthinkable and beyond the pale, even for many who would otherwise be sympathetic to Caesar.

One key fact must not be overlooked in analyzing this critical period. Granted communications were slow and sometimes unreliable, Caesar was still clearly occupying towns and sending colleagues to occupy others at exactly the same time that he was engaging in negotiations. Certainly a Caesarian could point out that Pompey was levying troops simultaneously. But Pompey was also not engaging in any dissimulation about that, whereas Caesar does not seem to have been noting anything about these takeovers while he was engaged in discussions about a peace deal.

Both Pompey and Caesar were making blunders, the result of the pressures of not knowing everything, and of the fear of the unknown and the need to take certain measures for immediate security. Caesar no doubt judged that he was in a stronger position the more towns he held, but the heavy price was that he was playing into the narrative that he was a bully and an invader. Pompey either was caught by surprise at any number of junctures, or he did not inform the senate of what his strategy was. His withdrawal south (whether premeditated or not) gave him the opportunity to paint Caesar as the aggressor, but it also surrendered the initiative in Italy and could reasonably be interpreted as a sign of weakness.

Pompey's departure from Rome was accompanied by word to the senate and other interested parties that it was time to evacuate. The consuls and a senate majority left on 18 January, the very day after Pompey. Whenever he had first spoken of leaving, if we can believe the vivid narratives of our sources, it did not allow for anything like an orderly departure. There was barely time for the consul Lentulus to empty the treasury into carts. Again, some of this may have been staged for the sake of arousing popular animus. But no doubt many people even at the higher levels of government were in a daze, unable to believe that things were happening so quickly. It is noteworthy that not all the contents of the treasury were taken; whether out of vain hopes or deliberate intention to return, there would be riches left behind. It is possible that the departure was so makeshift that logistically not everything could be removed. We hear of such a state of panic at the rumour and report that Caesar was near, that Lentulus overreacted out of anxiety and fled before he could do the logical thing and clear everything out.

Pompey was able to confer at length with Labienus. On 22 January, Pompey was at Teanum Sidicinum, not far from Capua; here he seems to have been able to be updated on the situation with Caesar, at least to the best of Labienus' knowledge.[12] The defector seems to have indicated that Caesar was by no means invincible, and that taking a stand in Italy to destroy him was both feasible and advisable. Labienus was courageous, for all his faults; no doubt there were many

How to Start a Civil War   245

Pompeians who could not imagine abandoning Italy without a fight. Honour seemed to demand nothing less.

Plutarch notes that Cato reminded Pompey that he had warned him about Caesar; Pompey is said to have responded with humility, admitting that Cato had been a prophet, while asserting that he had been friendly.[13] Pompey was perhaps surprised that Caesar had been invading Italian towns, perhaps not. But whatever his views on Caesar, this was not the moment to start a civil war within a civil war; for better or worse, Pompey had thrown in his lot with the Catonians, the very men from whom respect had come so grudgingly.

Cato, at any rate, had an excuse to leave Rome; he was on his way to Sicily to take up his provincial governorship. Plutarch observes that people from outside the city were flooding into Rome, while people from within were seeking to escape.[14] Everyone was giving Pompey unsolicited advice. If Pompey had aspired to be the 'first citizen', he had certainly achieved that status. Finally, in the most dubious of circumstances, Pompey was *princeps*, and suddenly the republic was looking for answers from one man. After spending so much time worried that Pompey would be a dictator, or that Caesar intended to be a dictator, now the republic was looking for a solution from a solitary saviour.

Octavian was in Rome when the chaos erupted; we hear that he was sent to the country for his protection.[15] The war between Pompey and Caesar would be a seminal event of his youth; even as the consuls and senate looked to Pompey to be *princeps* and saviour, the teenage Octavian would be spirited away to safety, a man who would one day do what neither Pompey nor Caesar could accomplish.

Pompey had the legion that had been reclaimed from Caesar in Apulia; not long after Rome was abandoned, efforts to levy troops may have been restricted to Capua and south thereof, the draft largely finding its inspiration from the person of Pompey. Cato had supported the designation of Pompey as the supreme commander of the armies of the republic; it would have been the last of the many extraordinary commissions that he had received from his beloved Rome. Pompey for his part had declared officially that there was a state of civil war. One could argue that there had been several such wars, including relatively minor crises (*pace* Cicero) like the Catilinarian conspiracy.

There was no official designation of supreme commander, such as we might think of when we consider titles like Supreme Allied Commander from the Second World War.[16] Pompey was not *dictator*. Indeed, one of the problems that hampered the republicans this fateful winter was that they were a republic, one in which Lucius Domitius, for example, was technically Pompey's equal.

Plutarch makes the important observation that there were more people who left Rome to follow Pompey's banners than those who were actually interested in fighting for liberty.[17] Pompey had a personal following, the same as Caesar.

Still, one should not underestimate the significance of the shouts and cries that Rome would soon be under attack.

Some have wondered as to the extent of manipulation of Pompey, in particular the question of negotiation with Labienus before he left Caesar's provincial territory. There is some evidence that the Catonians were in touch with him, and the theory has been proposed that Labienus' potential information was used as part of an effort to convince Pompey that Italy was in fact defensible. One thing is for sure: Pompey did set out on 23 January with Labienus for Larinum in the north of Apulia. Cicero was given the encouraging report that he might soon be moving back to Rome, and that the republican forces might be able to proceed to Pompey's native region of Picenum.[18]

Did Pompey change his strategy simply because of a few hours with Labienus? Leaving Rome made sense to avoid the chance of a siege, to give bad press to Caesar as an invader, and to buy more time to recruit forces. Operations were conceivable.

The reply that Caesar had sent back with Roscius and Lucius Caesar finally reached Pompey. The proposed terms of reconciliation, as we have seen, were more than reasonable given the dreadful alternative of full-scale war. If Caesar had made a mistake, it was in seizing more towns than just Ariminum. He had played a delicate balancing act: if he took one town, he might not be taken seriously. Taking several made him a threat, and it is noteworthy that his own commentaries make it sound as if Ariminum had been the only meal on his menu.

The reply that was sent back to Caesar via the same two go-betweens was that the terms were acceptable, but that Caesar needed to withdraw from the towns he had occupied; in the meantime, levying troops to defend the republic would continue. It was basically another demand that Caesar disarm. As for Caesar's original peace proposal, we have noted that it is by no means clear that it was a genuine offer, as opposed to a means to buy time; the game now was arguably one of calling Caesar's bluff, though he could always claim that the conditions imposed by the Catonians were to blame, and that Pompey had become a puppet of the hardline senators who had always been keen to stir up unnecessary troubles out of jealousy and resentment of successful and ambitious men.

We can be sure that Caesar was annoyed at the reply, which did not exactly accord with his vision of blaming everything on his adversaries. In the meantime, the priority for Pompey was probably the continued effort to raise troops, which was frustratingly slow. The draft was sudden and lightning quick; besides the usual aversion of many to being signed up to fight, there must have also been an element of paralysis combined with a desire to wait to see if negotiations could avert a wider war.

Pompey was trying to raise troops. Recruitment, meanwhile, was more and more of a challenge as men realized that they were likelier to be signing up to travel abroad with Pompey than to fight for their land. Caesar was intent on seizing more towns, and he was meeting with much success.[19] Iguvium (the modern Gubbio) was the next target. Curio was Caesar's legate, in charge of advancing toward the locale; Quintus Minucius Thermus was defending it. Thermus had experience in Asia and was a member of the old senatorial guard; at Iguvium, however, he had less than seasoned recruits. Thermus was in no mood to fight, and his men were soon to desert to Caesar. According to Caesar, the inhabitants of Iguvium were well-disposed toward Caesar. Thermus lacked trust in the population and sought to leave; his men deserted on the way and returned home. After Iguvium fell, there was no realistic chance of holding Camerinum; Umbria and Etruria were essentially indefensible now.

Auximum was another easy victory; once the people heard that Caesar was approaching, the local commander Publius Attius Varus was given a lecture on how Caesar had not been treated fairly by the senate, and that the town was open to him; Varus abandoned the town with his garrison. Caesar's general attitude in this period was his celebrated, studious clemency; he was open to accepting all to his ranks.[20] These were, to be sure, the cities of the front line, the towns that had become the impromptu first prizes of civil war. They were not strongly defended, and they correctly discerned that they had no chance of offering effective resistance. Caesar was a popular man; no doubt there was a healthy mix of those who were genuinely happy to see him, and those for whom fear was a more powerful motivator than any sincere affection.

Cingulum both surrendered without a fight and offered any help it could give. Labienus had founded the town, and no one seemed to care. Lentulus Spinther had been defending Asculum; he had some of his own taste of the experiences of Thermus and Varus, with troop desertions and being forced to depart. Pompey's own region of Picenum was now falling to Caesar, and again without bloodshed.

By early February, the situation in northern Italy was dire for the republicans, and central Italy was on the edge of the blade. Caesar's victories were probably due in large part to that familiar aversion to fighting one's own countrymen. There was also the fact that the men of northern and north-central Italy were being asked to fight for ideas (liberty, republicanism), and for the *optimates*. Coupled with the prospect of fighting fellow Romans, it is not entirely surprising that the front line folded so readily.

Pompey may have had hopes of fighting forthwith and establishing a defensive perimeter, but the prospect was looking increasingly unrealistic.[21] Caesar's main body was on the move, ready to join their commander, whose forces were now being increased by the desertions from Pompey's garrisons. The republicans clearly needed a plan for evacuating Italy, if standing up to Caesar were not possible; Brundisium would be the obvious port of embarkation, and Pompey needed to anticipate that Caesar might try to drive straight down the Adriatic coast to cut off any hope of escape. If offensive operations were not possible in Italy, there would need to be a defensive line, and as many men as possible needed to be organized and assembled for the mass exodus from the peninsula.

Arguably Pompey had succeeded in making sure that Caesar was likelier to take greater blame for the war than he. Opinions would be widely varied though; perhaps more people were inclined to blame the Catonians above all. But whatever the opinions on culpability, the real mess for the republic was that they were at present fighting a defensive engagement; Caesar had all the initiative. And if anyone were thinking that Pompey always intended to evacuate, then it must be admitted that the master of logistics had displayed astonishing incompetence.

Again we see how Caesar, for all the odds that were very much stacked against him, had the easier task in the immediate. Pompey was no doubt feeling like his mentor Sulla, imagining a world where he, too, would be returning from the east to restore the republic to Italy. Mentally he may have been reviewing the map and how he could cut off Caesar. Some senators were clearly expecting that if Italy were abandoned, it would be for Spain. Pompey was more astute; he correctly judged that Greece was a wiser place to go, so as to envelop the peninsula more effectively.

Metellus Scipio was entrusted with securing Brundisium at once. Lucius Domitius was at Corfinium. Efforts were commenced to retrieve all the abandoned treasure of Rome; now there was no doubt that an exodus was in motion. Pompey's cousin Gaius Lucilius Hirrus was on his way from Camerinum; he was bringing forces and linking up with the bulk of the republican forces in Italy. Lucius Vibullius Rufus originally had been sent to Picenum to hasten the levying the troops and to see to the feasibility of operations against Caesar; now that matters had changed so quickly, he was on his way to Pompey with additional forces.

January of 49 had been eventful, but February would be no less decisive, indeed in some ways even more critical. Once again the primary problem was a lack of awareness of exactly what was going on in every place at every time (Caesar of course had the same handicap), coupled with having too many chefs in the kitchen (a problem from which Caesar suffered to a far less appreciable degree).

Our knowledge of exactly what was going on must largely be pieced together from weighing the evidence of Cicero's correspondence with that of Caesar's commentaries. Pompey was at Luceria; he urged Cicero to join him there, arguing that it was the safest place for the orator.[22]

Lucius Domitius had been assigned to succeed Caesar in Transalpine Gaul; in a sense it would be appropriate that the first real opposition to Caesar would come at Corfinium, where his would-be successor Domitius had been charged with the city defence. Corfinium was located near the modern Corfinio, in the Abruzzo region. Corfinium was unquestionably of great strategic significance; it was a key location in the infrastructure leading from the Adriatic coast of Italy to Rome.[23]

Pompey had a problem though: he needed to defend strategic points (if only to cover an exodus), and he had to be ready to face Caesar if necessary with sufficient forces. Corfinium was more important than Luceria, strategically speaking. Here is what we know: Domitius was originally planning to join up with Pompey, but abruptly he changed his mind and decided to stay where he was. Scholars have tried to determine what was going on in his mind, and in Pompey's. Was Domitius fully aware that the plan now was to abandon Italy? Was Domitius convinced that Caesar was not strong enough to take Corfinium, especially if Pompey were to come to help in its defence? Was Domitius being pressured (like most everyone else in command) not to allow his men to suffer the potential losses of their property and farms without a fight?

Through it all, the abiding problem in terms of speedy execution of good logistical plans was the fact Pompey did not feel it right to treat Domitius like a subordinate; he was a colleague. The man who had been feared as a would-be dictator was displaying his best republican virtues at exactly the hour when some would say the security of the republic demanded a dictator. But that, needless to say, was exactly what the Catonians would never have been willing to suggest or to countenance. To be fair, this was not entirely unreasonable of them: to make Pompey a dictator to prevent Caesar from being one (especially after years of accusing Pompey of the same ambition) would seem to be the actions of those possessed more by disdain for Caesar than love for the republic. A would-be dictator could not be defeated by a legally sanctioned one.

By 13 February, Pompey was sending news to the consuls, who were at Capua. He made clear that he intended a major crossing from Brundisium across the Adriatic to Dyrrhachium, the modern day Durrës in central Albania. He planned for a second crossing, from Campania; this contingent would head to Sicily.[24] One consul was to go with each main group; the Campanian group would include Faustus Cornelius Sulla, the only surviving son of Pompey's mentor. By 16 February, Pompey was hearing from Domitius about the plan that he had settled on: he would come to help Pompey if Caesar seemed to be aiming for him, but if Caesar seemed to be lingering near Corfinium, he intended to make a stand.

Wisely, Pompey was concerned about a 'divide and conquer' situation. No doubt Pompey was also of the view that Domitius was not competent enough to stand up to Caesar. If Domitius came to him, there would be a sizable force to join Pompey; the price is that Corfinium would fall – a price that Pompey was willing to pay, given his intention to leave Italy.

In some ways it was all a moot point; Caesar was not waiting for the post office to do its work. By 15 February he was commencing a siege of Corfinium.[25]

Was Pompey truly afraid that if he simply told Domitius he planned to evacuate Italy, there would be a mass defection of even more soldiers overnight for Caesar? Quite possibly. Was he steadfastly avoiding any hint of dictatorial rule both to appease the fragile coalition he was part of, and (again) to forestall any chance of losing Domitius and/or his men to Caesar? All of this and more must have been on his mind. Pompey could not make everyone happy in the most strategically sound manner at one and the same time. Given that reality and the behaviour of both commanders and men, the best choice was to leave Italy. But it was understandably problematic to admit that.

Pompey learned of the siege on 17 February; an 'I told you so' message was sent to Domitius. The core of the letter was the same as before: do your best to get to me. Pompey was concerned about the fact that Caesar had veteran troops, trained on the battlefields of Gaul; new recruits and levies could not fight him. Pompey was daring, but he was no fool. He realized that if he seriously organized the forces he had and aimed for a pitched battle, say near Corfinium, he would probably lose, and with that loss the war effort would be at minimum seriously cobbled. Domitius was clearly fixated on the idea that Corfinum was strategic, and he must have been wondering why Pompey seemed to think that Luceria was more important. Even if he thought that an exodus was not a bad idea, he may have thought that it was almost shameful simply to abandon everything and run without a fight, or even token resistance.

Pompey must have been increasingly frustrated in this period. Likely he was envisaging disaster, and disaster could come in many ways.

Siege operations were always difficult and tedious; they consumed time and resources, and the order of the day was speed. Caesar had done what he had done because he had prized alacrity above all. Domitius realized that he was trapped in a city with an army that was of dubious loyalty; there was no clear way to get out at this point, except by combat. Domitius quickly came to the conclusion that he needed to abandon the city, with a few close associates.

On the list of disasters that Pompey could or should have contemplated, in some regards this would be the worst imaginable.

Chapter Twenty-One

The Road to Dyrrhachium

It would have been a miracle if Domitius had been able to escape Corfinium, and it was not a month for marvels. If there were a wonder to behold, it was that Domitius could even contemplate trying to flee. The man who had been firm in hoping to stand on the defensive line against a Caesarian takeover was now planning something that could only have led to the defection of his army. No doubt he was terrified, and fear expelled reason.

Corfinium was a gift for Caesar in several ways, not least the chance to display his much vaunted clemency. Domitius, not surprisingly, was caught by either the people of Corfinium or his own men in his efforts to abandon them. What had happened? Nearby Sulmo had been taken by Mark Antony; the people there had shown no desire to fight.[1] There were skirmishes before the siege of Corfinium; some resistance was at least offered, but it was probably token. Domitius' attempted flight sealed what was probably already inevitable: his men went over to Caesar. Domitius would be allowed to leave; he was useful now as a demonstration of the clemency of Caesar, who was eager to demonstrate that he was a reasonable man, not a Sulla come to order the deaths of fellow Romans. With Domitius would go a number of senators and others; Caesar made sure to note in his commentaries that he not only dismissed them with the money that Domitius had brought to the public treasury to maintain his soldiers, but also after having shielded them from the anger of those whom they planned to abandon.[2]

It was theatre, but it was good theatre; Domitius had been the stage manager helping Caesar in his performance. One can only imagine how frustrated, even livid Pompey must have been when he learned how everything had been so supremely mismanaged.

Caesar at this point had two main goals, and they had names: Pompey and Cato. The one was in Luceria, and the other in Sicily; the forces in Corfinium that were made to swear a new oath of allegiance to Caesar amounted to some thirty-one cohorts, a sizable number that Caesar earmarked to prepare to secure Sicily. He himself would lead his veteran force toward Pompey.

Pompey's plan seems to have been regroup, withdraw, secure the empire, blockade and then launch a massive and decisive attack. It was a slower strategy than Caesar now envisioned, which was a quick move to seize Italy and to catch up to the ringleaders of the opposition. As for the rest of the Mediterranean world, the logic was that once Pompey was removed as the figurehead of the cause, everyone would more or less willingly come to terms with Caesar, if only to avoid a long and costly civil war.

Pompey meanwhile faced some criticism that he had not gone to aid Domitius; probably on the whole his logic was sound. He had no realistic chance of winning some hasty pitched battle before Corfinium. He was being methodical and careful, which was what needed to happen given the coalition around him. But the risks were also enormous, as more and more people seemed to bleed away in favour of the Caesarians.

Pompey left Luceria on 19 February to meet the consuls at Canusium; the agenda would have included adjustments to the aforementioned plan to make a departure from both coasts for Dyrrhachium and Sicily, as well as to discuss the Corfinium disaster that made the changes warranted. By 24 February or thereabouts he was at Brundisium.

Pompey had repeatedly argued that it was best to avoid being conquered piecemeal, and he now judged (again, no doubt correctly) that the prudent plan would be to have as many people as possible head to Brundisium, where he would organize a departure in what would be two waves: the weaker or more unreliable forces would go first (i.e., the newest of the recruits, led by the consuls), and the stronger ones last (Pompey and the more experienced soldiery). This would allow for the possibility that Brundisium needed to be defended; Caesar was known for lightning attacks, even when such forays left him seriously exposed to risk. Brundisium might well be targeted any day, and the exodus could be under fire. Pompey knew that one way to fight Caesar's penchant for lightning strikes was to frustrate him with delays and to tax his patience.

By 8 March, the first wave had sailed for Greece. Part of the logistical problem that required the double sailing was the fact that there were simply too few transport vessels to suffice for what must have been a stressful, even makeshift flight. No one knew exactly when Caesar would appear.

The mystery would be solved on the ninth: the first wave had basically missed Caesar by as little as a day. It had taken a little more than two weeks for one of his classic rapid advances; along the way there were other forces to collect: defection was still the order of the day for those forces who had not made it to Brundisium either by accident or design.

One of Pompey's engineers, Nonius Magius, was among those captured on the route to Brundisium. Caesar expressed a good point: it was not useful to have messages conveyed back and forth by subordinates; what was needed was for Pompey and Caesar to have a conference in person. This was a reasonable suggestion, one that invites rich speculation as to alternate histories. Thus begins another critical juncture. We are frustrated by a lack of knowledge as to the exact nature of Pompey's response, but suffice to say it was clearly not a refusal to have discussions. Magius was sent back to Caesar, and there would be another message from the invader's camp.

I say 'invader' speaking from the perspective of Pompey. There seems to be good reason to believe that as winter turned to spring, Pompey was undergoing a decided turn from openness to conciliation to harshness. He was not becoming a Catonian, exactly, but he was clearly increasingly irritated and frustrated.

What would negotiation have meant at this point? Caesar was in control of significant swathes of Italy. He had sizable armies, and a population that was largely averse to civil war, if not happy to see Caesar in power. Those with significant economic interests in Italy had no interest in seeing their estates and lucrative farm operations threatened by war. Pompey himself may have felt insecure for his personal safety. We hear from this period of comments to the effect that if Sulla could launch proscriptions, why not Pompey? What may well have been expressed was resentment: Pompey had not inaugurated proscriptions or murderous reprisals, and yet Italy had slipped away from him without a fight. If he had expected that armies would refuse to defect, preferring to flee on the double to Brundisium or wherever the republic's banner beckoned, he was wrong.

Most galling of all must have been his native Picenum. He had been able to raise troops there as a young man. He was able to provide Sulla with significant support from places like Auximum, places that had opened their gates to Caesar with little if any resistance. Was this the republic he had agreed to risk everything to save? Was this the reward of virtue, the merits of republican valour? Was he facing ignominy and death for an idea with no substance? What exactly were the Catonians droning on about while men like Caesar were finding popular favour, or at least lack of resistance to their initiatives? Did no one remember what Caesar had done when he was a consul? Were Caesar's authoritarian actions simply the justifiable responses any reasonable man would offer to the intransigence of a Cato? If Pompey severed his ties to the Catonians, what future awaited him? A retirement that would have no honour?

All of this and more likely would have been on Pompey's mind during the latest brief interlude of negotiations. Neither Pompey nor Caesar could afford to look as if they were unwilling to talk. From January to March, civil war had been waged without much if any blood; no one could predict what would happen if and when the real fighting commenced. Caesar, for the moment at least, had no idea of Pompey's strategy. Maybe there were logistical reasons for why he was still at Brundisium with so many men; maybe he intended to hold the port and other strategic points in Italy while also controlling Greece.

Both Caesar and Pompey were skilled at managing the work of engineers and siege engines.[3] Caesar commenced operations to try to block the exits of the harbour by erecting moles and other means of impeding port operations; Pompey responded by trying to destroy the obstructions. These operations would have been the first actual instances of hostility directly supervised by the two opposing commanders; negotiations were ongoing, with Magius as the go-between, and the situation must have been unimaginably tense. Pompey would have worried about defections; he was seriously outnumbered, and he could not count on everyone in his force being happy or enthusiastic about abandoning Italy and their native soil.

Caesar takes pains in his commentaries to emphasize that he was willing to continue negotiations even though strategically it weakened his efforts.[4] More accurately, both sides laboured under the aforementioned problem of public scrutiny: neither general could afford to appear intransigent. Caesar utilized Lucius Scribonius Libo as an additional negotiator; Libo was one of Pompey's close associates, and a close friend of a partisan of Caesar, Gaius Caninius Rebilus. Rebilus was told to try to persuade Libo that he could be a key figure, indeed the most important agent, in resolving the war. Caesar claims that he proposed through Libo that both men should confer about laying down their arms simultaneously.

Allegedly the response of Pompey to these overtures was that the consuls needed to be consulted. Besides the weighty matter of not wanting to appear to be unwilling to talk, both commanders had serious difficulties. Pompey needed to wait until boats returned from Dyrrhachium, so that he could ferry across his armies. Caesar was now for the first time in a situation where every passing hour made it clearer that Brundisium would not be taken without a fight. If Caesar appeared open to talks, it also allowed him time to prepare a more effective siege; if Pompey delayed for negotiations, his transport fleet had more time to arrive and to start taking on men and material.

Coming to an agreement was at this point probably impossible, even if both men were seriously open to the possibility. There would still be non-negotiable conditions on both sides. The fact that the consuls were now in Dyrrhachium was not an insurmountable issue, but it did not help. It also allowed Pompey another chance to make his position clear in public opinion: the choice was between a republic or a monarchy; either you defend the republic, or you prepare to submit to Caesar. The argument came with a note of warning, at least implied: Caesar may seem to be accommodating and clement now, but that is only because he is trying to have things his own way; as soon as there is resistance, the iron fist in the velvet glove will come down.

We have not mentioned Caesar's entering Rome. Plutarch's life of Pompey is likely misleading; he presents Pompey as ordering the hasty evacuation of Rome, only for Caesar to enter the city unopposed a few days later, all before the siege of Brundisium.[5] The biographer hastens through the story, with no delay to discuss Corfinium. Caesar's own narrative has him going to Rome after Pompey's flight from Brundisium, which would make more sense strategically. Rome had been left undefended. Capturing it, even unopposed, played into the hands of those who painted Caesar as an invader. He could not avoid taking it indefinitely, but he also needed to try to prevent Pompey from leaving Italy. It was far more pressing to advance down the Adriatic coast as quickly as possible, trying to cut off any chance of exodus from the great harbour, while also making sure (insofar as it was feasible) that he could cut off any marches along the western coast.

Pompey, meanwhile, was executing his departure plans. Frontinus describes the method by which Pompey covered his exodus: archery units were used in force to harass any besiegers; they would be the last forces to escape, fleeing in light craft as they made their way under fire.[6] Our sources are filled with the predictable, dreary catalogue of all the omens and dire portents that accompanied Pompey's departure. He would not return to Italy, until his head was sent for burial at his beloved Alban villa.

We hear that the citizens of Brundisium were a threat to Pompey and his forces as he made his way. We cannot dismiss the possibility that Caesar painted a picture for posterity of an oppressed citizenry, eager to help Caesar because of insolent, abusive behaviour from Pompey and his men. Brundisium had almost overnight been transformed into an armed camp, under what amounted to a type of martial law; given the steady drumbeat of reports of defections and surrenders without a fight, it is easy to believe that Pompey's men were not remotely friendly. The truth was likely once again complicated; there were no doubt plenty of Brundisians who were happy that there would be no siege, no battle, no serious calamity. Pompey lost some two ships in the operation; all things considered, it was a success for him. By 17 March, it was all over. The city had been fortified with sunken stakes and other boobytraps; Caesar was warned about them by the population, and in general he avoided exploring Brundisium. He had much to do, and no need to linger. His target was gone.

Ancient historians were not oblivious to the fact that what was happening was the exact opposite of what had happened when Pompey had returned from the east.[7] He had landed then at Brundisium, and had immediately made everyone feel reassured when he disbanded his armies. Now he was heading east at the head of a large force, civil war an all too palpable reality. Lightning bolts may not have killed some of his men before he would make it to Dyrrhachium, and spiders may not have eerily appeared on his standards, but no one – least of all the commander – could have failed to appreciate the ominous import of what was happening.⁸ If anything, this was an hour where people needed to be reassured that in fact, Pompey had numerous and significant advantages, and Caesar was by no means master of all.

To this period is assigned the death by natural causes of Marcus Perperna, who had served as consul in 92 BC.⁹ Dead at ninety-eight, Perperna could say that while he had not played a particularly memorable role in the great events of his lifetime, he was a survivor. Some viewed his death as signalling the end of an age; one blessing would be that he would not live long enough to see the destruction of Pompey. He had outlived almost all his political colleagues.

What was the strategic situation for Caesar as it became clear that he would not be able to prevent Pompey's departure? He had no navy to speak of, and so pursuit was not feasible. He also needed to fear the Pompeian forces in Spain. Italy was also notoriously fickle, as Pompey had just been reminded; Caesar's victories, such as they were, could not be counted on without consolidation. As we have noted, Caesar had a list of problems no less serious than Pompey's.

The first order of business for Caesar was to deal with the sizable number of officials who had not fled. One of the most prominent of those who had not embarked for Dyrrhachium was Cicero. Ever a complicated man, his critics both in life and in his long *Nachleben* have accused him of being a weathervane, all too susceptible to the changing political winds. He was among the first people on Caesar's list to visit. If we can count on Cicero's account of events, Caesar wanted to win by persuasion; he wanted Cicero to say what Caesar might as well have drafted for him, but he wanted it said without compulsion.¹⁰ An opponent of Caesar would call it voluntary servitude. Cicero was not above criticizing Pompey; again, his critics would say he was playing both sides. In reality he was likely a nervous sort, incapable of remaining silent. He was no fan of Caesar at this point. But he was annoyed with Pompey as well, and he was certainly worried about what the current war would mean for him and his standing.

Both Pompey and Caesar must have been under serious stress for many reasons, but on the issue of finances, Caesar probably had less worries in the immediate. Pompey's frankly incompetent senatorial allies had failed, as we have noted, to clear out the treasuries in Rome. In their defence, Pompey had by no means been crystal clear as to the plan to abandon Italy. That said, there had been plenty of time to evacuate the treasure, and if the consuls were willing to evacuate Italy, they should never have left so much wealth behind. They could claim rightly that they were afraid of being seized along with the gold and silver, or that logistically and in terms of security, it was impossible to safeguard the wealth.

Whoever was to blame, the consequence was economic crisis. Pompey had a massive fleet compared to Caesar's essentially nonexistent navy. But someone had to pay to maintain it. Large numbers of infantry had fled Italy; they, too, would need to be paid. There would have to be heavy levies and taxes; Pompey first of all would need to start spending his enormous fortune in support of a war that was being fought for the republic, but which was also very much his war. He had the extensive list of client kings from the east, and they would respond to the calls of their benefactor. But they, too, would need to spend resources, and to levy their own taxes and military drafts. The ledger sheet probably showed Pompey as having superiority in forces as war loomed, while Caesar's ability to seize the treasury in Rome would likely enable him to have greater financial security in the immediate.

Plutarch says that Caesar was shocked that Pompey fled, while others considered it to be a brilliant trick.[11] Again, Pompey knew Caesar all too well. Caesar was at his best when problems needed to be resolved immediately. Patience was difficult for him. Cicero was among the critics of the strategy, which seemed to scream weakness and defeat; he would live to reconsider his initial verdict. Certainly Pompey was taking a serious risk, but then again so had Caesar. With every day that passed now, a diplomatic solution was appreciably less likely.

All things considered, arguably Pompey had won the first stage of the war simply by frustrating Caesar with his departure from Italy. This was exactly the scenario that Caesar desperately wanted to avoid. This was now very much a world war, and Caesar's much vaunted and justly celebrated love of seizing the initiative was less helpful. Figuring out how to seize Italy was not difficult, especially when your enemy was willing and ready to abandon it, and when the population was loath to see life and property endangered by war.

Plutarch offers what became a celebrated vignette of Pompey in this period.[12] The older man was happy to train among the greenest of recruits, practising equestrian manouevres and with the javelin. He inspired his men by acting as if he, too, were one of the men most in need of training. Between age and the number of years since he had seen serious combat, no doubt he needed the practise. But he was raising morale by acting like a conscript.

That said, if Brundisium displayed anything, it was that when Pompey was actually in charge, he was extremely formidable. When he felt that he needed to be diplomatic and deferential with a Domitius, there he had found problems. The war would provide yet another arena in which to display the weaknesses of the republican system, the government for which many were being called to lay down their lives.

The armies that Pompey had transported needed intense training. For Spain, the immediate concern was defending the Pyrenees against any plan of Caesar to invade Iberia; likewise, Caesar needed to worry about a strike toward Gaul and Italy from that theatre. Given in particular that Ptolemaic Egypt would need to be counted on as supporting Pompey, food supplies and resources would be a concern for Caesar. The eastern entrances to Italy in Illyricum constituted a problem not dissimilar to Spain; especially with Pompey in Dyrrhachium, Caesar needed to worry about an invasion from that direction, and vice versa. Africa was another problem for both men; here much would depend on the actions taken by the client kingdom of Numidia.

The problem with having appreciable power in the west and the east is that you cannot manage both theatres in person simultaneously. Pompey would need to trust on the competence of others to manage Spain (not to mention Africa), while he marshalled the enormous power and wealth of the east. It would not have taken much time for Pompey to realize that Spain would be Caesar's first main target; Pompey had taken so many ships that we can believe our sources when they say that there were barely any available for Caesar to utilize at once. Caesar could have tried an immediate land invasion of Greece, but this would have been exceedingly tedious: march up the Adriatic coast, down through Illyricum and toward a formidable enemy, losing momentum and time while you need to worry that the republican forces in Spain might launch their own strike at Gaul and Italy. Of course Pompey could also plan his own land war against Italy, but he would need time. Caesar, ever given to trying to seize the initiative, could also not be on two fronts at once. Spain would ideally be seized rapidly. Meanwhile it helped neither party that March was still not the ideal season for naval operations.

In Rome, as news filtered in about the departure of Pompey and the coming of Caesar, there was fear that the old days of the proscriptions were about to return. Any such worries were addressed when Caesar came and spoke as if moved by his trademark clemency. But the story we hear about the tribune Lucius Caecilius Metellus and the treasury shows the dropping of the mask. He tried to resist Caesar's taking of the money, allegedly only to be threatened with his life.

Caesar said that he had saved Rome from the curse of the treasury; since the Gauls had captured Rome in the fourth century, it was the place of the conqueror of Gaul to put an end to all superstitious scruples about seizing its riches. Lucan's brilliant purple poetry is on vivid display as he dramatizes both the issue of the money, and of the fear in Italy of the rebirth of the worst times of Sulla, Marius, and Cinna.[13]

Mark Antony, not surprisingly, was assigned responsibility for maintaining order in Italy; by now he had established himself as one of Caesar's most trusted legates, if not his closest political and military confidant. Curio was to be sent to

Sicily to replace Cato; others were to head for Sardinia, Illyricum, and Cisalpine Gaul, while the money and resources that had been seized were to be put to immediate use: Caesar commissioned a fleet for both coasts of Italy, to begin to address his serious deficiency on the sea.

Needless to say, both Pompey and Caesar presented what they were doing as being for the good of the republic. Since the consuls were with Pompey, he had the easier job here in theory. But those dissatisfied with government and with the Catonians in particular found Caesar's case the far more persuasive one. Most people, it may be imagined, simply wanted to avoid being swept up by war and its consequences.

Sicily and Sardinia would be like Italy: they fell without a fight, the Pompeians simply evacuating.[14] This made sense: they were largely indefensible without concerted effort. Arguably some such effort should have been taken, since every bloodless conquest made Caesar's position more secure, and increased the calls for negotiation to avoid bloodshed.

Caesar also tried to make use of Aristobulus, the would-be King of Judaea who had had so checkered and adventurous career: civil war against his brother Hyrcanus, prisoner of Pompey, escapee, would-be rebel, prisoner of Gabinius.[15] Caesar hoped to use him as his own client king in the east, helping to weaken Pompey's strong power base by doing what he did best, namely instigate rebellion and foment civil chaos. Off he went with his son Alexander on Caesar's orders; and ultimately off would go the head of Alexander. Aristobulus was poisoned by Pompeian supporters, and his son would be decapitated at Antioch. Caesar's attempted foreign coup was averted.

Caesar himself was aiming to deal in person with Spain, worried as he was both for Italy and for the security of Gaul for which he had spent so many years labouring. Lucius Domitius had been assigned to be Caesar's replacement in Transalpine Gaul. After the debacle at Corfinium and Caesar's release of Domitius and his entourage, the would-be proconsul in theory could have joined Pompey at Brundisium, but he was seriously conflicted: furious at Pompey for not helping him at Corfinium, he was also by no means a fan of Caesar. Further, his job was to take command in Gaul, and this is exactly what he endeavoured to do. He travelled to Cosa in Etruria first, and then sailed to Massilia, the modern Marseilles. Caesar meanwhile sent Quintus Fabius Maximus and Quintus Pedius to see to the start of operations both defensive and offensive in the Spanish theatre. Massilia could be bypassed for the sake of the priority of guarding the Pyrenees invasion routes, but the city could by no means be ignored for long.

Indeed, by the time Domitius arrived, Caesar had commenced a siege operation after the Massilians had made clear that they were not opening their gates to Caesar as he made his way down toward Spain.[16] The siege began toward the latter half of April; Caesar entrusted it to Gaius Trebonius, while leaving naval operations in the hands of Decimus Junius Brutus, the distant cousin of the more famous Marcus Brutus. Decimus Brutus had had naval experience serving under Caesar in the Gallic campaigns; here he faced a massive task: build a fleet, fight the Massilians on the sea, help to secure a surrender on land.

Domitius would arrive in time to help defend the city. Pompey was able to send help from his vast naval resources; it seems that Curio was not particularly competent about guarding the Sicilian straits to keep Pompey from being able to intervene.

In the end, Massilia was clearly going to fall, the only question was how long it would take, and at what cost. The operations would be another instance of the kind of fighting that Caesar did not like to manage in person: much of the work was tedious and frustrating. Massilia managed to hold out until early September; the Caesarians would lose about 1,000 men, and their enemies some 4,000. Domitius is said to have been among the last to escape; he was able to flee by sea to join Pompey.

Cicero and other senators who had been less than anxious to leave Italy now prepared to depart to join Pompey. We cannot be sure of the influence on their decision of Caesar's having left Antony in charge of Italy; Caesar's legate was never as popular as his master, and with Caesar heading for Spain, Italy was probably a less pleasant place for anyone not firmly in the camp of the *populares*.

Pompey's commanders in Spain, Afranius and Petreius, had made their camp near Ilerda, the modern Llleida/Lérida in the northeast of Spain, in the Roman province of Hispania Citerior. Quintus Fabius and Lucius Plancus had some early engagements with the Pompeians, which did not go entirely well for the Caesarians; the situation was more or less stable, however, in the advent of Caesar.

The Battle of Ilerda was fought in June of 49 BC, as part of a late spring/summer campaign that for Caesar was meant to ensure that Spain would be no threat to him, so that he would be able to move east to confront Pompey. Broadly speaking, the first stage of the campaign consisted of Pompeian attacks on Caesar's lieutenants, and the second the initial skirmishes with Caesar's force on arrival. The Spanish campaign under Caesar's direction was conducted simultaneously with the Massilian siege and naval operations; Caesar would be able to finish handling the Spanish front and return to Gaul before Massilia was seized.

Caesar's Spanish campaign merits its own book.[17] It is a tale that includes the tragic aspects of civil war (the Pompeians being worried about fraternization, and ordering the rounding up and killing of Caesarians who had been mixing with their men when encamped nearby), the brilliant skill of Caesar when confronted with engineering and logistical problems (late spring floods and resultant bridge collapses), the clemency of Caesar (Afranius and Petreius would surrender, only to go on to fight in subsequent engagements of the war), and the participation of the celebrated polymath Marcus Terentius Varro. A true survivor, Varro was older than Pompey by about a decade; he would live until 27 BC, earning a reputation as one of the greatest scholarly minds in Roman history, and certainly as one of the most prolific of writers. Varro commanded the Pompeian forces in Hispania Ulterior; like Afranius and Petreius, he would surrender and go on to fight again and to be pardoned by Caesar again; later in life he would survive proscription in the days of the Second Triumvirate, finally to find and enjoy security to pursue his academic interests under Augustus.

Overall, the campaigns in Spain and Massilia were Caesarian victories that made for a successful summer of 49. The present volume is not a history of the war, and it is focused on Pompey not Caesar. This much can be said about Pompey and the engagements in Spain and Massilia. Pompey knew Hispania well; he was also aware of the relative abilities of his colleagues as opposed to Caesar. He had to anticipate that there could be major setbacks; he needed time, and the Spanish operations afforded him a chance to strengthen his position in the east especially, as well as in Africa. He could hope for the best in Spain, but he could also not be everywhere at once. Caesar had the advantage in the west, simply because he was there.

Pompey was not alone in having to trust less than masterful subordinates. The weak link in the Caesarian chain was probably Curio. Curio's main problem was how to confront the Pompeians in Africa, where the republic had a significant ally in King Juba I of Numidia. Juba owed much to Pompey, who had been responsible for securing the throne of his father Hiempsal II in 81 BC. Juba is said to have loathed Caesar because of an episode of personal insult when he visited Rome during a trial in which Caesar was defending a client against Hiempsal. Curio had also exercised his notoriety for saying too much when he openly talked about Numidia being annexed.

Curio was always prone to being a victim of his arrogance, coupled with a capacity for incompetence and underestimation of his foes. Africa was under the control of Publius Attius Varus, so that the campaign there would be one of legate against legate; neither Caesar nor Pompey would personally intervene.

Curio sailed from Sicily for Africa, leaving behind a sizable amount of his force; this was indeed perhaps done out of contempt for Varus, but he may also have been seriously concerned about the security of Sicily. The bulk of Curio's available forces were the men who had defected at Corfinium; Curio himself had very little experience in the field or in command of armies, and Caesar knew this. He sent Gaius Caninius Rebilus with him, but at some level he must have known that he was in the same position as Pompey, forced to depend on underlings. The difference was that Curio would not be facing Pompey.[18]

Varus and Juba were an effective team in organizing Africa in support of Pompey and the republic. Curio seems to have been worried about how affairs would turn out in Spain before casting his own die of destiny on African sands. The Mediterranean is vast and difficult to control effectively; there were efforts to hinder Curio's advance to Africa, but by August he was on his way to what is today northeastern Tunisia.

The Battle of Utica would be a Caesarian victory. Curio would enjoy the peak of his short-lived, ill-fated career. There were signs of trouble; talk of mutiny and of seriously disaffected soldiers would prove to be a major problem for Curio as he prepared to engage with Varus in what he hoped would be a decisive victory. Arguably, Curio's main problems were three. He did not have enough men. The men he had were potentially of appreciably dubious loyalty. And third, he was impulsive and not given to making the necessary reconnaissance and threat assessment that the dangerous situation entailed. He was also rightly nervous and anxious; his lack of experience was displayed all too clearly when he was often seemingly at a loss as to how to follow up on successes.

Utica was another headline of good news for the Caesarians, but it would take its place in the annals of those battles that are followed by a complete reversal of fortune. Curio did the right thing by sending for reinforcements from Sicily, but of course he should have done that in the first place.

What precipitated Curio's fatal disaster was that he was not in control of proper intelligence about the approach of Varus' own reinforcements, namely the main body of Juba's army. He was under the impression that Juba's commander Saburra was approaching with a smaller contingent of Numidian cavalry; in early skirmishes, Curio's men did so well that again the commander was flush with success when he learned of the victory, and he was determined to strike hard, hoping to wipe out what he thought was a manageable force. Juba meanwhile was ready to send help from his main body to reinforce Saburra. Saburra was more strategically gifted than Curio; he correctly judged that after his initial success, Curio would move quickly to hit him. The stage was set for what history knows as the Battle of the Bagradas River. It was still August; Curio would not live to see the end of the month.

Saburra ordered his men to feign a retreat when Curio appeared, so as to encourage the Caesarians in their misconception about what they were facing. It was North Africa in August; weather did not work in favour of men not acclimated to the conditions. Saburra turned and engaged the Romans, but his basic strategy soon became all too apparent: retreat, return to fight, retreat, wear down Curio's men, and supplement your own forces with a flood of fresh cavalry from Juba.

One thing may be said in Curio's defence. When it became clear that he had a disaster on his hands, our sources are in agreement that he fought bravely to the end. He would be slain the battle, allegedly arguing to those urging him to flee that he could never face Caesar after having lost a major part of his army.[19]

Rebilus was among the few who would escape the aftermath of the stunning reversal; Horace's friend Gaius Asinius Pollio was also a survivor of the African disaster. Juba pursued the Caesarians; the men who would be able to boast that they escaped were the ones who had been able to get to their transports in time. Varus was of a mind to spare the Caesarians who were less lucky, but Juba killed the prisoners, arguing that this was a war against public enemies. Caesar, needless to say, would retaliate by declaring that Juba was a public enemy; Pompey and his supporters would hail the saviour of the African front as friend and ally of Rome, King of Numidia and bulwark of the republic's outposts in the desert. Both Juba and Saburra would go on to fight again, and to die for the republic.

By the end of the summer of 49 BC, of the major fronts of the war outside Italy, Caesar could boast of victory in Spain, while Pompey had won in Africa; the African campaign had been a success even without Pompey's personal oversight. Both sides had reason to feel confident, but the African loss was far more substantial in men than what Pompey's side had incurred in Spain.

Caesar meanwhile had no time to waste in heading for Pompey. 49 BC had already been a dramatic year, and events would continue to unfold at a rapid pace. There was more trouble in the news: besides Africa, Mark Antony's brother Gaius was having his own difficulty guarding Caesar's position in Illyricum. He ran afoul of two of Pompey's commanders, Marcus Octavius and Lucius Scribonius Libo, who were in control of the republic's naval forces in the Adriatic and Ionian Seas. Octavius and Libo engaged Caesarian ships under the command of Publius Cornelius Dolabella; their victory allowed them to trap Gaius Antonius and his land forces on the island of Curicta, the modern Krk in Croatia.[20] Strategically it was dreadful news, especially as Octavius managed to win some initial victories in seizing locations in what was, after all, Caesar's province of Illyricum. He would suffer his own defeats and losses, largely at the hands of the local population; by winter he would be ready to withdraw to join Pompey at Dyrrhachium. But with Libo, he had secured the surrender of fifteen cohorts of Caesarians, dominating a key theatre, even if not with permanent occupation.

Caesar suffered a mutiny at Placentia, the modern Piacenza; we are not sure of the exact nature of the uprising, but it seems that the disaffected were annoyed at not being free to plunder the towns where the army advanced.[21] The mutiny seems to have required Caesar to leave Massilia quickly to suppress it in person;

there were certainly executions and reprisals, as one would have expected for the sake of maintaining order, even given Caesar's usual attitude of trying to appear forgiving (even if only as a façade).

When Caesar went west to deal with Spain, he is said to have commented that he was proceeding to face an army without a leader, and that when he returned, he would be dealing with a leader without an army.[22] The witticism bore an element of truth, but in fact his own adjutants did poorly in Africa and Illyricum, and they did not even face Pompey. As summer waned, Caesar needed more than ever for the war to be finished as soon as possible. The year would still hold surprises, as the republic continued to feed on itself with increasing frenzy.

Chapter Twenty-Two

Dictatorship and Dyrrhachium

One of the problems with a civil war is the question of constitutional legitimacy. The consuls of 49 BC were with Pompey; they were at the head of a government in exile. Caesar and his allies could not ignore the niceties of political life indefinitely; at some point the normal machinery of republican government required that there be elections for the year 48. Things were not normal, of course. But something needed to be done with the status of what exactly Caesar's initiatives were vis-à-vis the republic. The longer questions of this sort remained unanswered, the easier it was for Caesar to be denounced as a robber of the republic, not its would-be restorer and saviour.

The expedient that Caesar's associates devised (no doubt with his approval, if not impetus) was for their hero to be declared dictator.[1] That was the time-honoured Roman office for dealing with emergency situations. Pompey must have found the news especially interesting, given how often he had been denounced by his opponents and foes as being a dictator in waiting. Caesar had had ties to Marius; he was by no means a Sullan. Now he was stepping into exactly the shoes of the threatening, hostile presence of his formative years in political and military life. To be sure, he was carrying on a programme of actively avoiding any semblance of violence or proscription of enemies; this was being advertised as a benevolent dictatorship that wanted ultimately only peace. But dictator he was.

The praetor who saw to the legal farce that was orchestrated was Lepidus, in another of those moments where like some ghost he flits in and out, haunting some of the most important moments in Roman history.

In the end – and this, too, may have been the deliberately orchestrated theatrical performance of the hour – Caesar would hold office for eleven days. This was but a brief dress rehearsal for the day when 'dictator for life' was the title he sought. The eleven days would allow for elections for the new consular year; no one could have been surprised that Caesar would be one of the winners. His colleague would be Publius Servilius Vatia Isauricus; almost everyone considered him to be a mere puppet to maintain the formalities of republican government. He would be in charge of affairs in Rome while Caesar prosecuted his war.

In his commentaries, Caesar blithely notes that this was the year in which he was permitted by law to stand for the consulship.[2] One wonders if a smile crossed his face as he made note of the fact, a legal nicety amid the realities of civil war. For Caesar, survival demanded that everything be made to seem as appropriate and fitting as usual; he needed to demonstrate that nothing out of the ordinary was happening that was not otherwise unavoidable. Dictatorship was a mechanism to be able to make himself a consul; the election season of 49 was by no means a shining example of the republican tradition in action.

Caesar could truthfully say that he resigned the dictatorship; soon enough he was planning to travel to Brundisium, to prepare for the campaign against Pompey. There were significant financial and economic matters to settle, and Caesar managed them adroitly. But for the moment, the pressing matter was how to end the war successfully.

Some later chroniclers would argue that Caesar was the first of the Roman emperors, and for a subset of those writers, the dictatorship of 49 was the commencement of his reign.[3] This is inaccurate, as is dating it from the Battle of Pharsalus in 48; while an argument can be made that Caesar inaugurated something that could be referred to more or less loosely as 'empire,' it is important to remember that there are good reasons why the date of transition from republic to empire is controversial, as opposed to that of the more straightforward (at least relatively speaking) transition from monarchy to republic.

I would prefer 27 BC as the key date for any such change; if a dramatic battle scene is needed to date the momentous event, let it be Actium in 31, with the aftermath in Alexandria in 30 (such as it was in terms of military resistance). But the matter is complicated for us just as for those who lived through it and in its shadow and under its consequences. This was still a republic, and Caesar would have agreed. He might even have believed it.

Meanwhile exiles were recalled; this was an agenda item in the pursuit of presenting Caesar as a gentler sort of autocrat, and of painting previous administrations as harsh and vindictive. There was talk of sending a peace delegation to Pompey, but Caesar's consular colleague opposed the idea; this was probably more theatre: better to have the other consul be the one who was appearing to be intransigent. The reality was that the time for negotiation was passed; events were now moving too fast, besides taking on a life of their own. It was inevitable that there would be a clash between Caesar and Pompey; until such a decisive engagement, nobody could seriously consider what the terms of a negotiation would even look like.

One of the exiles who was recalled was Aulus Gabinius. He was in an interesting position given his long tenure of loyal service to Pompey. Now, however, he owed much to Caesar; in the prosecution of the civil war, Caesar would not use him in offensive operations against Pompey.

Cato, meanwhile, was giving his own advice to Pompey. He urged that the war be protracted; he was concerned that any defeat would imperil the very existence of the republic.[4] He was resolutely of the view that Pompey should make sure that no Roman would be killed, except in battle; likewise he wanted to see no city plundered. Whatever his personal feelings, Cato was aware that Caesar was playing a powerful propaganda game. He was also aware of the reputation of the *adolescentulus carnifex*, and he wanted to make sure that Pompey did not seem in any way prone to violence, either from vengeful thoughts or frustration. Of all the advice that Cato had given, this set of admonitions may represent the high point of his counsel.

Cicero acquired a certain negative reputation during this no doubt tense period. Residing in Pompey's camp, he seems to have given in to his fondness for jokes and what he thought to be amusing remarks.[5] Needless to say, his sense of humour was not always appreciated.

Omens, not surprisingly, accompanied Caesar's departure from Rome.[6] There were warnings that he would be destroyed if he remained, but fortunate and successful if he left; we are given an insight into the games of children, when we hear that some boys were playing 'Caesarians versus Pompeians', with the Caesarians winning.

Caesar had made sure that he was named consul for 48 BC; the republicans would not be true to their name if they had not made sure to choose their own magistrates. They kept to the traditions and formalities of republican practise, though in fact they elected the same officials as for the preceding year – a time-honoured custom in time of war. The real problem they faced from a legal point of view was that while they could rightly assert that they had a senate, they did not have a people of Rome, and so elections could not actually be conducted. They were scrupulous about legality: the new officials were called promagistrates, not magistrates, since they were not, technically, magistrates once their terms expired. Caesar must have been amused when he learned of this expedient, and he would not have been alone in finding the situation a source of black humour.

There was no question at this point that Caesar was in charge of his side; as for Pompey, in some regards certainly he was the man in whom was invested the most power and responsibility. Was he in the position of greatest authority? Some would say yes, but likelier is that to the very end of his life, he laboured under conditions appreciably different from Caesar in the matter of being able to give orders to subordinates and to make unilateral decisions, even if senate awarded him supreme command of the war effort.

There was one unavoidable problem in all this. If Pompey were to have supreme command of the forces of the republic, then it was increasingly difficult to argue that this was not a war between two highly ambitious men. The war was becoming harder and harder to explain as a fight of a republic against a rebel; it was eerily reminiscent of Marius and Sulla, even if circumstances were markedly different, and the new rivals quite different from their respective antecedents.

In Pompey's ideal strategic situation, he would be able to blockade Caesar in Italy until he was ready to take the initiative. That wish had been partly snuffed out by events in Spain, though Africa and Illyricum provided some compensation. Caesar was always looking for the dramatic, swift gesture, indeed never more so; increasingly it was clear that he would go on the offensive and not allow himself to need to worry about grain supplies being cut off from Italian ports by Pompey's pesky formidable navy.

Speaking of grain supplies, during this period relations between Ptolemy XIII and his sister Cleopatra continued to deteriorate; Egypt was on the verge of its own civil war, or more accurately, the transition from a cold to a hot one.[7] In the crucial months from late 49 to mid-48 BC, the situation in Egypt would become increasingly problematic, with direct consequences looming for both the Caesarians and the Pompeians. In no small measure, the civil war that would erupt in Alexandria would be just as momentous in its consequences for Rome as that raging between the two Romans.

Dyrrhachium and other towns of Epirus, meanwhile, were prepared as veritable warehouses of supplies for a long campaign. As winter approached, the stormy season would have spelled trouble for both sides. Caesar would be taking enormous risks to think about a crossing of the Adriatic like Pompey had done the previous spring, and the maintenance of a naval blockade would pose its own problems.

We have noted that Pompey's force was supremely expensive, given the size of his fleet. Financially and logistically, it may have been increasingly difficult to maintain the blockades and watches needed to guard the Adriatic. The real problem, however, was that in an age without satellites and other devices of espionage, learning exactly where your enemy plans to disembark is impossible when dealing with something as immense as the Italian coast.

Did Pompey fail to anticipate that Caesar was exactly the sort of commander who would try to make a winter crossing? Was Pompey in a position where there was little anyone could do to hinder Caesar's sailing? As ever the truth likely rests in a combination of factors. There was no question that with some luck and tolerably navigable seas, Caesar could cross. The question was whether he would be sailing to his doom, given how Pompey could realistically hope to be better prepared for regaining the initiative quickly, once he learned where Caesar had appeared.

Probably it was always in Caesar's mind that he would go for the jugular and prepare for a swift transit to Greece. Caesar arrived at Brundisium sometime just after the winter solstice; he was hoping for a voyage across the Adriatic in early January of 49 BC.

Pompey's plan for the winter of 49-8 was to send his armies into winter quarters, while maintaining coastal surveillance and naval operations insofar as possible in that season. He had already set up a massive training facility at Beroea, the modern Veroia in central Macedonia in northern Greece; after landing his forces at Dyrrhachium, he had moved quickly to take positions in Thessaly and Macedonia. The Roman Alexander must have thought it fortuitous to be occupying the ancestral lands of Alexander the Great and of Achilles; this was sacred soil for the dreams of heroes.

The clash that was imminent was not exactly one of east and west; certainly Pompey viewed it as one of Rome versus an upstart who had shown his true colours during his first consulship, and who had seized a second term of office after the ludicrous game Lepidus played with naming him dictator for less than a fortnight. Especially galling was every memory of how Pompey had faced severe criticism and opposition, even threats of violence, for being a would-be dictator. He could take some pitiful degree of satisfaction in pointing out that Caesar was now giving the republic an education in what dictators can do. At least Sulla had been honest; Caesar was playing his infuriating game of pretending to be clement, when in fact he was a megalomaniac, intent on seizing supreme power. Sulla had retired; Caesar was showing no such inclination, at least not until he had a handpicked successor. Such may have been the thoughts of those who spent those anxious months in Greece, waiting to see what the result would be when the two warlords finally clashed.

Our sources are divided on a major point in this crucial winter: where did Pompey send his forces to spend it? Appian[8] states plainly that Pompey divided his forces between Thessaly and Macedonia, which certainly did provide the best places to be in the general region in terms of comfort and security. But Caesar is surely right: Pompey dispersed his men in the cities and towns of Epirus where first they had landed: Dyrrhachium, Apollonia, etc.[9]

If Pompey had kept his men in Thessaly and Macedonia, he would have been making a mistake that Caesar would have been the first one to condemn. He would have been discounting the possibility that Caesar might try to cross the Adriatic at exactly the worst season for the voyage. No; it was one thing to train and to set up a massive central nexus of locations for the shipment of provisions and treasure, and quite another to abandon the strategic towns of Epirus and trust that Caesar would avoid winter sailing.

The clear strategy was to spend the summer of 49 BC building one's forces and accumulating resources, maintain and hopefully triumph in other theatres, and enact at least something approaching a successful blockade to create economic problems in Italy and logistical difficulties for Caesar in supplying his armies.

Placentia must have been a particularly good bit of news: the men who had mutinied were veterans, in theory sufficiently disciplined and orderly. Caesar had had to raise armies of recruits alongside the forces that had defected to his cause. There was always the possibility that any man's troops might rebel or switch sides, but after the initial shock of the fall of Italy, arguably Caesar was the one who might have more to worry about as he planned an invasion of Greece.

Bibulus, meanwhile, was assigned to maintain the coast guard presence in the Adriatic. Again, it was impossible to be everywhere at once, but what is certain is that Pompey was not caught sleeping that winter.

Not sleeping is not the same thing as being impervious to any surprise. Credit must be given where credit is due: Caesar was daring, and his daring was a tremendous success. He would be able to cross the Adriatic in the stormy season, and he would be able to bring across a significant force without major catastrophe. Readers of Lucan will be treated to the image of Caesar like a god, battling storm and tempest as if he were one of the rebels against the Olympian order.[10]

Pompey had been heading westward to join his troops in their winter quarters. At some point he sent away his beloved wife Cornelia; she had been with him in Thessalonica, and now she would be sent to Mytilene on the island of Lesbos. Again Lucan makes the most of the dramatic potential; likely, however, there was an orderly dismissal of non-combatants like Cornelia and Sextus Pompey.[11] Gnaeus Pompey Minor stayed with his father; he would be a veteran of many of the great campaigns of the war. Bibulus established his main naval base on Corcyra, the modern Corfu.

Palasë, Albania today is a small and hospitable village, largely populated by ethnic Greeks. Corcyra is in the distance; the entire area is mountainous (= the region of Ceraunian or 'Thunderbolt' Mountains), with quite rugged terrain. From antiquity to the modern age, the question of where an invasion force will land is often the key mystery in the unfolding of a major amphibious operation. Ancient Palaeste was as good as any place for the Caesarians to land in the east; it qualified as remote and difficult of access, and it was likelier than not that there would be no republican forces in the vicinity; the greatest threat would likely be a naval one, not anything on land. Lucan certainly thought it was where Caesar arrived (following the commander's commentaries), and many have agreed with him; others have preferred the Bay of Vlorë (Vlorë = the ancient Aulon) to the north, and this may be right.

What happened deserves to be considered in depth. Caesar was essentially trying to do what Pompey had done earlier in the year: move a large force across the Adriatic, and make sure that said armies had plenty of supplies for a long and difficult campaign. This took time; Pompey had faced significant challenges in his crossing, but Caesar's were appreciably greater. Even if he landed successfully, he would need to do what Pompey had done and to send back the original ships to help with the ferry operations; this was a fleet-opposed invasion, which at any time could have been hampered by Pompeian ships. And once the forces had managed to land, they would need more supplies than they could have carried with them. They would need to start seizing territory.

We hear of initial attempts to sail that were retarded by wind and wave, before Caesar was finally able to depart Brundisium. Having arrived just after the solstice, he tried to depart at once, only to have to wait until early January (probably the fourth). The delay allowed more time for more of his forces to arrive, so that he could encourage them further in person. Caesar certainly portrays a picture of having caught Pompey by surprise. It is likely that the wind and wave contributed not only to a relatively brief delay, but to uncertainty as to where exactly he would land; again, he was certainly taking risks, even reckless ones. The men were told to travel light, so as to maximize the number of forces that could be conveyed in each transport.

Caesar says that Bibulus was lacking in confidence and too disorganized and his forces too dispersed to be able to hamper the landing; despite having 110 ships, he did not assembly his fleet in time to do any good.[12] There were additional republican naval forces at Oricum; these, Caesar notes, he challenged with a nearly equal force of his vessels, such that they did not decide to come out to engage.

This was again Caesar against subordinates; he had won a victory over his onetime consular colleague Bibulus, even if trying to impede an operation of this sort in rough seas is exceedingly difficult. Preventing Caesar from crossing in winter would have been a challenge for anyone. That said, even Caesar could not conceal the success that Bibulus did attain in dealing with empty transports that were departing Epirus for the return leg to pick up more men in Brundisium. Bibulus was able to strike at this fleet, destroying some thirty vessels in the rear of the body of ships as they tried to flee; the ships were destroyed with the loss of their crews. Filled with frustration that he had not been able to engage with Caesar, Bibulus was all the more zealous to distribute his forces and to begin operations to hamper the approach of additional Caesarian ships. Caesar would not be able to say that his D-Day had been a bloodless landing.

We have noted the dissension in our sources as to Pompey's intentions and whereabouts. Dio would have us believe that Pompey was not even aware that Caesar was in Italy, having assumed that he was still occupied in Spain; according to this logic, Caesar intended to wait until spring to sail from Brundisium, but when he realized that he had caught Pompey asleep, he decided on his winter crossing (again, we remember that what we call 4 January would actually have been in November, still very much a stormy season, perhaps more so usually than early January).[13]

Dio's version defies belief, both in light of other sources, and for its assumption that Pompey was receiving basically no reports of any value to think that Caesar was still in Spain, etc. Interestingly, Dio's narrative does include the detail about Bibulus catching some of Caesar's transports as they returned to Italy, noting that the episode reminded Caesar that luck and fortune had been his guides.[14]

The account in Dio is perhaps based on trying to explain how after a summer and autumn of intense preparations, Caesar was able to slip through the net, as it were; it would be easy to assume that someone had been asleep on guard duty. One of Caesar's strengths as a commander was that he was willing to do the unexpected, even when it might mean losing everything; Pompey was also daring, but generally speaking he was not given to quite the same level of risk-taking that Caesar displayed.

An interesting bit of news appears to have crossed Pompey's desk at this juncture. Caesar sent Lucius Vibullius Rufus to deliver a message: this was the moment for making peace, given that roughly equal losses had been suffered on both sides, that both commanders had impressive forces in the field, and that there was no reason to continue a civil war.[15] He proposed that both men should disarm, and that the senate and the people of Rome should draft a plan for lasting peace.

We have seen how negotiations can be used to stall for time. In the present scenario, one could argue that Caesar was the one who needed more time; at the very least, he was in as much need of it as Pompey was. There was also no mention of the fact that he was currently consul, and that his consular colleague was firmly in his pocket. Caesar held far more cards than Pompey if this were a game to be played out in the senate and the forums of Rome; Pompey would be the one in a vastly inferior position.

We would argue that Caesar was being more or less duplicitous in his efforts to secure a peace treaty. Public opinion was always a consideration, and proposing peace meant that Pompey would be in the position of having to be the man who said no to something that could spare so many from harm and destruction. Pompey would have been correct in judging that Caesar and he were not evenly matched; on paper at least, Pompey was in the stronger position. If we imagine the exact same scenario in terms of forces in the summer of 31 for Octavian in place of Caesar, and Antony in place of Pompey, we would think that Antony would have stood an excellent chance of seizing ultimate power.

No, Pompey likely realized that Caesar were trying primarily to buy time, and secondarily to win more popular support as the would-be voice of reason and champion of peace. There was no advantage to Pompey in accepting Caesar's deal; it would have spelled his own ruin and defeat.

Caesar's messenger Vibullius had the dubious distinction of having had to surrender to Caesar first at Corfinium and again in Spain; now he was entrusted with this frankly embarrassing charade of an amicable embassy. Meanwhile, Caesar's own commentaries tell a story that is eerily reminiscent of what had happened in northern Italy. First Oricum and then Apollonia fell to Caesar without any real resistance.[16] Caesar depicts the inhabitants of neither town as being interested in fighting against Rome; he presents himself as the representative of Roman authority, as indeed he was if he was to be considered a lawful consul.

Caesar does not bother to explain or to justify how once again he had proposed peace, only to proceed to start seizing towns. He needed supplies badly; soon enough logistics and access to resources would be a major problem for him if he made no move to capture the provisions he could plunder. But his actions once again belied his avowed interest in making peace; he was doing nothing but stall until he could be in a stronger position.

Pompey's situation was seriously compromised by the bloodless takeover of the two strategic towns; he would be able to prevent any chance that Caesar would reach Dyrrhachium first, but again we are reminded that neither commander could be in every place at once, and that wherever Caesar was, Pompey's legate or colleague tended more or less to do poorly.

Caesar was not having everything his way, especially on the water. Appian says that at Oricum, Pompey had naval vessels guarding merchant vessels with grain; whatever ships could not be used for escape to Dyrrhachium, they destroyed so that Caesar would be deprived of supplies he desperately needed.[17]

The clock was ticking now; this was not Italy where one commander would seize towns and cities largely unopposed, and the other prepare for a mass exodus. Now it was the start of a great campaign of manoeuvres, skirmishes, and full-scale engagements, a long sequence of events that would be dominated by the Dyrrhachium campaign and then Pharsalus. It would all be over by August; at that point, Pompey would be in the unenviable position of leaving Greece, and not in the position of relative strength with which he left Italy.

Our sources about the preliminary encounters between the enemy forces offer a more or less coherent narrative, even if they do not agree as to the details.

Caesar was always at his best when he was able to move with rapidity; his having landed near the Ceraunian Mountains may have inspired him with thoughts of lightning-fast strikes. He became more frustrated when there was tedious delay, and the loss of the initiative in seizing Dyrrhachium, coupled with the problems of supplies and logistics, would have contributed to his annoyance, not to mention the lack of a response from Pompey to his latest attempt to buy time via negotiation.

Pompey's men would have been stressed and potentially demoralized at the awareness that Caesar had landed and was establishing a camp and seizing cities. But it is telling that Caesar made no attempt to force a battle at this juncture; he realized that he was in no position to engage in what would have been an uneven contest. That said, Pompey had his own reasons for avoiding battle. Caesar had fewer but better troops; despite the rigorous summer and autumn training, Pompey was not prepared to commit his men to a decisive battle without improving his advantages even more. Caesar was waiting for men; so was Pompey: he was expecting legions from Syria.

We hear of a famous anecdote from this period, one that Lucan embellishes with his customary flair and brilliance, casting Caesar as a would-be god defying the forces of nature, reminiscent of some rebellious giant challenging the Olympian order.[18] The situation was simple: Caesar needed the rest of his forces as soon as possible, but he knew that now that Pompey knew that he was in Epirus, and especially once spring came and the seas were open to patrols, there would be extreme difficulty in transporting more troops. And so he disguised himself as a common man, and between his disguise and the help of servants he carried out a plan to procure a speedy ship, claiming that a messenger was being sent from Caesar.

It was stormy and conditions completely averse to sailing; the vessel was in danger and the helmsman dispirited. Caesar revealed his identity to the shocked sailor, and inspired his courage. Dawn came too quickly to avoid the risk of capture; Caesar needed to return. Pompey was fast to try to anticipate Caesar's reinforcements; we hear of two of his men who were slain by Caesarians were reconnoitring the best place to ford the River Apsus. Pompey is said to have considered this inauspicious, and so he refrained from fighting at once. Other stories tell of an attempt to bridge the river that failed because of an engineering mishap or overloaded structures that collapsed with casualties.

Caesar's men were astonished at what he had done, and criticized the risks that he was willing to take. The reckless act would be followed by a second crossing, this time entrusted to a legate to urge the rest of the army to move quickly to reinforce him. Pompey was criticized by his men, too, for his failure to offer battle at once.

Romantic stories of adventure aside, in reality both men were skittish about fighting immediately, for the reasons we have noted. But as with Pompey's departure from Italy, the problem was that one always risked being thought cowardly or unsure about the odds of victory. It was a brief moment where the two men were in something of a state of equipoise. They were both in need of time and a pause; they were too closely encamped for the air they both needed to breathe. The ledger showed both positives and negatives for them both, and in a sense the situation by the stormy winter sea in Epirus was a microcosm of the insanity and the horror of civil war.

Lucan makes much of the dramatic potential of both the risky voyage, and of sending away Cornelia on the eve of battle; certainly the second of these is poetic licence more than historical fact.[19] The reality of the moment was a tense waiting game above all. Pompey encamped to the south of the Apsus. We hear of cavalry skirmishes, the time-honoured method or consequence of probing one's adversary for weaknesses.[20] Pompey may have entertained early hopes of smashing whatever small advance force he might have been able to corner, but such hopes would have brief.

Some have credited Caesar with knowing that the astronomical season was out of synchrony with the calendar, and that a crossing would be feasible; this is to underestimate how stormy 'true November' can be. Some have argued that Bibulus was hardly a hero of the first and crucial days of the operation; in their estimation, more could and should have been done from Corcyra to stop Caesar. That said, the ex-consul more than made up for any dozing on the job; he was so exemplary in trying to maintain the guard and blockade on the coasts that he may have driven himself to exhaustion, coupled with the demands of maintaining naval operations in winter. He seems to have fallen ill; he would be dead before the end of winter, a casualty of natural causes on Corcya in early 48.[21] He was relatively young, but the last decade or so of his life had not been particularly easy, and the strain of the war and his difficult command responsibilities seem to have been too much for him.

Bibulus lived long enough to learn of some potentially hopeful developments. Caesar's supply problem was acute; to give a sense of how bad it was, at one point he needed to travel at least 100 miles to try to forage safely. He saw Buthrotum, in the very south of modern Albania; today it is a major archaeological site, and there was mythological lore associating it with the Trojans and their westward journeys. Simply put, Caesar needed to venture far and wide to find the wherewithal to maintain his armies, and behind his back, Pompeian naval forces were able to try to negotiate as they sailed into the harbour at Oricum, for example, hoping to reverse Caesar's takeover of the town. Whatever work had started before pneumonia or whatever else it was had ended Bibulus' admirality, it continued vigorously under Libo. Libo was successful in harassing the key Caesarian embarkation port of Brundisium; Antony would certainly have been compelled to admit that he had suffered significant harassment from the

Pompeian navy. It is not hard to imagine how Bibulus could fall sick and die; he was a formidable presence on the water, but it was both a bad time to be on the water weather-wise, and Caesar was making it increasingly difficult to land to find water and supplies.

Through it all, there were ample reminders that luck does play a role in war, sometimes a huge one. There were moments when Caesar was the first to admit that he owed it to fortune and not to skill that he did not suffer devastating losses in trying to bring over his armies.[22] Gaius Coponius performed admirably, for example, in conducting Pompeian naval operations against Antony in the spring of 48.

Dio says that Antony was hesitant to try to cross over to reinforce Caesar as long as Bibulus was alive, fearing the hazard from his patrol boats; once Libo succeeded him, Antony felt more confident and continued the ferrying of men.[23] There were engagements and setbacks for both sides; the weather conspired against them both initially; it would be early April before Antony was able to be ready to join Caesar in operations outside Dyrrhachium. Likely the better weather was the key contributing factor in Antony being able to provide appreciable supplement to Caesar's forces. Coponius was more a victim of wind than of Caesar's subordinate; even Caesar in his commentaries would admit that fortune was his ally, which of course he took as a sign of divine favour for his enterprise.[24]

Pompey meanwhile had worked on perfecting the fortification of a strong camp. Here he was in the superior position: with his back to the sea and superiority on the water, Pompey could expect to be able to be supplied as and if necessary by his navy. Caesar needed to rely on scouts and foragers, as well as on what he had brought from Italy and what he had seized from Oricum and Apollonia; Dyrrhachium was the real prize he coveted for sustaining his forces.

Pompey's problems increased appreciably once Antony managed to land, but so did Caesar's. It was all about resources: Pompey's were virtually inexhaustible, while Caesar and Antony faced formidable challenges. Caesar and Antony needed to try to unite their forces; Pompey ideally would have tried to prevent this. Scholars debate exactly where the Caesarians met; it was likely a day's march or so east of Dyrrhachium. Antony's original landing was at Lissus (the modern Lezhë) in Illyria; he needed to move swiftly to secure the town and to rendezvous with Caesar, which meant that Caesar needed to allow himself to be distracted from other agenda items (e.g., keeping an eye on Oricum) while trying to connect with Antony.[25] Once again fickle locals played a role in events; the Pompeian commander Marcus Otacilius Crassus was forced to abandon Lissus when it was clear that the inhabitants were ready to open their gates to Caesar, and Pompey faced significant opposition from the locals as he tried to

Dictatorship and Dyrrhachium 277

prevent Antony from being able to join with Caesar. For many of the Greeks, the issue was not partisanship in favour of Pompey or Caesar, but a desire not to have their towns and farms destroyed by war. With that motivator, it was a case of siding with the first person who showed up bent on attacking. Any harshess in maintaining order/martial law would also have turned the locals against the Pompeians.

Through it all, both Pompey and Caesar engaged in displays of their mastery of logistics and control of supply lines. The scene near Dyrrhachium was rife with opportunities for trying to cut off water supplies, to prevent animals from grazing, from allowing cavalry plenty of open ground for manouevres, for putting one's enemy on the defensive, at least to the eyes of potentially fickle locals.

If Pompey's first hope was to destroy Caesar's initial landing force, his second was to force a battle on terms favourable to him. An element of that strategy was wearing down the enemy by trying to deprive him of access to resources. For Caesar, if Pompey could not be initially crushed, the strategy was a similar one. It was a familiar waiting game of sorts, one in which there is a constant hope that the enemy will make a mistake. Meanwhile, the work of building fortifications continued unabated.

Dyrrhachium, we have noted, was a long series of intertwined campaigns and manouevres, both on sea and land. It has been the deserved subject of extensive research. Caesar would come close to destruction; in some regards, Pompey would lose his best opportunity to finish the war at one stroke. The weaknesses of both men as commanders would be cast in sharp relief; all things considered, a case could be made that it was a poor showing all around. But it was a Pompeian victory. Overall, Caesar's famous estimation that Pompey failed to know how to make use of his victory was correct; had Pompey become more like Caesar at the end, the war may have turned out differently; conversely, had Caesar been more like Pompey at the start, he may not have found himself in dire straits.

Amid the ongoing action and news, Caesar would make much of one episode. Marcus Octavius laid siege to Salonae, and soon found himself in a difficult position; Gabinius had come across not by sea but by land, and he assisted in the defence. Octavius would be forced to withdraw; Caesar, not surprisingly, would glorify the victory as if it were tantamount to the heroic exploits of yore.[26]

Gabinius merits extended comment here. He had enjoyed a long and varied career in different theatres. After his exile, thanks to the civil war he had another chance to take his place on the world stage. Conflicted because of loyalties to both sides, he played a significant but sideshow role in the Balkan campaigns, dealing with hostile Dalmatian tribes on the difficult land march toward Greece, and then with Octavius' siege operations. Like Bibulus, it seems that Gabinius would succumb to natural causes; they were both roughly the same age, and both of them seem to have exerted themselves overmuch. Gabinius died either in the latter part of 48, or possibly early in 47.[27] He did not enjoy a dramatic last achievement, but his record would include the defence of Salonae: he had added to his resume.

Illyricum should have been a source of more success to Caesar, but at the time when Caesar was supposed to be governing it, he had been more than occupied with the conquest of Gaul. In the current war it was something of an embarrassment; Octavius was able to achieve some success along the Dalmatian coast, even if Salonae would not fall; on the seas, the Caesarians had fared badly. Caesar could not count on the land route from Italy down into the Balkans; the region was by no means safe and pacified from native tribes anyway (again, its governor had had more than enough to do in the west), and the Pompeians were active and effective. On that front, at least, Pompey's subordinates either held their own or were in a superior position.

The Syrian proconsul Scipio, meanwhile, was a key player in the unfolding drama. We hear of the not surprising harshness of the financial and other exactions he imposed on his province to help fund and support the war effort; he needed to raise men and material quickly, and the means by which he did so must have been increasingly unpopular.[28] We have noted his beheading of Alexander of Judaea at Antioch; in this same period he was facing revolts and the omnipresent Parthian threat, which no doubt increased his impatience and frustration. He was informed by Pompey immediately of Caesar's arrival in Greece, and that he should come at once with whatever force he had collected; this required a swift and arduous advance toward Macedonia: in some sense he was playing Antony to Pompey's Caesar.

Caesar was aware of the threat posed by Scipio's forces, and he sent Lucius Cassius Longinus and Gnaeus Domitius Calvinus toward Thessaly and Macedonia, hoping to intercept Scipio and prevent his reinforcement of Pompey. We hear of reports that some towns in Thessaly and its environs contacted Caesar, indicating that there was a chance of some locales switching sides if Caesar were to send forces; Cassius Longinus was entrusted with looking into that matter, while Domitius Calvinus was supposed to hunt for Scipio.[29] At the same time, Gaius Calvisius Sabinus was assigned to head into Aetolia, principally to start managing supply gathering and logistical lines together with Cassius. Once again we are reminded that great commanders cannot be everywhere at once; these were exceedingly arduous tasks, and of critical strategic importance. The operations that would commence in Macedonia and Thessaly would be the prelude to the ultimate clash of Pompey and Caesar in Thessaly.

The decision to send major units deeper into Greece meant that Caesar needed to reduce his presence at places like Oricum, at harbours that were less of a strategic priority now that Antony had been able to land. As soon as the word spread that the defences in the area were thin, the Pompeians launched one of their more daring exploits: the naval raid of Pompey's son Gnaeus on Oricum.

The main goals of Pompey's son were to destroy the Caesarian ships at Oricum, and then, if possible, to proceed to do the same at Lissus with the vessels that had brought over Antony and his reinforcements. The operation would be Gnaeus' first chance to prove himself as a competent fighting son of his great father, and he performed splendidly. Gnaeus had brought ships from Egypt. Caesar admits that at Lissus, Gnaeus was able to destroy thirty merchant vessels. Attempts, however, to storm the town failed, and Gnaeus retreated. Caesar characteristically underplays the significance of the deeds of Pompey's son, but much had been done to make life harder for the Caesarians both in terms of supply lines, and with respect to a vexing question: was Italy really secure? The deeper Caesar ventured into Greece, the more worried he would need to be that the fickle pendulum would swing back; for all he knew, the Pompeians were planning to use their naval superiority to launch an invasion of Italy, which would have been a good strategy and one that would have seriously compromised Caesar's position, at least potentially.

In the virtual stalemate at Dyrrhachium in the period before Antony was able to reinforce Caesar, we hear again of fraternization between the armies, as had happened at Spain; Caesar allegedly encouraged this, mindful that it had helped his cause on that other front; the defector Labienus played a key role in ending the overly friendly relations.

Pompey's camp was on the height of Petra, a place that was virtually retardant to attack. What continued to unfold for weeks was one of the most memorable experiences of trench warfare in Roman military history, where the hard work of preparing, maintaining, and strengthening defensive fortifications is accompanied by occasional skirmishes, mostly between probing cavalry units.

Caesar gives his readers the impression that the location of Pompey's camp was the result of his having been cut off from Dyrrhachium by Caesar's trademark swiftness and gift for interception.[30] In reality, it is likelier that Pompey was committed to using Caesar's own talents against him, by making sure that his own supplies were inexhaustible by sea, while compelling Caesar to take more and more risks to continue to feed his hungry men. Even Caesar confesses that he now saw that the war would be prolonged: this was exactly the scenario that he had tried to forestall by landing so quickly in Epirus. Throughout this period, one gets the impression that Pompey and Caesar strongly complemented each other; together, they would have made a formidable force, being able to balance and to counteract each other's flaws and weaknesses. Civil war meant that it would be a contest to see whose deficits would prove deadlier, and, as always, to see who would be luckier. To the extent that they were evenly matched in plusses and minuses, the balance sheet would be increasingly at the mercy of fortune.

Pompey had more auxiliaries than Caesar, more archers and slingers. As Caesar attempted to invest Pompey's positions by taking hill positions, Pompey tried to drive him off, always being careful to be lured into a trap. Caesar describes one such clash, where men of his ninth legion were forced to give up a hill position, noting that Pompey is said to have remarked that he did not mind being called a bad commander, if he were able to drive Caesar away from positions that he had rashly tried to seize.[31] In other words, Pompey was playing conservatively, seeking to frustrate his onetime protégé, and to goad him into being even more reckless than usual.

The battle in question was probably fought in the middle of June of 48 BC, for the hill of Paliama. The comment attributed to Pompey is circumstantial evidence of the criticisms he would have been subject to from his own impatient men, and from those who thought that he was afraid to face Caesar in a pitched battle. The ninth legion was one of Caesar's most experienced units, commanded by Antony. While his performance was skilful, Caesar and Antony were also liable to the accusation that they were hesitant to engage in a straight fight with the enemy. In truth, all parties had good reason to resist the temptation to clash.

Caesar attests to the continuing problem of hunger by noting the makeshift bread his men made from unappetizing roots mixed with milk; the Pompeians are said to have made fun of this, which prompted Caesar's men to hurl the loaves at their jeering enemy.[32] Caesar had food supply issues, and Pompey faced the threat of bad water from the efforts that Caesar could make to divert and cut off his freshwater supply; Lucan has a characteristically vivid account of the outbreaks of disease in Pompey's camp, probably both dysentery and typhus.[33]

Whether or not it was typhus, disease was a greater threat to Pompey's forces than Caesar. Morale must have been seriously threatened, and the sense that Pompey's men were under siege was enough of a problem. At some point, there would need to be a breakthrough, and lice-borne illness was a powerful motivator to try to initiate some plan to put an end to the interminable stalemate.

The problem we face in analyzing the Battle of Dyrrhachium is that our sources are so contradictory and not entirely clear; a coherent narrative can be reconstructed, but not a definitive one. Lucan is as ever a valuable source, but his epic poetry is so redolent with the spirit of the rhetorical schools that it can be difficult to glean a clear sense of strategy amid all the bombast and hyperbole. Caesar certainly seems to have hoped that Dyrrhachium would be betrayed to him or would surrender, like Oricum, Apollonia, and so many other places in his lucky past. Pompey and Caesar were both interested in continuing to try to seize strategic hill positions, so as to strength the circumvallation of the enemy. And there was the great trench and fortification works of the main camps.

Pompey seems to have tried to use the element of surprise with a decoy effort: convince Caesar that Dyrrhachium was ready to surrender to him, to lure away forces so that simultaneously Pompey could launch an assault on Caesar's fortification lines, which seems to have been a three-pronged operation. This is the scenario that allowed for the celebrated episode with the centurion Scaeva. He was said to have been compelled to take command of his defensive fort when senior commanders were injured. He famously (if improbably) could boast of 120 holes in his shield, standing as a stalwart defender and managing a counteract, blinded in one eye and seriously wounded, the living incarnation of loyalty to Caesar and of literally blind madness to serve his commander.[34] Scaeva would be promoted, lavishly rewarded, and treated as a valiant hero; while his story was no doubt exaggerated (for Lucan, it becomes fodder for one of his most incredible narratives, a powerful commentary on the nature of fury),[35] he was clearly the most singularly outstanding of the defenders of Caesar's fortifications.

Lucan casts the whole series of operations as a Pompeian offensive, and this is surely right; the Caesarians were decoyed as to the situation in Dyrrhachium, and Pompeian naval units were able to help to ambush Caesar's forces that tried to advance toward what they thought would be a surrender. In the end, Pompey faced a serious problem. Caesar indicates that there were six separate operations, three at the siege lines, and three at Dyrrhachium. Scaeva succeeded as the leader in beating back an assault, though he did not press home his advantage; this decision was criticized by some and praised by others. Pompey's men were able to execute a retreat under fire.

In the end, we hear that Pompey lost something like 2,000 men in the whole affair, and Caesar twenty – but our source for this is Caesar, and the numbers are clearly an exaggeration.[36] The problem was that at best, the operations had resulted in the status quo ante: there was still a stalemate, and Pompey still had to contend with typhus or whatever diseases were afflicting his camp.

The pressing question is what Pompey had hoped to achieve. It would have been unrealistic to expect that the decoy operation (backed by naval forces) and frontal assault could result in some victory of combined arms that would result in the collapse of Caesar's position. It was likely that he was trying to achieve two goals, one of them psychological. The principal intention would be to expand the territory under Pompeian control, thus putting serious constraints on Caesar. Secondarily, it would be to show that Pompey was not afraid of confronting Caesar offensively. The seizure of additional territory would allow for better access to fresh water, thus alleviating the problem of disease and thirst; Pompey would also be able to have a better chance of provoking Caesar into making a mistake. The goals were limited in scope, but of appreciable significance; they reflected the classic Pompeian strategy of exercising caution while getting a job done. In this case, the job was improving the situation of his army, while also reassuring the fearful that he was more than willing to challenge Caesar.

Did Pompey's operations fail? On the whole, yes. But Caesar was still in dire straits. His need for supplies was exacerbated by the reality that the daring commander had landed his army in a vice that was wholly unnecessary. He was essentially laying siege to Dyrrhachium, salivating for its rich stores of supplies and provisions. But at the same time, he was under siege from a massive Pompeian army that had fewer worries about supplies on the whole, an army that was virtually impregnable owing to its superior position. Yes, Pompey needed to worry about water and disease. But Caesar had grave worries, too, and his situation was likely to worsen faster than Pompey's. The major clashes that had broken out may have cost Caesar fewer men, but that was the price to be expected for a frontal assault; Caesar had been able to hold his position, but that was tantamount to a stalemate, especially for someone who was best at lightning offensives.

It is of the utmost interest that in the aftermath of these operations, Caesar soon faced the defection of two of his allies, Gallic cavalry chieftains.[37] Obviously any defection would mean that Pompey would have access to information about the weaknesses in Caesar's fortifications and trenchworks, and there was the boost to morale that came from a major switch of allegiance. The Allobrogres who defected were probably sick of living on the makeshift rations and in the poor conditions of Caesar's camp; they were defecting to a position that was also in trouble, but anything may have seemed better after weeks of bad bread and constant worry about supplies. They may have calculated that the recent engagement had shown that Caesar was just as stymied in the immediate as Pompey, and that in the long view Pompey was in the better position. They may have had ties to Labienus or other Pompeians, and they may simply have come to dislike Caesar. He accuses them, as would be expected, of being little more than criminals and unsavoury types, and perhaps they were. But neither Pompey nor Caesar could boast the moral high ground in that area; both commanders were happy to have what help they could muster.

Pompey had to have been thinking of his next steps even before the defection of the Gallic cavalry, but no doubt at least some aspects of his plans were modified as a result of their intelligence and the supplementary forces. What he planned was essentially another three-pronged attack, having given little respite to the Caesarians. He was clearly determined to show that he was now taking the initiative; probably the Gallic chieftains had been able to update him and provide reliable information about where Caesar's defensive lines were weak.

The target this time was not the centre of Caesar's lines, where no doubt men were quickly working to restore damaged fortifications and palisades in fear of a second wave. Showing once again that he was a master of combined arms and amphibious operations, Pompey decided to strike at the south of Caesar's line, near the sea; ideally he could launch a frontal assault, backed by a seaborne force behind the lines. It was a daring raid, of the sort that served to remind everyone that Caesar was not the only one capable of such bold manouevres.

This would be a classic attack at the first light of dawn. One of the most memorable details of the attack is how Pompey made sure that his men were equipped with wicker visors, the idea being that the defensive accoutrement would provide protection against slingshot fire.[38] In other words, Pompey had done his job at making sure he knew how the Caesarian forces were armed.

Pompey's plan was also a demonstration of his meticulous attention to logistical detail. He had several objectives: destroy Caesar's fortifications, kill as many men as possible, if possible embarrass the enemy by capturing a standard, and most of all be ready immediately to start constructing a Pompeian camp and fortification, so that when the attackers were ready to withdraw if they were overwhelmed by enemy reinforcement, they would be able to escape into a prefabricated camp, a new base that would have the classic Pompeian fondness for access to the sea, a new threat on Caesar's southern flank.

The fact that Caesar had stationed elements of the ninth legion in this sector shows that he recognized the strategic importance of the site, not least because he knew that Pompey could utilize his superior naval forces to help attack and resupply the zone. The initial defenders were overwhelmed; Antony had to rush to the rescue, and in the end Caesar himself had to come, a sure sign of the seriousness of the crisis. Pompey's men were able to withdraw to the new outpost that had been swiftly set up; all in all, it was a stunning achievement of combined arms, engineering prowess, and daring. And for Caesar, it was a weakening of his defensive lines, one that came with a significant loss of manpower.

But the real problems for Caesar were only commencing. The obvious task for both sides now was to do the tedious, hard work that had already filled so many days: fortify and dig trenches. The Caesarians had repair work to do, indeed complete rebuilding; the Pompeians needed to start reinforcing their makeshift first camp into a formidable defensive barrier. Caesar the impatient was probably chafing at the failure of his men to provoke the full-scale pitched battle he craved; the kind of war that was dragging on near Dyrrhachium was not the sort of engagement in which he excelled, and for the moment he had seriously lost the initiative.

At some point in this process of construction and defensive preparations, scouts seem to have informed Caesar that a large Pompeian force was moving to occupy an abandoned camp by the River Lesnikia. The goal that Caesar instantly set on was to try to regain offensive momentum by launching a surprise attack on this force, all the while giving the impression that his men were occupied fully with the ongoing defensive labours. If he could pounce on the Pompeian forces and rout them, at the very least there would be another stalemate; he might even have luck again on his side and be able to inflict serious losses.

Caesar led away a portion of his force, included men from the shattered ninth legion, which had suffered such serious losses in the Pompeian attack. The total force that Caesar brought to the Lesnikia camp was about three times the size of his enemy; he was able to strike the camp, which despite a hard fight was soon ready to be taken.

The first problem, however, that the Caesarians faced must have filled them with instant aggravation as well as anxiety. There was a second line of fortifications; the Pompeians had erected something of a camp within a camp, and so the rout now once again turned into a classic siege. Antony's men who had succeeded in breaking down the first layer of defences now began striking at the second, and they enjoyed continued success. It must have seemed to both Caesar and Antony that the operation was going well, and that the critical losses they had incurred were being made up for in the slaughterhouse that the Lesnikia camp was at risk of becoming.

Time was of the essence, and the 'camp within a camp' defensive situation was taking all too long to sack, despite all the progress. Pompey meanwhile had learned of the assault, and he was on the way to reinforce his men, in a scenario that would be something of a miniature panorama of the Dyrrhachium campaign: Caesar the besieger would be besieged.

Caesar seems to have had emergencies with which to grapple. The first and arguably most serious was the arrival of Pompey and his fresh troops. The second was the fact that Antony's men had not succeeded in routing the Pompeians who were taking refuge in the inner camp; they were still a formidable force, especially when their spirits were buoyed by the realization that Pompey had galloped to the rescue.

Caesar now faced an attack from two sides: the Pompeians inside the camp drove hard at the right flank of his force, and it seems that before long there was a serious panic for both Caesar's cavalry and his infantry. The spectrum of emotions ranged from anxiety to terror; the Caesarians did not want to be trapped between two Pompeian armies, and the logistical problem with having destroyed camp fortifications is that now you cannot quickly manouevre amid all the destruction and wreckage of ramparts.

One cannot underestimate the scale of the disaster that was in the making. Caesarian units were in full flight; Caesar tried valiantly to rally his men and to urge them to hold the line, but we hear of one standard-bearer from Caesar's army who went so far as to attack Caesar: the commander was trying to prevent the flight of the eagles, and the *signifer* was not going to let anyone stand in his way. The man's arm was hacked off by Caesar's retinue; he had probably come frighteningly close to killing his general.

Fighting too passively and defensively carries risks, and so does being reckless. Caesar had behaved with characteristic vigour to the news of what he thought would be a juicy, irresistible target; the Pompeian force may not have been bait, but it might as well have been. Caesar did not have complete intelligence about what he would be facing, and he was unprepared for the rapid advance of significant relief forces under Pompey. It was an avoidable disaster, perhaps one of the worst performances by Caesar in his long and justly celebrated military career.

Before long, Caesar was also in flight. He knew that his situation was untenable; there was no realistic chance of rallying his men and holding position. There are two possibilities: either the whole engagement had unfolded by happenstance, or the force that went to the Lesnikia was meant to be nothing other than a lure for Caesar. We cannot be sure, but either way, what doomed Caesar's men was his recklessness. He had not sought out proper intelligence about the camp layout; he did not prepare for the eventuality of Pompey arriving to reinforce his beleaguered men. Yes, maybe if Antony's forces had fought harder, or if his men had not buckled and then fled, it could have been salvaged. But the blame for the defeat rested with Caesar, and while his commentaries sometimes seem to read as little more than a chance to blame everyone else for disasters, even the most partisan admirer of Caesar would have trouble defending the oversight of this battle. The loss was born of frustration with how the Dyrrhachium campaign had been proceeding; impatience and a tendency to impulsive, lightning strikes had conspired to doom Caesar's dreams of avenging the losses from the dawn raid.

Here begin the recriminations and occasional words of praise for Pompey. It is a tribute to the strength of Caesar's ultimate victory over Pompey that the historical record is marked more by criticism of Pompey at this juncture than by blame for Caesar for the disaster. Pompey did not press home his victory; he did not pursue Caesar. Allegedly, he could have won the war if he had known how to use his win; failure to know how to be a victor meant that the victory would lead ultimately to defeat.[39] Polynaeus says that Caesar's humiliated men presented themselves to their commander for decimation; Caesar refused to inflict the penalty, and ever after his soldiers fought with particularly fierce vigour.[40]

Lucan is often understandably dismissed as being ridiculous when he argues that Pompey refrained from pursuing and destroying Caesar because of the Roman virtue of *pietas*.[41] By this line of thought, Julia's widower could not bring himself to kill his father-in-law; he was too honourable and decent a man. Some have tried to assert that Pompey was trying actively to win as a bloodless a victory as possible; this was true for Caesar as well. It was part of the propaganda machinery for how you manage civil wars; you cannot appear too bloodthirsty when the blood is Roman.

Certainly the possibility existed that the rout of the Caesarians and the embarrassing flight of Caesar would inspire mass defections to the republican armies, and the effective end of the war. Pompey knew how fickle the Romans could be; if victory were the only god they loved, then he could expect the treatment due the hero of the hour.

Pompey as hero was hailed as *Imperator* by his men; famously, he is said to have refused to use the title, and not to have used the laurel of victory on his *fasces*.[42] The victory, after all, had been over fellow Romans. Labienus, it is true, is said to have had some Caesarian prisoners slain publicly in the wake of the debacle; it is likely that scholars are right to see these as Gallic and Germanic auxiliaries of Caesar, not Roman citizens. Still, there would be those who would resurrect the criticisms of Pompey as being the true protégé of Sulla, ready to sanction brutality against his opponents.

The campaign at Dyrrhachium arguably was the lowest point of Caesar's career on the battlefield; the month that would one day bear his name had not been lucky for him. While Caesar seemed ready to blame everyone (not to mention the fickle goddess Fortuna), in many regards he had only himself to blame, and his cause was at serious risk.[43] At the absolute minimum, he would need to abandon his original plans. The first order of business was to withdraw to Apollonia; initially he left a sizable force to cover the retreat. For Pompey, the priority agenda item was to determine what Caesar was doing; that would help with determining the next course of action for the republicans.

Pompey had every reason to be justly proud of his accomplishments, whether or not he had baited Caesar into striking the camp within a camp at the Lesnikia. But whatever elation he may have allowed himself to feel for even a brief moment would be exceedingly fleeting.

Chapter Twenty-Three

Toward Pharsalus

Plutarch says that Caesar lost 2,000 men in his defeat, and that Pompey was either incapable of taking Caesar's camp, or afraid to do so.[1] Pompey was well aware that at the very least, Caesar's supply problems were now critically exacerbated; he needed to get away from Dyrrhachium.[2] The mood of the republican elites was jubilant; word was sent to Cornelia to update her that her husband had been successful.[3] There was talk of sending men to Rome to prepare for proper elections and the resumption of normal republican business; indeed there were those who thought that Pompey needed to go to Rome in person to reassert that Caesar did not speak for the republic, and that in fact he was a public enemy who now happened to be a fugitive.

Afranius was one of the voices calling for a return to Italy; he was convinced that Italy, Sicily, Sardinia, Spain and Gaul would all readily fall to the republican forces after so great a showing. Pompey was determined to be the pursuer, however, and not to seem to be running away from Caesar again; he also expressed worry about his forces in Thessaly and Macedonia, not to mention the general security of the east. There was no real question, at least strategically; despite the farce that Caesar had perpetrated with Lepidus regarding the elections for 48, Pompey could not have seriously considered abandoning a final showdown with Caesar. And at least in the immediate aftermath of his victory, there was that aforementioned hope that Caesar's armies would slip away from him.

Indeed, Thessaly and Macedonia constituted an important theatre of war during the long sieges at Dyrrhachium. We have noted how Lucius Cassius Longinus and Gnaeus Domitius Calvinus had been out to deal both with Caesar's supply problems and with the threat from Scipio. The former suffered a defeat at the hands of Scipio's forces, and his colleague had setbacks in Macedonia; they were able to regroup and to draw on local support from the Locrians and the Aetolians to prepare for counterattacks, in which they were more successful. Caesar intended to try to link up with these forces and to seek a more stable source of provisions. He commissioned Quintus Fufius Calenus to try his luck with places like Delphi and Thebes, which he was able to win over to the Caesarian cause.

Caesar emphasizes that he had tried to initiate peace talks with Scipio; it is reasonable to be suspicious of these overtures as a stalling device.[4] In his account, Scipio was open to negotiation, but was forced by other republicans to abandon the effort; Caesar notes that he learned of this after the war – when we might wonder how many people were trying their best to polish their credentials with the victor.

Caesar says that after the disaster at Dyrrhachium, he needed to go to Apollonia to leave his wounded and sick, to pay his men, and to encourage them.[5] Certainly he needed to get to a place of safety and provision as soon as possible; he probably was not trustful of the devotion of his men, and the fear of losing them to Pompey by mutiny must have been acute. Pompey launched a pursuit, and there is no question that Caesar was masterful in executing his flight; within a matter of three or four days, it was clear that terrain cooperated with Caesar in making it increasingly unlikely that a cavalry force could gallop after the fleeing forces.

Caesar realistically had no option but to proceed into Thessaly and Macedonia. To stay anywhere on the Adriatic coast was to invite disaster. To leave Greece for Italy would be to admit defeat; to try to hope that he could raise more forces to cross over from Brundisium would be playing into the active summer naval operations of the Pompeian fleet. His only choice was to head east.

When he had first arrived in the Balkans, Caesar had had every hope of forcing a decisive confrontation with Pompey somewhere in what is today Albania. He was zealous and preoccupied as ever with speed; he needed to worry about provisions, but he was more interested in destroying the main body of the republican army as soon as possible. All of that had changed between spring and high summer; now he was desperately in need of provisions for what he needed to fear might be a long campaign.

He did, however, need to worry about Italy. The Adriatic coast at least gave one the ready sense that Italy was close. Now he was heading deeper inland, away from Rome and to an uncertain destiny. But it was also a land rich with resources, and that was the priority.

Pompey had ruled out the idea of returning to Italy, and Caesar would have learned about this decision sooner rather than later.[6] Devotees of alternative histories have delighted in doing what Pompey must have done, namely wargame the scenarios if he had decided to turn west. In one sense, it would have been to trade situations: Pompey would be abandoning the incredible wealth and resources of the east, and he would be inviting Caesar to start rebuilding. He may even have remembered the lessons of the war with Mithridates: one needed to finish a job, and to let Caesar run amok in the east was to risk everything. Caesar could easily have rebuilt his forces and profited from the limitless treasures of the vast regions that Pompey rightly considered to be his conquests for Rome.

All in all, it seems that Pompey made the right decision in moving to finish the war. Caesar would never be weaker than he was right now, and every passing day in the field made him stronger. The voices of Afranius and the others pushing for a return to Rome did not have a bad case; Pompey simply had a better one.

The obvious strategy for Pompey would be to enjoy the rich resources he had accumulated at Dyrrhachium and elsewhere, to link up with Scipio, and to destroy Caesar's army one way or another before it could regroup and refresh itself. If he were fortunate, the Caesarians would give up, ready to defect rather than to fight against overwhelming odds.

Pompey duly notified all relevant authorities and powers about what had happened at Dyrrhachium. He did not inform the parallel so-called republican officials in Rome, since neither he nor the magistrates of the government in exile recognized them. Rome would be left to find out the news unofficially; Pompey was more concerned about receiving continuing support from his many and powerful allied potentates and client kings.

We should not omit mention of one of those monarchs, a man who knew how to take advantage of distraction and crisis. When last mentioned in our story, Mithridates' youngest son Pharnaces had been responsible for helping Pompey with the finishing touches on the Third Mithridatic War; he had been responsible for seeing to the assassination of his father and the takeover of the Cimmerian Bosporus. Now Pharnaces showed something of his father's spirit for empire as he commenced his own conquests and takeovers, an imperial enterprise that was aided by the fact that the Romans had the attention of so many of the eastern monarchs. While Pompey and Caesar were preoccupied in Greece, Pharnaces would make his move.[7]

The dreams of Pharnaces would not come to lasting fruition; he was doomed by destiny to be a future conquest of Caesar, who is said to have taken satisfaction in vanquishing a parricide. But for the moment, the troubles in the east were a classic symptom of the instability occasioned by distractions of the civil war; it is small wonder that the poet Lucan and others would note ruefully that the Romans could have conquered so much of the world, had they decided not to turn the sword against themselves.

Not far from what is today the town of Mouzaki in Thessaly is the site of the ancient city of Gomphi. That locale has the distinction of having incurred the wrath of Caesar, or, perhaps better to say, the cold reality of the man once the mask of clemency was dropped. Gomphi had apparently decided that once the news of Caesar's defeat had arrived, it made more sense to side with the victor; the only problem was that neither Pompey nor Scipio was closer to its walls than Caesar. For Caesar, Gomphi offered a chance to make an example for the edification of the Thessalians; if he could seize the town and allow his men to plunder it, other towns would be less likely to resist. Caesar's men would be able to seize treasure and resources; it was a terrible invitation to them to vent their frustrations on the civilian population. Caesar claims that he commenced his siege in the midafternoon, and was able to complete it before sunset; he had made a speech to his men encouraging them to be vigourous in pursuing the attack, making clear that they could sack the town.[8]

The lesson worked; nearby Metropolis had planned to shut its gates to Caesar, but thought differently once the news arrived about the fate of Gomphi.[9] The episode illustrates well the straits in which Caesar found himself as he tried to secure provisions and to keep ahead of any threat from the Pompeians.

Caesar was presenting object lessons: he was scrupulous about sparing Metropolis from harm, to provide an example of what Caesarian armies did with accommodating cities. Some have wondered or marvelled at how Caesar was able to manage and control his forces, succeeding in ordering them to spare one place after giving free rein to their viler instincts at the other. But even sadists can become bored with savagery, and perhaps we should not be too quick to be impressed with Caesar as restrainer of would-be savages.

Caesar's own commentaries paint a picture of Pompey as being especially cautious in this crucial period, and as the object of increasing criticism from his colleagues as he seemed to be slow about forcing an end to the war; allegedly there were those who claimed that Pompey simply enjoyed being in supreme power.[10] Likely there were many who thought that the war was all but finished.

Our sources do not offer a coherent picture or clear narrative of everything that the rival forces were doing elsewhere in Greece during the main event around Dyrrhachium. The Caesarian strategy we have already described was an obvious one; there was a need for provisions and a need to keep Scipio's men from reinforcing Pompey. Pompey's concerns were both simpler and more complicated; Scipio needed to join Pompey, but he also needed to make sure that the Caesarians did not obtain provisions, and, at the same time, that some crisis did not develop in the heart of Greece that would allow for another front to open against Pompey's main body.

Scipio has been appraised as a commander by countless scholars and readers since Caesar and his commentaries. Scipio has received negative press for failing in a key duty of any Roman governor of Syria, namely guarding against trouble from Parthia. The criticism has validity, in that every Roman official should have been worried about Parthia and taking efforts to guard against trouble on that border. But fairness to Scipio demands that we ask what he was supposed to do. Staying on Parthian watch would have meant that he could not have assisted Pompey in any appreciable way. Scholars have been kinder to Scipio in vindicating him from one of the more absurd criticisms made by Caesar. Scipio had intended to take the treasures from the celebrated temple of Artemis at Ephesus, only to be prevented by the urgency with which Caesar needed him; Caesar was thus responsible for saving the temple. The fact that Caesar had ransacked the Roman treasury is what has led some to conclude that Caesar was consumed by particular disdain for Scipio; that said, there is no question that the aforementioned taxation and other levies throughout his province made Scipio susceptible to negative press.[11] Caesar was probably quite annoyed by the fact that he had failed miserably in trying to buy time by entering peace negotiations with Pompey's father-in-law.

Scipio was able to find assistance in the able cavalry of the allied Thracian monarch Cotys. If we trust Caesar, Scipio and his allied support were seriously deficient; other sources speak of Caesarian defeats, but there is confusion as to who lost what where. One thing seems clear: the Caesarians were by no means successful in preventing Scipio from establishing himself in Thessaly. Conversely, the Pompeians did not manage to evict Caesar's lieutenants.

Pompey had taken the main body of his force after Caesar, while leaving Cato to guard Dyrrhachium and the coastal regions. One wonders if he was happy to be rid of Cato for the decisive pursuit and prospective engagement with Caesar; if there were criticism of Pompey in this period, Cato may have been one of the more vocal in challenging the details of the commander's strategic decisions.

Plutarch lays special attention on even more ominous concerns regarding Cato and Pompey's attitude.[12] Allegedly, there were rumours that some in the army were asserting that as soon as Caesar was eliminated, then it would be time to be done with Pompey as well. Again we see the persistence of the argument that Pompey was really a dictator at heart; of all the problems that Pompey faced in the civil war, it must have been especially galling to hear anyone accuse him of being little better than Caesar.

Plutarch alludes to those who thought that the real reason for leaving Cato with the supplies at Dyrrhachium was to prevent him from demanding that Pompey surrender his command the moment Caesar was defeated.[13] For those who remember the Pompey who gave up his military power as soon as he had returned from the east, it was further evidence of never-ending suspicion of the man. No matter what he did or how scrupulous he was in displaying the best of republican sentiments, he was never able to exorcize the ghost of Sulla, or the reputation (deservedly or not) that he acquired as a young man in his service.

Lucius Domitius Ahenobarbus was the dutiful brother-in-law of Cato, and he would be something of Cato's voice during the period before Pharsalus. We hear that he started calling Pompey 'Agamemnon,' as if he were set on prolonging war for the sake of accruing and maintaining supreme power; Afranius is said to have added to the insults and criticism, seeking revenge for what had been said against him for the loss of Spain.[14] The diehard Catonian Marcus Favonius continued to complain about the failure to return to Italy. Matters were complicated by the fact that there was dissension even among those carping at Pompey; Afranius was held in low regard by some because of Spain. Rather astonishingly, we hear of arguments as to who should replace Caesar after the war in his pontifical capacity. In the event, one probably does not have to be a partisan of Pompey to sympathize with his having left Cato behind on the Adriatic coast.

Plutarch's analysis of Pompey is that he was a slave to the opinions of others, such that the complaints levelled against him affected his judgment and reason.[15] The fact is that at a fundamental level, to the end Pompey may indeed have been a slave, but not of uncritical acceptance of the views of others. He may have been convinced that if he tried hard enough, he would one day be accepted as a true republican, with no suspicion or stain of fear about would-be dictatorship. Or, it may be that he was simply doing what was required of a republican commander, aware that it would weaken his cause and expose himself and his forces to a charge of hypocrisy if he did otherwise.

If Pompey had been a slave to his republican colleagues, he would have returned to Italy, which was easily the preferred option of a strong contingent of senators. Some have wondered if Caesar would have tried sooner (perhaps rather than later) to move into Italy through Illyricum in that eventuality. Illyricum would have been a difficult march for Caesar, at any point; there were hostile tribes, and the terrain did not make for an easy march. But all of this was now speculation; Pompey was in Thessaly, and the forces of the republicans and the Caesarians were converging.

Calvinus, for his part, would have a close call; we hear that he learned about the imminent approach of Pompey from some of the Gallic cavalry that had defected to the republicans.[16] The cavalry had informed Calvinus of Pompey's advent for uncertain reasons; they are said to have come upon fellow Allobroges, and they were either sympathetic to their countrymen, or given to boasting about what they had just participated in at Dyrrhachium. Whatever the truth, Calvinus was able to escape and to make his way toward Caesar.

Calvinus was already demonstrating his penchant for survival. His future would be one of varied but overall not bad fortune. A loyal Caesarian, he was destined to tangle with Pharnaces. Probably the wisest decision of his long career was to be one of the first to support Octavian; he would hold office under the Augustan restoration, and he would live at least to 20 BC, a man who lived through defeats and reversals in battle and storms at sea, who at times could be accused of mediocrity, but who in the end managed to succeed in an age in which it was all too easy to be slain.

Pompey arrived at Larissa, that storied ancient city; there he made his rendezvous with Scipio. Larissa was Thessaly's heart; in mythology, it was associated with Perseus' grandfather Acrisius, and with Peleus and his son Achilles. It was an auspicious place, one redolent with the spirit of heroism and martial glory.

Auspicious is not the word to apply to the predictable catalogue of omens and portents that are recorded as alleged harbingers of the coming doom of the republic. Lucan invests his treatment of Pharsalus with everything from omen to witchcraft to necromancy; it is a brilliant tour de force of his rhetorical art and epic splendour.[17]

Significantly, after their meeting at Larissa we hear that Pompey treated Scipio as an equal. This was another instance of theatre, and again a good one. It was a tribute to republicanism, a reminder of what the armies were ostensibly fighting to preserve. It was a pointed criticism of Caesar, who was not engaging in such displays of tradition and venerable custom.

It was also a nod toward the fact that many of those who had wanted to go back to Italy were in part motivated by the desire to resume political careers and, yes, that treasured republican pastime of political fighting. Pompey must have thought that some of the senators and other officials travelling with him were living in something of a dream world; for them, the war was all but finished now, and it was high time to be thinking about the elections for 47 BC.

It was the very end of July when Pompey entered Thessaly; Pompey had not been close enough to help the poor citizens of Gomphi, but at least their disaster served to confirm roughly where Caesar was. From Scipio, Pompey was able to learn that Caesar was now in the Enipeus river valley, in the plain of Pharsalus. It was destined to be one of the most important locations in Roman republican history.

Time was of the essence. There was now no complication with naval operations or one side or the other being necessarily cornered into a difficult location because of recent landing or the need to respond to news of enemy arrivals. The situation was appreciably different as both sides prepared for their fateful clash. Thessalian plains would allow for exactly what both sides wanted: a fair fight in an open, pitched battle.

Farsala today is a town of modest size in southern Thessaly; the locals take immense pride in their association with the legends of Achilles and one of the greatest clashes in Roman history. The town is about two dozen miles south of Larissa. There is some debate as to the location of the battle, in part because some sources refer to it as having taken place at 'Palaepharsalus' or 'Old Pharsalus,' which is perhaps to be identified with the village of Krini (formerly Driskoli), several miles north of Farsala.[18]

As one might expect, there are many references to the battle and several accounts of its progress from our ancient sources.[19] While some details are open to debate, the general course of the engagement is not a source of major mysteries. Indeed, the aforementioned problem of determining exactly where it was fought is the major controversy.

It would have been difficult for anyone in Pompey's position to delay fighting. There were considerations of season. Keeping in mind the need to adjust the calendar, the grain was not yet ready for harvesting; once it was, Caesar would have no problem with supplies and provision. Pompey had reinforcements at least theoretically arriving from his distant allies and clients, to be sure. But all things considered, to delay fighting would only have benefited Caesar, at least in the long run. There could be debates about the exact timetable, but it would have made Pompey look worried and fearful if he did not display haste and vigour in putting an end to the war.

Labienus was a prominent voice in the discussions in the Pompeian camp before the war. He had long been a disparager of Caesar, especially of Caesar's cavalry strength. He was a strong advocate of taking decisive action, and there was certainly no question that in horses, Pompey had an appreciable advantage over Caesar.

A good place to commence a study of this final battle of Pompey's life is Caesar's own narrative of the engagement.[20] Caesar highlights his attention first to securing supplies and to allowing his men sufficient time to rest after their disastrous experience at Dyrrhachium. He wanted to test the will of the Pompeians to engage in a pitched battle, and so every day he would take out his army, advancing a little more *de die in diem*. Pompey had taken a somewhat elevated, hilly position; Caesar would move ever closer, affording every opportunity for the other side to make a move to accept the clear challenge. His men thus became more confident, seeing themselves in the role of practically taunting the republicans, one might think.

Caesar acknowledges his deficiency in cavalry (this would have been especially true after the defection of the Allobroges); he mingled lightly armed, first-rank men among the horse, to increase chances for practise. Caesar claims that his effective training technique allowed 1,000 cavalry to confront 7,000 without fear. Further, there were cavalry skirmishes in this period, in which the Gallic defectors lost one of their two leaders.

Pompey, for his part, kept drawing up his force on the lower spurs of his hill position, waiting to see if Caesar would continue to approach on unfavourable terrain. Caesar decided that his best option was to withdraw his army from the vicinity, so that he could continue to bring in supplies, keeping his army constantly on the move, and ideally fatiguing the Pompeians by leading them around in Thessaly and Macedonia. Caesar claims to have been on the brink of breaking camp and departing when he noticed that the Pompeians were now the ones advancing, so that an engagement could be fought on even ground.

Caesar reports what he claims to have learned after the battle.[21] Pompey indicated to his men that he planned to attack Caesar's right wing, utilizing his marked superiority in cavalry to effect an outflanking manouevre. Labienus encouraged everyone, deprecating Caesar's army as being significantly weaker compared to the days of the war in Gaul.[22]

Caesar delineates how the opposing forces were deployed.[23] On Pompey's left wing were the two legions that Caesar had handed over at what he considers to have been the start of the troubles: the first and the third legions, under Pompey's command. Scipio was in the middle with the legion he had brought from Sicily. The Cilician legion and Spanish cohorts from Afranius were on the right; these were the men in whom Pompey was most confident. 110 additional cohorts were between the centre and the wings, for a total of 45,000 men. Distributed throughout the whole force were some 2,000 reserves. Seven more cohorts guarded his camp. His right wing was protected by the river; all his cavalry and missile weapons were on the left.

Caesar had his mighty Tenth on the right, and the Ninth on the left.[24] The Eighth supplemented this second legion, since it had suffered so many losses at Dyrrhachium. Eighty cohorts made for 22,000 men in all, with seven cohorts in camp. Antony was on the left, Publius Cornelius Sulla on the right, and Domitius in the centre. He faced Pompey. Worried about the threat of a cavalry flanking operation, he made a fourth line out of his third, instructing them that the outcome of the day depended on how they responded to the threat from the enemy cavalry, ordering them to be ready for counter operations.

There was one noteworthy soldier, Gaius Crastinus, who had served in the Tenth.[25] He promised that whatever happened, he would be especially noteworthy in valourous performance. 120 men voluntarily shouted that they wanted to follow him, come what may.

Pompey is said to have been advised by Gaius Valerius Triarius to order his lines to wait and to absorb Caesar's first charge, so that the enemy lines might be broken and dispersed, and the republicans would be able more easily to attack a scattered opponent.[26] The logic was also that Pompey's men would be less fatigued, given that they would not have had to charge the same distance as Caesar's. Caesar criticizes this strategic analysis, arguing that men are more vigourous and courageous if they are on the move.

The signal was given, and the battle commenced. The Caesarians quickly realized that the enemy was not advancing, so they halted to ensure that they would not, in fact, be significantly exhausted relative to their foe. Then they proceeded again, having taken a moment to catch their breath. Missile weapons were hurled; swords were drawn. The republicans remained disciplined and did not break ranks; their javelins were hurled and exchanged for swords.

As expected, Pompey's cavalry on the left made their strike, supported by archers. The Caesarian cavalry was driven back. This manouevre drew in the republican horse, as Caesar planned; the fourth line infantry counter was then sprung. These six cohorts struck Pompey's cavalry; the horses fled, and the auxiliary troops with their missile weapons were left unprotected and were all slain. The six cohorts were now in a position to be the ones doing the outflanking, and they began to try to envelop Pompey's left.

Caesar now gave the signal to his third line to move in aggressively, since they were fresh and unwearied. They charged forth, driving the Pompeians back. For Caesar, the entire victory had rested with the men he had posted in those six cohorts of infantry, who were assigned to the duty of serving as a counter to the cavalry charge.

When Pompey saw that his much vaunted cavalry had been driven back, he considered the battle lost and made his retreat, giving the order to defend the camp. Caesar notes that the battle had been long, lasting until noon; it was hot and his men were by now exhausted, but he urged them to attack the camp.[27]

The date was the ninth of August; the calendar is misleading, as always, given it is pre-reform. It was likelier the sixth of June. But even two months earlier than the dog days of August, it can be uncomfortably warm and humid in southern Thessaly, and a brutal battle had been waging for hours, likely on the morning after a heavy downpour. Even if the hottest time of day had not arrived, we can readily believe that conditions were not pleasant.

Pompey's camp was strongly guarded, both by the men he had left behind, and by Thracian and other auxiliaries. The men fleeing from the battlefield were not thinking of defending the ramparts, but of flight; eventually, even the zealous defence of the camp was not enough, and the republican forces were seeking refuge in the hill positions.

Overall, Caesar's account is the most extended of the surviving records of the battle. He credits his victory to the effective use of infantry to check a cavalry outflanking manouevre, a classic tactic that requires both good timing and the ability to maintain proper control of other sectors of the battlefield to press home an advantage.[28]

Caesar wrote a book, and Pompey did not; throughout the history of the civil war, the question of how far we can trust Caesar's version of events is a weighty problem. Before we try to piece together what really may have happened on that momentous summer day, it is necessary to assemble the rest of our evidence. Here we have a range of material, including both continuous narratives and incidental details.

We may begin our look at other extant sources by considering Appian's account of Pharsalus.[29] Caesar is said to have noted that Pompey seemed to be hesitant to fight, and so he sent his men out to forage – three legions in all. He recalled his forces when he saw that Pompey was preparing to draw up in order of battle, happy that clearly he had been pressed into fighting. Appian's Pompey is described as being dejected and morose, noting that no matter what happened, there would be troubles henceforth for Rome; some interpreted this as meaning that he intended to retain supreme power if victorious.[30]

Appian concludes that Caesar had 22,000 men, 1,000 of them cavalry; Pompey had more than double that, with 7,000 horsemen.[31] He notes the disagreement in his sources on this key matter. Caesar had Gallic allies as well as some Greeks; Pompey had far greater foreign contingents. For Appian – who notes that Ptolemy and Cleopatra had sent sixty warships, which were idling at Corcyra – Pompey was foolish to entrust his fortune to a land battle when he had such dominance on the waves.[32] And just as he says that Pompey seemed melancholic before the battle, so he argues that his men seemed to be in a daze, disorganized and not up to their best – all classic indicators of reading back into events from a study of the outcome.

Caesar assigned 2,000 of his oldest men to guard his camp. The rest destroyed their fortifications; some of the less experienced with Pompey thought they were planning to flee, but Pompey knew it was a sign of boldness. Pompey left 4,000 men to guard his camp; the rest were drawn up between the town and the River Enipeus. Each side had Italians in front, arrayed in the traditional three lines, in the classic formation of deploying infantry in the centre and cavalry on the wings, with missile weapons intermingled.

Pompey stationed his Greek auxiliaries near his Italians, considering them to be well-disciplined and reliable fighters. The rest were arrayed to prepare for the chance to envelop the enemy or to attack the camp; Caesar is said to have anticipated this. The Pompeian centre was commanded by Scipio, the left wing by Domitius, and the right by Lentulus; Afranius and Pompey guarded the camp (we shall return to this significant error of Appian). Caesar took the right wing of his forces, with Antony and Publius Cornelius Sulla as his fellow commanders.

When the Pompeians saw the deployment of Caesar's forces, they transferred their best cavalry to face Caesar. Caesar countered by assigning 3,000 infantry with the task of being ready to engage these horsemen when they tried to outflank him. The Caesarians invoked Venus, and the Pompeians Hercules as their champions for the watchword.[33]

The day was advancing; both sides were arrayed for some time as if contemplating the other and meditating on the tragedy of civil war. Pompey's allies began to grow restless, and so Pompey ordered the signal for battle; Caesar responded. The mighty forces advanced; the usual missile fire was discharged. The cavalry charged, and the Pompeians began to outflank Caesar's infantry as expected; he gave the signal to the waiting footmen, who rose from their ambush and drove off the horses. Pompey's left flank was then hit, bereft of its cavalry shield.

Pompey gave the order for the infantry to stand their ground and to open their ranks; Appian notes that some people claim that this is indeed the best manouevre in such cases, while Caesar himself criticizes it in his correspondence, arguing that stationary men are less vigourous and make easier targets. Caesar's analysis is said to have been true at least in this instance, since now was the beginning of his victory. The allies are said to have watched everything in a sort of daze, shocked at how disciplined Romans are in battle; there was not even a move to attack the Caesarian camp.

Pompey's left began an orderly retreat, but the allies started to flee in disorder at the sight; they destroyed their own fortifications as if they were plundering the enemy camp, so disorganized, chaotic, and frenzied was their behaviour. The rest of Pompey's Italians were also orderly as they began to draw back, which inspired the Caesarians to press their pursuit. Caesar gave the word to spare fellow Romans and to kill auxiliaries, hoping to end the war quickly by extending even battlefield clemency. It was over, and Pompey was like Telamonian Ajax as he entered his camp in dejection.

After Appian, we may consider Dio.[34] He also records the long delay before the battle, the motionless stare from men who were as if lifeless. The allies began first after the signal was given; the Romans were said to have been in a state of horror and dejection at what was happening. Many are said to have sent messages home by the very men who killed them; Dio makes full use of his training in the rhetorical schools, though we would welcome more detail about the battle and less demonstration of his ability to compose memorable, pithy remarks.

Dio notes the Pompeian superiority in cavalry and archers, and how they would launch attacks and then retreat. For a very long time the battle continued with even odds; there were numerous casualties on both sides. Pompey was at last defeated.

Few of Dio's narratives are as frustrating as Pharsalus, where we have haunting reflections on the eerie prosecution of a battle in a civil war, but almost no clue whatsoever as to how the battle progressed; the fact that Pompey lost is almost tacked on as an addendum, and is followed by a lengthy note on how anyone could have predicted the ending, given the dire portents and omens beforehand.

Plutarch in his life of Pompey records that Scipio was in the centre, with Pompey on the right intending to face Antony; Domitius was on the left with most of the cavalry.[35] We hear of the plan to envelop Caesar's powerful Tenth legion, and of Caesar's stationing six cohorts of infantry to be ready to counter the horses. Caesar had some 22,000 men, and Pompey a little more than twice as many. Pompey is said to have erred in Caesar's estimation by ordering his front ranks to stand and to absorb the enemy's first onrush; this allegedly dampened their ardour. Once the signal was given, there was a serious reflection on the horror of civil war as the clash commenced; one of Caesar's centurions is said to have been the first to dart forth; he had been the first man Caesar had seen as he left camp, and the man had said that Caesar would be victorious, while he would be laudable, whether he lived or died. He earned his praise by his suicidal plunge into the Pompeian front lines, where a sword to the mouth brought him immortality.

The battle was then an even match for some time. But Pompey was slow to bring up his right wing, nervously watching as he was for what happened with his cavalry on the left. These horsemen tried their outflanking manouevre, which Caesar's infantry ambush countered. Caesar let these cavalry flee; Plutarch notes that they retired quickly given their inexperience.[36] Caesar then aimed for the unprotected infantry they were no longer covering. The Tenth legion struck them frontally, while the anti-cavalry cohorts aimed for the flank. Pompey saw that he was defeated, and returned to camp quoting Homer about Zeus striking fear into Ajax.

In his life of Caesar, Plutarch notes that Calvinus held his centre, with Antony on the left and Caesar on the right with his vaunted Tenth legion, with Scipio in Pompey's centre, Domitius on the left, and Pompey on the right.[37] In his life of Antony, the biographer notes that Antony was given the plum position because of his competence.[38] From the Brutus biography, we learn about the alleged partiality that Caesar showed to his future assassin, the object of gossip about his mother Servilia's affair with the dictator: Caesar is said to have instructed his men not to harm Brutus in battle; if he gave himself up voluntarily, he was to be taken prisoner, but if he tried to resist, they were to let him go.[39] Appian also notes the order to save Brutus, again in the context of the ironies of later history;[40] Dio also cannot resist including the detail.[41]

Among Latin writers, Velleius makes a point of noting that a brief work like his does not permit details about the engagement; he singles out the point that Caesar was clement to the enemy, before noting that the thanks he received was being stabbed by the likes of Brutus.[42] In other words, the Tiberian era historian makes laudatory note of Caesar's mercy, with no other information about the actual battle. In his life of Caesar, Suetonius observes that Caesar commented on the deaths of the Pompeians with the rueful note that he would have suffered the same fate, had he not turned to his men to defend him.[43]

Frontinus in his *Strategemata* notes Pompey's triple line of battle, each one ten men deep, and how the most trustworthy infantry were on the wings and in the centre, with the recruits filling in the spaces between them.[44] On the right there were 600 cavalry, along the river (where the terrain was difficult); the rest were on the left with the auxiliaries. Caesar's triple line had legionaries in front, his left flank resting on marshland to avoid being outflanked. Cavalry were deployed on the right, with infantry especially skilled at speedy cavalry manouevres. Six cohorts were stationed for ambushing enemy cavalry attacking his right. Frontinus credits this classic anti-cavalry counter as being the key to Caesar's success.

Lucan, as always, offers his own counterpoint to Caesar in *Pharsalia* 7. Lentulus Spinther held the Pompeian left, with Domitius on the right and Scipio in the centre. Caesar's much vaunted centurion is the first to stain Thessaly with Roman blood. Pompey's forces were thickly crowded; Caesar's men exceptionally swift as they charged forward. For Lucan, Caesar's side was the guilty one, and so it is not surprising that they should be hot and lustful for battle.

Pompey's cavalry on both wings began to attempt to outflank the enemy, forming arcs on either side of the battlefield, while his light-armed infantry moved forward. Caesar had his reserve cohorts positioned obliquely, ready to meet the cavalry manouevres. The republican cavalry fled in fear once Caesar engaged them with his cohorts; in Lucan's estimation, this is what happens when you entrust civil wars to barbarian forces.

A slaughter ensued, but Pompey still had his powerful centre under Scipio, which was the real heart of his strength. The Caesarians were in trouble, but everywhere Caesar was encouraging his men to acts of savage violence, driving on his men to counter the republican advance. Great men of the republic fell one by one, and before long it was all over. The field would be littered with corpses, and Lucan's Caesar was not inclined to allow burial for the slain.

From all of these major and minor sources, we can glean a coherent picture; there is an appreciable degree of consistency as to what happened, though as one would expect, there are questions to be asked about why things turned out the way they did.

The first question we may consider is the apparent lack of interest in joining battle allegedly displayed by Pompey's forces. Arrayed on slopes, the army may have hoped that the often rash and reckless Caesar would attack; it would have been a fatal blunder, so bad a move that it was highly unlikely that Caesar would commit it. That said, given the question of his supplies, he would either need to fight or to move on to try to secure provisions. So one way or another, what seemed like dithering and dilatory behaviour by Pompey was purposeful.

Pompey would need to fight sooner rather than later: we have mentioned the grain issue and the impending harvests. There was also the security of Larissa to consider. Pompey had a more unwieldy army, to be sure. But the longer Caesar survived in the field, the more threatening he could become. Pompey never underestimated him; after Dyrrhachium, a lesser commander would have had insurmountable difficulties recouping losses like those sustained by Caesar, but now time was on his side.

Since antiquity, Pompey has been liable to the charge of superstition and giving in to omens; this has been taken as the explanation for his allegedly dejected and depressed mood. But ancient sources, as we have seen and again, find it irresistible to talk about baleful prognostications of disasters, and we should be hesitant to believe such stories. Both sides were certainly worried, anxious, and concerned; the weather was not pleasant, the battlefield was not really the most inviting place to think thoughts of ready retreat, and indeed it was a war between countrymen. Even if we allow for appreciable rhetorical exaggeration about the horrors of civil war and the shuddering of men on both sides from engaging fellow Romans, surely there was an estimable degree of dejection and melancholy all around. This was the reality of internecine strife on a grand scale; perhaps there were even dreamers on either side who wondered if even at this late stage there could be a deal. As for portents, if there was indeed a thunderstorm the night before the battle – which would accord perfectly well with the weather for that time of year – both the comfort and the mood of the men would have depressed, and the ground may not have been so accommodating for cavalry manouevres.

Numbers can be deceiving. All of our sources agree that Caesar was at a serious disadvantage in this regard; exact totals may be disputed (and usually the correct decision is to accept lower rather than higher figures), but Pompey had more men. This is not to say that he had better men; certainly many of the Pompeians were raw recruits in the truest sense. Caesar had reason to worry about the cavalry deficit, but again, we should perhaps pay significant attention to the ground conditions after torrential rains, if indeed that was the weather situation.

The surviving evidence of the battle concurs on the decisive role played by the Caesarian cohorts that countered the Pompeian cavalry. There seems to be no question that the republicans seriously botched the outflanking manoeuvre. It was to be expected; this is what cavalry did, especially cavalry that outnumbered the enemy seven to one. The republicans had to be aware that Caesar was competent enough to try to find a way to counter the threat, and the only way to counter it was with trained infantry. Some of the sources specify that Caesar had ordered these cohorts to strike at the faces of the Pompeian horsemen, trying to scare off young men who would be concerned about disfiguring wounds.[45] But there need not have been any special instructions. Caesar just needed to make sure that he had some of his finest anti-cavalry veterans ready, and if the weather had made conditions less than ideal for cavalry, then his job would have been appreciably easier. Labienus is credited in the sources with being exceptionally confident and quick to denigrate Caesar's force (especially his cavalry); he was probably both overconfident and hampered by conditions.

Caesar says that 15,000 Pompeians fell in the battle; again, this number is no doubt greatly exaggerated.[46] But it was clearly a disaster for the republicans. For Caesar and other ancient historians, Pompey had fallen victim to the bad advice and demands of his colleagues, who had imposed a hasty battle on him which he knew in his heart he was not ready to fight. But what was Pompey supposed to do? More time would allow for more training, but at the same time it would open the door to Caesar being able to provision himself indefinitely. Dyrrhachium had been a rout; the longer Caesar was allowed to remain at large, the more dangerous he became. Naval forces would probably not have mattered much in the end. If Pompey had set guards on the Aegean coast – and likely he did – those units would have been of little consequence one way or the other in a Thessalian ground war.

No, Pompey needed to fight, and sooner rather than later. Nor was he any more despairing of victory than Caesar was before the climactic engagement at Dyrrhachium. Especially if Pompey had lured Caesar into a trap there, Pharsalus was simply a chance for Caesar to do something of the same with Pompey's cavalry. Labienus needed to be a better cavalry commander, and Pompey's horsemen needed to do a better job. Both failed, and the collapse was devastating.

Caesar's men fought better than Pompey's at Pharsalus. Commanders must do their part correctly, and subordinates must do theirs. In the 1963 *Cleopatra* film of Joseph Mankiewicz, a cinematic depiction of the history of the age that opens in the aftermath of Pharsalus, history is often ignored for the sake of artistic licence.[47] But one line is likely all too accurate. Rex Harrison's Caesar tells the leading Pompeian prisoners, 'as field officers you fought miserably for Pompey.'

The source that we should most like to have about Pharsalus is the civil war history of Horace's friend Pollio, who actually fought at the battle on Caesar's side; this would have made for fascinating comparison with Caesar's account. Both Appian[48] and Plutarch,[49] for example, cite Pollio for the figure of 6,000 Pompeian dead, much lower than Caesar's estimate of 15,000, though Pollio specifies that he is speaking of Italian dead, while Caesar may have been including auxiliaries, in which case some 9,000 of the archers and slingers, e.g., would have died. Caesar claims that he lost only 200 men, including thirty centurions; that figure is surely absurdly low.[50]

While the general course of events, as we have see, is reasonably clear, there are questions even on fundamental issues, such as why Appian makes his error about where Pompey was; most would agree that Domitius have must been his subordinate, just as Sulla would have been for Caesar.

As for debates about strategy, anyone in Pompey's position would have tried to capitalize on the overwhelming superiority he enjoyed in cavalry. What has not been much appreciated in studies of the battle from antiquity to modernity is that in a sense, Caesar took a lesson from the disaster at Dyrrhachium. There, his men had struck hard with superior numbers at what seemed to be a soft target. Only after they seemed to have routed the foe and to have been on the verge of victory did they realize that there was a camp within a camp. At Pharsalus, the republican efforts to perform a classic cavalry outflanking manouevre were countered by the existence of a quasi-secret 'fourth battle line', which could only be formed by weakening the other infantry lines.

Caesar's infantry displayed particular strength and resilience in holding their own: all they really needed to do was to fight for a draw, until the republican cavalry could be routed. Then they could take full advantage of the situation and press forward with all the vigour that comes from knowing that your side has the advantage and momentum. Did Caesar really tell his anti-cavalry units to strike at the face so as to drive away vain and proud young men who were afraid of facial injuries? Perhaps. All that needed to happen was to set in motion a cavalry retreat, which would throw Pompey's infantry into confusion.

Caesar has been followed by many in condemning Pompey for his order to his men to hold fast; the argument that Caesar makes about the need to inspire your men with vigour for the fight by making them charge is often taken as one of his vintage *dicta* about how to wage a war, for the simple reason that on this occasion, it worked. One could find many reasons to debate the wisdom of the strategy had the reverse been true; vigourous onrush had spelled doom for Caesar at Dyrrhachium. A healthy dose of luck had helped Pompey there, and a similar good fortune smiled on Caesar at Pharsalus.

Pharsalus was arguably going very well for Pompey in the stages of the battle just before the cavalry charge against Caesar's flank. The brilliant response of the Caesarians to this attack – and brilliant it was – surely spelled the beginning of the end. It was inevitable that the auxiliaries would easily be cut down in the wake of the rout of their cavalry screen; this is the sort of battle sequence where superior numbers begin to dissipate with frightening speed and bloody horror. In the space of not so very long, the cavalry and the missile units become mere sideshows, and what is left is the classic case of infantry clashing with infantry.

The factors involved in the rout of the cavalry included first and foremost the respective performance of Pompey's horsemen and Caesar's infantry cohorts, as well as the terrain, which probably worked against Pompey if the ground were saturated. Caesar's plan to counter the enemy horse was a sound one, but it was by no means guaranteed to succeed.

It is clear that when the cavalry charge had failed so spectacularly, the republican left was now in serious trouble. Pompey's centre and right were not; they may even have been doing their part in assuring a republican victory. But once the left was in danger of being outflanked by the infantry that had countered the cavalry and driven them off into a confused rout, the entire front was at risk. Pompey could have tried to send forces from the centre and right, diverting them to help his beleaguered and faltering left. Caesar, however, could use his third line to replace his ranks with fresh troops, and any attempt to orchestrate a transfer of men to relieve the crisis on the left would have jeopardized Pompey's ability to hold back what was quickly becoming a complete rout.

The question of when exactly Pompey and his retinue fled the battlefield has been debated. Not surprisingly, Caesar has the decision to flee come after the rout of the cavalry.[51] But surely Appian[52] and Plutarch[53] (probably if not certainly following Pollio on the point) are right in saying that it was after it was clear that the infantry were giving way. The cavalry rout on Pompey's left was not, in and of itself, fatal to his cause. It was the beginning of the end, but with a fair amount of luck, things could have stabilized, if only to result in a draw.

Should we be surprised that the republicans did not defend their camp? The shock of the rout clearly had them (rightly so) in fear for their lives. The camp was defended by fresh troops, and if enough men and officers had stopped to reason things out and to trust a healthy amount in the odds, there would have been a chance for a successful defence. But such things rarely work in a situation where most everyone is literally fleeing for dear life. The camp was going to be seized, and few stalwarts were likely to be ready to die in defence of the rich treasures that Caesar takes care to describe as part of his not so subtle denigration of the eastern pomp of Pompey's allied and client kings.

Pompey's thoughts would have been predictably overwhelming and conflicting, but one sentiment likely stuck in his mind: he would be blamed by everyone for the disaster; even if people were ready to criticize subordinate commanders, he bore the lion's share of the responsibility for everything that happened.

Among those subordinates, special notice must be made of Lucius Domitius Ahenobarbus. In his *Philippics*, Cicero records that Antony killed Domitius at Pharsalus as he was trying to escape; he was the most prominent republican to fall at the battle.[54] Lucan makes him a major character in his epic; he was one of the handful of senators to die, and so it was inevitable that a poem about the victory of a dictatorial, quasi-monarchical Caesar over a republic would prominently feature him. Caesar records him as a casualty, but without mention of the fact that it was Antony who had killed him, noting only that he was struck down by the cavalry. Lucan, needless to say, turns Cicero's passing insult of Antony into a richly dramatic opportunity to showcase Domitius against Caesar's subordinate.[55]

We have noted the rich wealth reputedly captured in the republican camp. Caesar notes in his commentaries that he was immediately concerned about making sure that his men would not waste valuable time in plundering it; the whole point now was to capture Pompey and to put an end to the war.[56] Caesar left some units to guard the camp, with others assigned to return to watch his own; four legions were to go with him to hunt for Pompey.

Caesar says that Pompey tore off his command insignia and prepared to gallop away to Larissa.[57] Some Pompeians were caught seeking refuge on a hill position; these were surrounded and preparations were made for a siege, but surrender negotiations soon commenced, with some senators fleeing under cover of night. Caesar presents the picture of the next morning as one of the classic instances of his display of mercy: the Pompeians were begging for mercy, and Caesar bid them to be of good cheer, reassuring them that both their lives and their property would be protected. Sources also allude to Caesar's burning of documents; this was a time-honoured way of demonstrating that one did not intend to launch proscriptions or to hunt down enemies.[58]

In another snippet of surviving information about Caesar's attitude in the aftermath, in his life of Titus Pomponius Atticus, Nepos records the neutrality of his biographical subject, who was a close friend of Pompey, yet had accepted no special honours from him, taking advantage of the fact that he was about sixty years of age to avoid being summoned to follow the republican armies.[59] Caesar was said to be so impressed with Atticus' neutral behaviour that he accepted his request to release Quintus Cicero together with his own sister's son from Pompey's camp. Again, our sources are united in attesting to Caesar's generally mild mood at this juncture. He had no reason to be vindictive, and every stimulus to pursue a benevolent course, especially while Pompey was still alive and there were formidable republican forces remaining.

On the night of 9 August 48 BC, both Pompey and Caesar would have been aware that the war was by no means finished. The republicans still had considerable forces, as well as extensive resources. As it became clearer to Caesar that Pompey had managed to escape, the realization that the war would be continuing for some time would have been increasingly apparent. Caesar had ample reason to be both relieved and even exultant in his victory. But Pompey still had good cause to hope that even now, all was not lost.

Chapter Twenty-Four

Endgame in Egypt

The young man who had been known as Alexander was destined to end his life not like Paris of Troy, but like Priam. Pompey had rejected the invitation to go to Egypt when invited to intervene in internal Ptolemaic affairs on his return from successfully prosecuting the Third Mithridatic War. Some would argue that he should have ventured to Alexandria when he was offered the chance to do so; as we have seen, his refusal then was rooted in his determination not to act as if he were some would-be dictator.

In the immediate aftermath of Pharsalus, the list of things to do was long and difficult; outpacing Caesar was first and foremost. Communications would be slow and tedious as usual; news would be travelling far and wide soon enough about the disastrous defeat. Pompey would have been worried in the immediate about the security of his wife Cornelia and son Sextus on Mytilene. There was the question of Cato at Dyrrhachium, as well as of the many survivors of Pharsalus, both the soldiers and the senators and other republican officials. There were the allied kings to consider. Across the chessboard of civil war, there was the question of who would be inclined to make a deal with Caesar, who at least in the minds of his supporters was at present one of the consuls.

We have noted that all was by no means lost. As a good and timely example of that, around the time of the Pharsalus campaign, Gaius Cassius Longinus succeeded in heading to Sicily, where he succeeded in a major naval strike that did significant damage to Caesar's fleet operations there.[1] He was then able to expand operations against Caesarian vessels in Italian waters. Caesar admits the disaster in his commentaries, noting that only the arrival of news of the victory at Pharsalus rallied the Caesarians, such that Cassius needed to withdraw.

When Cato learned of Pharsalus, he indicated to those with him that if Pompey were alive, he would keep his forces intact to continue the war; otherwise, he would ensure that his men were conveyed to Italy, while he would seek exile for himself, determined as he was not to live in a world that was Caesar's. He proceeded from Dyrrhachium to Corcyra, where he offered command of the forces to Cicero, on the grounds that Cicero had been a consul, while he had only been a praetor. It was good republicanism, though perhaps in the immediate, highly uncertain times he had no desire to be the one making executive decisions.

Cicero, however, had no interest in being in charge; given his occasional mercurial and melancholic tendencies, we should not be surprised.[2] Interestingly, we hear that Gnaeus Pompey was inclined to kill anyone who intended to run away, including Cicero; Cato needed to give private counsel to Pompey's older son, urging him to calm down and not to be rash at this critical juncture.[3] It may have been the first time in his political career that Cato was the one seeking to soothe the temper of someone who was burning with republican zeal.

Cicero himself claimed that after Pharsalus, he was interested in advocating for peace; his critics would be of the view that he was a weathervane, always ready to seek accommodation with the rising star.[4] The accusation was not entirely fair, but needless to say, Cicero was one of the voices urging reconciliation and the casting aside of arms. All that said, Cicero is also quick to note in his *Philippics* that he only spoke of Pompey reverentially, and with regret for his destiny; he claims that Pompey acknowledged that Cicero had been more far-sighted, while he had allowed himself to indulge in dreams and hopes.[5] We cannot know for sure what if anything Pompey really said or wrote to this effect; Cicero may have been engaging in some more or less slight historical revisionism. In Rome, Caesar's men held the power, both by force of arms and in the person of his consular colleague; we hear of how Caesar was hesitant to report the victory, or at least that he laboured for some time over the problem of how to characterize it. Care was of the essence: this had been a defeat of fellow Romans, and even now civil war remained a deeply distasteful enterprise.

Plutarch notes poignantly that Pompey, for his part, now had a chance to experience defeat and flight after a lifetime of success.[6] The biographer says that he passed by Larissa, proceeding to Tempe, heading for the coast. Caesar's account is less romantic. He mentions his pursuit of Pompey, noting that at Amphipolis, there was an edict in his name, urging Greeks and Romans to assemble; it was unclear whether this was done for the sake of making it seem as if Pompey intended to stay in Greece, planning to raise troops and to hold Macedonia. Pompey is said to have stopped at Amphipolis to raise money, before hastening to depart for Lesbos and his family. Dio adds the information Pompey avoided entering Larissa on his way from Pharsalus, out of concern that Caesar would take vengeance on the city; he urged them not to challenge the victor, and merely took provisions that were graciously offered and took his leave.[7] He may have been all too hesitant to enter because he wanted to escape as soon as possible from the haunting association of the place with Achilles; any thought of either Achilles or Alexander at this juncture would have been a source of sorrow and self-recrimination.

Pompey is said to have told his servants to go to Caesar and to turn themselves over to him without concern; he took with him only a small number.[8] If there is one thing that has not been much studied, it is the speed with which everything seemed to evaporate for Pompey. Obviously he would have expected that the Roman soldiers who surrendered would be given the chance to give up with honour; he would not have had any illusions about mass escapes or anything of the sort that would leave him with intact forces. The senators and other civilians might have had more of an ability to stay with him, but those who were not physically in his retinue would have had a difficult time in the immediate learning where he was going. He could not dare take his time with flight; he knew that Caesar was looking for him, and unlike Caesar after Dyrrhachium, he did not have a force that had fled with him. Pharsalus may not have been the slaughterhouse (at least for the Roman legions) that the ancient sources depict, but it was an unmitigated disaster from a strategic point of view. There was no realistic hope for Pompey to remain in Thessaly, and Macedonia was just marginally better as an option. And if Caesar knew where his family was, he would have been consumed with worry about finding them, even if he did not think that there was any physical threat to them. Caesar would not harm them, but he could not be sure that they would be safe from others in a world where he was the most hunted of men.

Plutarch says that on arrival at the coast, Pompey stayed in the hut of a fisherman; then travelled in a river vessel until he found a merchant ship.[9] There is a clear effort here to cast Pompey as a victim of a classic reversal of fortune; this was, after all, the man who had rid the seas of the pirate menace, and who had such impressive naval forces still at his disposal. The merchant ship was captained by a Roman named Peticius; he is said to have recognized Pompey from a dream he had had. The group was small; it included Lentulus and Favonius. As the boat departed, allegedly it stopped to rescue King Deiotarus of Galatia, when he was seen running along the shore seeking help. Favonius had been known earlier for his criticisms of Pompey; now when he saw the man bereft of slaves and taking off his own shoes, he began to serve him and to minister to his needs. The vessel coasted near Amphipolis, before heading toward Lesbos.

It is vintage Plutarch, full of charm and vivid, memorable imagery; how much of it is true is uncertain. Certainly Pompey had fled with a small number; everyone was making their way as best they could and in accord with whether or not they were interested in coming to terms with Caesar. Did Pompey need to depend on some passing merchant vessel? They were by no means rare, though there was always the worry that someone would decide to assassinate him, depending on how quickly news travelled. Pompey had not planned for this eventuality, and so this was no case of having a ship ready for a quick departure.

Pompey was on his way to Lesbos and his wife and son; Cornelia had lost her first husband at Carrhae, and now she would learn of the defeat of her second spouse at Pharsalus. We recall that Pompey had written to her of his success after Dyrrhachium; she would hear the dire update in person.

Who was to blame for it all? Probably the most significant deficit for Pompey at Pharsalus had been what it had always been in the civil war: his men were simply not as competent as Caesar's. Caesar had fewer but significantly better soldiers. Certainly it did not help Pompey that he had to deal with more of republican reality than Caesar did, but this was a distant second to the problem of veterans and military quality. Caesar had the great advantage of fighting in the immediate aftermath of Gaul; there was no respite for him. Caesar's military acumen and experience was fresher; this, too, would have been a factor.

At Pharsalus itself, arguably Pompey performed just as respectably as Caesar as a strategist and tactician. Luck and fortune always play a role, but in the end, in our estimation the fundamental problem for Pompey was the handicap of his relatively inexperienced men. Dyrrhachium, in contast, had been a campaign where Caesar had made mistakes, indeed blunders; these errors were serious enough that his other advantages could not compensate for them.

No ancient historian or modern scholar can be sure what Pompey's longtime strategy was in what would be the last weeks of his life. We know of his immediate, family priority. One problem would be that the already challenging realities of efficient communication would now be a serious problem. His colleagues needed to make decisions, and reaching Pompey would be exceedingly difficult, just as he would be hampered in his efforts to reach out to them. As he arrived at different venues, he could bring news and receive what updates were available. But he was essentially on the run until he had more definitive information, or until he was in a secure place.

Plutarch lavishes his usual rhetorical skill on the scene of Pompey reuniting with Cornelia.[10] She is depicted as blaming herself for bringing doom first on Publius Crassus, and then on Pompey; she laments that she had not committed suicide as she wished in the wake of the loss of her first husband. Pompey replies with an admonition that they must bear up under the bad fortune as well as the good, and that he had hopes that he would have a chance to resume his once high stature.

As at Larissa, so at Mytilene Pompey was unwilling to enter the city; he urged them to make their peace with Caesar. The point here was the same as at Thessaly; if Caesar came after Pompey to Lesbos, as in Thessaly there would be no hope of resistance, and loyalty to Pompey would mean another Gomphi. Pompey is said to have had a discussion with the philosopher Cratippus about the nature of providence. Plutarch notes that Cratippus was careful not to cause depression or anxiety in Pompey, by asking questions of the sort that he could raise, such as whether the republic had been so badly managed that now it needed one ruler, or whether if he had won, Pompey would have been any better than Caesar.[11]

Next on Pompey's itinerary was Attaleia in Pamphylia, the modern Antalya on the south coast of Turkey. Triremes were there from Cilicia, together with some sixty senators and a force of soldiers. Pompey had arrived there by stopping at unspecified harbours only for the sake of provisions and water; Attaleia was the first city that he entered. He may have received word that this was a secure republican stronghold. Lucan has a different version, in which Phaselis was the city.[12] But the sentiments of the entire region were sympathetic to Pompey, whose legacy of kindness remained a potent force: Caesar was by no means the only Roman commander who knew the value of exhibiting clemency and compassion.

Attaleia is where Pompey seems to have learned the first detailed and substantial news about the aftermath of Pharsalus. The two main pieces of news seemed to be that the navy was still intact, and that Cato was on his way to Africa with a large republican force. It is at this juncture that Pompey is said to have made the lament that he should never have allowed himself to be induced to fight a land battle, and that if it were impossible to avoid a land engagement, he should have ensured that it would be fought somewhere where he would be able to use his superior navy to help to support his operations. Plutarch concurs with the assessment, arguing that this was Pompey's greatest mistake, and Caesar's clearest demonstration of how able a strategist he was.[13]

Let us begin by assuming that Pompey really did express these views. Having just lost a major land battle, it would make sense that after arriving at Attaleia and seeing ships (and hearing that unlike his land forces, his navy was still intact), he would express rueful remarks about sea power. If so, he was being harsher on himself than he deserved. Certainly he was a master of combined arms and amphibious operations; certainly he had far more experience than Caesar in warfare on the high seas.

But Caesar could not be defeated so easily with a naval strategy. Winning the civil war would require control of both land and sea, and there was no way that Caesar could be beaten without decisive land engagements, far from coastal regions. After Dyrrhachium, it would not have been so easy for Pompey to lure Caesar into battle in some locale where naval power could support the land engagement, and time was of the essence before the harvest. If anything, Pompey's reflections were reflective of the fact the war was by no means finished; Caesar had much to worry about that late summer of 49 BC, and there were good reasons for Pompey to have hopes for victory.

At Attaleia, Pompey had the chance to confer with five dozen senators; he was still the republican commander, making decisions insofar as possible in a collaborative manner. The main point of discussion was the issue that had weighed on him since the collapse of his army in Thessaly: where was he to go? Plutarch lists the options and the pros and cons that were raised by different parties.[14] The debate was an interesting one; Africa and Juba's Numidia was raised as a possibility.[15]

Leaving aside any consideration of what Pompey thought about the prospect of joining Cato in a potentially awkward and contentious rendezvous, Africa had real advantages, but it would of course have diverted Pompey from the east, which remained his greatest source of wealth and manpower. The tension of the east was that it was a complicated patchwork of kingdoms and political regimes, and the loyalty and security of each place needed to be taken into consideration.

Parthia is said to have been Pompey's preference. If this is correct, it shows at least a passing flash of brilliant analysis, regardless of its seeming impracticality, not to say impossibility. Pompey had never resolved the Parthian question during his great eastern commission. Scipio had been criticized for leaving the east at the potential mercy of Parthia while he was on his way to Greece to help Pompey.

If Pompey could come to some accommodation with the great power to Rome's east, he would be well on his way to resolving both the civil war and the Parthian question, for the betterment of the republic. It was a grand vision. It was worthy of the Roman Alexander.

But let us be realistic. Parthia was geographically nowhere near the great naval forces that were the veritable lynchpin of a Pompeian victory. To argue that one was a defender of the Roman republic meant that one should be a mortal enemy of Parthia, ready to destroy Rome's major eastern rival if accommodation could not be made with her on Roman terms, on the basis of a treaty favourable to Rome. Caesar mentions how Pompey's legate Gaius Lucilius Hirrus had been sent to Parthia before Pharsalus; one did, after all, need to continue diplomatic initiatives with the great power, especially during time of civil war. Securing Parthian peace and Parthian support was always a goal of Roman foreign policy: ultimately, either there was going to be a major war, or there was going to be a major peace treaty that secured the east for generations to come. For Pompey to consider Parthia as a potential formidable ally of the republic was not madness, and it was not mutually exclusive with his goal to shore up and to maintain support elsewhere in the Roman world. The deadly game in which Pompey and Caesar were engaged in was not a zero sum contest. Parthia may not have been on the immediate itinerary for a host of reasons, but that did not mean that Parthia was inconsequential to the chessboard. On the contrary, she was a key player to keep in consideration, for either side.

One of the most consequential men in Roman history is not a household name, even among those who are devotees of the subject. Theophanes of Mytilene was a scholar and historian, a friend to Pompey and author of a laudatory history of the Asian campaigns.[16] He was granted Roman citizenship by Pompey, and had served as a *praefectus fabrum*; he had taken Pompey's name. He had come to Rome with Pompey, and had followed him back to the east when the civil war erupted. For years, he had been a trusted advisor to Pompey. Now he was once again in a position to make suggestions. Whatever had been the extent of his wisdom then and now, his last recommendation would be disastrous, even if all things considered, it was sound.

Sound, we might say, for one whose information was *au courant*. Theophanes suggested heading to Ptolemaic Egypt. That kingdom, unfortunately, was embroiled in its own civil war, between the sibling spouses and co-rulers Ptolemy and Cleopatra. The situation in Egypt had long been tense; it is quite possible that brother and sister never enjoyed any amity in their relationship. Given the age difference, some have questioned whether the union ever actually occurred. But incestuous sibling marriage dated back for centuries in the monarchy, and while certainty is impossible, at least in name the nuptials were probably contracted.[17] Cleopatra had become queen in 51 BC; born in 70–69, she was about seven or eight years older than Ptolemy (born c. 62). Relations were clearly strained between the official co-rulers; there is evidence that by as early as late August of 51, documents were already being issued in Cleopatra's name alone.[18]

Complicating matters, there was a younger brother, Ptolemy XIV; he had been born around 59. He would be especially ill-fated, and was probably poisoned by his sister in the summer of 44. When Cleopatra was in conflict with Ptolemy XIII, the other brother was useful as a potential ally. While we are woefully ignorant of all the details of the story, tensions bubbled over in 51 and 50, with Ptolemy enjoying the powerful backing of a number of key allies: the general Achillas, the tutor Theodotus of Chios, and the eunuch and tutor Pothinus. There seems to have been a brief period in which Ptolemy was the one signing documents with his older sister named after him, and then a complete takeover by Ptolemy and break with Cleopatra sometime in 49.

It is not clear how much of this information was known to Pompey and his entourage (or, for that matter, to Caesar and the other leading Romans). We have noted that Ptolemaic Egypt sent some sixty warships to aid Pompey in the civil war; this was done with the agreement of both Ptolemy and Cleopatra. Troops were also sent, including members of the 'Gabiniani' who had not been involved in the murder of Bibulus' envoys in 50.

But while Pompey and Caesar were fighting their war from January of 49, Ptolemy and Cleopatra were well advanced in theirs. Cleopatra was compelled to flee Alexandria; she seems to have travelled first to Thebes and then into Roman Syria, accompanied by her sister Arsinoe IV.[19] She was able to muster a force that was ready to try to evict Ptolemy, but she was soon delayed at Pelousion, facing her brother's men and, yes, the remaining Gabiniani.

Egypt, in short, was in a state of crisis; had the Roman civil war not intruded on the Egyptian, it is unclear what would have happened in Alexandria. Once again alternative histories invite contemplation; could Cleopatra have defeated her brother? Such questions would soon be rendered academic.

Theophanes pointed out to Pompey that Egypt was a three-day voyage, and that Ptolemy owed him much. In contrast, the Parthians were criticized as being unworthy of trust and likely to betray Pompey. It was a good argument, and one that would have been sound, were it not for the ongoing mess in Ptolemy's capital. Plutarch argues that the significant factor in Pompey's final decision was when Theophanes argued that it was dangerous to bring Cornelia to Parthia.[20] For all we know, there may have been a thought to the potential insensitivity of bringing the young Crassus' widow to the very kingdom that had been responsible for the death of her first husband. Indeed, the idea sounded shocking enough to Dio that he states outright that he does not believe the report that Pompey ever seriously considered it. Pompey, at any rate, settled quickly on Egypt; it would have the advantage of being relatively close to his strong position in Africa, and this consideration may have also weighed on him, even if none of the ancient sources notes it.

To Plutarch's account we may add some details gleaned from Appian. He notes that when Pompey met Cornelia on Lesbos, he was able to make use of four warships that had come to him from Rhodes and Tyre; these would perhaps have been forces that had come to ensure the safety of Cornelia and Sextus.[21] Appian also knows the report about Pompey's planned Parthian mission; he claims that Pompey proceeded as far as Cilicia before tentatively raising the idea, only to be dissuaded at once by his associates.[22] He then suggested Egypt or Africa; Juba was dismissed as not being of sufficient prominence as client kings go, while Ptolemy offered greater potential in terms of men and material, what he owed to Pompey, and, implicitly, the fact that Egypt was a place of mystique and mytho-historical renown, not least because it was the place that held the body of Alexander.

Velleius says that Pompey was offered the last and most significant of the many suggestions and admonitions of his life; some men recommended Parthia, others Africa; Egypt was finally chosen.[23]

Caesar has a short account of this fateful sequence of events in his commentaries; he gives the detail that bad weather delayed Pompey's departure from Mytilene for two days, before he could proceed first to Cilicia and then to Cyprus.[24] There Pompey is said to have learned that messages had been sent out from Antioch that Pompey was not welcome there, and that it was clear that Antioch was a perilous place for any of the republicans to visit. Rhodes is said to have passed similar exclusionary edicts against Pompey's supporters. Caesar further adds that news was being sent abroad of his approach; this would have been the parallel set of announcements to when Pompey had declared his victory at Dyrrhachium.

It would have been challenging to be in some of these communities at that time, learning from day to day of the changing fortunes of the civil war, and having the problem of needing to respond to which victor *du jour* might appear at one's gates. Caesar was now the man of the hour.

In Caesar's narrative, Pompey would have gone to Syria, had he not heard of the decisions taken at Antioch and elsewhere.[25] And so having raised a force of some 2,000 men and a supply of wealth with which to pay his army, he proceeded to Egypt.

Pompey's itinerary, then, is a matter of some uncertainty; this was a likely consequence of how much of what was happening was ad hoc. But Caesar seems to have thought (or at least wanted his readers to think) that Pompey had intended to go to Syria; this is not mentioned by the other sources we have cited. Caesar's main concern was to convey the sense that support for Pompey was evaporating, even in his eastern strongholds. News of Pharsalus would have travelled as fast as any serious announcement could, and certainly the events that Caesar describes could have happened with lightning-fast speed. Syria may have been the planned destination for one interested in opening talks with Parthia, and in Caesar's certainty about Syria, we may have evidence of that possibility.

What of the Cyprus stopover? Plutarch has Pompey's final voyage as being from there to Egypt; he notes that at Cyprus, Pompey boarded a Seleucian warship with Cornelia, while others in his entourage travelled either in similar vessels, or in merchant ships.[26] Speaking of those who had left Greece with Pompey, Deiotarus, for his part, left his patron for Galatia; in his oration on his behalf, Cicero takes pains to note that the king considered that he had satisfied the demands of duty, and that he saw no reason to continue to support a defeated cause.[27]

Pompey was not contemplating abandoning the fight. Efforts were made to continue to further the war effort both economically and militarily; this had to be done in tandem with investigating where key individuals stood after Pharsalus. Why did he not go to Corcyra, where he would have found his large fleet, not to mention Gnaeus Pompey Minor? This may have been viewed as too risky: not only was there a chance (however unlikely) of engagement with Caesarian ships, there was also the problem of the east. On the other hand, it was the destination of Scipio and other prominent republicans, and it was probably given serious consideration by Pompey. Scipio would join Cato in Africa; Gnaeus Pompey would have his eyes set on Spain. Cato had been willing to yield command to Cicero because of his consular rank; he would do the same with Scipio.

Any bad news from Antioch in particular would have served as a warning of a threat of which Pompey was only too aware: the east could slip away from him, all his great work at establishing ties of patronage undone with breathtaking speed.

How serious were Caesar's efforts to track him down? Quite intense, one might think, and at a time of year for which sailing and naval operations were ideal. Pompey would have needed to find a place where he could actually start making effective plans, without worrying about the arrival of a Caesarian force. Cyprus was a natural stopover if one were heading to Egypt or not: it was a potential source of money from tax revenues and other sources, and at any rate, any harbour call allowed for more information to be gathered.

As for the question of Caesar's pursuit, like Caesar we are somewhat in the dark as to the exact means and routes by which every leg of Pompey's flight from Pharsalus was executed. Scholars debate, for example, whether he really did go to Amphipolis (a major detour for someone determined to see one's wife on Lesbos), or how many ships he was able to requisition or commandeer when he left the Greek mainland. Caesar would also need to obtain vessels for any search overseas; heading to the Hellespont would be its own significant roundabout hunt for his prey. Pursuit over land by the impressively speedy Caesar would still allow Pompey a much needed respite to continue his journeys; August and September were months of little rest for either commander. And, albeit for altogether different reasons, neither Pompey nor Caesar knew exactly where the map would lead.

All this said, Pompey did not have a particularly long list of choices for his destination. If he seriously did consider Parthia, it would have been at variance with his reported laments at Attaleia that he had not utilized his superior naval forces. But this may have been an element of the attraction: inland locales would force Caesar to continue to challenge him on land, while his older son and others could continue to force the issue on the sea, not to mention from the strong African base that Cato was establishing. We can only speculate, but the range of possibilities was relatively limited. Ptolemy and Cleopatra were young, and they were among the monarchs who had not come to fight and lose alongside Pompey at Pharsalus. Egypt, in the end, was by no means an illogical choice; Pompey may have reasoned or been persuaded by his advisors to think that the republicans could all but take over business in Alexandria.

Pompey's miniature navy proceeded south, to the destination that he had scorned all those years before, when he was returning to Italy as a feared conqueror, with many worrying what he would do with his formidable armies when he landed at Brundisium. Hauntingly, he was going to his death in the very same legendary land of the tomb of Alexander.

Caesar was an expert at how to do things swiftly. If he was not by any means Pompey's equal in naval operations, he was certainly highly competent at preparing what he needed to commence operations both by land and sea. We have some knowledge of his activity in this period, not least from his own pen.

Not surprisingly, Caesar emphasizes his alacrity in trying to find Pompey, so that he could put an end to the war as expeditiously as possible.[28] He made it to Asia, where he boasts of once again saving money from the treasury of Diana at Ephesus.[29] He stayed a few days in the region before word arrived that Pompey had been seen in Cyprus; at once he claims to have conjectured that his enemy must have decided to head to Egypt. And so he headed there, with one legion that he had brought from Thessaly, and another that he had ordered from Achaea, with 800 cavalry, ten Rhodian warships, and a few vessels from Asia. This would be the force with which he proceeded to what would be the Alexandrian War.

Appian, for his part, says that after Pharsalus, Caesar remained in the vicinity for two days, giving his men a rest; we can be sure that in the interim he lost no time sending out word to try to find Pompey.[30] The Athenians who had fought for Pompey were dismissed with a pardon, as well as with a sarcastic remark alluding to how once again the ancient glory of the city of the goddess Athena had saved them. He then headed east after Pompey in person.

We can be sure about Caesar's having sent out pursuing parties immediately, and in different directions. He did have immediate business to settle with the army and his many prisoners, but he could not afford to give Pompey a two-day lead without any intelligence gathering or attempt to follow.

Appian tells an interesting story in accord with one of Caesar's own favourite topics, namely how he was a child of good fortune.[31] He had proceeded east, and at the Hellespont he encountered Cassius, who was on his way from his aforementioned Sicilian and Italian operations to head toward Pharnaces. Cassius had seventy warships, and Caesar nowhere near anything sufficient to do battle with such an armada. But news had been spreading about Caesar's victory at Pharsalus, and Cassius surrendered to him. Caesar makes clear that he could have been destroyed at that juncture, had fortune not smiled on him again.

Caesar learned that Pompey had decided on Egypt as a destination; he sailed on to Rhodes as he continued his pursuit. He did not wait for the rest of his army, but prepared to go to Alexandria to confront Pompey.

Dio also mentions the pressing business that Caesar needed to complete immediately after Pharsalus.[32] He also records the encounter with Cassius, and how Caesar was incredibly lucky in his ability to cow a vastly superior force into surrender. Caesar entered Asia in safety, and began raising money, though in a way that scrupulously sought to avoid offending anyone or bringing back memories of the alleged harshness of Scipio's exactions. Soon enough he learned that Pompey was heading to Alexandria.

We have a significant problem in our sources. Appian makes clear that the 'Cassius' involved in the odd episode at the Hellespont was Gaius Cassius, best known to history as one of the assassins of Caesar.[33] But Dio, like Suetonius, says that it was Lucius Cassius.[34] Suetonius says that Caesar was crossing the Hellespont in a single passenger boat (shades of the image of Pompey fleeing to Lesbos in a merchant ship), when he met Lucius, who had ten warships; Caesar made no attempt to flee, but went to Lucius and persuaded him to surrender.[35] Lucius begged for mercy and received it.

Besides the question of which Cassius was at the Hellespont coincidentally just when Caesar happened to be there, we may wonder about how a Pompeian navy (whether composed of ten or of seventy ships) could be induced to surrender to Caesar as if he were a mesmerizing deity.

Lucius Cassius was Gaius' brother; he had been forced to retreat from Thessaly in the face of Scipio's advance, and he joined Calvisius in Aetolia. Gaius, for his part, was destined to play a role for a time on the Caesarian side, but he would retire to Italy and politics (including increasingly close ties to Cicero, and the slow and steady march toward the Ides of March), with no participation in the campaigns against Cato and Scipio in Africa. What may have happened in the historical record is this. It would be all too easy for some sources to confuse the two brothers, especially when one started out on the Caesarian side, and the other came over to it later, albeit likely quite halfheartedly. When Gaius learned of the disaster at Pharsalus, he abandoned his operations in the central Mediterranean, and may have headed toward his brother as much as toward the Hellespont and Pharnaces. It defies credulity to imagine that Caesar encountered Cassius by happenstance, and that Caesar was able to convince the man who had just performed brilliantly for Pompey at Sicily to surrender, let alone to throw himself on Caesar's mercy. At the same time, clearly Cassius was not some diehard like Cato; he was not going to make sure that his fleet continued to prosecute the war. He was among the many who were done with civil war, at least when it came to fighting fellow Romans.

The calendar would not have permitted much time for negotiation, and one wonders at the extraordinary logistics involved, but it is possible that Cassius withdrew from operations in Italian waters as soon as he heard about Pharsalus; he then decided to move toward where he had learned that his brother was now operating. By the time he arrived at the Hellespont, he knew that he would be ready to make clear to Caesar that he was not interested in continuing to fight against him; likewise, he was ready to tell anyone – including Caesar – that he was not willing to go to Africa to fight Cato and Scipio on Caesar's behalf. In other words, the truth likely involved both brothers, rapid negotiation, and an agreement that Gaius Cassius was not going to try to follow Pompey to Alexandria, or anywhere.

Caesar was hampered in his pursuit of Pompey mostly by the problem of receiving accurate information, and by the fact that like Pompey, he had made no ready plans for a seaborne departure from Greece. Certainly he had fewer naval resources than Pompey overall, though he was not entirely bereft of options, and the win at Pharsalus would have inspired even the otherwise unwilling to help him: throughout this crucial window, the fate of Gomphi would have continued to be instructive.

Ptolemaic Egypt would have been more than a mere brief obstacle to Caesar, had the court of Ptolemy XIII decided to help Pompey and the republic. The Alexandrians had a formidable army, and especially an appreciable navy. It is true that they were embroiled in a civil war, but Caesar did not exactly have a large force ready to take Alexandria on short notice; by the time he would be able to amass a force, Pompey could also have summoned allies. It is true that as soon as Caesar learned about Pompey's Egyptian destination, he set the ball in motion and was preparing for any eventuality in Egypt. But the situation was complicated and challenging for both larger than life Romans, and Egypt was by no means some trivial kingdom that could be expected to be dispensed with quickly. Soon enough Cleopatra would prove to be a key factor in Caesar's engagement with the Alexandrians, but the mere fact that he had appreciable difficulties navigating the Egyptian civil war gives a clue to the resources that were available at least potentially to Pompey.

We have mentioned the geographical consideration of the relative closeness of Egypt to Cato's forces in Africa. Likewise, holding Egypt would put serious pressure on Syria and the east, on Cyprus and southern Asia Minor (where Pompey had significant strength and widespread sympathy). All in all, Pompey's last voyage was by no means unsoundly planned.

Plutarch records that Pompey heard that Ptolemy was at Pelousion, and so he put in there, sending word ahead to the king of his arrival.[36] Pompey had sailed into a civil war; Ptolemy's forces were seeking to pin down and to destroy Cleopatra's attempted takeover of the monarchy. Appian says that it was the luck of the winds (or, we might say, the bad luck) that Pompey landed near Casium, close to Ptolemy's position; seeing a large army encamped near the coast, he realized that the king must be there.[37] Dio (like Caesar) simply says that he arrived at Pelousion, with no explanation of how or why he went there.[38] It is possible that Alexandria was the original destination, as one would expect;

Pompey or his advance guard would have been told that the king was in fact at Pelousion with his court and his army. It is also possible that Pompey had received information in Cyprus about the general situation in Egypt, and the location of the king and his forces. If it had all been accidental and fortuitous, lovers of alternative histories might wonder what would have transpired had Pompey landed behind Cleopatra's lines instead of Ptolemy's; the two were quite close together at this point. Strabo notes that Casium is a sandy promontory without water, the site of a temple to Zeus; he records the burial of Pompey there.[39]

We do not have an exact sense of chronology; it seems likely that Pompey met his end just before what would have been his fifty-fourth birthday, probably in fact the day before: 28 September, 48 BC.[40] From his family he had Cornelia and Sextus with him; Egypt was not thought to be a dangerous place to bring any of them.

Plutarch rightly deplores the tragedy that the fate of such a man as Pompey was decided by the three counsellors of Ptolemy: the soldier Achillas, the academic Theodotus, and the eunuch Pothinus.[41] Naturally there was disagreement as to what to do about this frankly unwelcome arrival. Whoever the Roman was who landed in Egypt, the arrival was supremely inconvenient; the courtiers of the king had a civil war to fight, and they had no idea how any Roman commander would respond to the situation he encountered. It was supremely bad luck for all parties; while Pompey would be eliminated, the king's advisors would find themselves in their own serious mess of a crisis once Caesar came swiftly in his wake.

The options were essentially three. Ptolemy's court could agree to help Pompey; indeed, he might have been able to help them to crush Cleopatra. The Alexandrians could try to drive him away, making it clear that like Antioch and Rhodes, the Pompeians were not welcome in Egypt. Or they could kill him, for the obvious reason that it seemed at least to some that it would secure their future with Caesar. The smart decision does not require hindsight to discern, one might be tempted to think: they should simply have refused to receive him. Every available option carried risks, but that was the one that posed the least hazard. If, that is, Cleopatra were not in the picture. She complicated everything.

Let us take a step back, and imagine the scene in Ptolemy's court. Plutarch indicates that while the other courtiers were divided between either receiving Pompey or not welcoming him, it was Theodotus who raised the idea of killing him.[42] Perhaps (it is impossible to be sure), Pothinus had advocated for not admitting him, and Achillas for opening the door. The military would have appreciated the need not to fight with both Cleopatra and Pompey's admittedly small force, and there was another consideration: if Pompey were not welcomed, there was every chance he would go to Cleopatra's camp and throw his weight behind her. That was probably a decisive factor in the decision making, and indeed it would have been the main sticking point for Achillas, Pothinus, and/or Theodotus. Probably it was thought unrealistic if not impossible to try to seize Pompey as a prisoner, holding him for Caesar.

Theodotus is said to have argued that sending Pompey away would incur Caesar's wrath, once he learned that his search could have been concluded far sooner. He was also worried about having Pompey as an enemy; in his estimation, not admitting him meant having both powerful Romans as enemies. Lucan, not surprisingly, casts the eunuch Pothinus as the principal villain of the dark hour for the republic.[43]

Theodotus urged his colleagues, then, to summon Pompey to his assassination. Chillingly, we hear that he reminded them that dead men do not bite. This quote is used in Mankiewicz's *Cleopatra*, when Theodotus urges Caesar to accept the 'gift' of the jar with Pompey's head.

Ptolemy's men were in an impossibly difficult situation. If Cleopatra and the civil war were not a factor, the choice would have been far easier. But the camps were so close together, and any rejection of Pompey risked his going to her. From his perspective, the boy and his adolescent sister were supposed to be co-rulers. When he first drew near to Alexandria, he may have asked first after the male ruler, learning at once where he was, and quickly being informed by Ptolemy's supporters of the civil war, from their point of view. If they accepted him, there would have been a chance (indeed, the necessity) to do what he had refused to in years before – intervene in the Alexandrian civil war. But to make it clear that Ptolemy was no friend would practically invite Pompey to side with the other co-ruler. He could not be expected to leave so precious a prize as Egypt to the handlers of a boy, and he would have to expect that Caesar was on his way, and that he would settle Alexandrian affairs to his liking. No, to deny admittance to Pompey was to give Cleopatra a potentially powerful ally at exactly the moment when the sycophantic courtiers of the boy king wanted her dead. They could not have known that the decision to murder Pompey so treacherously would be a key factor in the rise of Cleopatra; the girl they hated so much whose forces were encamped not so far off was destined to be one of the inadvertent beneficiaries of the assassination.

Theodotus likely did not have much trouble persuading the others of the alleged wisdom of his plan; indeed, there may have been less dissension than Plutarch indicates. Caesar professes to have no certainty as to what they were thinking; he says that perhaps they were afraid that welcoming Pompey meant having him take over the kingdom, or maybe they scorned someone who was obviously down on his luck. Appian blames Theodotus for the plot to have

Pompey killed, but gives no analysis as to why the fateful decision was taken.[44] Dio is also distinterested in exploring the mindset of Magnus' murderers.[45]

The decision was made; the execution of the grim plan was easier.[46] As the chief military official at Ptolemy's court, Achillas was chosen to be in charge of the assassination. Plutarch says that he recruited Septimius, a former tribune under Pompey, and the centurion Salvius, with three or four servants; they set out in a vessel toward Pompey's ship.[47] Pompey's entourage is said to have been suspicious from the start, because Theophanes had predicted that the Alexandrians would welcome Pompey with honour, and here was a small group in a fishing boat. But Achillas' craft was allowed to draw near, and Septimius hailed Pompey with that classic title of Roman respect for a military commander: *Imperator*. It would be the last time that Pompey would hear so treasured an honourific. Achillas spoke to Pompey in Greek, urging him to come abroad the fishing vessel, noting that the shallows were hazardous and extensive, and that Pompey could not safely draw near to shore there in a trireme. If Pompey was deeply suspicious of the whole scene, it was too late to do much about it; whether Achillas and the others were good actors was irrelevant at this point. Achillas' pretext about the shallows was a legitimate one; still, Ptolemy's men must have been greatly relieved that Pompey was not accompanied personally by a powerful contingent.

Simultaneously, the king's own vessels near the shore were being loaded with men, as if to make sure that there would be no realistic chance for Pompey to decide to try to escape what he judged to be a trap. Cornelia was embraced; not surprisingly, Plutarch portrays her as crying and mourning what she was certain to be his impending death – in other words, the usual claims of such biographical narratives of momentous dire events.[48] Pompey ordered two of his centurions to precede him into the boat, together with his freedman Philip, and a servant named Scythes; if we remember that Pompey had dismissed his original servile staff, Scythes must have been picked up somewhere along the commander's last journey. Pompey is said to have turned one last time to Cornelia as Achillas was stretching out his hand, quoting Sophoclean tragedy; in a way, he had been like a man in a dream for some weeks now.[49]

The fishing boat set off for shore, and along the short way Pompey turned to Septimius and expressed his recognition of his veteran tribune. Septimius nodded, with no response; the whole mood must have been ominous and chilling, even as it was awkward and full of anxiety on all sides. Pompey had a scroll on which he had been composing a Greek address to deliver to Ptolemy; he began studying it as the boat was rowed to shore. Cornelia and the retinue with her were watching; they saw that there was a growing assembly on the coast, and they were initially heartened that perhaps this was, after all, the honourable welcome that the Roman Alexander merited in Alexandria.

Pompey took the hand of the freedman Philip as he prepared to stand up to disembark. At that moment, Septimius struck him behind, and then Salvius attacked. The third assassin was Achillas. In Mankiewicz's movie, Caesar comments to Achillas that surely the death of Pompey was not by his hand; the solemn-faced soldier comments that Caesar should know better, if he indeed he had had accurate reports about him. Nothing could be more untrue; whatever Achillas' initial recommendation as to what to do about Pompey, he was certainly among his killers.[50] He would join that dubious cast of historical names remembered most for participation in treacherous assassinations.

Plutarch's Pompey shielded his face with his toga in the honourable gesture of one facing his end; he groaned, but said or did nothing to his discredit.[51] Plutarch says that he was fifty-nine, and that he died a day after his birthday; he was actually younger, and likelier just missed his anniversary by a day. The Roman Alexander breathed his last at the moment of stepping foot on the sands of the land that boasted the tomb of the Macedonian.

Caesar's account is broadly similar to Plutarch's.[52] He calls Achillas a man singular in his boldness; he named Lucius Septimius as the treacherous tribune. Indeed, one of the most tragic elements of the death of Pompey was that he was slain by a Roman hand; he was a victim of civil violence just as Caesar was doomed to be. Septimius was the bait; he had served as a centurion under Pompey in the campaign against the pirates, and now he addressed Pompey with respect as he came forward with Achillas. According to Caesar, these were the two killers; Lucius Lentulus is said to have been taken prisoner not so long thereafter, when he arrived to join Pompey; before long he was killed in prison.[53] Apparently it was not considered an option to keep him for Caesar; the same possibility clearly had been dismissed in the matter of Pompey. Likely Ptolemy's handlers were worried that Pompey still commanded sufficient respect that he would be far more dangerous as a prisoner; Theodotus' comment about dead men not being able to bite may have been a comment on just that sort of consideration.

Cuius infesto adventu urbe pulsus, in Pharsalia victus ad Ptolemaeum Alexandriae regem confugit. eius imperio ab Achilla et Potino satellitibus occisus est. Such is the laconic summary of the late antique *De Viris Illustribus*, describing the dramatic and highly consequential events that occurred in so brief a span of time.[54] Velleius would note in his history that after the death of Pompey, his name remained alive as a potent rallying cry for the continuation of the struggle against Caesar and his aspirations to dictatorship.[55] Once Caesar knew that Pompey was dead, he could breathe something of a sigh of relief that a major opponent of his ambitions had been eliminated. But the chessboard was still full of threats and potential traps. The fact that Caesar himself would be dead in less than four years is ample testament to how unhealthy the climate was throughout the Mediterranean. As for Caesar's reaction when he learned of the murder, it is easy to imagine conflicted feelings; Caesar's situation had been vastly simplified by Septimius' blade, but he would have been horrified by the indignity and shameful treachery of it all. The circumstances of the assassination, however, would afford him the chance to remind his Roman audience how clement he claimed to be; reverential treatment of Pompey's remains and the eventual death of Pothinus would be emblematic gestures to be highlighted in the mythology that was carefully curated concerning the magnanimous Caesar.

In the immediate wake of the brutal stabbing on the beach, Cornelia and Sextus needed to be spirited away to safety; there was no way that the small force with Pompey's family could challenge the Ptolemaic fleet. Plutarch says that the wind cooperated with the flight, and that the efforts of the Alexandrians to launch a pursuit came to naught.[56] The Alexandrians had been preparing to chase after Pompey if he tried to take flight out of fear of a trap; it is possible that once Pompey was in their hands and slain, the king's forces had no interest in chasing down his wife and son. Especially if there had been dissension as to what to do, it is likely that Achillas and the others did not want to risk having Caesar horrified that they had slain a woman and the young man. Cicero in his *Tusculan Disputations* would make a rather academic comment on the escape scene, using it as an example of a case where fear is the dominant emotion, surpassing even grief.[57] Sextus Pompey would prove to be exceptionally vigourous in his pursuit of something of the legacy of his father; his likely eyewitness place at the assassination scene would have been a powerful formative influence on his spirit and will. In Plutarch's life of Cato, we hear that it would be Sextus who would have the sad duty of announcing the death to him.[58] Cornelia now had the grim distinction of having lost two husbands to violence in the east; by marriage she was connected to the sequences of events that had seen the removal of two of the original three 'triumvirs.' At least in the case of Crassus' son, Cornelia had been nowhere near the scene, and the young hero had died in the context of a battle. This time she was a spectator to the macabre theatrical scene, reduced to fleeing for her life either to Cyprus or, possibly, initially Phoenician Tyre.

Pompey's body was decapitated (Appian specifies that the grisly act was performed by the servants of Pothinus);[59] the freedman Philip stayed with the headless corpse, washing and purifying it before gathering the remains of an old fishing vessel to try to fashion a funeral pyre.[60] An old Roman is said to have come upon the site, revealing that he had served with Pompey once upon a time, long ago; Lucan describes the poignant scene as Cordus paid tribute to his onetime commander. He would assist the faithful *libertus* on that desolate Alexandrian strand. The great republican hero had died not only the day before his birthday, but on the anniversary of his triumph in 61 BC, over Mithridates.[61]

Plutarch closes his life of Pompey by noting that Caesar on arrival would be presented with the head, and with the signet ring that was marked by a lion holding a sword in its paws.[62] Needless to say, the victor at Pharsalus was not pleased with the deed of Ptolemy's court; Livy's surviving epitome of the event says that Theodotus showed him the head, and that Caesar wept.[63] Ultimately Achillas and Pothinus would be slain; Ptolemy would disappear in battle, drowned or slain. Theodotus would manage to escape, until he was captured by Brutus, who ensured that the vengeance for Pompey was complete. Caesar would ensure that the head was sent to Cornelia, for honourable burial at the Alban villa of the man who had been his son-in-law, colleague, adversary, and above all fellow Roman.

Lucan closes his eighth book with a haunting passage that comes after a long diatribe against the land of Egypt.[64] A happier age will come, the Neronian poet of *Libertas* says, when Romans will think Egypt to be just as mendacious in claiming to have the grave of Pompey, as Crete in boasting of the grave of Jupiter. Pompey, after all, is to be considered as nothing less than a veritable god, a figure of divine inspiration in the quest for republican liberty.[65]

Chapter Twenty-Five

Magni Nominis Umbra

In death as in life Pompey would cast a long shadow.[1] The sequel volume to this work, *The Sons of Pompey*, is intended to continue the story for a dozen and more years, as the Roman civil wars continued to rage across the Mediterranean, and as the last surviving member of the so-called First Triumvirate went the violent way of his onetime colleagues. Pompey's sons Gnaeus and (especially) Sextus would be prominent in the ongoing internecine conflicts of the republic; the death of their father was as much the beginning as the end of the story of what would be nothing less than a transformation of the Roman world.

Already as word of his assassination spread, the legacy of Pompey has been debated and questioned; scholarly opinions on the man are exceedingly varied, as they are with respect to his protégé and eventual deadly rival Caesar.[2] The *optimates* had viewed Pompey with serious suspicion from his young manhood; in the crisis with Caesar, they belatedly realized (at least at some level) that he was willing to stand and to fight with them, indeed to cooperate with them in leadership. He was a republican to the end. Caesar would not be able to claim the same status, and it would be Caesar's fate to die at the hands of his countrymen. Pompey had been struck down by a Roman hand, a veteran of his glorious campaigns. But the Roman was little more than a hired hand for a client boy king, and unlike Caesar, Pompey did not die because he had been deemed a threat to the very existence of the republic.

Our analysis of the man is that Pompey was a key figure in the development of what ultimately would put an end to Rome's internecine strife (at least for a sustained period), namely the Augustan principate. Coincidentally, the future Augustus would don the *toga virilis* or toga of manhood in October of 48 BC, a few weeks after Pompey's death and possibly before the teenage Octavian had received word of the news.

According to this view, Pompey aspired at maintaining the republican system in such a way that would allow for the benevolent management of the machinery of government (especially of foreign affairs) by one man, a figure who enjoyed power more through *gravitas* than anything else. Titles mattered and were a key element of maintaining *auctoritas*, but what was of paramount importance was being hailed and venerated as the saviour of the people and of the state. For Augustus it would be victories over the enemies of Rome; from Parthian standards to the defeat of Cleopatra and other foreign threats real and exaggerated, the *princeps* was Rome's deliverer from harm and bringer of peace. For the *princeps* Pompey, it was much the same in the campaigns against the Cilician pirates and Rome's enemies in the east; ensuring the security of the grain supply was the quintessential salvific deed of a national hero. Ending civil wars was part of the equation as well, even if the idea of fighting fellow Romans required appropriate finesse and devotion to public relations and communications concerns.

Caesar, had he lived, may well have been a markedly different Roman ruler than Augustus proved to be. Caesar's assassination was followed by his deification; the hunting down of his assassins and the conspirators of the Ides was a duty of *pietas* for his adopted son. It may have been that Antony would have been more Caesarian than not had he been able to defeat his rival. Caesar's assassination made him a convenient figure for propaganda: all the good and positive, popular and praiseworthy deeds and acts of the man could be celebrated. Premature death had made him immortal; he was now a true descendant of Venus, adored and deified.[3] Negative associations of the man were easier to forgive and to ignore once he was dead; his lover Cleopatra and their son Caesarion would not be alive to complicate any neat picture of propaganda. The problematic Caesar fell to the daggers of the would-be *liberatores* on that March day; the admirable Caesar would become immortal, not only in his own divine honours, but in the principate of the man he was discerning enough to adopt.

In a world where Caesar was a god, Pompey occupied a problematic place. He had been defeated in battle by the future deity. Slain by treacherous so-called allies, in death he found tremendous sympathy; he would be one of the many recipients of Caesar's clemency, as he was treated as a man whose death deserved to be avenged, a hero of the republic who deserved respect even in defeat.

But if we may be permitted to speculate, it is possible that in Pompey the future Augustus found a potent role model, such that the slain Roman Alexander and republican martyr would have appreciated and admired the system that Augustus established, fostered, and did his best to set on a sure footing.[4] This is not to say that Caesar himself would not have been proud of the achievement of his heir. Nor was it principally a question of temperament; Pompey and Caesar were both alike in feeling at home in the field, military men to the core, while Augustus was never in quite the same league, for all his experience and successes. Inclination was perhaps the issue more than ability. The more noteworthy comparison would be between Pompey and Caesar in government. Here, there is no question that both commanders were often frustrated with the differences between the two worlds. Pompey, however, was more tolerant and willing to live according to republican conventions than Caesar. Caesar if anything displayed his true nature in this regard when he held his first consulship. While Pompey was often feared and distrusted for what he might do as a would-be dictator, it was Caesar who actually held the office; the eleven days of dictatorship in which Lepidus and he were engaged in orchestrating a political farce was mere prelude to aspirations to a more lasting tenure in quasi-monarchical power. A critic of Caesar could craft an argument that Pompey was often assailed for what he might do; we have seen that even in the question of Pharsalus, there were voices asking just how tyrannical Pompey would have been had he won the battle. And yet the civil war had commenced because Caesar was so unwilling to dismiss his armies; Pompey was justly indignant, given the vivid memory of how (contrary to the expectation of his political opponents) he had been willing to surrender his legions.

Augustus had the advantage of coming of age with an impressive range of *exempla* to follow, an array of luminaries both celebrated and reviled from which to learn; he came to power at the end of a century marred by civil wars. An heir of Caesar, his adopted name would endure as the title most associated with the rulers of Rome; Julius was the first of the Caesars, and what would endure as the Julio-Claudian dynasty would remain at the helm of empire for decades. Tacitus says that when the historian Livy celebrated Pompey with lavish praise, Augustus called him a 'Pompeian.'[5] The comment may have carried it with a great deal of significance as a reflection of one *princeps* on another; Augustus and Pompey were both 'first citizens' in different ways at different moments in history, and much of what had characterized Pompey in his life as a republican statesman would be mirrored and exemplified in the attitude of Augustus toward the republic. The premiere historian of the age was willing to praise Pompey, and Augustus likely would have had it no other way. Augustus had much in common with Pompey, far beyond the mere coincidence of late September birthdays. In historical memory, Caesar may have been remembered less than warmly not so much for the times when he was dictator, as for when he was consul the first time. At least there is a certain honesty and forthrightness to dictatorship; with Bibulus during the so-called consulship of Julius and Caesar, republicanism had been rendered farcical.

Pompey may have held a special appeal for Augustus for another reason. Pompey was betrayed and slain under the auspices of one Ptolemaic monarch, and Augustus cast his final victory and bringing of peace to the Mediterranean as the triumph of Rome over the forces of the other Ptolemaic monarch. Abolishing the monarchy of the Ptolemies was vengeance for Pompey; Augustus could take pride in having openly sought to avenge his father Caesar, and having implicitly secured revenge for Pompey. It did not matter that Cleopatra was actually at war with Pompey's killers at the time of his death, or that she had had nothing to do with his murder. It was the same Egypt, the same line of the Ptolemies; the fact that Cleopatra had been the embarrassing paramour of Caesar made the whole matter even more satisfying.

In short, while Pompey had failed in attaining his goals and succeeding in his ambitions, one could recognize much of the style of Pompey in the way in which Caesar's adopted son would manage Rome's affairs; Augustus would also be the one to be given back the standards that Crassus had lost to the Parthians, a tangible sign of the settlement of the east and the bringing of peace. What Pompey had aspired to do overseas was largely accomplished by Augustus.

When Augustus called Livy *Pompeianus*, he may well have been saying about his friend what he could not say about himself. His requiem in AD 14 would be more direct, via the import of its iconography. As Dio recalls, for the funeral procession there were images of prominent Romans, commencing with Romulus.[6] Caesar was not included among the *imagines* because he had been deified. But Pompey the Great was there, accompanied by likenesses of all the nations he had acquired or vanquished for Rome. The Roman Alexander had conquered a world for Rome; fittingly, his image was prominent at the valedictory rites for the man who had saved her.

Notes

Chapter 1
1. On the underappreciated question of any formative contact between the two future Roman luminaries, see A.M. Ward, 'The Early Relationships between Cicero and Pompey until 80 BC,' in *Phoenix*, Vol. 24, No. 2 (Summer, 1970), pp. 119–129; cf. the same author's 'Cicero and Pompey in 75 and 70 BC,' in *Latomus*, T. 29, Fasc. 1 (janvier-mars, 1970), pp. 58–71.
2. *Brutus* 239.
3. Indispensable for the study of the period covered in the present biography is J.A. Crook, A. Lintott, and E. Rawson, *The Cambridge Ancient History: Volume IX, The Last Age of the Roman Republic, 146–43 B.C.*, Cambridge, 1994 (second edition).
4. The surviving life of Pompey by the second-century AD author Plutarch provides a complete narrative; the biographer pairs him with the famous Spartan monarch Agesilaus II. Not surprisingly, Plutarch's lives have been translated many times; in both the Oxford World's Classics and Penguin Classics series, there are convenient collections arranged by period. More recent editions of Plutarch in translation have been careful to include the valuable comparisons of the Greek and Roman paired subjects. The Loeb Classical Library provides access to both Plutarch's lives and his *Moralia*. Herbert Heftner's *Plutarch und der Aufstieg des Pompeius: Ein historischer Kommentaar zu Plutarchs Pompeiusvita. Teil I: Kap. 1–45* (Europäische Hochschulschriften. Reihe III, Geschichte und ihre Hilfswissenschaften), Frankfurt: Peter Lang, 1995, provides detailed annotation on the first half of the life. Leach 1978, pp. 218 ff. provides a convenient selection of translations of primary sources related to the life of Pompey.
5. Cicero's works provide an invaluable, utterly fascinating window into his life and times. The complete surviving output is voluminous; for the study of Pompey's life, the speeches and the letters are the more important resources. The letters give what sometimes amounts to a running commentary on the events of a given period; the collection preserves letters that were composed by Pompey himself to his correspondent. The Loeb Classical Library offers Cicero's works in more than two dozen volumes, including the fragmentary speeches. For the letters, the Loeb edition is based on the massive Cambridge Classical Texts and Commentaries edition by D.R. Shackleton Bailey, which contains a commentary alongside a critical edition and English translation of the corpus. There are abridged editions of the letters in both the Oxford and Penguin series; Penguin originally published complete editions of the Shackleton Bailey translations, which are now regrettably out of print.
6. Caesar, like any ancient historian or commentator, must be read critically; indeed, given the fact that in his *Bellum Civile* he was writing about a war that he had conducted personally, his use as a source merits special caution; as we shall see in the preset study, not everything that Caesar says can be taken as gospel. Many editions exist of Caesar's work in the usual sets of translations (Oxford, Penguin, Loeb); the Aris & Phillips Classical Texts series offers a good two-volume *Civil War* (with useful notes), and in the popular *Landmark* series, Caesar is the first Roman author to be included.
7. Patrick McGushin's two-volume set for the Clarendon Ancient History series (1992, 1994) is a splendid resource here, with English translation and detailed historical commentary. John T. Ramsey's Loeb edition is richly annotated.
8. Sadly, the relevant books of the Augustan historian Livy do not survive, but we do have epitomes or summaries, the so-called *Periochae*; these are included in the Loeb Livy, and are the subject

of a massive new standard edition by David Levene for Oxford. The monumental works of the imperial Greek historians Appian and Dio Cassius are priceless troves of information, providing narratives of the foreign and civil wars of the Age of Pompey; alongside these two major Greek sources, we may note the Tiberian historian Gaius Velleius Paterculus, whose brief historical works sometimes display evidence of the use of sources independent of Livy. From the same age we have the *Factorum et dictorum memorabilium libri*, or 'Memorable Deeds and Sayings' of Valerius Maximus; there is a Loeb edition of this enchanting, addictive collection of anecdotes. The Caesar biography of Gaius Suetonius Tranquillus is one of the most popular surviving works of classical antiquity; there is also the epitome of Roman military history of Publius Annius Florus, which occasionally preserves precious snippets of information. We may note also the Greek historian Josephus, author of the extensive *Jewish Antiquities*; Josephus is our best surviving source of information for Pompey's wars in Judaea and its environs. The Loeb collection offers access to all that remains of this first-century AD author.

9. The Neronian Age poet Lucan constitutes another important source for the life of Pompey, given his extensive attention to and narrative of the civil war. Given the genre and nature of his work, Lucan must be treated with special care, but should not be dismissed out of hand as a valuable witness to the tradition that had developed around Pompey in the century after his death. There are translations available in the Loeb, Oxford's World Classics, and Penguin series; the Penguin includes the *Bellum Civile* from Petronius' *Satyrica*.

10. The standard scholarly English studies remain Greenhalgh's two-volume set and Seager's predominately political biography; Leach offers a thorough and incisive study on a smaller scale. The present work does not seek to rival Greenhalgh and Seager, but to provide something along the lines of Leach's book, with particular attention to the image of Pompey as model for several of the actions and reforms of Augustus. For those with German, Matthias Gelzer's *Pompeius: Lebensbild eines Römers* deserves to be as popular as his widely used Caesar biography.

11. This is not one of the better documented periods in Roman history; we have fragments of the imperial historian and author of curiosities, Granius Licinianus, which provide one of the best windows into the campaigns of Pompey's father.

12. A. Keaveney, 'Young Pompey: 106–79 BC,' in *L'Antiquité classique*, T. 51 (1982), pp. 111–139 gives a detailed account of what we know, with the author's customary sober analysis.

13. See B.X. de Wet, 'Aspects of Plutarch's Portrayal of Pompey,' in *Acta Classica*, Vol. 24 (1981), pp. 119–132, for a good introduction to the manner in which the biographer approaches his subject and uses his sources.

14. On Strabo's alleged rapacity and general unpopularity, cf. Valerius Maximus 9.14, Pliny, *NH* 7.54, Plutarch, *Mor.* 203B.

15. See further M. Griffith, *Aeschylus: Prometheus Bound*, Cambridge, 1983.

16. *Pomp.* 1.

17. *Pomp.* 1.

18. *Pomp.* 1; cf. *Mor.* 553B, Velleius 2.21, Orosius 5.19; the second-century AD historian Granius Licinianus also knows the story of a lightning strike (noting that it took off the top of his tent while he was sick inside), but records that he survived the bolt, only to die on the third day after his good fortune of a wasting disease. Appian (*BC* 1.68) says that he died along with other nobles from lightning.

19. For his life and mysterious end, note O.D. Watkins, 'The Death of Gn. Pompeius Strabo,' in *Rheinisches Museum für Philologie, Neue Folge*, 131. Bd., H. 2 (1988), pp. 143–150, T.W. Hillard, 'Death by Lightning: Pompeius Strabo and the Roman People,' in *Rheinisches Museum für Philologie, Neue Folge*, 139. Bd., H. 2 (1996), pp. 135–145, T.P. Hillman, 'Cinna, Strabo's Army, and Strabo's Death in 87 BC,' in *L'Antiquité classique*, T. 65 (1996), pp. 81–89.

20. *NH* 7.20. Pliny's *Natural History* is an encyclopedic work of immense value, not least for its preservation of otherwise unattested lore; besides the Loeb edition, we may note the extensive Budé series of French commentaries accompanying critical texts of the Latin with translation.

21. The Criterion Collection has an edition of Kubrick's *Spartacus*, which has been the subject of an appreciable bibliography. Martin Winkler's 2008 *Spartacus: Film and History* for Wiley-

Blackwell provides a comprehensive and reliable appraisal of the film and its relationship to the surviving ancient sources.
22. *Pomp.* 1.
23. Allen Mason Ward's *Marcus Crassus and the Late Roman Republic* (Missouri, 1977) is perhaps the finest general study of the man; Peter Stothard's *Crassus: The First Tycoon* (Yale, 2023) is a brief, excellent introduction; note also B.A. Marshall, *Crassus: A Political Biography*, Amsterdam: Adolf M. Hakkert, 1976.
24. For the Roman reception of the image of Alexander note Jennifer Finn, *A Determinist History of Alexander the Great in the Roman Empire*, Ann Arbor: The University of Michigan Press, 2022.
25. *Pomp.* 2.
26. Conversely, cf. the criticisms of effeminacy recorded by Ammianus Marcellinus (17.11), and the historian's defence of Pompey; for the charge see Seneca Rhetor, *Contr.* 7.4 (citing Calvus), and note Plutarch, *Pomp.* 48.
27. The topic was of perennial interest and concern to the ancients; see further Francesca Romana Berno's *Roman Luxuria: A Literary and Cultural History* (Oxford, 2023).
28. Recommended for further reading here are Christopher J. Dart, *The Social War, 91 to 88 BC: A History of the Italian Insurgency against the Roman Republic*, Oxford-New York: Routledge, 2016 (first published 2014, Ashgate), and Philip Matyszak, *Cataclysm 90 BC: The Forgotten War That Almost Destroyed Rome*, Barnsley: Pen & Sword Military, 2014.
29. Federico Santangelo's *Ancients in Action: Marius* (London-New York: Bloomsbury Academic, 2016) is a good start for further research.
30. Arthur Keaveney, *Sulla: The Last Republican*, Oxford-New York: Routledge, 2005 (second edition of the 1982 Croom Helm original) offers an incisive, standard account of Pompey's mentor; the edited volume *Sulla: Politics and Reception* by Alexander Thein and Alexandra Eckert (Berlin-New York: Walter de Gruyter, 2019) is a collection of studies on his legacy. Note also L. Telford, *Sulla: A Dictator Reconsidered*, Barnsley: Pen & Sword Military, 2014, which seeks to rehabilitate its subject.
31. *Fasti* 6.563–4.
32. Strabo 14.560 notes that Aristodemus of Nysa was one of his teachers; cf. Athenaeus, where Atticus of Neapolis is cited as his tutor in gymnastics.
33. Cf. Appian, *BC* 1.50, Livy, *Per.* 75, Eutropius 5.3.
34. 5.18. The three-volume Budé edition with text, French translation, and notes may be recommended here; Peter Van Nuffelen's *Orosius and the Rhetoric of History* (Oxford, 2012) is the best scholarly study.
35. On the relevant chronology, source criticism, and question of Strabo's ambitions see A. Keaveney, 'Pompeius Strabo's Second Consulship,' in *The Classical Quarterly*, Vol. 28, No. 1 (1978), pp. 240–241.
36. Cf. Plutarch, *Pomp.* 4, Appian, *BC* 1.48, Florus 2.6, Orosius 5.18.
37. See Leach 1978, pp. 11–4, 218–20 for the text of an inscription at Asculum recording Strabo's grant of Roman citizenship to a squadron of Spanish horsemen that had distinguished itself in the Social War.
38. 2.21. Velleius may be found in the Loeb Library; there are major Cambridge editions of the 'Caesarian and Augustan Narrative (2.41–93),' and the Tiberian in the 'Cambridge Classical Texts and Commentaries' (orange) series. R. Seager, 'Velleius on Pompey,' in E. Cowan, ed., *Velleius Paterculus: Making History*, Swansea: The Classical Press of Wales, 2011, pp. 287–307 is indispensable for the study of the Tiberian historian as a source for late republican history.
39. Like most of the figures in our story, Mithridates has inspired an impressive range of studies; note especially Adrienne Mayor's *The Poison King: The Life and Legend of Mithridates, Rome's Deadliest Enemy*, Princeton, 2010, and Philip Matyszak, *Mithridates: Rome's Indomitable Enemy*, Barnsley: Pen & Sword, 2008, also Jakob Munk Højte's edited volume, *Mithridates VI and the Pontic Kingdom*, Aarhus, 2009.
40. Cf. Plutarch, *Sulla* 7, Appian, *Mith.* 22, Velleius 2.18, Eutropius 5.4.

41. See here Seager 2002, pp. 25 ff. for a good treatment of the problems that Pompey faced during the *Cinnanum tempus*.
42. Note here A.W. Lintott, 'The Tribunate of P. Sulpicius Rufus,' in *The Classical Quarterly*, Vol. 21, No. 2 (Nov., 1971), pp. 442–453, and J.G.F. Powell, 'The Tribune Sulpicius,' in *Historia: Zeitschrift für Alte Geschichte*, Bd. 39, H. 4 (1990), pp. 446–460.
43. See further here T.J. Luce, 'Marius and the Mithridatic Command,' in *Historia: Zeitschrift für Alte Geschichte*, Bd. 19, H. 2 (Apr., 1970), pp. 161–194.
44. Cf. Plutarch, *Sulla* 9, *Marius* 35, Appian, *BC* 1.57, Valerius Maximus 9.7, Florus 2.9.
45. B.M. Levick, 'Sulla's March on Rome in 88 BC,' in *Historia: Zeitschrift für Alte Geschichte*, Bd. 31, H. 4 (4th Qtr., 1982), pp. 503–508 considers the infamous deed in light of Sulla's attitude toward the senate.
46. 'The fine flower of the Sullan Restoration' (J. Macdonald Cobban, *Senate & Provinces 78–49 BC ...*, Cambridge, 1935, p. 99).
47. On Lucullus note especially A. Keaveney, *Lucullus: A Life*, London-New York: 1992, and L. Fratantuono, *Lucullus: The Life and Times of a Roman Conqueror*, Barnsley: Pen & Sword, 2017.
48. On the 'wrenching year' see B.R. Katz, 'Studies on the Period of Cinna and Sulla,' in *L'Antiquité classique*, T. 45, Fasc. 2 (1976), pp. 497–549.
49. For an excellent survey of his career in the context of Rome's domestic troubles, see M. Lovano, *The Age of Cinna: Crucible of Late Republican Rome* (Hermes Einzelschriften 158), Stuttgart: Franz Steiner Verlag, 2002.
50. Note here B.R. Katz, 'The Selection of L. Cornelius Merula,' in *Rheinisches Museum für Philologie*, Neue Folge, 122. Bd., H. 2 (1979), pp. 162–166.
51. Cf. Plutarch, *Sertorius* 4, *Marius* 41, Appian, *BC* 1.64–65, Velleius 2.20, Florus 2.9.

Chapter Two
1. *Pomp.* 3; cf. Cicero, *De lege Man.* 28.
2. Cf. Plutarch, *Pomp.* 4, Cicero, *Brutus* 230, and see H. van der Blom, 'Pompey in the *Contio*,' in *The Classical Quarterly*, New Series, Vol. 61, No. 2 (December 2011), pp. 553–573.
3. Note here T.P. Hillman, 'Notes on the Trial of Pompeius at Plutarch, *Pomp.* 4.1–6,' in *Rheinisches Museum für Philologie*, Neue Folge, 141. Bd., H. 2 (1998), pp. 176–193.
4. *Pomp.* 4.
5. See further here G.B. Miles, *Livy: Reconstructing Early Rome*, Ithaca, New York-London: Cornell University Press, 1995, pp. 188 ff.
6. *Pomp.* 5.
7. Cf. Appian, *BC* 1.74, Valerius Maximus 9.12, Florus 2.9.
8. Plutarch, *Pomp.* 5–6, *Mor.* 203B-C; cf. Cicero, *De lege Man.* 61, *Phil.* 5.43–4, Velleius 2.29, Appian, *BC* 1.80. Invaluable here is the 1992 Berkeley doctoral dissertation of Marianne Schoelin Nichols, *Appearance and Reality: A Study of the Clientele of Pompey the Great*.
9. See further here C.M. Bulst, "Cinnanum Tempus': A Reassessment of the 'Dominatio Cinnae,' in *Historia: Zeitschrift für Alte Geschichte*, Bd. 13, H. 3 (Jul., 1964), pp. 307–337, and C.H. Chimeno, 'Apiano, el *Cinnanum Tempus* y el nuevo régimen,' in *Aevum*, Anno 93, Fasc. 1 (Gennaio-Aprile 2019), pp. 155–174.
10. Cf. Plutarch, *Lucullus* 7, 34, *Sulla* 23, Appian, *Mith.* 52, Livy, *Per.* 82, Velleius 2.23–24.
11. Cf. Plutarch, *Lucullus* 4, *Sulla* 23–24, 43, Appian, *Mith.* 56–58, Velleius 2.23, Florus 1.40.
12. Cf. Plutarch, *Sulla* 25, Appian, *Mith.* 59–60, Velleius 2.24, Orosius 6.2.
13. Cf. Appian, *BC* 1.76–77.
14. *Pomp.* 5; cf. *Sertorius* 6, Appian, *BC* 1.78, Dio 45.47, 52.13, Livy, *Per.* 83.
15. See further here Seager 2002, pp. 26 ff.
16. *Pomp.* 8.
17. See here M.E. Deutsch, 'Caesar's First Wife,' in *Classical Philology*, Vol. 12, No. 1 (Jan., 1917), pp. 93–96.
18. Cf. Appian, *BC* 1.76–77, Livy, *Per.* 83.
19. *Pomp.* 6.

Chapter Three

1. Cf. Cicero, *De lege Man.* 61, *Phil.* 5.43–44, Ps.-Caesar, *Bellum Alexandrinum* 22, Diodorus 38.9, Appian, *BC* 1.80, Livy, *Per.* 85, Velleius 2.29.
2. *Pomp.* 6.
3. Cf. Plutarch, *Sulla* 27, Appian, *BC* 1.79, Livy, *Per.* 85, Velleius 2.24.
4. *Pomp.* 7.
5. Cf. Diodorus Siculus 38.9–10.
6. *Pomp.* 8.
7. Cf. Plutarch, *Pomp.* 8, *Crassus* 6 (where these early honours accorded to Pompey are cited in the context of exploring his older colleague's resentment and jealousy toward him), *Mor.* 806E, Valerius Maximus 5.2.9.
8. *Pomp.* 8.
9. For the definition of these controversial, problematic terms see M.A. Robb, *Beyond Populares and Optimates: Political Language in the Late Republic*, Stuttgart: Franz Steiner Verlag, 2010, Leach 1978, pp. 238–9 n. 3 (a good *précis*); note also G. Achard, 'Langage et société: A propos des optimates et des populares,' in *Latomus*, T. 41, Fasc. 4 (octobre-décembre 1982), pp. 794–800, N. Mackie, '*Popularis* Ideology and Popular Politics in the First Century BC,' in *Rheinisches Museum für Philologie*, Neue Folge, 135. Bd., H. 1 (1992), pp. 49–73, C. Tracy, 'The People's Consul: The Significance of Cicero's Use of the Term 'Popularis,'' in *Illinois Classical Studies*, No. 33–34 (2008–2009), pp. 181–199, R. Seager, '*Populares* in Livy and the Livian Tradition,' in *The Classical Quarterly*, Vol. 27, No. 2 (1977), pp. 377–390, and A. Yakobsen, 'Traditional Political Culture and the People's Role in the Roman Republic,' in *Historia: Zeitschrift für Alte Geschichte*, Bd. 59, H. 3 (2010), pp. 282–302.
10. *BC* 1.84.
11. For a good overview of the career and campaigns of the man, see P. Matyszak, *Sertorius and the Struggle for Spain*, Barnsley: Pen & Sword Military, 2013. Konrad's 1994 North Carolina historical commentary on Plutarch's life is invaluable for investigating the many difficulties (especially chronological) of the Sertorian War.
12. J. Strisino, 'Sulla and Scipio 'not to be trusted'? The Reasons why Sertorius captured Suessa Aurunca,' in *Latomus*, T. 61, Fasc. 1 (janvier-mars 2002), pp. 33–40 is helpful here.
13. Cf. Plutarch, *Pomp.* 7, Appian, *BC* 1.87, Orosius 5.20.
14. *BC* 1.87.
15. *BC* 1.84.
16. Cf. Plutarch, *Sulla* 28, Diodorus 38.15, Appian, *BC* 1.87, Livy, *Per.* 87, Velleius 2.26, Florus 2.9.
17. *BC* 1.87.
18. *BC* 1.88.
19. Cf. Appian, *BC* 1.89, Livy, *Per.* 88, Velleius 2.28, Pliny, *NH* 8.221.
20. *BC* 1.89.
21. *BC* 1.90.
22. Cf. Appian, *BC* 1.90, Livy, *Per.* 87.
23. *BC* 1.91.
24. *BC* 1.92.
25. Cf. Plutarch, *Sulla* 28, Appian, *BC* 1.92, Livy, *Per.* 88.
26. A. Thein, 'Booty in the Sullan Civil War of 83–82 BC,' in *Historia: Zeitschrift für Alte Geschichte*, Bd. 65, H. 4 (2016), pp. 450–472, explores the impact of Sullan plundering of Italian towns, with thorough examination of the extant evidence.
27. *BC* 1.92.
28. *BC* 1.93.
29. Cf. Plutarch, *Sulla* 33, Appian, *BC* 1.98–99, Velleius 2.28. For the emergency expedient of dictatorial powers and other extraordinary offices of republican government, see Golden 2013.
30. On an interesting topic, see M. Barden Dowling, 'The Clemency of Sulla,' in *Historia: Zeitschrift für Alte Geschichte*, Bd. 49, H. 3 (3rd Qtr., 2000), pp. 303–340, and E. Thein, 'Reflecting on Sulla's Clemency,' in *Historia: Zeitschrift für Alte Geschichte*, Bd. 63, H. 2 (2014), pp. 166–186.

31. Cf. Plutarch, *Sulla* 33, 40, Appian, *BC* 1.100–101, Dio 37.10, Livy, *Per.* 89.
32. *BC* 1.101.
33. Cf. *Pomp.* 9, *Sulla* 33.
34. See further here S.P. Haley, 'The Five Wives of Pompey the Great,' in *Greece & Rome*, Vol. 32, No. 1 (Apr., 1985), pp. 49–59.
35. *Pomp.* 9.
36. On this episode from Caesar's early life note R.T. Ridley, 'The Dictator's Mistake: Caesar's Escape from Sulla,' in *Historia: Zeitschrift für Alte Geschichte*, Bd. 49, H. 2 (2nd Qtr., 2000), pp. 211–229.
37. *BC* 1.96.
38. *Per.* 89.
39. *Pomp.* 10.
40. Cf. the censure of Pompey's action by Valerius Maximus 5.3 (with 6.2, 9.13). Pompey's oversight of the deaths of Sullan opponents is also mentioned at Eutropius 5.8 and Orosius 5.21.
41. For Pompey's establishment of order in Sicily cf. Plutarch, *Pomp.* 10, Diodorus 38.20, Cicero, *De lege Man.* 30, 61, Pliny, *NH* 7.96.
42. Cf. Appian, *Mith.* 65, Livy, *Per.* 86.

Chapter Four
1. Cf. Plutarch, *Sulla* 28, Appian, *BC* 1.92, Livy, *Per.* 88.
2. *Pomp.* 11.
3. Tacitus, *Ann.* 16.1–3.
4. *Pomp.* 12.
5. Cf. Plutarch, *Pomp.* 12.
6. *Pomp.* 12.
7. *Pomp.* 13.
8. See further here T.P. Hillman, 'Pompeius in Africa and Sulla's Order to demobilize (Plutarch, *Pompeius* 13,1–4),' in *Latomus*, T. 56, Fasc. 1 (janvier-mars 1997), pp. 94–106.
9. For the appellation cf. *Pomp.* 13, 23, *Sertorius* 18, *Crassus* 7, 12, Livy 30.45.
10. Cf. Plutarch, *Pomp.* 14.
11. The story is considered in detail by G. Mader, 'Triumphal Elephants and Political Circus at Pompey, *Pomp.* 14.6,' in *The Classical World*, Vol. 99, No. 4 (Summer, 2006), pp. 397–403. It is known to Granius Licinianus.
12. For the fantastic wealth on display at Pompey's celebration, cf. Pliny, *NH* 37.13.
13. Note here E. Badian, 'The Date of Pompey's First Triumph,' in *Hermes*, 83. Bd., H. 1 (1955), pp. 107–118, and the same author's 'Servilius and Pompey's First Triumph,' in *Hermes*, 89. Bd., H. 2 (1961), pp. 254–256.
14. For her death in childbirth (with her former husband's child) after only a few months of marriage, see Plutarch, *Sulla* 33.
15. Cf. *Pomp.* 42.
16. Cf. Plutarch, *Sertorius* 7.
17. See further here J. McAlhany, 'Sertorius Between Myth and History: The Isles of the Blessed Episode in Sallust, Plutarch & Horace,' in *The Classical Journal*, Vol. 112, No. 1 (October-November 2016), pp. 57–76.
18. Cf. Plutarch, *Sertorius* 10–11, Appian, *Hisp.* 101, *BC* 1.108, Livy, *Per* 90, 96, Eutropius 6.1, Orosius 5.23.
19. On their amicable tenures cf. Plutarch, *Sulla* 6, *Mor.* 202E, Appian, *BC* 1.103.
20. Cf. Plutarch, *Sulla* 34, Appian, *BC* 1.3, 103–105, 2.138
21. *Pomp.* 15.
22. Helpful here is C. Steel, 'The Roman Senate and the Post-Sullan *Res Publica*,' in *Historia: Zeitschrift für Alte Geschichte*, Bd. 63, H. 3 (2014), pp. 323–339.
23. A. Rosenblitt, 'The Turning Tide: The Politics of the Year 79 B.C.E.,' in *Transactions of the American Philological Association (1974–2014)*, Vol. 144, No. 2 (Autumn 2014), pp. 415–444

considers the significance of this year with respect to the continuing pervasive fear of Sulla, and the rise of Lepidus.
24. Cf. Plutarch, *Pomp.* 15, *Sulla* 34.

Chapter Five
1. See further here Greenhalgh 1980, pp. 30–9.
2. The political and social concerns of the post-Sullan period have been the subject of extensive study and debate; for an overview of the problems, see especially F. Santangelo, 'Roman Politics in the 70s B.C.: a Story of Realignments?,' in *The Journal of Roman Studies*, Vol. 104 (2014), pp. 1–27.
3. Cf. Plutarch, *Lucullus* 1, 4, *Sulla* 6, 37, *Pomp.* 15, *Mor.* 805E-F. The surviving fragments of the memoirs may be found in the magisterial edition of T.J. Cornell, *The Fragments of the Roman Historians*, Oxford, 2013 (three volumes), with detailed commentary.
4. Granius Licinianus records the event; cf. Sallust, *Hist.* 1.57–58, Florus 2.11.
5. See further here Rosenblit 2019, pp. 45 ff. P. Burton, 'The Revolt of Lepidus (*cos.* 78 BC) Revisited,' in *Historia: Zeitschrift für Alte Geschichte*, Bd. 63, H. 4 (2014), pp. 404–421, seeks to offer a wide-ranging reappraisal and rehabilitation of its subject, arguing that in fact Lepidus was a rigorous defender of Sullan legislation, convinced that therein lay the best chance for a lasting peace in Italy. Burton's work follows on (*inter al.*) L. Hayne, 'M. Lepidus (*cos.* 78): A Re-appraisal,' in *Historia: Zeitschrift für Alte Geschichte*, Bd. 21, H. 4 (4th Qtr., 1972), pp. 661–668.
6. Cf. Appian, *BC* 1.107, Sallust, *Hist.* 1.67.
7. Cf. Suetonius, *Divus Iulius* 3.
8. See further here T.P. Hillman, 'Pompeius and the Senate: 77–71,' in *Hermes*, 118. Bd., H. 4 (1990), pp. 444–45.
9. Cf. Plutarch, *Pomp.* 16, Appian, *BC* 2.111, Livy, *Per.* 90, Valerius Maximus 6.2, Orosius 5.22.
10. Cf. Plutarch, *Pomp.* 16, Appian, *BC* 1.107, Livy, *Per.* 90, Florus 2.11.
11. *Pomp.* 16.
12. Cf. Plutarch, *Brutus* 4 (in the context of why the son might be expected to support Caesar and not the man responsible for the death of his father), Appian, *BC* 2.111, Orosius 5.22.
13. *Pomp.* 16.
14. Frontinus, *Strategemata* 1.9 alludes to Pompey having to deal with a massacre of senators of Mediolanum by his troops; this atrocity may date this period, but we cannot be certain.
15. Cf. Plutarch, *Pomp.* 13, 17, Appian, *Hisp.* 101, *BC* 1.80, 108, Cicero, *Pro lege Man.* 62, *Phil.* 11.18, Livy, *Per.* 91, Valerius Maximus 8.15, Eutropius 6.12, Orosius 5.23.
16. Cf. Plutarch, *Sertorius* 15, Appian, *BC* 1.107, Orosius 5.24.
17. Cf. Appian, *BC* 1.109.
18. The story is one of the most popular and oft-studied of the episodes from the younger Caesar's life; see further J. Osgood, 'Caesar and the Pirates: Or How to Make (and Break) an Ancient Life,' in *Greece & Rome*, Second Series, Vol. 57, No. 2 (October 2010), pp. 319–336.
19. The classic article of L.R. Taylor, 'Caesar's Early Career,' in *Classical Philology*, Vol. 36, No. 2 (Apr., 1941), pp. 113–132, provides an excellent overview.

Chapter Six
1. Cf. Cicero, *De lege Man.* 28, Caesar, *BC* 1.35.
2. Greenhalgh 1980, pp. 40–57 is invaluable for its coverage of Pompey in Spain.
3. *Pomp.* 18.
4. *Pomp.* 18.
5. Plutarch, *Pomp.* 18, *Sertorius* 18, Appian, *BC* 1.109, Florus 2.10, Orosius 5.23. The campaign is ably surveyed in Greenhalgh 1980, pp. 46–8.
6. Cf. Plutarch, *Sertorius* 18.
7. Cf. Frontinus, *Strategemata* 2.5, Appian, *BC* 1.109.
8. *Pomp.* 18.

9. Cf. Sallust, *Hist.* 2.82.
10. The battle is featured at Plutarch, *Pomp.* 18, Orosius 5.23, and is alluded to by Cicero at *Pro Balbo* 5.
11. Cf. Frontinus, *Strategemata* 2.3.
12. Plutarch, *Pomp.* 19, *Sertorius* 19, Appian, *BC* 1.110, Orosius 5.23. Livy, *Per.* 92 also alludes to this inconclusive battle.
13. Plutarch, *Pomp.* 19.
14. *Sertorius* 19.
15. *Sertorius* 21.
16. *BC* 1.110.
17. C.F. Konrad, 'Segovia and Segontia,' in *Historia: Zeitschrift für Alte Geschichte*, Bd. 43, H. 4 (4th Qtr., 1994), pp. 440–453, is useful for disentangling the major interpretive problems.
18. *Pomp.* 19.
19. Cf. Plutarch, *Sertorius* 11.
20. Frontinus, *Strategemata* 2.7.
21. Cf. Plutarch, *Pompey* 19, *Sertorius* 21, Livy, *Per.* 92.
22. Cf. Plutarch, *Sertorius* 22.
23. Cf. Plutarch, *Sertorius* 22.
24. *Sertorius* 22.
25. Cf. Plutarch, *Sertorius* 21.
26. Cf. Plutarch, *Pomp.* 20, *Lucullus* 5, Appian, *BC* 1.111.
27. Cf. Plutarch, *Caesar* 2, Suetonius, *Divus Iulius* 4, Velleius 2.41, Valerius Maximus 6.9.
28. Cf. Appian, *Mith.* 7, 71, *BC* 1.111, Velleius 2.4, 39.2, Festus, *Breviarium* 11, Eutropius 6.6.
29. On their negotiations regarding coordination of attacks on Roman interests, cf. Plutarch, *Sertorius* 23, Appian, *Mith.* 68, 72, 76, Cicero, *De lege Man.* 9, 46, *Pro Murena* 32, Livy, *Per.* 93, Orosius 6.2.
30. Appian, *BC* 1.112.
31. Appian, *BC* 1.112; cf. Livy, *Periochae* 93.
32. *Sertorius* 22.
33. Plutarch, *Pomp.* 20, *Sertorius* 26, Livy, *Per.* 96, Eutropius 6.1, Orosius 5.23.
34. Cf. Plutarch, *Pomp.* 20, *Sertorius* 27, Appian, *BC* 1.115, Orosius 5.23. Ammianus Marcellinus 26.9 alludes to Perperna's pitiful end.
35. Cf. Cicero, *Verr.* 2.5.
36. Cf. Plutarch, *Pomp.* 21, Strabo 3.160, Pliny, *NH* 3.18, 7.96.

Chapter Seven
1. B.D. Shaw, *Spartacus and the Slave Wars: A Brief History with Documents*, Boston-New York: Palgrave Macmillan, 2018 (second edition of the 2001 original) is the best and most reliable overall starting place for further investigation; note also B. Baldwin, 'Two Aspects of the Spartacus Slave Revolt,' in *The Classical Journal*, Vol. 62, No. 7 (Apr., 1967), pp. 289–294.
2. Cf. Plutarch, *Crassus* 9, Appian, *BC* 1.116, Livy, *Per.* 95, Florus 2.8, Orosius 5.24.
3. Cf. here P. Piccinin, 'Les Italiens dans le *Bellum Spartacium*,' in *Historia: Zeitschrift für Alte Geschichte*, Bd. 53, H. 2 (2004), pp. 173–199.
4. B.A. Marshall, 'Crassus' Ovation in 71 B.C.,' in *Historia: Zeitschrift für Alte Geschichte*, Bd. 21, H. 4 (4th Qtr., 1972), pp. 669–673, considers the controversies and problems related to Pompey's involvement in suppressing the Spartacus revolt, with particular focus on the genesis of any enmity between Crassus and his younger colleague.
5. Cf. Plutarch, *Crassus* 10, 36, Appian, *BC* 1.118, Livy, *Per.* 96, Florus, 2.8, Orosius 5.24.
6. For the persistent economic troubles of the period see C.T. Barlow, 'The Roman Government and the Roman Economy, 92–80 BC,' in *The American Journal of Philology*, Vol. 101, No. 2 (Summer, 1980), pp. 202–219, and cf. A. Collins and J. Walsh, 'Debt Deflationary Crisis in the Late Roman Republic,' in *Ancient Society*, Vol. 45 (2015), pp. 125–170.
7. Cf. Plutarch, *Crassus* 11, Livy, *Per.* 97, Orosius 5.24.

8. Cf. Plutarch, *Pomp.* 21, *Crassus* 11, 36, Appian, *BC* 1.120, Eutropius 6.7, Orosius 5.24.
9. Cf. Plutarch, *Pomp.* 21, 31, *Crassus* 11, Appian, *BC* 1.119.
10. Cf. Plutarch, *Pomp.* 22, 45, *Crassus* 11, Cicero, *De lege Man.* 62, Velleius 2.30, Pliny, *HN* 7.96, Eutropius 6.5.
11. Not surprisingly, the election of the two is well documented; note Plutarch, *Pomp.* 21–22, 44, *Crassus* 12, Appian, *BC* 1.121, 3.88, Dio 77.5, Cicero, *Verr.* 1.45, *De lege Man.* 62. Livy, *Per.* 97, Valerius Maximus 8.15.
12. R.J. Evans, 'Pompey's Three Consulships: The End of Electoral Competition in the Late Roman Republic?,' in *Acta Classica*, Vol. 59 (2016), pp. 80–100 studies the problems related to just how Pompey succeeded politically given the ambitions of his peers.

Chapter Eight
1. Cf. Appian, *BC* 1.121 and Plutarch, *Crassus* 12.
2. *Pomp.* 22.
3. See here especially David Stockton, 'The First Consulship of Pompey,' in *Historia: Zeitschrift für Alte Geschichte*, Bd. 22, H. 2 (2nd Qtr., 1973), pp. 205–218.
4. *Pomp.* 22.
5. Cf. Plutarch, *Pomp.* 24, Cicero, *Pro lege Man.* 33.
6. For an interesting that Rome's involvement in Cilicia in Asia Minor commenced from the suspicion that there was eastern instigation for servile uprisings, see A.L. Beek, 'The Pirate Connection: Roman Politics, Servile Wars, and the East,' in *TAPA*, Vol. 146, No. 1 (Spring 2016), pp. 99–116.
7. Cf. Plutarch, *Caesar* 5, Suetonius, *Divus Iulius* 6.
8. *Pomp.* 23.
9. Cf. Plutarch, *Caesar* 5, 11, *Mor.* 206B, Suetonius, *Divus Iulius* 7, Dio 37.52, 41.24.
10. *Pomp.* 24.
11. On the controversial political machinations attendant on the decline of Lucullus and the rise of Pompey, see R.S. Williams, 'The Appointment of Glabrio (*cos.* 67) to the Eastern Command,' in *Phoenix*, Vol. 38, No. 3 (Autumn, 1984), pp. 221–234; cf. L. Hayne, 'The Politics of M'. Glabrio, Cos. 67,' in *Classical Philology*, Vol. 69, No. 4 (Oct., 1974), pp. 280–282
12. Invaluable here is E.W. Sanford, 'The Career of Aulus Gabinius,' in *Transactions and Proceedings of the American Philological Association*, Vol. 70 (1939), pp. 64–92; cf. R.S. Williams, 'The Role of *Amicitia* in the Career of A. Gabinius (Cos. 58),' in *Phoenix*, Vol. 32, No. 3 (Autumn, 1978), pp. 195–210, which considers Gabinius' career advancement in light of his bond of friendship with Pompey.
13. Cf. Plutarch, *Pomp.* 25–26, Cicero, *De lege Man.* 44, 52–53, 56, 59, 67, Livy, *Per.* 99, Velleius 2.31–32, Valerius Maximus 8.15, Florus 1.41, Appian, *Mith.* 94, Dio 36.23–37.2
14. *Pomp.* 25.
15. Cf. Plutarch, *Pomp.* 26, Appian, *BC* 2.1.
16. Cf. Appian, *Mith.* 94.
17. *Mith.* 95.
18. For an appraisal of the political considerations of the extraordinary commission in the context of Rome's imperial expansion and maintenance thereof, note M. Tröster, 'Roman Hegemony and Non-State Violence: A Fresh Look at Pompey's Campaign against the Pirates,' in *Greece & Rome*, Second Series, Vol. 56, No. 1 (Apr., 2009), pp. 14–33.
19. *Pomp.* 26.
20. Note here Greenhalgh 1980, p. 91.
21. *Pomp.* 27; cf. Dio 36.37.
22. On the visit and the report of divine honours offered to him, see Michael Hoff, 'Athens honours Pompey the Great,' in L. de Blois, J. Bons, and T. Kessels, eds., *The Statesman in Plutarch's Works, Volume II*, Leiden: Brill, 2005, pp. 327–36.
23. Plutarch, *Pomp.* 27, Strabo 11.492.
24. *Mith.* 96.

25. *Pomp.* 28.
26. 2.32.
27. 1.41.
28. *NH* 7.93.
29. 1.41.
30. *Pomp.* 29.
31. 2.34, 40.
32. 1.42.
33. *Sic.* 6.6.
34. 36.17–19.
35. 36.18.
36. See further here E. Rawson, 'L. Cornelius Sisenna and the Early First Century B.C.,' in *The Classical Quarterly*, Vol. 29, No. 2 (1979), pp. 327–346, also E. Candiloro, 'Sulle *Historiae* di L. Cornelio Sisenna,' in *Studi Classici e Orientali*, Vol. 12 (1963), pp. 212–226, and C.B. Krebs, 'Caesar's Sisenna,' in *The Classical Quarterly*, Vol. 64, No. 1 (MAY 2014), pp. 207–213 (on the possible intertextual relationship between the authors).
37. Cf. Plutarch, *Caesar* 5, Suetonius, *Divus Iulius* 6.
38. See Morrell 2017, pp. 57 ff. for how Pompey's eastern campaigns continued the emphasis in his consular year on sound provincial administration.

Chapter Nine
1. See further here C. Goldsberg, 'Decimation in the Roman Republic,' in *The Classical Journal*, Vol. 111, No. 2 (December 2015–January 2016), pp. 141–164.
2. E.S. Gruen, 'P. Clodius: Instrument or Independent Agent?,' in *Phoenix*, Vol. 20, No. 2 (Summer, 1966), pp. 120–130 treats his reader to an important study of one of the key questions posed by Clodius' checkered career; W. J. Tatum, *The Patrician Tribune: Publius Clodius Pulcher*, Chapel Hill-London: The University of North Carolina Press, 1999, may be recommended without reserve.
3. Cf. Plutarch, *Lucullus* 38, Cicero, *Pro Milone* 73.
4. On 'Rome in the Absence of Pompeius' see Seager 2002, pp. 63 ff., with thorough consideration of the political scene in this pivotal political period.
5. For the eastern campaigns note Greenhalgh 1980, pp. 164–79.
6. On the question of the exact origins of the apparent mutual dislike between the men, note T.P. Hillman, 'The Alleged *Inimicitiae* of Pompeius and Lucullus: 78–74,' in *Classical Philology*, Vol. 86, No. 4 (Oct., 1991), pp. 315–318.
7. 2.33.
8. Plutarch, *Pomp.* 2.
9. 2.33.
10. Cf. Livy, *Per.* 100.
11. *Pomp.* 30.
12. *Pomp.* 31.
13. Cf. Plutarch, *Pomp.* 31–32, Dio 36.46, 37.49.
14. *Pomp.* 31.
15. 36.46.
16. Cf. Plutarch, *Lucullus* 37, *Pomp.* 46, Athenaeus 2.50–51, Pliny, *NH* 14.96, 15.102, 34.36, Ammianus Marcellinus 22.8.
17. *Pomp.* 32.
18. E.L. Wheeler, 'Roman Fleets in the Black Sea: Mysteries of the *Classis Pontica*,' in *Acta Classica*, Vol. 55 (2012), pp. 119–154 gives a thorough account of the history of Roman navies on the Euxine from 64 BC through the third century.
19. *Pomp.* 32.
20. For a detailed examination of the diplomatic history and background, see A. Keaveney, 'Roman Treaties with Parthia circa 95–circa 64 B.C.,' in *The American Journal of Philology*, Vol. 102, No. 2 (Summer, 1981), pp. 195–212.

21. 36.45.
22. 36.51.
23. One of the seven cities he founded in the east, which included a Pompeiopolis in Paphlagonia. See further here Greenhalgh 1980, pp. 152–3.
24. *Pomp.* 32.
25. *Pomp.* 32.
26. Cf. *Pomp.* 32. S. Asirvatham, 'Plutarch, Ἀνδρεία, and Rome,' in *Illinois Classical Studies*, Vol. 44, No. 1 (Spring 2019), pp. 156–176 considers the biographer's presentation of the bold concubine.
27. *Mith.* 99–101.
28. 36.49.
29. *Mith.* 98.
30. *Breviarium* 16.
31. *Pomp.* 32.
32. *Pomp.* 33.
33. *Pomp.* 33.
34. *Mith.* 105.
35. *Mith.* 105.
36. 36.45.
37. 36.48–49.
38. 36.50.
39. 36.51.
40. Cf. 37.5.
41. *Pomp.* 36.
42. 37.5–6.
43. On this famous appellation see J.G. Griffiths, 'βασιλεὺς βασιλέων: Remarks on the History of a Title,' in *Classical Philology*, Vol. 48, No. 3 (Jul., 1953), pp. 145–154.
44. 37.6.
45. 37.6.
46. *Pomp.* 36.
47. Helpful here is M. Dreher, 'Pompeius und die kaukasischen Völker: Kolcher, Iberer, Albaner,' in *Historia: Zeitschrift für Alte Geschichte*, Bd. 45, H. 2 (2nd Qtr., 1996), pp. 188–207.
48. *Pomp.* 34.
49. 36.54.
50. 6.4.
51. 36.54.
52. *Pomp.* 34.
53. *Pomp.* 34.
54. 37.1–2.
55. Cf. *Mith.* 101–103.
56. *Pomp.* 35.
57. *Pomp.* 35.
58. *Mith.* 103.

Chapter Ten
1. *Divus Iulius* 9.
2. Cf. Sallust, *Bellum Catilinae* 18, Dio 36.44.
3. On the scholarly debate cf., e.g., F.L. Jones, 'The First Conspiracy of Catiline,' in *The Classical Journal*, Vol. 34, No. 7 (Apr., 1939), pp. 410–422, R. Seager, 'The First Catilinarian Conspiracy,' in *Historia: Zeitschrift für Alte Geschichte*, Bd. 13, H. 3 (Jul., 1964), pp. 338–347, and E.S. Gruen, 'Notes on the 'First Catilinarian Conspiracy,' in *Classical Philology*, Vol. 64, No. 1 (Jan., 1969), pp. 20–24.
4. *Pomp.* 36.
5. *Pomp.* 36–7, Appian, *Mith.* 107, Dio 37.7.

6. *Pomp.* 37.
7. Cf. Appian, *Mith.* 102.
8. 36.33.
9. 12.549.
10. *Pomp.* 38.
11. 37.11.
12. See further here J.M. Madsden, *From Trophy Towns to City-States: Urban Civilization and Cultural Identities in Roman Pontus*, Philadelphia: University of Pennsylvania Press, 2020.
13. T.N. Mitchell, 'Cicero, Pompey, and the Rise of the First Triumvirate,' in *Traditio* Vol. 29 (1973), pp. 1–26 discusses the political machinations and undercurrents behind the arrangement.
14. Cf. Appian, *Mith.* 107.
15. *Mith.* 107.
16. *Mith.* 109.
17. Cf. Plutarch, *Pomp.* 41, Appian, *Mith.* 109, Florus 1.40.
18. 37.12.
19. *Mith.* 106; cf. Dio 40.20.
20. Cf. Appian, *Mith.* 105.
21. Cf. Strabo 16.751, Festus, *Breviarium* 16.4, Eutropius 6.14.
22. On the background of these issues see G. Downey, 'The Occupation of Syria by the Romans', in *Transactions and Proceedings of the American Philological Association*, Vol. 82 (1951), pp. 149–163.
23. Cf. Appian, *Syr.* 70.
24. It is doubtful, but just possible, that he = the Philip considered as a potential husband of Berenice IV in 56 BC.
25. Cf. Josephus, *Antiquitates Iudaicae* 14.38–40, Festus, *Breviarium* 14.2, 16.3, Eutropius 6.14, Orosius 6.6.
26. See further here Smallwood 2001.
27. Cf. Plutarch, *Pomp.* 41, Appian, *Mith.* 106, Dio 37.14–15, Florus 1.40, Orosius 6.6.
28. *Bellum Iudaicum* 1.128.
29. *Bellum Iudaicum* 1.131–133.
30. For Mithridates' end, cf. Appian, *Mith.* 110–112, Dio 37.12–14, Florus 1.40, Festus, *Breviarium* 16, Eutropius 6.12, Orosius 6.5.
31. Cf. Pliny, *NH* 25.5–7, 62–63, 65, 127, 29.24.
32. *Pomp.* 39.
33. *Pomp.* 41. On Pompey's reaction to the news see Mayor 2010, pp. 352 ff.
34. Cf. Plutarch, *Pomp.* 39, Josephus, *Bellum Iudaicum* 1.139–40, *Antiquitates Iudaicae* 14.54–57, Dio 37.15.
35. Appian, *Syr.* 50 gives a laconic account of the grim history of the city's various calamities.
36. On the historiographical problems and the challenges of analyzing Josephus' attitude toward the Roman actions under Pompey, note J. Bellemore, 'Josephus, Pompey, and the Jews,' in *Historia: Zeitschrift für Alte Geschichte*, Bd. 48, H. 1 (1st Qtr., 1999), pp. 94–118
37. *Bellum Iudaicum* 1.152–153.
38. *Bellum Iudaicum* 1.145–148, *Antiquitates Iudaicae* 14.64.
39. *Bellum Iudaicum* 1.153.
40. *Bellum Iudaicum* 1.153 emphasizes Pompey's hopes to conciliate the people by allowing Hyrcanus some title.
41. *Antiquitates Iudaicae* 14.73.
42. *Pomp.* 39.

Chapter Eleven
1. See further here B. Levick, *Ancients in Action: Catiline*, London-New York: Bloomsbury Academic, 2015, and Carney 2023.
2. L. Hayne, 'The Political Astuteness of the Antonii,' in *L'Antiquité classique*, T. 47, Fasc. 1 (1978), pp. 96–105, considers the diverse fortunes of members of the extended family.

3. On Cato note especially F. Drogula, *Cato the Younger: Life and Death at the End of the Roman Republic*, Oxford, 2019; for his depiction in Caesar's narratives see D.C. Yates, 'The Role of Cato the Younger in Caesar's *Bellum Civile*, in *The Classical World*, Vol. 104, No. 2 (Winter 2011), pp. 161–174.
4. Cf. Plutarch, *Cicero* 12, Appian, *BC* 2.3, Florus 2.12.
5. See here K.R. Bradley, 'Slaves and the Conspiracy of Catiline,' in *Classical Philology*, Vol. 73, No. 4 (Oct., 1978), pp. 329–336.
6. On the speeches, note A.R. Dyck, *Cicero: Catilinarians*, Cambridge, 2008, with text, detailed commentary, and scholarly introduction.
7. Cf. Sallust, *Bellum Catilinae* 57–61, Livy, *Per.* 103, Appian, *BC* 2.7, Dio 37.39–40.
8. *Pomp.* 42. On Pompey's theatre note Leach 1978, p. 134, and Greenhalgh 1981, pp. 54–7.
9. V.L. Holliday, *Pompey in Cicero's Correspondence and Lucan's Civil War*, The Hague-Paris: Mouton, 1969, is essential for close study of the depiction of Pompey in both sources.
10. M. Siani-Davies, 'Ptolemy XII Auletes and the Romans,' in *Historia: Zeitschrift für Alte Geschichte*, Bd. 46, H. 3 (3rd Qtr., 1997), pp. 306–340 explores the question of this monarch's reputation in primary and secondary sources. For the controversies surrounding the numbering of the Ptolemies, see Greenhalgh 1980, pp. 141 ff.
11. *Pomp.* 42.
12. *Divus Iulius* 50.
13. R.T. Ridley, 'Antiochos XIII, Pompeius Magnus and the Unessayed Coup,' in *Ancient Society*, Vol. 36 (2006), pp. 81–95, offers a simple explanation for why the fears of a Pompeian seizure of power were unwarranted: Pompey had no need to make such an attempt.
14. On the difficult question of Crassus' political strategy in this period, see E.J. Parrish, 'Crassus' New Friends and Pompey's Return,' in *Phoenix*, Vol. 27, No. 4 (Winter, 1973), pp. 357–380.
15. *Pomp.* 43.
16. Cf. Plutarch, *Cato* 26–28, *Cicero* 23, Dio 37.43.
17. *Cato* 30.
18. *Pomp.* 46.
19. *Pomp.* 44.
20. See here M.E. Deutsch, 'Pompey's Three Triumphs,' in *Classical Philology*, Vol. 19, No. 3 (Jul., 1924), pp. 277–279.
21. *Pomp.* 46.
22. For the immense wealth that also accrued to Pompey and his friends, see Greenhalgh 1980, pp. 168 ff.
23. *Pomp.* 46.
24. 40.4.
25. 'The Dedicatory Inscription of Pompeius Magnus in Diodorus 40.4*: Some Remarks on an Unpublished Manuscript by Hans Schaefer,' in *Acta Classica*, Vol. 28 (1985), pp. 57–75.
26. For how much the bad press about Clodius is influenced by Cicero's hostility, cf. W.M.F. Rundell, 'Cicero and Clodius: The Question of Credibility,' in *Historia: Zeitschrift für Alte Geschichte*, Bd. 28, H. 3 (3rd Qtr., 1979), pp. 301–328, and D. Mulroy, 'The Early Career of P. Clodius Pulcher: A Re-Examination of the Charges of Mutiny and Sacrilege,' in *Transactions of the American Philological Association (1974–)*, Vol. 118 (1988), pp. 155–178.
27. 'Marcus Licinius Crassus and the Trial of Publius Claudius Pulcher,' in *Electrum*, Volume 8 (2004), pp. 91–103.
28. Appian, *Mith.* 120.
29. T. Rising, 'Senatorial Opposition to Pompey's Eastern Settlement: A Storm in a Teacup?,' in *Historia: Zeitschrift für Alte Geschichte*, Bd. 62, H. 2 (2013), pp. 196–221, explores whether the root problem was considering the initiatives individually or as a bloc.
30. Cf. Suetonius, *Divus Augustus* 3.
31. See here M.P. Charlesworth, 'Some Fragments of the Propaganda of Mark Antony,' in *The Classical Quarterly*, Vol. 27, No. 3/4 (Jul. - Oct., 1933), pp. 172–177.

32. See further here S.J. Chrissanthos, *The Year of Julius and Caesar: 59 BC and the Transformation of the Roman Republic*, Baltimore: Johns Hopkins University Press, 2019.
33. On the prosopographical problems of clarifying the identities of bearers of the name 'Lucceius,' see W.C. McDermott, 'De Lucceiis,' in *Hermes*, 97. Bd., H. 2 (1969), pp. 233–246.
34. For a valuable study of this intriguing, enigmatic figure see L. Morgan, 'The Autopsy of G. Asinius Pollio,' in *The Journal of Roman Studies*, Vol. 90 (2000), pp. 51–69.
35. On the Varronian reference see R. Astbury, 'Varro and Pompey,' in *The Classical Quarterly*, Vol. 17, No. 2 (Nov., 1967), pp. 403–407.
36. See further here H.A. Sanders, 'The So-Called First Triumvirate,' in *Memoirs of the American Academy in Rome*, Vol. 10 (1932), pp. 55–68.

Chapter Twelve
1. *BC* 2.10.
2. Cf. Plutarch, *Caesar* 14, *Cato* 31–32, Appian, *BC* 2.10, Dio 38.1–2. For an overview and analysis of the tensions posed by Caesar's consulship, see especially Seager 2002, pp. 86 ff.
3. *BC* 2.11.
4. 38.1–3.
5. G.R. Stanton and B.A. Marshall, 'The Coalition between Pompeius and Crassus 60–59 B.C.,' in *Historia: Zeitschrift für Alte Geschichte*, Bd. 24, H. 2 (2nd Qtr., 1975), pp. 205–219, provides helpful background on how the two older members of the arrangement came to terms.
6. *Divus Iulius* 21.
7. *Pomp.* 47.
8. *Divus Iulius* 20.
9. Cf. Plutarch, *Pomp.* 47, 70, *Caesar* 5, *Cato* 31, Appian, *BC* 2.14, Dio 38.9, Velleius 2.44, Suetonius, *Divus Iulius* 21
10. *Divus Iulius* 50.
11. 2.44.
12. See further here W.C. McDermott, 'Vettius Ille, Ille Noster Index,' in *Transactions and Proceedings of the American Philological Association*, Vol. 80 (1949), pp. 351–367, W. Allen, Jr., 'The 'Vettius Affair' Once More,' in *Transactions and Proceedings of the American Philological Association*, Vol. 81 (1950), pp. 153–163, and L.R. Taylor, 'The Date and the Meaning of the Vettius Affair,' in *Historia: Zeitschrift für Alte Geschichte*, Bd. 1, H. 1 (1950), pp. 45–51.
13. 38.9.
14. *Lucullus* 42.
15. *Divus Iulius* 20.
16. Appian, *BC* 2.12.
17. *In Vatinium* 42–46.
18. Cf. Plutarch, *Caesar* 14, *Cato* 33, *Pomp.* 48, *Crassus* 14, Appian, *BC* 2.13, Velleius 2.44.

Chapter Thirteen
1. Loyal yes, successful in accomplishing the goals of his patron, not always; cf. here R.S. Williams and B.P. Williams, 'Cn. Pompeius and L. Afranius: Failure to Secure the Eastern Settlement,' in *The Classical Journal*, Vol. 83, No. 3 (Feb. - Mar., 1988), pp. 198–206.
2. E.S. Gruen, 'Pompey and the Pisones,' in *California Studies in Classical Antiquity*, Vol. 1 (1968), pp. 155–170, offers a fine study of the relationship (and implications thereof) of our subject to one of the most celebrated and prominent of republican families.
3. Cf. Plutarch, *Cicero* 31, 53, *Cato* 35, Appian, *BC* 2.15, Dio 38.17, 45.17.
4. The best modern study is E.G. Huzar's *Mark Antony: A Biography* (Minneapolis: The University of Minnesota Press, 1978); see now W.J. Tatum, *Mark Antony, Civil War, and the Collapse of the Roman Republic*, Oxford, 2024.
5. Cf. Plutarch, *Cato* 34, Appian, *BC* 2.23, Dio 38.30, Florus 1.44, Festus, *Breviarium* 13.1, Ammianus Marcellinus 14.8.
6. Cf. Plutarch, *Cato* 35–36, Appian, *BC* 2.23, Dio 39.22.

7. On the work on the island of 'the stormiest petrel of Roman politics in the last age of the Republic' see S.I. Oost, 'Cato Uticensis and the Annexation of Cyprus,' in *Classical Philology*, Vol. 50, No. 2 (Apr., 1955), pp. 98–112.
8. Cf. Plutarch, *Pomp*. 49, Dio 39.12.
9. Cf. Plutarch, *Pomp*. 48–9, Dio 38.30, Cicero, *Pro Sestio* 69, *In Pisonem* 27–30, *Pro Milone* 18–9.
10. For a valuable, incisive account of the relationship between the two men, see A.W. Lintott, 'Cicero and Milo,' in *The Journal of Roman Studies*, Vol. 64 (1974), pp. 62–78.
11. Cf. Plutarch, *Cicero* 33, Appian, *BC* 2.15, Dio 38.17, 39.11.
12. Cf. Plutarch, *Antony* 3.
13. Cf. Dio 39.56.
14. Cf. Plutarch, *Pomp*. 49, Appian, *BC* 2.18, Dio 39.9, 54.1, Livy, *Per.* 104.
15. 39.9–10.
16. 39.22.
17. 39.24–25.
18. *Pomp*. 50.
19. *Pomp*. 51.
20. Cf. Plutarch, *Pomp*. 51, *Caesar* 21, *Crassus* 14, *Cato* 41, Appian, *BC* 2.17, Dio 39.24–26, Suetonius, *Divus Iulius* 24.
21. For the argument that what happened at the conference (and, more generally, in political events in Rome) was strongly influenced by Caesar's military actions abroad, see J.F. Lazenby, 'The Conference of Luca and the Gallic War: A Study in Roman Politics 57–55 B.C.,' in *Latomus*, T. 18, Fasc. 1 (janvier-mars 1959), pp. 67–76.
22. For a start to the vast bibliography, see C. Luibheid, 'The Luca Conference,' *Classical Philology*, Vol. 65, No. 2 (Apr., 1970), pp. 88–94, Seager 2002, pp. 110 ff.
23. Cf. Plutarch, *Lucullus* 43–44.

Chapter Fourteen
1. Cf. *Crassus* 51.
2. *Pomp*. 53.
3. 39.55.
4. 39.57.
5. Cf. Plutarch, *Antony* 3–4, Appian, *Syr.* 51, Dio 39.55–56, 58, 45.26.
6. Strabo 17.796.
7. 39.58.
8. *Antony* 3.
9. For a good, scholarly introduction to a popular topic, see G. Webster, *The Roman Invasion of Britain*, London-New York: Routledge, 1993 (revised edition of the 1980 B.T. Batsford first edition).
10. Plutarch, *Crassus* 2.
11. Cf. Plutarch, *Cicero* 25.
12. Cf. Plutarch, *Pomp*. 40, Dio 39.38, Pliny, *NH* 7.34, 158, 8.20–21, 53, 64, 70. 36.41, 115.
13. Cf. Dio 39.38.
14. Cf. Dio 39.54.
15. Cf. Plutarch, *Pomp*. 52, *Crassus* 15, Appian, *BC* 2.18, Dio 39.33–35, Eutropius 6.18, Orosius 6.13.

Chapter Fifteen
1. *Bellum Iudaicum* 1.179.
2. *Crassus* 17.
3. Cf. Caesar, *Bellum Gallicum* 5.1, Dio 40.1, Orosius 6.9.
4. Cf. Cicero, *Phil*. 2.48.
5. Cf. Josephus, *Bellum Iudaicum* 1.179, *Antiquitates Iudaicae* 14.104, Appian, *Syr.* 51.
6. Cf. Plutarch, *Pomp*. 53, *Caesar* 23, Appian, *BC* 2.19, Velleius 2.47, Florus 2.13.

7. A. Chiu, 'The Importance of Being Julia: Civil War, Historical Revision and the Mutable Past in Lucan's *Pharsalia*,' in *The Classical Journal*, Vol. 105, No. 4 (April-May 2010), pp. 343–360 explores the mythologized and politicized *Nachleben* of Pompey's spouse.
8. *Pomp.* 53.
9. Plutarch, *Pomp.* 53.
10. Cf. Plutarch, *Pomp.* 53 and Dio 39.64 (girl), Velleius 2.47 (boy).
11. Cf. Appian, *Syr.* 51, Dio 39.55, 62.2, Valerius Maximus 8.1.
12. See here E. Fantham, 'The Trials of Gabinius in 54 B.C.,' in *Historia: Zeitschrift für Alte Geschichte*, Bd. 24, H. 3 (3rd Qtr., 1975), pp. 425–44; cf. R.S. Williams, '*Rei Publicae Causa*: Gabinius' Defence of His Restoration of Ptolemy Auletes,' in *The Classical Journal*, Vol. 81, No. 1 (Oct. - Nov., 1985), pp. 25–38.
13. *HN* 2.147.
14. Cf. Dio 39.60, 61.3–4.
15. *Pomp.* 54.
16. Note here J. Carlsen, 'Cn. Domitius Calvinus: A Noble Caesarian,' in *Latomus*, T. 67, Fasc. 1 (mars 2008), pp. 72–81.
17. On the possible significance of the dedication in light of the politics of the day see further D.W. Roller, 'Gaius Memmius: Patron of Lucretius,' in *Classical Philology*, Vol. 65, No. 4 (Oct., 1970), pp. 246–248.
18. For detailed analysis of the campaign, see G.C. Sampson, *The Defeat of Rome: Crassus, Carrhae, & the Invasion of the East*, Barnsley: Pen & Sword Military, 2008.
19. Cf. Plutarch, *Crassus* 20.
20. Cf. Plutarch, *Crassus* 18.

Chapter Sixteen
1. Cf. Plutarch, *Crassus* 18–19.
2. 40.20.
3. *Crassus* 20–22.
4. *Breviarium* 17.
5. On the battle and its aftermath, in addition to Sampson 2008 see S.P. Mattern-Parkes, 'The Defeat of Crassus and the Just War,' in *The Classical World*, Vol. 96, No. 4 (Summer, 2003), pp. 387–396 (cf. D. Frendo, 'Roman Expansion and the Graeco-Iranian World: Carrhae, Its Explanation and Aftermath in Plutarch,' in *Bulletin of the Asia Institute*, New Series, Vol. 17 (2003), pp. 71–81), and J.M. Schlude, 'The Parthian Response to the Campaign of Crassus,' in *Latomus*, T. 71, Fasc. 1 (mars 2012), pp. 11–23.
6. Plutarch, *Crassus* 22.
7. Cf. Plutarch, *Crassus* 25.
8. Cf. Plutarch, *Crassus* 30.
9. Cf. *Crassus* 31.
10. Plutarch, *Crassus* 33.
11. Cf. Plutarch, *Crassus* 19, Appian, *BC* 4.59, Dio 40.28, Velleius 2.46, Eutropius 6.18, Orosius 6.13.
12. *Pompeius* 54.
13. Cf. *Bellum Gallicum* 6.9.-10, 29, Livy, *Per.* 107.
14. Cf. Plutarch, *Pomp.* 55.
15. Suetonius, *Divus Iulius* 27.
16. Cf. Plutarch, *Pompeius* 55.
17. Invaluable here is the work of G. Wylle, 'The Road to Pharsalus,' in *Latomus*, T. 51, Fasc. 3 (juillet-septembre 1992), pp. 557–565.
18. Besides Cicero's account in his *Pro Milone*, cf. Appian, *BC* 2.20–1, Dio 40.48.
19. G.S. Sumi, 'Power and Ritual: The Crowd at Clodius' Funeral,' in *Historia: Zeitschrift für Alte Geschichte*, Bd. 46, H. 1 (1st Qtr., 1997), pp. 80–102.

20. R.D. Weigel, *Lepidus: The Tarnished Triumvir*, London-New York: Routledge, 1992 is the standard scholarly study. On his participation in a crucial period see K.E. Welch, 'The Career of M. Aemilius Lepidus 49–44 B.C.,' in *Hermes*, 123. Bd., H. 4 (1995), pp. 443–454.

Chapter Seventeen
1. J.T. Ramsey, 'How and Why was Pompey Made Sole Consul in 52 BC?,' in *Historia: Zeitschrift für Alte Geschichte*, Bd. 65, H. 3 (2016), pp. 298–324, is invaluable here.
2. *Pompeius* 54; cf. Appian, *BC* 2.23, Dio 40.50, Livy, *Per.* 107.
3. For the Latin text (with detailed introduction and commentary) see T.J. Keeline, *Cicero: Pro Milone*, Cambridge 2021.
4. Cf. Plutarch, *Cicero* 35, Livy, *Per.* 107, Suetonius, *Divus Iulius* 30, Appian, *BC* 2.24, Dio 40.54.
5. Cf. Asconius 54–55.
6. *Pomp.* 55.
7. Cf. Appian, *BC* 5.10, Dio 40.30.
8. R. Morstein-Marx, 'Caesar's Alleged Fear of Prosecution and His *Ratio Absentis* in the Approach to the Civil War,' in *Historia: Zeitschrift für Alte Geschichte*, Bd. 56, H. 2 (2007), pp. 159–178, reconsiders 'this old chestnut' about just how worried Caesar was about legal vulnerability.
9. Our principal source for this great rebellion is Book 7 of Caesar's *Bellum Gallicum*; Christopher Krebs' 2023 edition of the book for the 'Cambridge Greek and Latin Classics' series provides text, commentary, and detailed introduction.
10. Cf. Caesar, *BC* 1.9, Appian, *BC* 2.25, Dio 40.51, 56.2, Livy, *Periochae* 107–108, Suetonius, *Divus Iulius* 26.
11. Cf. Plutarch, *Pomp.* 55, Appian, *BC* 2.25, Dio 40.51.
12. Cf. Caesar, *Bellum Galllicum* 7.89, Plutarch, *Caesar* 27, Dio 40.41, Florus 1.45, Orosius 6.11.
13. Cf. Caesar, *Bellum Gallicum* 7.90, Dio 40.50.
14. Cf. Plutarch, *Crassus* 33.
15. 3.28.
16. Cf. Caesar, *Bellum Gallicum* 6.1, 8.54, Plutarch, *Caesar* 25, Suetonius, *Divus Iulius* 24, Orosius 6.10.

Chapter Eighteen
1. *BC* 2.25.
2. Cf. Plutarch, *Caesar* 20, Cicero, *Ad Att.* 5.11, Suetonius, *Divus Iulius* 28, Appian, *BC* 2.26.
3. Cf. Caesar, *BC* 3.108, Ps-Caesar, *Bellum Alexandrinum* 33.
4. Cf. Plutarch, *Antony* 86, Cicero, *Ad Fam.* 8.4.
5. Cf. Dio 40.59.
6. *Ad Att.* 5.21.
7. Cf. *Ad Att.* 5.20, 21.9, *Ad Fam.* 3.5, 6.6.
8. Cf. Cicero, *Ad Att.* 5.7, 11.3, *Ad Fam.* 8.4, Dio 40.59.
9. *Divus Augustus* 8.
10. *Ill.* 3.12.
11. Cf. Cicero, *Ad Att.* 5.20, Appian, *BC* 5.10, Dio 40.30.
12. Cicero, *Ad Fam* 8.8.
13. R.D. Weigel, 'The Career of L. Paullus, Cos. 50,' in *Latomus*, T. 38, Fasc. 3 (juillet-septembre 1979), pp. 637–646, examines Paullus' *curriculum vitae*, with consideration of both his paternal and fraternal connections to the revolutionary of 78 and the future triumvir.
14. There is a wealth of useful analysis and information in C.L. Babcock, 'The Early Career of Fulvia,' in *The American Journal of Philology*, Vol. 86, No. 1 (Jan., 1965), pp. 1–32. C.E. Schultz, *Fulvia: Playing for Power at the End of the Roman Republic*, Oxford, 2021 offers a comprehensive biography.
15. See further here R.J. Rowland, Jr., 'Crassus, Curio, and Clodius in the Year 59 B.C.,' in *Historia: Zeitschrift für Alte Geschichte*, Bd. 15, H. 2 (Apr., 1966), pp. 217–223.

16. L. Logghe, 'The Gentleman Was not for Turning: the Alleged *volte-face* of Gaius Scribonius Curio,' in Latomus, T. 75, Fasc. 2 (2016), pp. 353–377 offers an extended reappraisal of the evidence for Curio's attitude toward Pompey and Caesar in this period.
17. Cf. Cicero, *Ad Fam.* 8.6, Dio 40.60–61.
18. Cf. Caesar, *BC* 3.110, Valerius Maximus 4.1, Seneca, *Dial.* 6.14.
19. For an intriguing study that offers learned analysis of the question of whether our sources preserve evidence for nothing less than a nervous decline (not to say collapse) of the ex-consul, see M.J.G. Gray-Fow, 'The Mental Breakdown of a Roman Senator: M. Calpurnius Bibulus,' in *Greece & Rome*, Vol. 37, No. 2 (Oct., 1990), pp. 179–190.
20. Cf. Plutarch, *Pomp.* 57, Appian, *BC* 2.28, Dio 41.6, Velleius 2.48.
21. *Pomp.* 57.
22. *BC* 2.28.
23. Cf. Dio 41.6.
24. Plutarch, *Pomp.* 57.
25. *BC* 2.29–30.

Chapter Nineteen
1. Cf. Plutarch, *Pomp.* 58.
2. Cf. Julius Obsequens 62, Orosius 6.14, 7.2.
3. Cf. Cicero, *Ad Fam.* 16.12, *Phil.* 2.24, Plutarch, *Pomp.* 59, Cicero 37, Caesar 31, Antony 5, Appian, *BC* 2.32, Velleius 2.49.
4. Cf. Plutarch, *Pomp.* 58.
5. Cf. Appian, *BC* 2.32, Suetonius, *Divus Iulius* 29.
6. Cf. Cicero, *Ad Att.* 7.4, 15.3, *Ad Fam.* 16.12.
7. 2.48.
8. *Ad Att.* 7.8.
9. Cf. Plutarch, *Pomp.* 59, *Mor.* 810C, Appian, *BC* 2.34, Dio 41.3, Caesar, *BC* 1.6, Livy, *Per.* 109.
10. Cf. Velleius 2.49, Florus 2.13.
11. Cf. the analysis of D.W. Knight, 'Pompey's Concern with Pre-eminence after 60 B.C.,' in *Latomus*, T. 27, Fasc. 4 (octobre-décembre 1968), pp. 878–883.
12. Cf. Plutarch, *Pomp.* 59, Caesar 30, Antony 5, Appian, *BC* 2.32, Dio 41.1–2, Caesar, *BC* 1.1–3.
13. R.W. Westall, *Caesar's Civil War: Historical Reality and Fabrication*, Leiden-Boston: Brill, 2018 may be recommended as an excellent, detailed study of Caesar's work, especially the problematic issue of his reliability in view of his obvious prejudices. Cf. A. Peer, 'Julius Caesar and the Roman *stasis*,' in *Hermathena*, No. 199 (Winter 2015), pp. 71–92, which presents a compelling case for Caesar's modelling his account of the civil war on Thucydides' work, with the Pompeians cast in the role of villain.
14. Cf. Plutarch, *Caesar* 31, *Antony* 5, Appian, *BC* 2.33, Dio 41.3, Caesar, *BC* 1.3–5, 7, Livy, *Per.* 109, Suetonius, *Divus Iulius* 31, Orosius 6.15.

Chapter Twenty
1. R.T. Ridley, 'Attacking the World with Five Cohorts: Caesar in January 49,' in *Ancient Society*, Vol. 34 (2004), pp. 127–152, discusses Caesar's bold act in striking when he was not in the most advantageous position in terms of resources.
2. F.A. Sirianni, 'Caesar's Decision to Cross the Rubicon,' in *L'Antiquité classique*, T. 48, Fasc. 2 (1979), pp. 636–638 considers the role of *dignitas* in the fateful decision; more generally note here Fezzi 2019, G.R. Stanton, 'Why Did Caesar Cross the Rubicon,' in *Historia: Zeitschrift für Alte Geschichte*, Bd. 52, H. 1 (2003), pp. 67–94, A. Rondholz, 'Crossing the Rubicon: A Historiographical Study,' in *Mnemosyne*, Fourth Series, Vol. 62, Fasc. 3 (2009), pp. 432–450, and J. Beneker, 'The Crossing of the Rubicon and the Outbreak of Civil War in Cicero, Lucan, Plutarch, and Suetonius' in *Phoenix*, Vol. 65, No. 1/2 (Spring-Summer/printemps-été 2011), pp. 74–99. On the immediate strategy of Caesar, the brief appraisal of T.P. Hillman ('Strategic Reality and the Movements of Caesar, January 49 B.C.,' in *Historia: Zeitschrift für*

Alte Geschichte, Bd. 37, H. 2 (2nd Qtr., 1988), pp. 248–252) is very helpful. On the reaction of Pompey and the *optimates*, cf. Seager 2002, pp. 152 ff.
3. Cf. Plutarch, *Pomp*. 60, *Caesar* 32–3, *Cato* 52, *Antony* 5–6, Appian, *BC* 2.35, Dio 41.3, Caesar, *BC* 1.7–8, Velleius 2.49, Eutropius 6.19, Orosius 6.15.
4. *Pharsalia* 1.183–391. On the implications of the depiction of Caesar and Roma by the poet note the insightful article of E.V. Mulhern, 'Roma(na) Matrona,' in *The Classical Journal*, Vol. 112, No. 4 (April-May 2017), pp. 432–459.
5. No surprise, then, that in Virgil's underworld, in the vision revealed by the shade of Anchises, Caesar and Pompey will be relegated to a description that focuses on the horror of civil war, with an appeal to both men to refrain from such internecine struggles (6.826 ff.).
6. Cf. Appian, *BC* 2.35.
7. *Pomp*. 60.
8. Cf. Plutarch, *Pomp*. 64, *Caesar* 34, Dio 41.4.
9. Cf. Caesar, *BC* 1.8–11, Dio 41.5.
10. On 'how this loose broom got his chance to change history,' see D.R. Shackleton Bailey, 'The Credentials of L. Caesar and L. Roscius,' in *The Journal of Roman Studies*, Vol. 50, Parts 1 and 2 (1960), pp. 80–83. On the problems posed by the recurring negotiations to avoid/settle problems, see F.A. Sirianni, 'Caesar's Peace Overtures to Pompey,' in *L'Antiquité classique*, T. 62 (1993), pp. 219–237.
11. On the departure cf. Plutarch, *Pomp*. 60–61, 83,, *Caesar* 33–34, 56, *Cicero* 37, Appian, *BC* 2.36, Dio 61.6.9, Caesar, *BC* 1.14, Suetonius, *Divus Iulius* 75, Orosius 6.16.
12. On Labienus in this crucial period see W.B. Tyrrell, 'Labienus' Departure from Caesar in January 49 B.C.,' in *Historia: Zeitschrift für Alte Geschichte*, Bd. 21, H. 3 (3rd Qtr., 1972), pp. 424–440.
13. *Pomp*. 60.
14. *Pomp*. 61.
15. Nicolaus of Damascus fr. 127.4.
16. E.J. Vervaet, 'The Official Position of Cn. Pompeius in 49 and 48 BCE,' in *Latomus*, T. 65, Fasc. 4 (octobre-décembre 2006), pp. 928–953 discusses the evidence for what we know about Pompey's legal status in this period.
17. *Pomp*. 61.
18. Cf. *Ad Att*. 7.16. On Cicero after the Rubicon see P.A. Brunt, 'Cicero's *Officium* in the Civil War,' in *The Journal of Roman Studies*, Vol. 76 (1986), pp. 12–32.
19. Cf. Caesar, *BC* 1.11–13, 3.73, Suetonius, *Divus Iulius* 34, Dio 41.4, 44.44, Orosius 6.15.
20. C.C. Coulter, 'Caesar's Clemency,' in *The Classical Journal*, Vol. 26, No. 7 (Apr., 1931), pp. 513–524, gives an introduction to this alleged signal virtue of the would-be master of Rome, with particular attention to that we know of its manifestations apart from the evidence of Caesar's own pen.
21. K. von Fritz, 'Pompey's Policy before and after the Outbreak of the Civil War of 49 B.C.,' in *Transactions and Proceedings of the American Philological Association*, Vol. 73 (1942), pp. 145–180, seeks to argue that Pompey had made the decision to evacuate Italy in the event of war with Caesar long before the Rubicon was crossed. Cf. L.G. Pocock, 'What Made Pompeius Fight in 49 B.C.?,' in *Greece & Rome*, Vol. 6, No. 1 (Mar., 1959), pp. 68–81.
22. *Ad Att*. 8.11a; cf. *Ad Att*. 7.20 (Pompey is at Luceria).
23. A. Burns, 'Pompey's Strategy and Domitius' Stand at Corfinium,' in *Historia: Zeitschrift für Alte Geschichte*, Bd. 15, H. 1 (Jan., 1966), pp. 74–95, presents the problems of this key episode in the early stages of the civil war.
24. On the significance of islands in the strategies of the Roman civil wars see E. Deniaux, 'Le contrôle de la mer et des îles de la Sicile à l'Adriatique, de l'époque des Guerres Civiles à Auguste,' in *Pallas*, No. 96, Le monde romain de 70 av. J.-C. à 73 apr. J.-C. (2014), pp. 127–144.
25. Cf. Caesar, *BC* 1.15–23, Plutarch, *Caesar* 34–35, Appian, *BC* 2.38, Dio 41.10–11, Livy, *Per*. 109, Velleius 2.80, Suetonius, *Divus Iulius* 34, Orosius 6.15.

Chapter Twenty-One

1. Cf. Caesar, *BC* 1.18.
2. *BC* 1.23.
3. Cf. Caesar, *BC* 1.25–26, Plutarch, *Pomp.* 62, *Caesar* 35, Appian, *BC* 2.40, Dio 41.12–14, Livy, *Per.* 109, Suetonius, *Divus Iulius* 34, Florus 2.13, Orosius 6.15.
4. *BC* 1.26.
5. Cf. *Pomp.* 62–63.
6. *Strategemata* 1.5.
7. Cf. Dio 41.13.
8. Cf. Lucan, *Pharsalia* 1.524–695, Pliny, *HN* 2.147, 17.243–244, Dio 41.14.
9. Cf. Valerius Maximus 8.13, Pliny, *NH* 7.156, Dio 41.14.
10. Cf. *Ad Att.* 9.18.
11. *Pomp.* 63.
12. *Pomp.* 64.
13. Cf. *Pharsalia* 3.112–68.
14. Cf. Dio 41.18.
15. Cf. Josephus, *Bellum Iudaicum* 1.183, *Antiquitates Iudaicae* 14.123, Dio 41.18.
16. Cf. Caesar, *BC* 1.36, Dio 41.19, Livy, *Per.* 110, Suetonius, *Caesar* 34, Florus 2.13, Orosius 6.15.
17. Cf. Caesar, *BC* 1.31–47, Appian, *BC* 2.42, Dio 41.20.
18. On the campaigns in Africa cf. Caesar, *BC* 2.23–44, Appian, *BC* 2.44–46, Dio 41.41–42, 42.56, 43.30, Livy, *Per.* 110, Velleius 2.55, Florus 2.13, Orosius 6.15. On Lucan's account in *Pharsalia* 4, note P. Asso, *A Commentary on Lucan, De Bello Civili IV*, Berlin-New York: Walter de Gruyter, 2010.
19. Cf. Caesar, *BC* 2.23–44, Livy, *Per.* 110, Velleius 2.55, Florus 2.13, Orosius 6.15, Appian, *BC* 2.44–46, Dio 41.41–42.
20. On the reconstruction of this relatively poorly attested encounter, see H.C. Avery, 'A Lost Episode in Caesar's Civil War,' in *Hermes*, 121. Bd., H. 4 (1993), pp. 452–469.
21. Cf. Appian, *BC* 2.47, Dio 41.26–35, Suetonius, *Divus Iulius* 36. For how Lucan treats the episode at *Pharsalia* 5.237–373, see E. Fantham, 'Caesar and the Mutiny: Lucan's Reshaping of the Historical Tradition in *De bello civili* 5.237–373,' in *Classical Philology*, Vol. 80, No. 2 (Apr., 1985), pp. 119–131, and see further A.V. van Stekelenburg, 'Lucan and Cassius Dio as Heirs to Livy: The Speech of Julius Caesar at Placentia,' in *Acta Classica*, Vol. 19 (1976), pp. 43–57.
22. Suetonius, *Caesar* 34.

Chapter Twenty-Two

1. Cf. Caesar, *BC* 3.1, Plutarch, *Caesar* 37, Appian, *BC* 2.48, Dio 41.36, Florus 2.13.
2. M.T. Boatwright, 'Caesar's Second Consulship and the Completion and Date of the *Bellum Civile*,' in *The Classical Journal*, Vol. 84, No. 1 (Oct. - Nov., 1988), pp. 31–40, examines the references in Caesar's commentaries to his second term, and the implications for the question of when the work was commenced and completed.
3. Cf. e.g. Ps.-Eusebius, *Chron.* 129.
4. Cf. Plutarch, *Pomp.* 65, *Cato* 53–54.
5. Cf. Cicero, *Phil.* 2.37–40, Plutarch, *Cicero* 38, *Mor.* 205D, Quintilian 6.3, Macrobius, *Sat.* 2.3.
6. Cf. Caesar, *BC* 3.2, Appian, *BC* 2.48, Dio 41.39.
7. Cf. Caesar, *BC* 3.103, Strabo 17.796, Plutarch, *Caesar* 48, Appian, *BC* 2.84, Livy, *Per.* 111.
8. *BC* 2.50–52.
9. *BC* 3.5.
10. *Pharsalia* 5.476–702.
11. *Pharsalia* 5.460.
12. *BC* 3.7.
13. 41.44.
14. 41.44.

Notes   349

15. Cf. Plutarch, *Pomp.* 65.
16. *BC* 3.10–12; cf. Plutarch, *Pomp.* 65, Appian, *BC* 2.54–55, Dio 41.45.
17. *BC* 2.54.
18. Cf. Plutarch, *Caesar* 38, *Mor.* 206C-D, 319C-D, Appian, *BC* 2.56–58, 150, Dio 41.45–46, Valerius Maximus 9.8, Lucan, *Pharsalia* 5.476–702, Suetonius, *Divus Iulius* 58, Florus 2.13, Ammianus Marcellinus 16.10.
19. R.T. Bruère, 'Lucan's Cornelia,' in *Classical Philology*, Vol. 46, No. 4 (Oct., 1951), pp. 221–236 is a classic study.
20. A.O. Anders, 'The 'Face of Roman Skirmishing,"' in *Historia: Zeitschrift für Alte Geschichte*, Bd. 64, H. 3 (2015), pp. 263–300, serves as a valuable study of this often ignored preliminary aspect of major pitched battles.
21. Cf. Caesar, *BC* 31.14–18, Orosius 6.15.
22. On the theme and its appearance as a veritable Caesarian emblem see E. Tappan, 'Caesar's Luck,' in *The Classical Journal*, Vol. 27, No. 1 (Oct., 1931), pp. 3–14.
23. 41.48.
24. *BC* 3.26.
25. Cf. Caesar, *BC* 3.25–30, Plutarch, *Caesar* 39, *Antony* 7, Appian, *Ill.* 12, *BC* 2.59, Dio 41.48.
26. *BC* 3.9; cf. Dio 42.11, Orosius 6.15.
27. Cf. Ps.-Caesar, *Bellum Alexandrinum* 26, Appian, *Ill.* 12, 27–28, *BC* 2.59.
28. Cf. Caesar, *BC* 3.31–33.
29. Caesar, *BC* 3.34.
30. *BC* 3.41–42.
31. Cf. Caesar, *BC* 3.45.
32. *BC* 3.48.
33. Cf. *Pharsalia* 6.80–117, Caesar, *BC* 3.47–49, Plutarch, *Caesar* 39.1–3, Suetonius, *Divus Iulius* 68, Velleius 2.51, Pliny, *NH* 19.144, Florus 2.13, Appian, *BC* 2.61.
34. Cf. *BC* 3.53.
35. *Pharsalia* 6.1138–262.
36. *BC* 3.53.
37. Cf. Caesar, *BC* 3.59–61.
38. Cf. Caesar, *BC* 3.63.
39. Cf. Plutarch, *Pomp.* 65.
40. *Strategemata* 8.23.
41. Cf. *Pharsalia* 7.45 ff.
42. Cf. Caesar, *BC* 3.71.
43. Cf. *BC* 2.68.

Chapter Twenty-Three
1. *Pomp.* 65.
2. Cf. Caesar, *BC* 3.73–79, Plutarch, *Caesar* 39, Appian, *BC* 2.64, Dio 41.51, Velleius 2.52, Orosius 6.15.
3. Cf. Plutarch, *Pomp.* 66.
4. *BC* 3.57.
5. *BC* 3.78.
6. Cf. Caesar, *BC* 3.82, Plutarch, *Pomp.* 66, *Cato* 55, Velleius 2.52, Appian, *BC* 2.65–66, Dio 41.52–54.
7. Cf. Plutarch, *Caesar* 50, Strabo 11.498, Appian, *BC* 2.91, Dio 42.45, Eutropius 6.22.
8. *BC* 3.80–81; cf. Plutarch, *Caesar* 41, Appian, *BC* 2.64, Dio 41.51, Florus 2.13.
9. Cf. *BC* 3.81.
10. *BC* 3.82.
11. Cf. *BC* 3.33 and 105.
12. *Pomp.* 67.
13. *Pomp.* 67.

14. Cf. Plutarch, *Pomp.* 67.
15. *Pomp.* 67.
16. Cf. Caesar, *BC* 3.79.
17. The battle has been the subject of a daunting number of studies, as one would suspect; recommended are W.E. Gwatkin, Jr., 'Some Reflections on the Battle of Pharsalus,' in *Transactions and Proceedings of the American Philological Association*, Vol. 87 (1956), pp. 109–124, and C.B.R. Pelling, 'Pharsalus,' in *Historia: Zeitschrift für Alte Geschichte*, Bd. 22, H. 2 (2nd Qtr., 1973), pp. 249–259.
18. See here J.D. Morgan, 'Palaepharsalus-The Battle and the Town,' in *American Journal of Archaeology*, Vol. 87, No. 1 (Jan., 1983), pp. 23–54.
19. Caesar, *BC* 3.85–97, 99, Plutarch, *Pomp.* 68–73, *Caesar* 44–46, *Antony* 8, *Brutus* 4, Velleius 2.52, Valerius Maximus 1.5, 4.5, Eutropius 6.20–21, Orosius 6.15, Appian, *BC* 2.69–82, Polyaenus, *Strategemata* 8.23, Dio 41.55–61.
20. *BC* 3.85–97.
21. *BC* 3.86.
22. *BC* 3.87.
23. *BC* 3.88.
24. *BC* 3.89.
25. Cf. Caesar, *BC* 3.91.
26. Cf. Caesar, *BC* 3.92.
27. *BC* 3.95.
28. *BC* 3.93.
29. *BC* 2.69–82.
30. *BC* 2.67.
31. *BC* 2.70.
32. *BC* 2.71.
33. F. Santangelo, 'Pompey and Religion,' in *Hermes*, 135. Jahrg., H. 2 (2007), pp. 228–233, considers a rarely surveyed aspect of Pompey's career, with good analysis of his inheritance of the treatment of religious questions by Sulla.
34. 41.55–61.
35. *Pomp.* 69.
36. *Pomp.* 71.
37. *Caesar* 44.
38. *Antony* 8.
39. *Brutus* 5.
40. *BC* 2.112.
41. 41.62.
42. 2.52.
43. *Divus Iulius* 30.
44. 2.3; cf. 4.7.
45. Cf. Plutarch, *Pomp.* 69.
46. *BC* 3.99.
47. On this film note G.N. Daugherty, *The Reception of Cleopatra in the Age of Mass Media*, London-New York: Bloomsbury Academic, 2023, pp. 89 ff.
48. *BC* 2.82.
49. *Pomp.* 72.
50. *BC* 3.99.
51. *BC* 3.94.
52. *BC* 2.80.
53. *Pomp.* 72.
54. 2.71.
55. R.C. Lounsbury, 'The Death of Domitius in the *Pharsalia*,' in *Transactions of the American Philological Association (1974–)*, Vol. 105 (1975), pp. 209–212, considers the poet's altered view of the circumstances of the slaying.

56. *BC* 3.97.
57. *BC* 3.96.
58. Cf. Dio 41.62.
59. 7.3.

Chapter Twenty-Four
1. *BC* 3.100–101.
2. Cf. Plutarch, *Cicero* 38, *Cato* 55, *Mor.* 205D.
3. Cf. Plutarch, *Cato* 55.
4. *Pro rege Deiotaro* 29.
5. 2.39.
6. *Pomp.* 73.
7. 42.2.
8. Cf. Plutarch, *Pomp.* 73.
9. *Pomp.* 73.
10. *Pomp.* 74.
11. *Pomp.* 75; cf. Aelian, *Varia Historia* 7.21.
12. *Pharsalia* 8.251.
13. *Pomp.* 76.
14. *Pomp.* 76.
15. Quintilian 3.8 cites the question of 'where should Pompey go?' as an example of a complicated deliberation.
16. Note here B.K. Gold, 'Pompey and Theophanes of Mytilene,' in *The American Journal of Philology*, Vol. 106, No. 3 (Autumn, 1985), pp. 312–327.
17. On a vast subject see S.L. Ager, 'Familiarity Breeds: Incest and the Ptolemaic Dynasty,' in *The Journal of Hellenic Studies*, Vol. 125 (2005), pp. 1–34, and the same author's 'The Power of Excess: Royal Incest and the Ptolemaic Dynasty,' in *Anthropologica*, Vol. 48, No. 2 (2006), pp. 165–186.
18. C.M. Peek, 'The Expulsion of Cleopatra VII: Context, Causes, and Chronology,' in *Ancient Society*, Vol. 38 (2008), pp. 103–135, presents a thorough account and analysis of the problems posed by our sources with respect to the breakdown of relations between the sibling rulers.
19. Cf. Strabo 17.796 (a valuable source).
20. *Pomp.* 76.
21. *BC* 2.83.
22. *BC* 2.83.
23. 2.53.
24. *BC* 3.102.
25. *BC* 3.102–103.
26. *Pomp.* 77.
27. *Pro rege Deiotaro* 13, 29.
28. *BC* 3.102.
29. *BC* 3.105.
30. *BC* 2.88.
31. *BC* 2.88–89.
32. 42.6.
33. *BC* 2.111; cf. 2.88.
34. 46.6.
35. *Divus Iulius* 63.
36. *Pomp.* 77.
37. *BC* 2.84.
38. 42.36.
39. 16.760; cf. 17.796.
40. For the dispute as to the exact date cf. Plutarch, *Mor.* 717C.

41. *Pomp.* 77.
42. *Pomp.* 77.
43. For his rendition of the death see *Pharsalia* 8.472–711.
44. *BC* 2.84.
45. Cf. Dio 42.3.
46. R. Westall, 'Pompeius at Pelusium: The Death of the Roman Lord of Asia,' in *Hermathena*, No. 196/197, *The Roman Civil Wars: A House Divided* (Summer–Winter 2014), pp. 309–340 provides a superlative study.
47. *Pomp.* 78.
48. *Pomp.* 78.
49. Cf. Appian, *BC* 2.84 and Dio 42.4.
50. See P. Hardie, *The Epic Successors of Virgil: A Study in the Dynamics of a Tradition*, Cambridge, 1993, pp. 37–8 for Lucan's play on Achillas-Achilles.
51. *Pomp.* 79.
52. *BC* 3.103–104.
53. L. Hayne, 'Caesar and Lentulus,' in *Acta Classica*, Vol. 39 (1996), pp. 72–76, provides a survey of the ill-starred career of the man, with particular focus on his portrayal in Caesar's commentaries.
54. 77.9. For this priceless work, the Budé edition provides the best access to text and commentary.
55. 2.54.
56. *Pomp.* 80.
57. 3.66.
58. *Cato* 56.
59. *BC* 2.86.
60. J. Mebane, 'Pompey's Head and the Body Politic in Lucan's *De bello civili*,' in *TAPA*, Vol. 146, No. 1 (Spring 2016), pp. 191–215, considers Lucan's depiction of the desecration of the body of hero as metaphor for the revolt of the body politic against its leader.
61. A.A. Bell, Jr., 'Fact and *Exemplum* in Accounts of the Deaths of Pompey and Caesar,' in *Latomus*, T. 53, Fasc. 4 (octobre-décembre 1994), pp. 824–836 is useful on how almost immediately, the death narrative became one of the classic dramatic sequences in Roman death theatre.
62. *Pomp.* 80.
63. *Per.* 112.
64. R. Mayer, *Lucan: Civil War VIII*, Liverpool, 1981, and Alessio Mancini, *Lucano Bellum Civile VIII: introduzione, testo, traduzione e commento* (*Texte und Kommentare, 70*), Berlin-Boston: De Gruyter, 2022, provide detailed annotation.
65. But cf. here D. Feeney, '*Stat magni nominis umbra*: Lucan on the Greatness of Pompey,' in *The Classical Quarterly*, Vol. 36, No. 1 (1986), pp. 239–243.

Chapter Twenty-Five
1. Not least, in the immediate, the work of his sons (the subject of the sequel of this volume). On the Pompeian legacy note K. Welch, *Magnus Pius: Sextus Pompeius and the Transformation of the Roman Republic*, Swansea: The Classical Press of Wales, 2012.
2. H.P. Collins, 'The Decline and Fall of Pompey the Great,' in *Greece & Rome*, Vol. 22, No. 66 (Oct., 1953), pp. 98–106, is a brief and insightful essay on the reception of Pompey.
3. Cf. here E.S. Ramage, 'Augustus' Treatment of Julius Caesar,' in *Historia: Zeitschrift für Alte Geschichte*, Bd. 34, H. 2 (2nd Qtr., 1985), pp. 223–245 and P.S White, 'Julius Caesar in Augustan Rome,' in *Phoenix*, Vol. 42, No. 4 (Winter, 1988), pp. 334–356.
4. In the example of Pompey, Augustus would have found a potent example of how provinces of the burgeoning republic should be governed; see further here Morrell 2017, pp. 22 ff.
5. L. Hayne, 'Livy and Pompey,' in *Latomus*, T. 49, Fasc. 2 (avril-juin 1990), pp. 435–442, considers the oft-debated problem of the historian's attitude towards our subject.
6. 56.34.

Select Bibliography

The following collection of secondary titles aims to provide an elementary guide for further reading on Pompey, his conflict with Caesar in particular, and more generally the history of the decline and fall of the Roman republic (especially the lives of its most famous figures); it provides a mix of popular as well as scholarly studies. Some titles are also included for those interested in exploring Lucan's epic in more depth. The bibliography on the last century of the Roman Republic is impossible to master, and any list is bound to be more or less abridged. Inclusion does not imply acceptance of an author's thesis; some titles demand serious appraisal and consideration, even if I remain unpersuaded by conclusions. Primary sources may be found conveniently in the Loeb Classical Library, which has complete editions on the Greek side of Plutarch, Appian, and Dio, and on the Latin of Caesar, Velleius Paterculus, Lucan, and Suetonius.

Adcock, Frank E. *Marcus Crassus, Millionaire*. Cambridge: W. Heffer & Sons, 1966.
Ahl, Frederick. *Lucan: An Introduction*. Ithaca, New York-London: Cornell University Press, 1976.
Arena, Valentina, and Prag, Jonathan. *A Companion to the Political Culture of the Roman Republic*. Malden, Massachusetts: Wiley-Blackwell, 2022.
Batstone, William, and Damon, Cynthia. *Caesar's Civil War*. Oxford, 2006.
Billows, Richard A. *Julius Caesar: The Colossus of Rome*. London-New York: Routledge, 2009.
Canfora, Luciano. *Julius Caesar: The Life and Times of the People's Dictator*. Berkeley-Los Angeles: The University of California Press, 2007 (English translation of the 1999 Italian original, with minor corrections).
Carney, James T. *Catiline: Rebel of the Roman Republic*. Barnsley: Pen & Sword Military, 2023.
Carter, John M. *Julius Caesar: The Civil War, Books I & II*. Liverpool, 2003.
Carter, John M. *Julius Caesar: The Civil War, Book III*. Liverpool, 2010.
Crook, J.A., Lintott, Andrew, and Rawson, Elizabeth. *The Cambridge Ancient History: Volume IX, The Last Age of the Roman Republic, 146–43 B.C.* Cambridge, 1994 (second edition)
de Ruggiero, Paolo. *Mark Antony: A Plain Blunt Man*. Barnsley: Pen & Sword Military, 2013.
Dinter, Martin T. *Anamotizing Civil War: Studies in Lucan's Epic Technique*. Ann Arbor: The University of Michigan Press, 2012.
Drogula, Fred. K. *Cato the Younger: Life and Death at the End of the Roman Republic*. Oxford, 2019.
Everitt, Anthony. *Cicero: The Life and Times of Rome's Greatest Politician*. New York: Random House, 2003.
Fezzi, Luca. *Crossing the Rubicon: Caesar's Decision and the Fate of Rome*. New Haven, Connecticut-London: Yale University Press, 2019 (English translation of the 2017 Italian original).
Fields, Nic. *Warlords of Republican Rome: Caesar Versus Pompey*. Barnsley: Pen & Sword Military, 2008.

Flower, Harriet I., ed. *The Cambridge Companion to the Roman Republic*. Cambridge, 2014 (second edition of the 2004 original).
Fratantuono, Lee. *Madness Triumphant: A Reading of Lucan's Pharsalia*. Lanham, Maryland: Rowman and Littlefield, 2013.
Fratantuono, Lee. *Lucullus: The Life and Times of a Roman Conqueror*. Barnsley: Pen & Sword Military, 2017.
Gelzer, Matthias. *Pompeius: Lebensbild eines Römers*. München: Franz Steiner Verlag, 2005 (reprint of the 1984 edition, with updates).
Gilliver, Kate. *Essential Histories 43: Caesar's Gallic Wars, 58–50 BC*. Oxford: Osprey Publishing, Ltd., 2002.
Golden, Gregory K. *Crisis Management during the Roman Republic: The Role of Political Institutions in Emergencies*. Cambridge, 2013.
Goldsworthy, Adrian K. *Caesar: Life of a Colossus*. New Haven, Connecticut-London: Yale University Press, 2006.
Goldsworthy, Adrian K. *Antony and Cleopatra*. New Haven, Connecticut-London: Yale University Press, 2010.
Goldsworthy, Adrian K. *Augustus: First Emperor of Rome*. New Haven, Connecticut-London: Yale University Press, 2014.
Green, Peter. *Alexander to Actium: The Historical Evolution of the Hellenistic Age*. Berkeley-Los Angeles: The University of California Press, 1990.
Greenhalgh, Peter. *Pompey: The Roman Alexander*. London: Weidenfeld & Nicolson, 1980. The University of Missouri Press editions of Greenhalgh are dated 1981 and 1982, which has occasioned some confusion in scholarly citations.
Greenhalgh, Peter. *Pompey: The Republican Prince*. London: Weidenfeld & Nicolson, 1981.
Griffin, Miriam, ed. *A Companion to Julius Caesar*. Malden, Massachusetts: Wiley-Blackwell, 2015.
Grillo, Luca. *The Art of Caesar's Bellum Civile: Literature, Ideology, and Community*. Cambridge, 2012.
Grillo, Luca, and Krebs, Christopher B., eds. *The Cambridge Companion to the Writings of Julius Caesar*. Cambridge, 2018.
Gruen, Erich S. *The Last Generation of the Roman Republic*. Berkeley-Los Angeles-London: The University of California Press, 1995 (paperback printing).
Heftner, Herbert. *Plutarch und der Aufstieg des Pompeius: Ein historischer Kommentar zu Plutarchs Pompeiusvita. Teil I: Kap. 1–45* (Europäische Hochschulschriften. Reihe III, Geschichte und ihre Hilfswissenschaften). Frankfurt: Peter Lang, 1995.
Holliday, Vivian L. *Pompey in Cicero's Correspondence and Lucan's Civil War*. The Hague-Paris: Mouton, 1969.
Humble, Noreen, ed. *Plutarch's Lives: Parallelism and Purpose*. Swansea: The Classical Press of Wales, 2010.
Kaizer, Ted, ed. *A Companion to the Hellenistic and Roman Near East*. Malden, Massachusetts: Wiley-Blackwell, 2022.
Keaveney, Arthur. *Lucullus: A Life*. London-New York: Routledge, 1992.
Keaveney, Arthur. *Sulla: The Last Republican*. Oxford-New York: Routledge, 2005 (second edition of the 1982 Croom Helm original).
Keavaney, Arthur. *The Army in the Roman Revolution*. Abingdon-New York, 2007.
Konrad, C. F. *Plutarch's Sertorius: A Historical Commentary*. Chapel Hill-London: The University of North Carolina Press, 1994.

Lange, Carsten Hjort and Vervaet, Frederik Juliaan, eds. *The Historiography of Late Republican Civil War*. Leiden-Boston: Brill, 2019.
Leach, John. *Pompey the Great*. London: Croom Helm Ltd., 1978.
Leigh, Matthew. *Lucan: Spectacle and Engagement*. Oxford, 1997.
Lovano, Michael. *The Age of Cinna: Crucible of Late Republican Rome* (Hermes Einzelschriften 158). Stuttgart: Franz Steiner Verlag, 2002.
Masters, Jamie. *Poetry and Civil War in Lucan's Bellum Civile*. Cambridge, 1992.
Matyszak, Philip. *Sertorius and the Struggle for Spain*. Barnsley: Pen & Sword Military, 2013.
Matyszak, Philip. *Julius Caesar in Egypt: Cleopatra & the War in Alexandria*. Barnsley: Pen & Sword Military, 2023.
McCall, Jeremiah. *Rivalries that Destroyed the Roman Republic*. Barnsley: Pen & Sword Military, 2022.
Morrell, Kit. *Pompey, Cato, and the Governance of the Roman Empire*. Oxford, 2017.
Morstein-Marx, Robert. *Julius Caesar and the Roman People*. Cambridge, 2021.
Osgood, Josiah. *Rome and the Making of a World State, 105 BCE–20 CE*. Cambridge, 2018.
Osgood, Josiah. *Uncommon Wrath: How Caesar and Cato's Deadly Rivalry Destroyed the Roman Republic*. New York: Basic Books, 2022.
Pelling, Christopher. *Plutarch Caesar: Translated with an Introduction and Commentary*. Oxford, 2011.
Raaflaub, Kurt A., ed. *The Landmark Julius Caesar: The Complete Works*. New York: Anchor Books, 2017.
Rawson, Elizabeth. *Cicero: A Portrait*. London: Bristol Classical Press, 2001 (reprint of the 1975 Allen Lane original).
Robb, M.A. *Beyond Populares and Optimates: Political Language in the Late Republic*. Stuttgart: Franz Steiner Verlag, 2010
Roche, Paul. *Reading Lucan's Civil War: A Critical Guide*. Norman: The University of Oklahoma Press, 2021.
Roller, Duane. *Empire of the Black Sea: The Rise and Fall of the Mithridatic World*. Oxford, 2020.
Rosenblit, J. Alison. *Rome after Sulla*. London-New York: Bloomsbury Academic, 2019.
Sampson, Gareth C. *Rome's Great Eastern War: Lucullus, Pompey, and the Conquest of the East, 74–62 BC*. Barnsley: Pen & Sword Military, 2021.
Sampson, Gareth C. *The Battle of Dyrrhachium (48 BC): Caesar, Pompey, and the Early Campaigns of the Third Roman Civil War*. Barnsley: Pen & Sword Military, 2022.
Sampson, Gareth C. *The Battle of Pharsalus 48 BC: Caesar, Pompey & their Final Clash in the Third Roman Civil War*. Barnsley: Pen & Sword Military, 2023.
Santangelo, Federico, ed. *Sir Ronald Syme: Approaching the Roman Revolution, Papers on Republican History*. Oxford, 2016.
Scullard, H.H. *From the Gracchi to Nero: A History of Rome from 133 BC to AD 68*. Abingdon-New York: Routledge, 2007 (reprint of the 1982 fifth edition of the 1959 Methuen original).
Seager, Robin. *Pompey the Great: A Political Biography*. Oxford: Blackwell Publishing, 2002 (second edition of the 1979 original).
Shackleton Bailey, D.R. *Cicero*. London: Duckworth, 1971.
Sheppard, Si. *Pharsalus 48 BC: Caesar and Pompey – Clash of the Titans*. Oxford: Osprey Publishing, 2006.
Smallwood, E. Mary. *The Jews under Roman Rule from Pompey to Diocletian: A Study in Political Relations*. Leiden-Boston: Brill, 2001.
Southern, Pat. *Pompey*. Stroud: Tempus, 2002.
Southern, Pat. *Mark Antony: A Life*. Gloucestershire: Amberley Publishing, 2012.

Spann, Philip O. *Quintus Sertorius and the Legacy of Sulla*. Fayetteville: The University of Arkansas Press, 1987.
Stevenson, Tom. *Julius Caesar and the Transformation of the Roman Republic*. London-New York: Routledge, 2015.
Strauss, Barry. *The Spartacus War*. New York: Simon & Schuster, 2009.
Swain, Hilary, and Davies, Mark Everson. *Aspects of Roman History, 82 BC–AD 14: A source-based approach*. London-New York: Routledge, 2010.
Syme, Ronald. *The Roman Revolution*, Oxford, 1960 (paperback edition of the 1939 original).
Tatum, W. Jeffrey. *The Patrician Tribune: Publius Clodius Pulcher*. Chapel Hill-London: The University of North Carolina Press, 1999.
Tatum, W. Jeffrey. *A Noble Ruin: Mark Antony, Civil War, and the Collapse of the Roman Republic*. Oxford, 2024.
van Ooeteghem, Jules. *Pompée le grand, bâtisseur d'empire*. Bruxelles: Palais de Académies, 1954.
Welch, Kathryn. *Magnus Pius: Sextus Pompeius and the Transformation of the Roman Republic*. Swansea: The Classical Press of Wales, 2012.
Westall, Richard. *Caesar's Civil War: Historical Reality and Fabrication*. Leiden-Boston: Brill, 2018.
Zampieri, Eleonora. *Politics in the Monuments of Pompey the Great and Julius Caesar*. Oxford-New York: Routledge, 2023.
Zander, Horst, ed. *Julius Caesar: New Critical Essays*. Abingdon-New York: Routledge, 2005.

Index

Abas, Battle of the, 123
Abgarus II, 196–7
Achillas, 219, 319–22, 324
Achilles, 269, 293, 307
adolescentulus carnifex, 61, 93
Adriatic, Caesar's crossing of, 270–2
Aemilia, 44–5, 54–5
Aeneas, 18
Aeschylus, 3
Afranius, *see* Lucius Afranius
Agamemnon, 291–2
Ajax, 298
Albanians, Caucasian, 119–20, 122–3
Alexander (freedman of Strabo), 19
Alexander (son of Aristobulus), 259, 271
Alexander the Great, 3, 5–6, 50, 70, 95–6, 106, 119–20, 123, 137, 147, 158, 194, 226, 269, 307, 313, 316, 328
Alexandria, 143, 162, 166, 170, 171–2, 187, 219, 227, 312
Allobroges, 282, 294
Alps, 71, 87, 243
Amazons, 123
Amphipolis, 307, 315
Anchises, 18
Annius Luscus, *see* Gaius Annius Luscus
Antioch, 130–1, 271, 313–15
Antiochus I, 130
Antiochus XIII Asiaticus, 130–1
Antistia, 19–21, 44–5
Apollonia, 273, 288
Appian, 8
Appius Claudius Pulcher (*cos.* 79), 61
Appius Claudius Pulcher (*cos.* 54), 181, 228
Apsus, River, 274–5
Archelaus, 170–1, 179
Aretas III, 131–3, 135
Ariamnes, 196–7
Ariminum, 223, 239–41

Ariobarzanes I, 130
Ariobarzanes II, 130
Aristobulus, 132–7, 147, 259
Armenia, buffer to Parthia, 118–19, 195
Arretium, 243
Arsinoe IV, 313
Artavasdes II, 195–7
Artemis, 147–8, 291
Artoces, 120–1
Asculum, 11, 247
Asinius Pollio, 151–2, 263
Athens, 99
Attaleia, 310, 315
Augustus/Octavian/'Thurinus', 151, 221, 292, 327–328
Aulus Gabinius (*cos.* 58), 97, 164, 170–1, 178–80, 183, 187–8, 211–12, 266, 277–8
Auximum, 247, 253

Bacchae, 200
Bagradas River, Battle of the, 262–3
Balearic Islands, 59
Batiatus, Lentulus, 86
Bellum Octavianum, 15–17
Berenice IV, 166–7, 170, 179
Bibulus, *see* Marcus Calpurnius Bibulus
Bithynia, 127
Bona Dea, 149–50, 157
Bovillae, 205, 210
Britain, 13, 106, 180, 185–6, 194
Brundisium, Pompey's landing at (62), 145
Brundisium, Pompey's departure from (49), 255
Brutus, *see* Marcus Junius Brutus

Caenum, 125
Caesar (Gaius Julius), 26–7, 45, 69–70, 82–3, 95–6, 98, 103, 124, 140, 144, 147–9, 151–5, 158–9, 161–4, 167,

175–6, 180, 186, 193–4, 202, 206, 210–15, 222, 224–6, 228–33, 241–2, 246–7, 265–6, 272, 294, 316
Calagurris, Siege of, 83
Calpurnia, 158–9
Camerinum, 247–8
Canary Islands, 59
Cannae, 76
Cappadocia, 130, 170
Capua, 86, 244, 249
Carbo, *see* Gnaeus Papirius Carbo
Carrhae, Battle of, 197–200
Carrinas, *see* Gaius Carrinas
Carthage, 49
Casilinum, Battle of, 34
Cassius (Crassus' quaestor), 200, 210
Castus, 90
Catiline (Lucius Sergius), 139–41
Catilinarian Conspiracy, 92, 124–5, 131, 139–40, 149, 157
Cato the Younger/Cato Minor, *see* Marcius Porcius Cato
Catulus, *see* Quintus Lutatius Catulus
Caucasus, 119
Censorinus, *see* Gaius Marcius Censorinus
Ceraunia, 270, 273
Cerisus, 108
Cicero (Marcus Tullius), 1–2, 69, 89, 94, 105, 124–5, 139–41, 149, 157, 159–61, 164–5, 167–9, 172–3, 193, 209, 216, 220–1, 232–3, 256, 260, 267, 306–307
Cilicia (Roman province), 127–8
Cilician pirates, 58, 82, 88–9, 94–101
Cingulum, 247
Cinna, *see* Lucius Cornelius Cinna
Cinnanum tempus/dominatio Cinnae, 22
Cleopatra (VII Philopator), 95, 162, 219, 227, 268, 297, 312–13, 319–20
Cleopatra V, 166
Clodius, *see* Publius Clodius Pulcher
Clunia, 81
Clusium, First Battle of, 38
Clusium, Second Battle of, 40
Colchis, 121
Colline Gate, Battle of the, 41
Commagene, 130
Coracesium, 100
Corcyra, 270, 275, 314

Corduene, 116–17
Cordus, 323–4
Corfinium, 248–52
corn commission, Pompey's, 172, 174–5
Cornelia (daughter of Cinna), 27, 45
Cornelia (daughter of Scipio), 203–204, 270, 306, 308–309, 313, 319, 321, 323
Cornelia (daughter of Sulla), 103
corona civica, 69
Cornelius Nepos, 305
Cosis, 122–3
Cossyra, 46
Cotys, 291
Crassus (Marcus Licinius), 26, 41–2, 88–9, 91, 124, 140, 143–5, 149–53, 161–3, 175–6, 180–1, 185, 187–9, 192–200
Cratippus, 309–10
Crete, 101–103, 324
Crixus, 86–8
Curio, *see* entries for Gaius Scribonius Curio, father and son
Cyprus, 165–6, 174, 314–16
Cyrnus, 119

Damascus, 132
Dardanos, Treaty of, 24, 47–8
Dasteira, 112
Decimus Junius Brutus (*cos.* 77), 67
Decimus Junius Brutus (son of the consul), 260
Decimus Laelius, 72–3
Deiotarus of Galatia, 308
Demetrius (freedman of Pompey), 6
Diana, 80, 316
dictator, 43, 60, 265–6, 269
Dido, 49, 51
Diodorus Siculus, 147
Dionysius of Tripolis, 133–4
Domitius, *see* Gnaeus Domitius Ahenobarbus/Lucius Domitius Ahenobarbus/Gnaeus Domitius Calvinus
Dyrrhachium 249, 254, 256, 268–9, 273, 277, 280–2, 284–5

Egypt, 142–3, 162, 178–80, 187–8, 313, 318
elephants, 53–4

Elymaeans, 119, 123
Ephesus, 147–8, 291, 316
Euripides, 200

Faesulae, uprising at, 64–5
Faustus Cornelius Sulla, 249, 295
fawn, Sertorius', 80
Fimbria, *see* Gaius Flavius Fimbria
First Mithridatic War, 11–12, 23–4, 47
First Triumvirate, 152–3, 163, 193
Flaccus, *see* Gaius/Lucius Valerius Flaccus
fleas, fable of the, 43–4
Fortuna, 286
Frontinus, 255, 300
Fucine Lake, Battle of, 10–11
Fulvia, 223, 226

'Gabiniani', 219, 227, 312–13
Gabinius, *see* Aulus Gabinius
Gaius Annius Luscus, 57–8
Gaius Antonius Hybrida (*cos.* 63), 131, 139–40
Gaius Ateius Capito, 181
Gaius Aurelius Cotta (*cos.* 75), 74
Gaius Calpurnius Piso (*cos.* 67), 97, 100
Gaius Calvisius Sabinus, 278
Gaius Caninius Rebilus, 254, 261, 263
Gaius Carrinas, 35, 38–40, 42
Gaius Cassius Longinus, 306, 316–18
Gaius Claudius Glaber, 86
Gaius Claudius Marcellus (*cos.* 50), 203–204, 223
Gaius Claudius Marcellus (*cos.* 49, cousin of the consul of 50), 231–5
Gaius Coponius, 276
Gaius Crastinus, 295
Gaius Flavius Fimbria, 21–4
Gaius Herennius, 75
Gaius Lucilius Hirrus, 189, 248
Gaius Manilius, 105
Gaius Manlius, 140–1
Gaius Marcius Censorinus, 36–7, 42
Gaius Marcius Figulus (*cos.* 64), 126
Gaius Memmius (brother-in-law of Pompey), 79
Gaius Memmius (praetor in 58), 190–1, 201
Gaius Norbanus (*cos.* 83), 27, 30, 34, 44

Gaius Octavius, 151
Gaius Scribonius Curio (*cos.* 76), 69
Gaius Scribonius Curio (tribune 50), 223–5, 229, 231–2, 235, 237, 260–3
Gaius Trebonius, 184, 260
Gaius Valerius Flaccus, 54, 56–7
Gaius Valerius Triarius, 295
Gaius Verres, 89, 94
Gallic chieftains, defection of, 282–3
Gannicus, 90
game, Caesar vs. Pompey children's, 267
Gaul, Caesar's campaigns in, 167, 175, 206, 210, 215, 222
Geminius, 6, 66
Glaber, *see* Gaius Claudius Glaber
Gnaeus Aufidius Orestes (*cos.* 71), 92
Gnaeus Calpurnius Piso, 125
Gnaeus Cornelius Dolabella (*cos.* 81), 46
Gnaeus Cornelius Lentulus Clodianus (*cos.* 72), 87
Gnaeus Cornelius Lentulus Marcellinus (*cos.* 56), 173–4
Gnaeus Domitius Ahenobarbus, 49–50
Gnaeus Domitius Calvinus (*cos.* 53), 190, 201, 278, 287, 292, 295, 299–300
Gnaeus Octavius (*cos.* 87), 15–17, 20
Gnaeus Octavius (*cos.* 76), 69
Gnaeus Papirius Carbo (*cos.* 85–84, 82), 24, 30–1, 35–40, 45–7
Gnaeus Pompeius (son of Pompey), 91–2, 143–4, 270, 314
Gomphi, 289–90, 293

Hannibal, 71, 76, 119, 232–3, 243
Helen of Sparta, 6
Heracles, 3, 123, 298
Hiarbas, 51
Hiempsal II, 51, 261
Hirtuleius, *see* Lucius Hirtuleius
Horace, 151, 263
Hypsicrateia/'Hypsicrates', 112–13
Hyrcanus II, 132–3

Iarbas, 51
Iberians, Caucasian, 119–20
Iguvium, 247
Ilerda, Battle of, 260
illness, Pompey's, 227–8

Illyricum, 222, 263, 278, 292
imperator, 32, 50–3, 82, 286, 321
Italica, Battle of, 76, 80

7 January 49, 238–9
javelin training, Pompey's, 257
Jericho, 132, 135
Jerusalem, 131–2, 135–7, 185
Josephus, 132, 136–7, 185
Juba I, 261–3, 311
Judaea, 131–3
Julia (daughter of Caesar), 27, 158, 165, 178, 186–7, 204
Julian *gens*, 4, 221

Kubrick, Stanley, 4, 44, 89–90, 237

Labienus, *see* Titus Labienus
Larissa, 293, 305, 307
Lauron, Battle of, 72–3
Lauron, burning of, 74
Lepidus, *see* Marcus Aemilius Lepidus
Lesnikia, River, 284, 286
Lessus, 276
lex Gabinia, 97
lex Licinia Pompeia, 213
lex Manilia, 105, 109, 128, 143, 183
lex Tribonia, 213
lex Vatinia, 213
Lissus, 276, 279
Livy, 328
Luca, Conference of, 175–7, 183–4
Lucan, 2, 239, 270, 274–5, 280–1, 286, 293, 300, 304–305, 310, 323–4
Lucania, 188
Luceria, 251–2
Lucius Aemilius Paullus Lepidus (*cos.* 50), 223, 226
Lucius Afranius (*cos.* 60), 77–8, 116–17, 148, 182, 196, 260–1, 287, 289, 295, 297
Lucius Aurelius Cotta (*cos.* 65), 124
Lucius Caecilius Metellus (*cos.* 68), 95
Lucius Calpurnius Piso (*cos.* 58), 158
Lucius Cassius Longinus, 278, 287, 317–18
Lucius Cornelius Cinna (*cos.* 87–84), 15–17, 20–2, 24–5
Lucius Cornelius Cinna the Younger, 65

Lucius Cornelius Sisenna, 102
Lucius Domitius Ahenobarbus (*cos.* 54), 178, 181, 190–1, 237, 245, 248–51, 260, 291–2, 297, 299, 304–305
Lucius Gellius (*cos.* 72), 87
Lucius Hirtuleius, 76, 79
Lucius Julius Caesar (*cos.* 90), 9
Lucius Julius Caesar (*cos.* 64), 126, 241–2, 246
Lucius Lentulus Crus (*cos.* 49), 231–2, 322
Lucius Licinius Murena (*cos.* 62), 47–8, 54, 140, 142, 216
Lucius Lucceius, 151
Lucius Manlius Torquatus (*cos.* 65), 124
Lucius Marcius Philippus (*cos.* 56), 68, 173–4
Lucius Octavius (*cos.* 75), 74, 102
Lucius Porcius Cato (*cos.* 89), 10
Lucius Roscius Fabatus, 241–2, 246
Lucius Scribonius Libo, 254, 263, 275–6
Lucius Terentius, 17
Lucius Valerius Flaccus, 21, 23
Lucius Vettius, 159–60, 223
Lucius Vibullius Rufus, 272–3
Lucius Volcatius Tullus (*cos.* 66), 105
Lucretius, 190
Lucullus (Lucius Licinius), 7, 15, 39, 63, 82, 92, 96–7, 104–108, 125, 148–9, 154, 156–7, 160, 176
Lucullus (Marcus), 34, 39, 83, 89–90
Luscus, *see* Gaius Annius Luscus
Lusitanians, 59

Macedonia, 151
Machares, 125
Madeira, 59
Maeotis, Lake, 128
Magnus, Pompey's title, 52
Mamercus Aemilius Lepidus Livianus (*cos.* 77), 67
Manilius, *see* Gaius Manilius
Manius Acilius Glabrio (*cos.* 67), 97
Manius Aemilius Lepidus (*cos.* 66), 105
Marcus Aemilius Lepidus (*cos.* 78), 62–8
Marcus Aemilius Lepidus (triumvir), 206–207, 265, 269
Marcus Aemilius Scaurus, 132–3

Index

Marcus Antonius (Mark Antony), 165, 185–6, 210, 223–4, 236–7, 243, 258–9, 276–7, 280, 284, 295, 297, 299, 304–305
Marcus Antonius Creticus, 95
Marcus Aurelius Cotta (*cos.* 74), 82
Marcus Caelius Rufus, 237
Marcus Calpurnius Bibulus (*cos.* 59), 151, 154–5, 158–60, 175, 208, 211, 220, 222, 227, 270–1, 275–6
Marcus Claudius Marcellus (*cos.* 51), 216, 218–19
Marcus Favonius, 292, 308
Marcus Junius Brutus, 158, 260, 299–300
Marcus Junius Brutus (father of the Caesarian assassin), 65–7
Marcus Licinius Crassus (son of Crassus), 187
Marcus Octavius, 263, 277
Marcus Otacilius Crassus, 276
Marcus Perperna (*cos.* 92), 256
Marcus Perperna Veiento, 47, 68–9, 73, 75–6, 79, 84–5
Marcus Petreius, 182, 260–1
Marcus Porcius Cato, 140, 142, 146–9, 155–6, 166, 174, 178, 180, 201, 208–209, 232, 236–7, 245, 251, 253, 267, 306, 314–15
Marcus Pupius Pisu Frugi Calpurnianus (*cos.* 61), 145
Marcus Saufeius, 210
Marcus Tullius Decula (*cos.* 81), 46
Marcus Valerius Messalla Niger (*cos.* 61), 146
Marcus Valerius Messalla Rufus (*cos.* 53), 201
Marius (Gaius), 9
Marius the Younger, 35–7, 42, 55–6
Marsians, 9
Massilia, Siege of, 259–60
Medea, 121
Menogenes, 4
Mesopotamia, 193, 195–6
Metellus, *see* Quintus Caecilius Metellus/ Quintus Caecilius Metellus Creticus
Metropolis, 290
Milo, *see* Titus Annius Milo
Minerva/Athena, 147, 316

Mithridates of Pontus, 12, 24, 47, 60, 82–3, 92, 96–7, 108–19, 1212, 125–9, 134–5, 151
Mithridates IV, 171, 180, 192–3
Mucia Tertia, 54–5, 143–4, 168
Mytilene, 270, 306, 309
Mytilene, Siege of, 69

Nabataean Arabs, 131
Neapolis, 227
Nepos, *see* Cornelius Nepos/Quintus Caecilius Metellus Nepos
Nicomedes IV, 82
Nicopolis (modern Koyulhasir), 112
Nola, 151
Nonius Magius, 252–3
Norbanus, *see* Gaius Norbanus
Numidia, 51, 261, 311

Octavia, 203–204
Oenomaus, 86–7
Oricum, 271, 273, 275, 278–9
Orodes II, 171, 180, 192–3, 196–7, 216, 222
Oroeses, 120, 122
Orosius, 10
Osroene, 192, 196

Palantia, 83
Paliama, 280
Panticapaeum, 128
Parthia, 109–10, 171, 185–6, 192, 200–201, 210–11, 222, 225–6, 311, 313, 315
paternal *pietas*, 18–19, 286
patron-client system, 21
Pelorus, Battle of the, 120–1
Pelousion, 318–19
Pentheus, 200
Perperna, *see* Marcus Perperna Veiento
Perseus, 293
Peticius, 308
Petra, 131, 135, 279
Petreius, *see* Marcus Petreius
Phanagoria, 134, 151
Pharnaces II, 129, 134, 151, 289
Pharsalus, Battle of, 293–305
Phaselis, 310
Philip, freedman, 322–3

Philip II Philoromaeus, 130–1
Philippus, see Lucius Marcius Philippus
Philodemus, 164
Phraates III, 109–10, 116–18, 123, 171
Picenum, 4, 22, 77, 253
Piso, see Gaius Calpurnius Piso
Placentia, 39
Placentia, mutiny at, 263–4
Pliny the Elder, 4, 188
Plutarch, 1–2
police, lack of a Roman republican force, 202
Pompeia (daughter of Pompey), 143
Pompeia (daughter of Quintus Pompeius Rufus), 103, 149
Pompeian *gens*, 4
Pompey,
   early military exploits, 30–1
   physical appearance, 5
   relationship with Sulla, 25, 28, 31–2
Posidonius, 99
Pothinus, 219, 319–20, 323–4
Praeneste, 36–8, 42
princeps, 230, 245
Pro Caelio, 237
Pro lege Manilia, 105
Pro Milone, 209
Pro Murena, 216
Prometheus, 3
Promona, 222
Ptolemy (son of Mennaeus), 133
Ptolemy XII, 142–3, 162, 165–7, 170, 174, 178–80, 219
Ptolemy XIII, 219, 227, 268, 297, 312–13, 318–19, 322–4
Ptolemy XIV, 312
Publius Antistius, 19
Publius Attius Varus, 247, 261–2
Publius Clodius Pulcher, 104–105, 139, 149–51, 157–8, 164–5, 167–70, 172–4, 177, 202–203, 205–206, 223
Publius Cornelius Cethegus, 29–30
Publius Cornelius Lentulus Spinther (*cos*. 57), 168, 174, 177, 244, 247, 300, 308
Publius Cornelius Lentulus Sura (*cos*. 71), 92
Publius Cornelius Sulla, 295, 297
Publius Fonteius, 157

Publius Licinius Crassus, 187, 192, 197–9, 203
Publius Plautius Hypsaeus, 203
Publius Rutilius Lupus (*cos*. 90), 9–10
Publius Servilius Vatia (*cos*. 79), 61
Publius Sulpicius Rufus, 14–15
Publius Varinius, 87
Publius Vatinius, 160–1

Quintus Caecilius Metellus, 33–5, 37, 39, 55, 60–1, 64, 66–8, 71–2, 74–84, 90–1
Quintus Caecilius Metellus Creticus (*cos*. 69), 94, 101–103, 106
Quintus Caecilius Metellus Nepos (*cos*. 57), 168
Quintus Caecilius Metellus Scipio, 210, 236, 248, 278, 288, 290–1, 293, 295, 297, 299–300
Quintus Cassius Longinus, 236–7
Quintus Fabius Maximus, 259
Quintus Hortensius Hortalus (*cos*. 69), 94
Quintus Lucretius Afella, 42–3
Quintus Lutatius Catulus (*cos*. 78), 63–4
Quintus Marcius Rex (*cos*. 68), 95
Quintus Metellus Celer (*cos*. 60), 148
Quintus Metellus Scipio, 203
Quintus Minucius Thermus, 247
Quintus Mucius Scaevola, 54–5
Quintus Pedius, 259
Quintus Pompeius Rufus (*cos*. 88), 11, 103
Quintus Sertorius, 34, 55–9, 68–9, 71–3, 75–7, 80–4

Ravenna, Caesar and Curio at, 235–6
Regium Lepidi, 66
Rhegium, 89
Rhodes, 142, 314
River Asio, Battle of the, 35
Rome, Caesar's entry in 49, 255, 258
Rubicon, crossing of, 239

Saburra, 262–3
Sacriportus, Battle of, 36
Salonae, 277–8
Sallust, 2
Salvius, 321
Samnites, 9, 41–2
Sampsiceramus, 130–1

Sardinia, 66, 68, 259
Scaeva, centurion, 281
Scaurus, see Marcus Aemilius Scaurus
Scipio Asiaticus (cos. 83), 27, 30–1
Second Mithridatic War, 47–8
Segontia, Battle of, 79–80
Segovia, Battle of, 79–81
Sena Gallica, Battle of, 36–7
Septimius, 321–2
Sertorian War, 59–60, 71, 79–80
Sertorius, see Quintus Sertorius
Servilia, 158–9, 299
Servius Sulpicius Rufus (cos. 51), 140, 216, 220
Sextus Julius Caesar, 9
Sextus Pompey, 143–4, 270, 306, 319, 323, 325
Sicily, fall of (49), 259
Silarius River, Battle of the, 90
Sisenna, see Lucius Cornelius Sisenna
Social War, 7–9
Sophocles, 321
Spartacus, 86–90, 129, 141
Spoletium, Battle of, 39
Strabo (father of Pompey), 3–4, 17–18, 139
Stratonice, 125
Sucro, Battle of, 77–8
Sulla (Lucius Cornelius), 9, 22, 24–5, 41–2, 52, 54–5, 60–1
Surena, 192, 196, 198–9, 216

Tacitus, 216
Talasio, 19
Tarcondimotus I, 127–8
Tarsus, 127
Teanum Sidicinum, 244

Tempe, 307
Theodotus of Chios, 219, 312, 319–20, 322, 324
Theophanes of Mytilene, 311–13, 321
Theatre, Pompey's, 181
Theseus, 123
Thessalonica, 169
Thessaly, 269
Third Mithridatic War, 105
Tifata, Battle of, 34
Tingis, 57–9
Tigranes the Great, 110–11, 114–18, 195
Tigranes II, 109–11, 114–16, 118
turmoil of 87 BC, 13, 15, 21
Titus Annius Milo, 169, 174, 203, 205–206, 209–10
Titus Labienus, 240, 243, 246–7, 282, 294
Titus Pomponius Atticus, 305
Trebonius, see Gaius Trebonius

Utica, Battle of (81), 50
Utica, Battle of (49), 262

Vaccaei, 82
Valentia, Battle of, 75–6
Vatinius, see Publius Vatinius
Venus, 147, 181, 298
Vercingetorix, 212
Verres, see Gaius Verres
Vettius, see Lucius Vettius

Xenophon, 37, 51
Xiphares, 125

Zela, 130
Zeus, 3, 319

Dear Reader,

We hope you have enjoyed this book, but why not share your views on social media? You can also follow our pages to see more about our other products: facebook.com/penandswordbooks or follow us on X @penswordbooks

You can also view our products at www.pen-and-sword.co.uk (UK and ROW) or www.penandswordbooks.com (North America).

To keep up to date with our latest releases and online catalogues, please sign up to our newsletter at: www.pen-and-sword.co.uk/newsletter

If you would like a printed catalogue with our latest books, then please email: enquiries@pen-and-sword.co.uk or telephone: 01226 734555 (UK and ROW) or email: uspen-and-sword@casematepublishers.com or telephone: (610) 853-9131 (North America).

We respect your privacy and we will only use personal information to send you information about our products.

Thank you!